AID AND POLITICAL CONDITIONALITY

T0330938

EADI BOOK SERIES 16
(This volume is also No. 82 in the series
Norwegian Foreign Policy Studies, Norwegian Institute of
International Affairs, Oslo.)

AID AND POLITICAL CONDITIONALITY

edited by
OLAV STOKKE

FRANK CASS • LONDON

in association with
The European Association of Development Research
and Training Institutes (EADI), Geneva

EADI

First published in 1995 in Great Britain by
FRANK CASS & CO. LTD.
Newbury House, 900 Eastern Avenue,
London IG2 7HH

and in the United States of America by
FRANK CASS
c/o ISBS
5602 N.E. Hassalo Street
Portland, Oregon 97213–3644

Transferred to Digital Printing 2006

British Library Cataloguing in Publication Data
Aid and Political Conditionality - (EADI
Series No.16)
    I. Stokke, Olav II. Series
338.91

ISBN 0-7146-4640-7 (cloth)
0-7146-4162-6 (paper)

Library of Congress Cataloging-in-Publication Data
Aid and political conditionality / edited by Olav Stokke
        p.   cm.
"Published in collaboration with the European Association of
Development Research and Training Institutes (EADI) Geneva."
    "Also no. 82 in the series Norwegian foreign policy studies" — Ser.
t.p.
    Includes bibliographical references.
    ISBN 0-7146-4640-7 (cloth) — ISBN 0-7145-4162-6
(pbk.)
    1. Economic assistance — Political aspects. 2. Economic
assistance — Political aspects — Case studies. I. Stokke, Olav,
1934–
HC60.A4526   1995   95–5860
338.9 — dc20   CIP

Contents

Introduction

OLAV STOKKE

The present volume results from a research and publishing project under the auspices of the Working Group on Aid Policy and Performance of the European Association of Development Research and Training Institutes (EADI). The decision to focus on aid and political conditionality was reached at EADI's Sixth General Conference, which took place in Oslo in June 1990. At that time, the first manifestations of a new policy trend were visible and posed a challenge for exploration. The Working Group was in the process of fulfilling its second major programme with a focus on evaluation of development assistance. In subsequent years, a series of three volumes was published in the EADI book series (Nos. 11, 12 and 14).[1] Previously, the Group had examined the aid policies of European countries, a task completed in 1984 with the publication of two volumes in the EADI book series (No. 4).[2]

Within EADI, the issue of aid conditionality attracted general interest. In mid-1992, a workshop in Vienna took a first shot at the *problématique*; and *The European Journal of Development Research* decided to devote a special issue to the theme (No. 1, 1993). The Working Group, therefore, did not need to start from scratch when the proposal for the current project was worked out.

The Working Group on Aid has established a mode of work. A design is worked out by the Convenor. Outstanding researchers in the field are asked for comments on the position paper. These

---

1.   Clay, Edward and Olav Stokke, eds., 1991, *Food Aid Reconsidered: Assessing the Impact on Third World Countries*, London: Frank Cass; Stokke, Olav, ed., 1991, *Evaluating Development Assistance: Policies and Performance*, London: Frank Cass; and Berlage, Lodewijk and Olav Stokke, eds., 1992, *Evaluating Development Assistance: Approaches and Methods*, London: Frank Cass.
2.   Stokke, Olav, ed., 1984, *European Development Assistance: Policies and Performance*, Volume I, Tilburg: EADI Secretariat/University of Tilburg; and Stokke, Olav, ed., 1984, *European Development Assistance: Third World Perspectives on Policies and Performance*, Volume II, Tilburg: EADI Secretariat/University of Tilburg.

consultations are followed by invitations to provide a component study. The draft studies are presented at a workshop to which, in addition to the authors, a selected group of experts are invited, representing the immediate environment of the chosen theme (researchers, top administrators and others in the specific field). It is the matured versions of drafts which have been scrutinised through this process and then edited that are published.

There have always been strings attached to development assistance, but these have been of different kinds, varying with the donor. The conditions set by the Bretton Woods institutions and major bilateral donors during the 1980s aimed at reform of the economic policy of recipient governments. They carried a strong neo-liberal baggage, boosting the market and reducing the role of the state, with structural adjustment lending as the major tool. In this volume, the main focus will be on second generation aid conditionality which in its present form was initiated in the late 1980s and took off in the early 1990s. This aims above all at policy reform, involving the system of government, democracy and participation, and human rights, in particular civil and political rights.

The evolving patterns of aid conditionality, somewhat different for the various categories of donors, are outlined in Chapter 1, and an extensive overview of the *problématique* and core issues involved in second generation conditionality is given. The concept is at first narrowly defined, restricted to the denial of aid if the conditions set are not met, but it is subsequently opened up for a discussion that transcends the stick and includes the carrot ('positive conditionality') and 'positive measures' as well. A distinction is drawn between the various levels of interference, and the main objectives associated with aid conditionality are identified, the emphasis being on those associated with second generation conditionality.

Against this background, normative and instrumental issues are discussed in greater detail. Normative issues transcend the question of the sovereignty of states; what is important here is the legitimacy of policy and of governments *vis-à-vis* the ruled. Of equal importance is the question: does conditionality work? Under what conditions is it likely to work and what may cause it to fail? The potential of the policy is explored from a theoretical point of departure and then discussed on the basis of empirical evidence from a few cases involving second generation conditionality and earlier experience of first generation conditionality.

For most of the objectives, essential aspects associated with an effective international regime seem to be missing. This in turn leads to an exploration of alternative strategies involving 'the carrot' or 'positive measures'. The under-explored concept of a development contract is seen as a possible way of reconciling conflicting aspirations and concerns; however, such a contract does not escape the demands associated with an international regime.

The objectives associated with second generation conditionality and the strategy to attain these objectives vary from one donor country to another; the policy blend and emphasis emerge from different national traditions. In this project, the focus has been on a few European donor countries which may shed an interesting light on the problem from a variety of perspectives.

Belgium's relations with its former colonies of Burundi, Rwanda and Zaïre involve aid conditionality related to issues on the second generation agenda. In Chapter 2, the experiences emerging from these relations are explored by Robrecht Renard and Filip Reyntjens. In the past, geopolitical and military factors motivated and determined Belgian aid policy, resulting in generous aid to the regime of President Mobutu in Zaïre regardless of its poor developmental record. However, the concerns associated with first generation conditionality, together with a new international situation (the end of the Cold War), made the Belgian government decide to pursue the more 'soft' values associated with second generation conditionality. Still, no coherent relationship between aid and human rights or democracy existed in the stated policy.

Nevertheless, aid to Burundi had been terminated in the 1970s and mid-1980s when fundamental human rights were violated, and aid conditionality was again applied in 1988. In relation to Rwanda and Zaïre, Belgium's concern for human rights took a new turn in 1989-90. This changed policy is attributed partly to the domestic political constellation in Belgium. In the case of Zaïre it was also partly caused by the brinkmanship of President Mobutu, and led to Belgium cutting off all aid. This policy was followed up by Belgium, particularly within the framework of the European Community. The authors, however, argue for a more differentiated approach: aid through NGOs and universities, in pursuit of poverty alleviation and supportive of domestic forces that aimed for political reform, should not have been cut off.

Germany has maintained a particularly high profile in the second generation conditionality drive, even with regard to policy implementation. It also played an active role in the case of Kenya, where President Moi was forced to change the one-party constitution and arrange for a multi-party election. In Chapter 3, Peter P. Waller describes the evolving policy of the 1990s. In 1991, respect for human rights, popular participation and rule of law were among the five conditions set for German development assistance; since then, aid to some extremely repressive regimes has been terminated, aid to some authoritarian regimes substantially reduced, and aid to some 'fragile reformers' increased.

The main lessons learned from the German experience are that political conditionality may work if certain requirements, on the donor and recipient side, are met. It is necessary for the donor to establish clear directives and procedures within its own administration and to ensure solid public support of the policy. Its success depends too on the recipient having weak bargaining power (being of little economic and strategic importance to the donor and heavily dependent on aid), on there being strong internal forces fighting for democracy, and on the major donors' ability to coordinate their aid. Waller argues, with particular reference to German-Kenyan relations, that an authoritarian regime which fights to stay in power will not be interested in 'positive measures' which will undermine its position. Measures in support of human rights and democracy may, however, play an important role in the reform process if combined with aid conditionality, and therefore being accepted by an aid-dependent government. Waller argues for accepting 'double standards': aid conditionality should be applied where it may work.

The Dutch and Nordic governments placed human rights and democracy on the aid agenda at an early stage; promotion of democracy was among the four overall objectives set for Swedish aid in 1962; and in the mid-1970s, both the Netherlands and Norway set observance of human rights as a criterion (condition) for the selection of main partners for bilateral aid.

In 1990, the Dutch government coupled continued aid with the human right performance of the Indonesian government with reference to the human rights violations in East Timor. In Chapter 4, Nico G. Schulte Nordholt explores the conflict from the perspective of past relations between the two countries, with particular reference to the crisis of 1963 when President Sukarno broke off relations with the West. He describes the main characteristics of the political and economic developments in Indonesia under President Suharto up to the massacre of peaceful demonstrators in Dili, and surveys the discussion on the role of human rights in Dutch foreign policy. Against this background, he analyses international and Dutch reactions to the Dili incident, and the reaction of the Indonesian government, leading to Suharto's decision to give the Netherlands one month to pull out of all aid engagements.

The conflict is, to a large extent, framed in the context of a confrontation between two prominent politicians, President Suharto and the Dutch Minister of Development Co-operation, Jan Pronk. The situation was unusual; for once, the traditional balance was not attained between the concerns of the Ministry of Foreign Affairs and those of the Ministry of Development Co-operation in forming Dutch policy towards Indonesia. This allowed Pronk a free hand to take a human rights stance. However, he had to wage this battle on political terrain that was unfamiliar to him, namely that of his Indonesian opponent.

In Chapter 5, the focus shifts to the aid policy formation of a small donor country. What makes Norway an interesting case are the contradictions inherent in its policy: it has, on the one hand, kept a high profile, in its stated policy, with regard to the core issues of second generation conditionality, particularly social justice and human rights. On the other, it has insisted that its bilateral aid should be genuinely recipient-oriented, both to ensure its sustainability and in order not to infringe the sovereignty of the recipient. This contradiction is shared with other Western middle powers, particularly the so-called like-minded, in contrast to major powers with a different justification for aid and different traditions with regard to interference. To what extent did the changed international agenda influence the Norwegian policy in the early 1990s? Was the response one of resistance or adaptation?

The focus, accordingly, is on continuity and change within the declared and implemented aid policy, with particular emphasis on the changes taking place in the 1980s and early 1990s. The international aid agenda of the early 1990s, Olav Stokke argues, strengthened one set of the conflicting values, particularly those related to civil and political rights, although the social justice rhetoric was not toned down. By the same token it weakened other traditional values, particularly those related to the sovereignty of recipient governments. However, this change was to a large extent self-generated and in progress in the early 1980s. Torn between competing values, Norway has given emphasis to 'positive measures' and taken the role of a hesitant free-rider in the international conditionality drive.

In Chapter 6, Jacques Forster describes the main features of Swiss aid policy with particular reference to second generation conditionality and the evolving Swiss interpretation of the basic concepts involved. These are portrayed against the background of Swiss neutrality which induced strict separation between the country's human rights policy and other dimensions of its foreign policy, in particular in the realm of international economic relations.

International sanctions are therefore avoided; it follows that Switzerland is reluctant to apply aid conditionality. This policy originates in the country's traditional reserve about making declarations or taking actions concerning political issues within other countries; the same is true in the area of human rights. In line with its aid policy, positive measures, and support for agents of change within the Third World country concerned, are preferred to sanctions; and dialogue is preferred to conditionality. This is also reflected in the implementation of policy; where the possibility to co-operate with the state is excluded, opportunities to support programmes benefiting the least privileged sections of the population are grasped, as in the case of Haiti.

In the following four chapters, the perspective is changed to that of governments being exposed to conditionality of different kinds. In Chapter 7, Samuel S. Mushi explores Nordic-Tanzanian co-operation since the 1960s. He finds that relations have changed over the years, from being basically recipient-oriented until the mid-1970s to being largely donor-oriented later. He confronts the human rights/ democracy rhetoric of Nordic governments with their funding in support of these purposes and concludes that the funding indicates a low priority for the pursuit of these objectives.

Nordic governments' political influence-*cum*-conditionality *vis-à-vis* Tanzania has taken four forms: quiet diplomacy, the use of the multilateral voice, assistance to political parties, human rights groups and civic organisations, and support for specific economic and political reform measures. However, there are both political and economic limits to conditionality; the proposition suggested is that the more donor-oriented aid practice becomes, the less the likelihood that conditionality relating to human rights will be applied vigorously. However, human rights and democracy will be asserted rhetorically.

In Chapter 8, Mosharaff Hossain twists the perspective. Taking the aid rhetoric at its face value, he asks to what extent donors have set conditions to make aid meet the development imperatives of Bangladesh, particularly the problems facing the rural poor. From this perspective, he traces aid provided to Bangladesh since the early 1970s. Aid conditions appear to have been founded on the implicit belief by the donors that, left to themselves, recipient governments would either 'waste' or misappropriate funds. Such conditions are related to micro-management problems and not to eliminating the real causes of arrested development in recipient countries. As such, they do not advance the process of sustainable development, and fail to satisfy either donors or recipients.

What is needed, Hossain argues, is a development contract between Bangladesh and the donor community involving a firm commitment to poverty alleviation through rapid and sustainable labour-intensive growth. This would presuppose a clear development agenda defined through a process of national dialogue on the basis of which a national consensus can be built.

In chapters 9 and 10, the focus shifts to experiences with first generation conditionality based on the cases of Egypt and Turkey. Egypt has been implementing stabilisation and structural adjustment measures since the mid-1980s, often in the absence of any formal agreement with the IMF or the World Bank. In 1991, the country reached formal agreements with the two Bretton Woods institutions and these together make up the backbone of Egypt's economic reform and structural adjustment programme (ERSAP). In Chapter 9, Gouda Abdel-Khalek and Karima Korayem outline the main elements of ERSAP and explore its impact on economic growth, poverty and equity.

Based on a 'before-after' analysis, the authors conclude, *inter alia*, that excessive conditionality faced less resistance than was expected, particularly with regard to trade liberalisation, price liberalisation and the reductions of fiscal deficit, only privatisation generated political opposition. The impact on the poor is harmful in the short term and the programme has a negative impact on wage-earners, while its income distribution impact on non-wage earners is less clear-cut.

The authors argue that, given the institutional underdevelopment and structural rigidity of the Egyptian economy, a structuralist approach would be more appropriate than the neo-classical one on which ERSAP was based. Such a package should include a more balanced mix of supply-augmenting and demand-reducing measures, with emphasis on increasing food supply; a better balance between market forces/price mechanism and planning/direct control; use of more instruments to promote better economic management; and a different sequencing, starting with reform of the real economy.

Turkey embarked on a trade liberalisation programme in 1980 as part of a large structural adjustment loan (SAL) provided by the World Bank. Its experience in the 1980s has been hailed as a success. Why was this the case in the 1980s, while previous reforms had not been sustained? This is the key question addressed by Oliver Morrissey in Chapter 10, examining the Turkish experience against general lessons derived from the experiences of adjustment programmes in other reforming countries. Patterns of aid to Turkey in the 1980s and the main features of the structural adjustment programme are analysed along with the economic policy reform taking place.

Adjustment in Turkey in the 1980s is considered a success in a number of senses. The principal targets were achieved: high rates of real export and GDP growth and elimination of the current account deficit. The structure of incentives was improved and the anti-export bias largely eliminated. Democracy was also restored during this period. However, the success is limited; public enterprises remain in need of reform and adjustment has been a failure with regard to income distribution as labour and agriculture are worse-off now than they were in the 1980s.

In the case of Turkey, the governing elites and the Bretton Woods institutions had a shared understanding of the nature of the economic crisis and the cure required to solve it when the programme was initiated. Morrissey attributes the success of aid conditionality, in terms of attaining the main targets set, to this favourable environment, which made direct intervention by the World Bank unnecessary and allowed flexibility for the government. The government was also in a position to resist the losers. The main lesson learned is that gradualism makes sense; it eases the process of adjustment, allows governments to alter some conditions and may allow a recipient to obtain subsequent loans without fully complying with conditions. For the World Bank, the main lesson is that it, too, should exercise flexibility and learn to see its role as a facilitator rather than an enforcer.

The perspective of the conditionality debate is extended to include Russian relations with the West. In Chapter 11, Stanislav Zhukov asks the crucial question: how do the conditions of Western governments and credit institutions correspond to the strategic twin goals of the on-going transition, namely to transfer from a central planning system to a market economy and simultaneously to create an open, democratic society? Zhukov identifies an apparent paradox: in discussions of the problem of debt repayments and a stabilisation policy in line with the recommendations of the Bretton Woods institutions, the Russian side was the one which devoted most attention to human rights and democracy consolidation, while the Western side concentrated on the economic problems of interaction involving the standard stabilisation package.

The hardship created by the strong medicine prescribed to attain the objectives of first generation conditionality, and the built-in conflict between the objectives of first and second generation conditionality, are both illuminated in the Russian case where the two generations are combined in a situation where a third of the population lives below the poverty line. To carry out such a programme, argues Zhukov, presupposes a military dictatorship or a civil leadership resting on overall national consensus; neither exists in contemporary Russia. In the prevailing circumstances, the Bretton Woods institutions, paradoxically, should devote a large part of their assistance to such an unusual task as the creation of a modern social system – in prosperous economies the natural task of the state. However, since traditional agencies such as the IMF and the World Bank were created to fulfil different tasks, the solutions for Russia have to be sought at the political level, involving the Group of Seven (G-7). This, Zhukov argues, may lead to a new paradigm of political conditionality.

Programme food aid is a form of commodity assistance usually provided as short-term balance-of-payments budgetary support. Since the immediate post-World War II era, it has been associated with various forms of conditionality. In Chapter 12, Edward Clay surveys the history of conditionality associated with programme food aid from the Marshall Plan up to recent attempts to integrate commodity assistance with support for structural adjustment programmes.

The United States and the European Community (EC) are the main providers of food aid. Their perspectives differ, and did so particularly in the 1980s. Exploring US policy back to the Marshall Plan, Clay finds that many elements in the present discussions of conditionality emerged with the major food aid programmes first in Europe and in Asia from 1948 and subsequently with PL480 from 1954 onwards. From being almost the single most important form of aid, programme food aid went through a checkered history of political misuse, attempts at sectoral conditionality, and integration into the mainstream of macro-development policy; by the early 1990s, it was being increasingly assimilated into broader packages of commodity assistance to countries involved in structural adjustment.

Europe should seek to avoid the US model where food aid accrued more and more stipulations advancing special interests. The general lesson, Clay argues, is the need for genuine realism amongst those whose 'realist' development practice involves an attempt to attach a complex set of conditions to a single instrument.

First and second generation conditionality involve relations between states and some major international organisations; but non-governmental organisations (NGOs) are also involved in various ways. They may be used by donors as alternative aid channels and they may be affected negatively by the decisions of both parties when conditionality involves brinkmanship; for such reasons, NGOs actively engaged as development agents also seek to influence policy, and other types of NGOs have such efforts as their main rationale.

In Chapter 13, Mark Robinson examines the implications of

political conditionality from three interrelated angles. The first is the direct repercussions of a reduction, suspension or termination of bilateral aid for NGOs and their clients, especially the poor. The second is the channelling of aid through NGOs to promote more accountable government and democratic reform. The third concerns NGO views on political conditionality as presently conceived and alternative conceptions of conditionality from an NGO perspective.

NGOs and human rights agencies could have a greater input than they have had hitherto into donor thinking about political conditionality. This will require a combination of lobbying and advocacy efforts, but NGOs and rights agencies would also have to prove that they have a positive contribution to make. The challenge, Robinson argues, lies in combining NGOs' knowledge of grassroots reality in developing countries with the legal expertise and monitoring capacity of the human rights agencies. The new policy agenda has created a space for a more effective exchange of ideas and a more wide-ranging combination of talents than existed before, which brings with it the possibility of fruitful engagement.

Among the core controversies in the conditionality discourse are the relationship between democracy and development, and the issue of double standards. The sovereignty issue, given a wide interpretation, also belongs to this group. These controversies are intertwined. The last two chapters of this volume enter into these discourses from different perspectives.

Second generation conditionality related to 'good governance' raises the broader issue of state formation. External involvement in state formation processes is no novelty; for the former imperial powers it has been the case since the inception of the decolonised states. However, during recent years, external interference into internal policy frameworks and the structuring of political processes in formally independent Third World countries has acquired a magnitude which adds a new dimension to the *problématique*: state formation under external supervision and direction. In Chapter 14, Martin Doornbos considers recent modes of external intervention with respect to the manner in which Third World countries are expected to structure their policy processes and public administrative frameworks and discusses the characteristics of 'good governance' in a wider developmental perspective.

It is quite possible, Doornbos argues, that one effect of the various external initiatives to promote 'good governance' in Third World countries is, paradoxically, to reduce rather than strengthen the capacity of Third World governments to devise and implement policy. The price of increasing external accountability may be the progressive erosion of policy-making capacity. What is currently being presented as a package of policy prescriptions for 'good governance' fails to recognise that there is no standard formula for fostering an acceptable level of state management and good government: the road to such a destination is mapped out by cultural factors that vary considerably from place to place and change constantly with the pressure of both internal and external dynamics.

In Chapter 15, Georg Sørensen addresses three controversies: the issue of double standards on the part of donors and recipients, the notion of democracy as a problem for policies that aim to promote democratic practice, and the relation between democracy and economic development with particular reference to Southeast Asia.

Donor countries are accused of 'foul play', applying conditionality only when it is politically expedient but not when their economic or security interests are at stake. However, this manifest lack of policy coherence, Sørensen argues, is balanced by a double standard on the part of Third World governing elites who call for respect of sovereignty in the form of freedom from outside intervention but enjoy foreign assistance without providing a development regime.

The debate on democracy in the Third World is both one-dimensional and based on a Western concept. However, a universally valid notion of political rights and civil liberties is gaining ground. If donors wish to give a genuinely high priority to the promotion of democracy, emphasis should be given to the micro level without completely disregarding the macro level, since lasting qualitative changes in the political superstructure require similarly fundamental changes in its basis: the structure of its economy and civil society.

What then of the consequences for economic development in democratic regimes? This debate, Sørensen argues, remains unresolved: it cannot be maintained that democracy as a form of regime is a necessary precondition for economic development, nor that undemocratic regimes are necessarily more successful in developing their economies than democratic ones. It is important not to draw misleading conclusions from the apparent economic success of authoritarian regimes in Southeast Asia.

*

The research and publishing programme has received much help and goodwill. The Ministry of Foreign Affairs in Oslo has generously contributed to the project by funding the major costs involved in organising the Berlin workshop. This grant is acknowledged with pleasure and appreciation. I am also indebted to the institutes with which the authors of the component studies included here are associated for their valuable contributions in kind to this project. Special thanks are due to the German Development Institute for its hospitality, in opening its premises for the workshop in mid-September 1993. The fertile interaction between administrators and researchers at that workshop resulted in a significant strengthening of almost all the papers that are now presented in this volume.

From the very beginning, the project has had the privilege of being integrated in the research programme of the Norwegian Institute of International Affairs in Oslo and has benefited from its institutional support. The project has, in its final stages, benefited from the editorial support of Eilert Struksnes and the efficient secretarial support of Liv Høivik. Warm thanks also go to Wendy Davies and Penny Ormerod for their assistance in editing the present volume.

1

Aid and Political Conditionality: Core Issues and State of the Art

OLAV STOKKE

I. INTRODUCTION

In the 1990s, aid donors have increasingly made official development assistance (ODA) conditional on political and administrative reform in recipient countries. The stated objectives for this second generation conditionality have been to promote democratic reform, human rights and administrative accountability in the South. The first generation conditionality, related to structural adjustment programmes initiated and driven by the International Monetary Fund (IMF)/World Bank, in addition to administrative reform and budget balance, had market liberalisation as the prime objective. The main distinction between the two is that while the first generation aimed at *reform of the economic policy* of the recipient country, the second aimed, above all, at *political reform* involving both systemic and substantive aspects.

Conditions of various kinds have been linked to aid, explicitly or implicitly, throughout the Aid Age. Some have had as their primary purpose to pursue the systemic and private sector interests – economic, cultural, ideological, strategic and/or political – of the donor country. Others have shown concern for effective and efficient aid, achieving the objectives set for it by the donor, including the stated developmental ones.

Note of acknowledgements. An earlier version of this chapter has been commented upon by friends and colleagues. I am grateful for stimulating and helpful comments by Edward Clay, Martin Doornbos, Jacques Forster, Oliver Morrissey, Robrecht Renard, Filip Reyntjens, Mark Robinson, and Peter P. Waller, who are authors of separate chapters in this volume, and by Tore Linné Eriksen of NUPI, Olav Schram Stokke of the Fridtjof Nansen Institute, and Arne Tostensen of the Christian Michelsen Institute. They have all contributed to improvements. Needless to state, I am alone responsible for the chapter, with its perspectives, value assessments and possible misinterpretations and shortcomings.

For the donor governments, development assistance has been – and still is – an instrument to pursue foreign policy objectives. The stated ones relate to economic, social, cultural and political development with an emphasis on poverty alleviation and sustainable development in recipient Third World countries. However, for most donor governments the objectives have been less altruistic and related to the pursuance of more selfish interests. This applies, in particular, to the main powers during the Cold War. For these, aid has been driven by security motives and, for the superpowers, these motives have probably been the most important ones [*Griffin, 1991; Love, 1992*].[1] However, as argued elsewhere [*Stokke, 1989abc*], for some Western middle powers, developmental objectives have been – and still are – the primary motive for providing aid. For these countries, humanitarian objectives (relief operations) probably rank second.

In this chapter, it is my intention to identify the many faces of conditionality related to aid, with particular reference to the 1980s and 1990s, above termed first and second generation conditionality. The two generations have long roots which also will be considered.

The starting point must be to define the core concept: what exactly do we mean when referring to aid conditionality? Conditionality is not an aim in itself but an instrument by which other objectives are pursued. What, then, are these objectives? In this sequence of questions, the next to be addressed concerns the legitimacy of the policy, and relates both to the objectives and the ways in which they are pursued. To what extent are the various combinations of objectives and tools legitimate in the relations between the actors involved? These normative aspects of aid conditionality will be examined.

---

1.   According to Carol Lancaster [*1993a:13*], security concerns were primary and remained the principal pillar on which the United States' aid programme has rested over the past 45 years. The US effort, in the late 1940s, had as the primary objective 'to bolster the economies of Greece and Turkey in the face of communist-led insurgency in the former country and Soviet pressures for territorial concessions from the latter country. The Marshall Plan soon followed aid to Greece and Turkey and was also motivated by a concern that lagging economic recovery in Western Europe would lead to an expansion of communist influence there. From the very beginning, US foreign aid has rested heavily on the need to respond to external threats to US and world security emanating from the Soviet Union. Indeed, it seems likely that without such threats, an insular American public and a sceptical Congress would have never acquiesced to a sizeable foreign aid programme in the years following the Second World War.'
      This justification of foreign aid may be found even in the rhetoric of prominent political actors. Thus, the Secretary of State (Schultz) in the Reagan Administration, introducing his foreign aid budget to Congress in 1984, stated that the programme was 'in effect, the foreign policy budget of the United States. It is that portion of the total Federal budget which directly protects and furthers US national interests abroad' (quoted in Riddell [*1986:32*]).

Effects and efficiency matter, too. Does the instrument work? Does it deliver the results asked for? Under which circumstances and for which objectives does it work and under which does it not? In addressing these questions, the main constraints have also to be identified. Since conditionality is not an aim in itself but basically a means to obtain a variety of objectives, the analysis would not be complete if alternative and supplementary strategies were not explored, both from instrumental and normative criteria. But first I shall briefly describe the evolving patterns of political conditionality – its coming to the fore among bilateral and multilateral aid donors, its rationale, major objectives and modalities.

II. AID AND CONDITIONALITY: EVOLVING PATTERNS

1. There is nothing new ...

The origins of today's foreign aid[2] – with its many open and hidden motives and objectives – are not easily traced. Gifts exchanged between sovereigns have a long tradition – and the real implications of such transfers have always been dependent on a wide variety of circumstantial factors. However, gifts have more often than not been used to buy and maintain friendship, forge alliances, in short, to pursue various objectives with a short- or long-term perspective. Such objectives have also varied in their more specific terms, according to the existing power relations between the parties to the transaction, whether these are characterised by hegemony and dependency, or equality and interdependence. In such relations, the gift, whether of a substantial or symbolic nature, has had as its primary function to secure or increase the power position of the donor or to fend off real or imaged threats – or both; in short, to promote what the donor perceives to be in its own interest.

Development assistance in its many and varied forms is a relatively new phenomenon, dating back to the late 1940s and early 1950s.[3]

2. In this chapter, the terms official development assistance (ODA), foreign aid, development assistance, and development co-operation are used as if they were more or less identical although there is a time sequence in their coining which may reflect conceptual differences. Foreign aid, in particular, may have connotations which transcend the ODA concept by including other types of aid. For a definition of ODA, see OECD [*1992a:A-99*]: 'grants or loans: – undertaken by the official sector; – with promotion of economic development or welfare as main objectives; – at concessional financial terms (if a loan, at least 25 per cent grant element).'
3. In the autumn of 1948, the UN General Assembly adopted two resolutions which had a bearing on aid to what then was termed 'underdeveloped' countries: one expressed the hope that the World Bank would begin providing development loans to

North-South relations, of course, have a much longer history; for several of the major European aid donors, aid relations (along with trade) continued when the colonial relations ended in a more or less orderly way. In the 1960s and 1970s, particularly, the main recipients of bilateral aid from former colonial powers were almost without exception the newly independent countries which had previously been their colonies [*Stokke, 1984a; chapters in Stokke, ed., 1984*]. The relations between an imperial power and its dependency differ in certain important ways from those that pertain following the independence of the latter; this also has a bearing on the concessional transfers involved. However, there are similarities too, which should not be overlooked. Thus France, for instance, included its concessional transfers to its remaining dependencies (the TOMs and DOMs) in its aid statistics up to 1992.

However, the traditions of today's donors differ quite extensively, as does the origin of their aid. Many of the present donor countries have no colonial past. The North-South relations of several of these countries were based on trade and Christian missionary activities. For the Scandinavian countries and several others, aid emerged primarily as a consequence of their international commitment within the United Nations, although also with roots in commercial as well as humanitarian traditions, including relief operations [*Stokke, 1984ab, Forster, 1984*].

A parallel to today's development assistance has also been traced to the Marshall Plan, involving huge financial transfers from the US government to a war-ridden Europe after World War II [*Lancaster, 1993a*]. This generosity was coupled with an enlightened self-interest in creating external environments that coincided with ideological aspirations, economic interests and, already at that time, the security interests of a great power aspiring towards a hegemonic position in an emerging bipolar world system.

---

these countries, and the other made the first allocation from the UN budget for a regular programme of technical assistance in the fields of economic development and public administration. In January 1949, the foreign ministers of the Commonwealth countries met in Colombo and launched the so-called Colombo Plan, arranging for development co-operation within that group of countries. Later that month, President Harry Truman opened his second term with an announcement that the United States should embark on a programme for the improvement and growth of 'underdeveloped areas', emphasising transfers of knowledge, talents and technical know-how through the United Nations and its specialised agencies. The signal was given: only two months later, the UN Economic and Social Council started the process which led to the creation of the Expanded Programme of Technical Assistance (EPTA) – the forerunner of the United Nations Development Programme (UNDP) – which started operations in July 1950, financed by voluntary contributions from member states.

This aid (though not termed development assistance at that time) was given on explicitly political conditions; the recipients had to commit themselves to a policy attuned to the objectives indicated above, with particular emphasis on an open market economy. More than that; as pointed out by Edward Clay [*this volume*], the Marshall Plan included most components of today's first and second generation aid conditionality and the traditional form of aid conditionality (including aid tying) as well. It aimed at protecting both the general economic interest of the United States and special sectional interests within that country, and was explicit about making use of surplus production. However, the bilateral arrangements in East Asia were more similar to the aid conditionality of today than the arrangements in Western Europe where the OEEC made up the principal institutional framework to ensure that the objectives were met. Only in this unique framework, Clay argues, have recipient governments genuinely participated in the decisions about the allocations among themselves of bilateral US aid.

In the early 1950s, the US government also used the mutual defence assistance programme as a lever *vis-à-vis* the participating European governments, with the objective of raising the level of their military expenditure, involving a redirection of public expenditure away from investments in recovery [*Clay, this volume*].

Development assistance became, from the very beginning, an instrument in the international power play between the emerging superpowers in the bipolar world system that evolved after World War II. During the late 1940s and early 1950s, Western powers were quite open about the fact that containing communism in the Third World was the primary purpose of aid – at that time, the United States posed as the most generous aid giver not only in absolute terms but in relative terms as well. The convincing force of the argument at that time is perhaps best illustrated by the fact that elements of it could be found even in the policies of Western countries with a tradition of neutrality.[4] However, it was not only the West which used aid as a foreign policy instrument; the USSR and the Eastern bloc used aid extensively, targeting it at strategically important governments and

---

4.   In the early 1950s, aid was linked to the East-West conflict even by Norwegian spokesmen in the UN. Aid was conceived as an instrument to contain Communism in the developing countries and as a means to promote democracy. In Norwegian domestic politics, particularly within the ruling party (Labour), aid played an additional role: its main function was to serve as a 'positive' foreign policy to balance the arms race between East and West – with rising allocations to defence in the Norwegian budget – and to keep busy those within the party who had been against Norway joining NATO [*Pharo, 1977; 1986*].

social structures. The fact that aid was used in this way contributed to a large extent to weaken this activity already during the USSR's perestroika period in the late 1980s: foreign aid was considered 'ideological' and therefore discredited [*Arefieva, 1990*].

For several Third World governments, this situation left them with at least three options: to enter into an alignment with one of the two superpowers and pick up the reward in terms of foreign aid, or to remain uncommitted and play one against the other and, with good luck, nerve and craftsmanship, obtain rewards from both. The strategic position of the individual Third World government, in military, diplomatic and political terms, influenced the outcome. However, there was little secrecy about the kind of game and stakes involved.

However, the superpowers and other major powers with global or regional aspirations were not alone. Several other governments entered the scene as aid providers with different perspectives with regard both to primary motives and objectives. During the 1960s and 1970s, this new international commitment took on dynamics of its own. Two interrelated factors were instrumental.

The most important single factor was the new, manifest presence of the Third World at world councils; in the 1950s and early 1960s, a large number of newly independent nations changed the face of the United Nations, bringing with them a concern for world poverty and the development needs of the South. The development issue attained top priority on the international agenda; it became of equal importance to the security concerns for which the United Nations was originally created. In turn, this created a new alertness in the North – including the superpowers – to the prevailing needs of the South and a commitment both from governments and within the general public to assist in solving these problems. Development aid emerged as the primary mechanism designed to address the task.

This new concern was manifest in many ways. The international community committed itself to a set of objectives and strategies to bring development home. In the formative years, the strategies which the United Nations adopted for the first and second development decades (the 1960s and 1970s) in particular, were of crucial importance, providing the normative foundation and ideological base for this new activity. The report produced by an international commission [*Pearson, 1969*] represented a milestone in this regard. Although many roots may be traced even here, the new international commitment did not spring from the tradition of power politics, but grew out of the tradition of international humanism [*Stokke, ed., 1989; Pratt,*

6

ed., 1989]. Poverty alleviation and development at the global level were identified as being a concern – and calling for a commitment – that transcended the boundaries of nation states.

During the formative years, a wide variety of conditions applied, in addition to those identified with the tradition of *Realpolitik* in the Cold War setting. Quite a few were associated with policy objectives within the donor society which competed with the developmental ones, particularly those emerging from private sector economic interests, as expressed in procurement tying of aid. Others were associated with the objectives set for aid, typically expressed in the project aid concept (which could easily coincide with the objectives driving the tying of aid), and others again associated with more lofty developmental objectives, such as poverty alleviation or even the promotion of social justice.

2. First Generation Conditionality: Economic Policy Reform

While conditionality, even political conditionality, therefore, is no new phenomenon, what may be seen as new since the late 1970s is that conditions prescribing reforms by recipients of aid are made open and transparent. What triggered this conditionality?

The causes explaining the first generation are different from those which gave rise to the second generation, although the architects and main proponents inhabited the same quarters. First generation conditionality focused on economic reform and came in the wake of the growing economic crisis of many Third World countries, particularly in Latin America and sub-Saharan Africa.

This is not the place for a detailed description of the deep-rooted economic crisis evolving in the late 1970s and early 1980s which has crippled the economy of many Third World countries ever since, nor for analysing the causalities involved. The sources were many and varied, with variations from one region to another, involving droughts (particularly in Africa), increases in the price of petroleum on which the economy of non-oil exporting countries had become dependent, the prolonged recession in industrial countries and the deteriorating terms of trade for raw materials. Early policy responses made the situation worse, not least by giving priority to short-term relief instead of what might serve these countries' longer-term interest, and keeping up the spending by extensive borrowing – even beyond the level required from a balance-of-payments perspective – from commercial and multilateral finance institutions which had petro-dollars in abundance and a relaxed attitude to traditional banking norms involving safety and capital returns.

With heavy debts and increasingly onerous debt-servicing as a result of rising interest rates – as well as continuously deteriorating productivity, terms of trade and market opportunities – the economic situation for many Third World countries became desperate. As a result, commercial financial sources dried up; the financial institutions abandoned their 'open purse' policy and insisted that loans were paid back as quickly as possible. The situation threatened the international financial system involving, in particular, commercial finance institutions in North America and also some in Western Europe.

In this situation the International Monetary Fund (IMF), designed for short-term stabilisation of balance-of-payments crises in the North (and not as a development finance institution), was brought into the picture. Its approach and prescriptions *vis-à-vis* the crisis-ridden Third World governments were much the same as those earlier applied to Northern governments in temporary crisis: they had to observe certain conditions before the IMF would agree to assist with short-term credits.

According to the IMF analysis, the crisis of individual Third World countries was caused by excessive government spending (an unbalance between spending and revenues), resulting in budget deficits and inflation; over-valued currencies; disproportionate imports in relation to exports; and insufficient attention to factors on the supply side. The prescription, accordingly, was to correct these areas of neglect: the domestic economic policy of individual countries had to be reformed.[5] Economic reform was made a condition of assistance through structural adjustment loans.

However, the recipe was not restricted to the conventional wisdom of domestic and foreign housekeeping: the mechanisms prescribed re-

---

5. The IMF (and also the World Bank, particularly during the early structural adjustment period) has all along been criticised for coming up with the same stereotype recommendations which failed to take into consideration the widely varying conditions applying in the countries concerned. The IMF itself has not been unaffected by such criticism, as reflected in the new set of guidelines which was issued after a comprehensive review in 1979, reaffirming that due regard should be paid to members' social, political and economic priorities and objectives, as well as their particular circumstances, including the causes to their balance-of-payments difficulties. Its policy recommendations (conditions for economic relief assistance) when dealing with Third World governments have been strongly and consistently criticised for not taking into account the wisdom reflected in these guidelines. For an early, soft-spoken critique along such lines, see Fahy [*1984:241*], who concludes that 'the IMF has adopted an increasingly standardized approach to economic adjustment programmes, which does not sufficiently reflect differences in the capacity to adjust nor variations in the magnitude of economic shocks among countries. ... the assumptions underlying the monetarist framework used by the IMF are not appropriate for all developing economies.'

flected a neo-liberal economic perspective and were therefore highly political. Structural adjustments of international economic relations were not part of the perspective; by the early 1980s, the programme for a new international economic order (NIEO), conceived in the mid-1970s, already belonged to the distant past. The World Bank joined forces with the IMF, the main bilateral donors and – in the second half of the 1980s – 'like-minded' governments also fell into line. With few other sources of finance, individual, debt-ridden Third World countries had little choice but to accept the conditions.

3. Second Generation Conditionality: Systemic and Policy Reforms

While the Third World's economic crisis of the late 1970s and early 1980s triggered off first generation political conditionality, the revolutionary changes which took place in the Second World towards the end of the 1980s – involving systemic transformation in Eastern and Central Europe and the disintegration both of the Soviet bloc and its core power, the USSR – triggered off second generation conditionality. However, although the new emphasis given to political reform as a condition for aid coincided in time with this revolution, the causalities involved are probably indirect.

The disintegration of the Soviet bloc and its core power implied that the bipolar international system which had dominated international relations and world politics since World War II belonged to the past and that the Cold War was over. In the emerging world order, with the competition between East and West for political influence and strategic positions in the Third World removed, Western governments felt freer than before to pursue basic political concerns *vis-à-vis* the governments of the South. Pursuance of predominant Western political norms and interests – relating in particular to governmental system (democracy, rule of law) and human rights, above all civil rights – and of the prevailing Western economic system, with the market keeping an upper hand in mixed economies, replaced security policy considerations as the primary concern.

Other processes worked in the same direction. There are inter-linkages between the first and the second generation aid conditionality. After years, the structural adjustment programmes had produced few result in terms of economic recovery, particularly in Africa. This led to a growing recognition, in the Bretton Woods institutions, that the main cause had to be sought in what Myrdal earlier had termed the soft state [*Myrdal, 1969*]; economic policy reform, accordingly, had to be combined with reform of the political and administrative systems [*World Bank, 1989*]. Of equal importance were developments which took place in the Third World itself. During the 1980s, internal pressures had been mounting in several countries primarily caused by the economic crisis and the hardships resulting from the prescribed cure. In Africa, such pressures were also nourished by the democratisation process which was taking place in Central and South America; towards the end of the decade, the revolutions in Eastern and Central Europe added fuel and kindled new hopes to those in opposition to autocratic malgovernment.

Another interpretation, which does not necessarily contradict the first, is that, in the absence of the Cold War, some major Western governments needed a new justification *vis-à-vis* their own electorate for continuing to give aid to the South. The promotion of values cherished in their own societies, in combination with other aspects included in the concept of good government ('good governance'), emerged as the answer [*Lancaster, 1993a*]. This explanation may, if correct, also explain why there are different brands of political conditionality at work and why the emphasis of different donors varies.

Other interpretations have been offered, including the argument that the new forms of conditionality have little to do with the West's desire for democracy; it is an ideological device seeking to replace the vision of socialism with that of capitalism world-wide while creating a new legitimacy for hegemony by participating in the removal of discredited regimes [*Barya, 1993; Gills et al., 1993*].[6] A concern for the

---

6. Barry Gills *et al.* [*1993:5*] maintain that 'the identification of capitalism with democracy is a not very well-hidden ideological bias of certain Western studies of Third World democracy. Today, the particular forms of democracy promoted by the West in the Third World are specifically tailored to serve the interests of global capital in these countries. Here, a political economic orthodoxy of hegemonic power holders is presented as being a matter of natural law, whether economic or developmental, rather than as a specific product of historical conditions, conflict over the pursuit of interests, and class struggle.' The US change of policy in the late 1980s – towards support for the democratisation process in countries run by authoritarian regimes which in some cases had previously received tacit or active US support – is seen as tactically motivated: a civilianised, conservative regime could pursue painful and even repressive social and economic policies with greater impunity and with less popular resistance than could an openly authoritarian regime. Thus, what is termed 'low intensity democracy' complements the economic policy offensive managed principally by the IMF with the primary aim to break down political barriers to the further transnationalisation of capital [*ibid.:8-9*]. It may be concluded, according to the authors [*ibid.:7*], that 'the new democratic facade [in Third World countries] will cloak new forms of authoritarianism, repression and conservatism, and legitimise further incorporation and subordination to global capital.'

With particular reference to the actual democratisation process taking place in Latin America during the 1980s, the authors [*ibid.:9*] refer to the 1982 'Crusade for democracy' speech by US President Reagan to the British Parliament and the subsequent double standard doctrine on authoritarianism of the US Ambassador to the UN, Jeane Kirkpatrick, justifying US support for capitalist authoritarianism in the context

effectiveness of aid and its legitimacy may also apply – corrupt practices by state administrations and malpractice of funds endanger the legitimacy of aid in donor societies [*Andreassen and Swinehart, 1992:xii*]. For some governments, an additional motive might well be to establish respectable arguments to justify further cuts in their ODA commitments [*Moore, 1993a:2-3*] or to transfer aid from traditional to other recipients in order to promote interests and values elsewhere.

III. SOME CHARACTERISTICS OF AID CONDITIONALITY

Political conditionality attached to development assistance is primarily associated with *state-to-state relations* and *international agency-to-state relations* involving development assistance: the donor sets certain conditions to be met by the recipient as a prerequisite for entering into an aid agreement or for keeping up aid. However, it may also affect ODA channelled through NGOs and the private sector in general. Actors within the private sector and NGOs of a donor country may set conditions for involving themselves in activities in a recipient country. And for an aid agency/ministry, NGOs and their own private sector may also offer themselves as alternative channels for aid when the authorities on both sides do not see eye-to-eye. These channels may be considered instrumental in pursuing the objectives set.

The *definition* of aid conditionality is, of course, crucial for the discussion and is itself controversial. The key element is the use of

---

of Cold War rivalry, which eventually gave way to a pragmatic preference to replace certain client authoritarian with 'democratic' successors: 'By the end of 1989, the dictatorships of Latin America, many originally put in place with US help and afterwards supported by it against their own people, had virtually all been replaced by "democratic" governments. In Central America, by 1990, there had been an overall consolidation by conservative civilian governments.' The Reagan Doctrine 'exemplified an aggressive foreign policy posture designed to halt any further progress of revolutionary forces anywhere in the world and, beyond that, to roll back revolution wherever feasible through various forms of covert or overt intervention'. According to the authors [*ibid.:17*], the 'crusade for democracy' was, in Central America, accompanied by 'state-sponsored campaigns of murder, torture and general barbarism. In most cases this war was waged from "within" by the military and paramilitary death squads. The main exception was Nicaragua ... At best, the US tolerated, and at worst directly promoted the most grotesque abuses of human rights in recent history throughout Central America.'

Samir Amin [*1993:78*] concludes in the same vein: the current offensive of the West is concealing the destabilising tendency of democracy and is 'not really an offensive in favour of democracy, but an offensive against socialism. The cause of democracy – in its impoverished form as a means of stabilizing an alienated society – is then mobilised as a tactical weapon.' See also *infra*, notes 31, 42 and 63.

11

pressure, by the donor, in terms of threatening to terminate aid, or actually terminating or reducing it, if conditions are not met by the recipient. Foreign aid is used as a lever to promote objectives set by the donor which the recipient government would not otherwise have agreed to. The donor may set the pursuit of such objectives, by the recipient, as a condition for entering into an aid relationship (*ex ante* conditionality); or expectations of the recipient's progress towards meeting these objectives may be expressed beforehand and followed up afterwards (*ex post* conditionality).[7] The objectives may vary; second generation conditionality includes far-reaching objectives such as systemic change, ultimately involving the very system of government, and policy changes, involving policy priorities and implementation, on the aid recipient side.

This definition places the emphasis on coercive aspects – *denial* of aid resulting from non-compliance on the part of the recipient government to demands for reform. Other definitions of the concept include also the carrot.[8] The type of reform requested may, however, vary.

---

7. The distinction between *ex ante* and *ex post* conditionality, as defined here, may indeed be blurred. *Ex ante* conditionality implies that the donor will not provide aid to a government if certain standards have not been met in the recipient government's previous behaviour (an *ex post* assessment) and/or unless there are reforms in order to meet such standards or an explicit commitment to undertake such reforms. However, *ex post* conditionality may presuppose that certain standards have been met in the recipient government's previous performance or even a tacit *ex ante* commitment to this end. *Ex post* conditionality implies an explicit understanding by both parties that continued aid (volume and form) at some *future* point in time will be dependent on the recipient government's performance *vis-à-vis* certain standards in the meantime, as assessed by the donor government (or the international agency) involved.

It may be argued that to the extent *ex ante* conditionality is based on past performance, aid – in this context – may involve an element of reward for good behaviour. This represents an argument in favour of including into the concept 'positive conditionality', as defined in the following footnote.

8. Several authors have come up with a broader definition which includes both the stick and the carrot – even authors included in this volume. This applies explicitly to Peter P. Waller [*this volume*], who uses the term 'negative conditionality' when aid is reduced if the human rights/democracy performance is reduced, and 'positive conditionality' when aid is increased as a response to an improving performance (termed by the Japanese government as 'positive linkage' – a reward for good behaviour [*Ball, 1992*]); in addition he refers to positive measures in support of these objectives (termed by Nelson and Eglinton [*1992:46*] 'democracy bonus' when that particular objective is involved), which are not included in his conditionality concept. Also Robrecht Renard and Filip Reyntjens [*this volume*], implicitly, adhere to a similar definition of the concept. Samuel S. Mushi [*this volume*] distinguishes between 'explicit' and 'implicit' conditionality, the first corresponding to Waller's 'negative conditionality', the second to 'positive measures'. Other prominent participants in the debate have applied even broader definitions; thus, John P. Lewis [*1993:41*] defines conditionality broadly as 'donor efforts of one kind or another to influence recipient policies.' Although it may identify a policy geared to certain objectives, the core mechanism, retained in Waller's definition (which excludes 'positive measures'), is then removed.

Although general, and therefore open to different interpretations as to what may or may not be included, this definition limits what can be included in the concept; it may even be too narrow to include interventions that deserve our attention. What may be termed *positive conditionality*, that is, interventions using additional aid as an argument for reforms – falls outside the definition, or may belong to a grey area. Policy dialogue also belongs to a grey area. It may qualify for inclusion the moment non-compliance is followed up by a reduction in the volume of aid; but what if a dialogue, the purpose of which is to explore whether the framework conditions for effective aid are met, discourages the donor?

This elaboration illustrates how difficult it is to operationalise the concept in a way that includes most manifestations associated with it. The following analysis and discussion will therefore not be restricted to those manifestations which clearly fall within the confines of the concept as defined; also other ways of attaining the objectives involved will be explored. Although a harmonisation of objectives has taken place among the bilateral and multilateral donors during recent years – both as regards first and second generation conditionality – there are still variations both with regard to substance and emphasis. And there are different agendas.

IV. LEVELS OF INTERVENTION AND MAIN OBJECTIVES

The roots of today's conditionality (Section II) clearly demonstrate that different types of aid conditionality apply, that conditionality applies at several levels and that it may have quite different objectives. It is also apparent that the current trend is towards increasing conditionality with an ever higher degree of political interference. However, donor countries have not been identical in their approach; whereas the major powers have, directly or indirectly, pursued policies involving conditionality at a high level of political intervention throughout the Aid Age, for others this represents a recent trend associated with the first and second generation conditionality of the late 1980s and 1990s.

1. Levels of Conditionality

It makes sense to distinguish between various levels of conditionality (the degree of intervention). One reason is the assumption that an intervention at a high level is more serious than interventions at lower levels; however, although the degree of an intervention matters, no linear relation applies since also other factors influence the degree of legitimacy or illegitimacy of an intervention. Six levels of conditionality may be distinguished:

(1) The highest degree of political intervention applies to *the systemic level*, involving the system of government and governing institutions. Several demands of the second generation conditionality belong clearly to this category; amongst these are the pressure for democratic reform and the introduction of a multi-party system and free and fair elections, as well as for improved human rights. They also include the 'good governance' agenda in general. Some of the conditions associated with the first generation conditionality also apply here, in particular, demands for an open economy and for the removal of traditional mechanisms of state interventions into the domestic market and those determining inter-state economic transactions. They include, too, prescriptions for a reduced role of the state in the economy in terms of owning and running productive enterprises (state enterprises and parastatals).[9]

(2) Attempts by foreign governments to change *national policies and priorities* represent an almost equally high degree of political intervention. Both first generation conditionality, involving the economic policy of the recipient country, and second generation conditionality, involving human rights, democracy and 'good governance', apply at this level.

(3) Attempts to change *specific policies* – within an area or a sector – represent a high degree of intervention. The borderlines between this and level 2 (above) may well be somewhat blurred, as sectoral policies may have a national bearing involving taxes (and duties) and prices, although limited to a specific sector or area. Legislation, although specific to a sector or policy area, belongs to the same grey area between (2) and (3). Still, a matter of *degree* is involved which marks the distinction: wide-spectrum economic policy reforms pursued within the context of the first generation conditionality clearly belong to (2), whereas specific price mechanisms involving, for example, an agrarian product clearly belong to (3).

(4) A fourth level of intervention refers to the *programme/project* level. The borderline between (3) and (4) may be blurred, particularly when sector programmes are involved. Conditions at this level may involve institutional reform, official regulations, and financial or per-

---

9. Political conditionality at this level of interference is not an invention of the 1980s; after World War II, democratic reforms were imposed on the losers (Germany, Japan) as a condition of support for their reconstruction efforts.

sonnel contributions with reference to the environments of the aid activity. These conditions determine how the recipient uses its own funds for investments and, particularly, for recurrent costs. The selection of project activities and technology influences policies and priorities at the recipient side.

(5) Financial conditions also apply; a basic distinction is between grants and credits, but also the terms of credits matter. Other conditions in this category include the financing of local costs, the financing of maintenance and recurrent costs and procurement tying. Thus a donor quite frequently declares interest in supporting a project only if a particular type of technology (available in the donor country) is used in implementing it.

(6) *Administrative conditions* also apply, involving procedures for the transfer of resources, accounting, reporting, evaluation, privileges enjoyed by technical co-operation personnel and project/programme-related imports, etc.

Although apparently 'technical', (5) and (6) encroach onto the policy arena of the recipient country.

Most aid agencies have always set conditions at the levels (4) to (6), with variations in degree and follow-up, and continue to do so. Current debate largely concerns levels (1) to (3), in particular (1) and (2), and involves most donors rather than being restricted to the major powers, as in the past.

2. The Main Objectives of Aid Conditionality

Objectives pursued through aid conditionality vary from one level of intervention to another. The assumption is that, in a development assistance relationship, some of these objectives are more legitimate than others; pursuit of established developmental objectives would be more legitimate than objectives which were less directly related to the development agenda. As indicated, some of the objectives pursued relate to the development agenda whereas others relate to the donor's interests and values, and the link to developmental objectives set for aid may be quite indirect if present at all.

At the three lowest levels of political intervention ((4)-(6)) – particularly level (4), the area where the aid agencies, according to Gus Edgren [*1984:161*], 'feel more at home in exercising our "petty imperialism" ' – the conditions set may to some extent aim to satisfy the selfish interests of the donor. However, most conditions set at these levels aim at the improvement of aid in terms of its effectiveness *vis-à-vis* the developmental objectives set and efficiency in terms of management and cost-effectiveness.

15

Conditions set in order to promote the donor's self-interest, particularly export promotion of commodities and services, have an impact on the real value of ODA to the recipient. Catrinus Jepma [*1993*] has calculated that aid tying reduces the value, on average, by 15-30 per cent. The recipient of tied aid may, however, be exposed to even more damaging effects due to ill-adapted technology. An example of this problem, now notorious, is the case of a water development programme in Kenya which received 18 different types of pumps from donors which had tied their aid. The problems involved in running such a programme when servicing and spare parts are required are easily imaginable [*Duncan and Mosley, 1985*]. With inappropriate technology, even grant aid can be expensive for the recipient.

2.1 Welfare and social justice

The devastating effects of some conditions imposed on the recipients of aid in order to satisfy donor self-interest deserve to be exposed. However, most conditions related to levels (4)-(6) are framed in a development perspective, in terms of the developmental objectives set by donor governments for their aid. Usually, the link is a quite transparent and direct one.

The particulars of the development agenda have changed over the years. In the 1960s and 1970s, *economic and social development* and poverty alleviation held a prominent position. During most of the 1960s, the main concern was economic growth, with the implicit assumption that benefits would 'trickle down': aid with a poverty focus was directed to poor countries. In the late 1960s and increasingly in the 1970s, the assumption of a 'trickle-down' effect was questioned. As a consequence, an economic growth strategy was coupled with the targeting of aid more directly to improve the lot of the poorer segments of the population, or aid was given other forms assumed to affect the welfare of poor people (health, education). In the mid-1970s, basic human needs emerged as the focal point for aid, particularly after the strategy adopted by the International Labour Organisation (ILO) had been endorsed by the OECD. Several bilateral donors targeted part of their aid to vulnerable social groups, children, women or the poorest groups in general. In his address to the 1973 annual meeting of the World Bank in Nairobi, Robert McNamara, then President of the Bank, identified the poorest 40 per cent of the population as the target group. A revival of this concern, after the preoccupation with macro-economic structural adjustments in the 1980s, is reflected in the focus on human development in the 1990s, driven by the United Nations Development Programme [*UNDP, 1990, 1991, 1992*]. It is also reflected in the more recent return to a poverty focus by the World Bank.[10]

The policy context obtaining in the individual countries is crucial for the success of aid with a poverty alleviation objective or, more generally, for the attainment of social justice objectives. In order to be effective, aid geared towards these objectives has to be integrated within government policies that are similar in orientation.

Governments with these kinds of policy are not in abundance in the so-called developing world. On the contrary, in most of the Third World the state has lost much of its legitimacy during the past three decades due to governments being run by people driven by the desire for self-enrichment and with little concern for the well-being of the nation, let alone a concern for the poorer segments of the population. Such governments have emerged both from traditional, *ascribed* elites and from the new economic and professional *achieving* elites – the

---

10. The policy positions of the IMF and the World Bank on structural adjustment conditions – as stated and followed up – have not always been identical; and the World Bank position has been inconsistent since the policy was formulated in the early 1980s. The policy was under fire from the outside, particularly for the hardship it caused to vulnerable social groups [*Cornia et al., 1987*], and the World Bank was brought on the defensive. For an interesting inside review of the evolving policy, with particular reference to Africa, see Serageldin and Faruqee [*1993*], a paper presented to the EADI workshop in Berlin.

The process leading to a propelling intervention is a particularly interesting one. When governments, in order to obtain loans, were requested to cut public spending, the first targets for most were social services and education. When criticised for destroying the social security net (also from inside the Bank), it approached the governments telling them that they should cut, but not in the way they had done. It then became a problem to get out of this intrusion trap, by transferring the 'owner-ship' of the policy to the governments themselves. As portrayed by Serageldin and Faruquee [*ibid.:8-9*]: '... in periods of economic stress, there is a heightened risk that the poor and the vulnerable will be the ones to bear the brunt of adjustment unless special efforts are made to guard against such an outcome. Unfortunately, many African governments have been dominated by powerful elites little concerned about the welfare of poorer strata of society. This has forced the Bank to confront some truly difficult choices. On the one hand, an effort has been made to build the government's "ownership" of the program, which meant allowing the government to play the lead role in drafting the program. On the other hand, the Bank was determined that actions be included in the adjustment program to protect the poor and vulnerable from undue hardship and to give them a chance to participate more fully in the ensuing period of income growth than had been the case in the past. In pursuing these two inherently contradictory objectives, the Bank often found itself drawn into pressing governments to spend more on basic health and education than the country's leadership would itself have chosen.'

For a brief survey of the policy, with particular reference to the World Bank's 'pro-poor aid' stance, see Lewis [*1993*]. For recent positions, see also a policy paper issued by the World Bank in 1991 [*World Bank, 1991*] and two progress reports issued in 1994 [*World Bank, 1994ab*].

power basis for quite a few of them has been their control of the coercive powers (the police and the military).[11]

Most donor governments have given high priority to poverty allevi- ation, seeking to contribute to lasting improvements in the lot of the worst-off. This is in no way limited to the front runners, the Scandi- navian and Dutch governments [*Stokke, ed., 1984; 1989*]. Since most aid is channelled through Third World governments, it makes sense to ask if the donor governments, in the past or more recently, have brought pressure to bear on the recipients in order to bring about policy reform for the benefit of the poor. More precisely, to what extent have they made aid dependent on the recipient governments' efforts to attain objectives included in the social agenda or on their performance in this regard?

Few, if any, donor governments have made ODA conditional on such policy reforms or on budgetary redistribution in favour of the poor.[12] However, in the 1970s a few set such regime features as cri- teria for the selection of main recipients of bilateral aid (see chapters on Netherlands, Norway and Sweden in Stokke, ed. [*1984*]), but this stated policy affected aid implementation only marginally, as argued in the case of Norway [*Stokke, this volume*].[13]

---

11. Commenting on the lack of legitimacy which characterises post-colonial African states, Georg Sørensen [*1993b:15-17*] refers to neo-patrimonialism – personal rule based on personal loyalty especially to the leading figure of the regime, the strong- man. All important positions in the state – political, bureaucratic, military, police – are filled by loyal followers, relatives, friends, kinsmen, tribesmen. Their loyalty is re- inforced by sharing the spoils of office. Political decisions are up for sale, the capacity of the bureaucracy is destroyed by its participation in the system of spoils. And the weakest point is the political elite itself. The core feature of the developmental state – the autonomy from groups involved in zero-sum activities including corruption – is turned on its head [*ibid.:17*]: 'the political elite is by far the strongest zero-sum group in society, and it has more than merely access to the state; it controls it directly. It is clear that very little in terms of *statecraft* seriously promoting economic development can be expected to emerge in this situation, neither from the bureaucracy enmeshed in the spoils system, nor from the political elite itself.'

For similar observations, see also Robinson [*1993b:88-9*], adding that despite the implicit recognition on the part of most aid donors of the deleterious effects of personalised and authoritarian rule, most were very generous with their development assistance which may have bolstered regime legitimacy and enabled authoritarian rulers to remain in power.

12. However, according to Lewis [*1993:36-40*], some governments (the United Stat- es, Germany, the Netherlands) have recently developed systems of aid criteria which take into consideration, when deciding the overall allocation of aid, how effectively recipients' policies strengthen the poor; this also applies, according to Lewis [*ibid.:32-4*], to the World Bank's IDA funding, and represents allocative condi- tionality.

13. John P. Lewis, formerly President of OECD's Development Assistance Com- mittee (DAC), has recently made a hesitant plea for making aid conditional on the recipient's social justice performance [*Lewis, 1993*]; he is fully aware of and

This is a striking observation, particularly since social justice has been the main justification and core objective of development aid, especially for the most ardent providers. Conditionality has come to the fore in connection with those objectives which now have gained the ascendancy but which were previously seen as secondary in the aid setting, namely economic and political reform involving neo-liberalism, human rights and democracy. This represents a change of perspective, even an overall change of priority, particularly as far as the governments most committed to aid are concerned.

2.2 Economic policy reform

During the 1960s and 1970s, a large share of aid – from bilateral and multilateral sources alike – was directed towards *projects* within a variety of areas and sectors and with a broad range of purposes. The distinction between projects and programmes may, however, be blurred; some projects may be extensive both in terms of scope and financial input, and some programmes which include several single projects, such as sector programmes, may have many of the character- istics associated with a project.

This focus on more circumscribed activities – which is the core characteristic of a project – contradicts the recognition of develop- ment as a holistic process, which in no way is a new one although it became more broadly accepted during the 1970s. Single projects might be successes within their limited settings without necessarily contributing much to the overall development of the recipient country or towards the overall aims set for aid by the donor. On the other hand, the degree of success or failure of a single project is not unaffected by circumstantial factors, at the national as well as the local level. During the late 1970s and early 1980s, it became broadly recognised in the aid community that national policy, particularly the economic framework conditions, mattered.

Crises tend to foster stocktaking and even invention and reform. The deep-rooted, structural economic crisis in large parts of the Third World at the end of the 1970s generated the first generation of condi- tionality. The main objective was crisis management: to put the eco- nomies of Third World countries concerned in order, that is, to restore their balance. This objective has not been contested. The controversy

---

appreciates the constraints involved, particularly the difficulty of operating a large number of conditions: the mechanism as such may be weakened involving a subsequent weakening of conditions of a higher ranking within the Bretton Woods institutions.

starts when it comes to the ways and means, involving burden-sharing and the other agendas (particularly the neo-liberal drive) which were integrated into this rescue operation and which turned into a programme for structural reforms of the economy.

The main components of this programme have already been indicated (II.2). Measures to tackle the immediate crisis – their economies had come out of control partly as a result of changes in the international economy, including a dramatic rise in interest rates, followed by galloping debts – were combined with measures that aimed at more fundamental and far-reaching policy reforms with ideological connotations: shifting the balance between the state and the market in the direction of the market, and scaling down the role of the state in the economy, both with regard to its traditional role of setting the rules of the game (calling, instead, for fewer restrictions) and its active role in the economy in terms of owning and running enterprises (demanding privatisation).

A crucial point in the context of our analysis concerns the relationship between the objectives pursued through aid conditionality and the objectives set for aid. Obviously the two sets of objectives may coincide: if the economy finds itself in disarray, aid may be of little use in terms of supporting sustainable development; at worst its effects may even be negative by delaying necessary reforms, at best it may serve as relief. In such a setting, measures to get the economy in balance are a precondition for aid to work. Stating this does not, of course, imply a blind acceptance of any measure proposed.

However, the two sets of objectives may also be conflicting. Such conflicts may be identified at the level of theory: although neo-liberal thinking received a boost in the 1980s, particularly in the Bretton Woods institutions and as far as some major Western governments were concerned, the blessings of the market and a reduced and different role of the state are in no way uncontested. On the contrary, it could be argued that a high degree of state intervention and regulations as well as an active role in facilitating an enabling environment for economic activities are necessary for crisis-ridden Third World countries to put their house in order, both with regard to the domestic and foreign economy – although, admittedly, the argument can draw little support from the way state powers have been used during the last decades by several Third World governments, particularly in Africa.[14] As argued by Leftwich [1994:373], sustained economic

---

14. For a comprehensive analysis, see Martin Doornbos [1990]. He observes that the expectations which, in the 1960s, were held, within both liberal and Marxist paradigms, to the developmental role of the state proved ill-founded, both *vis-à-vis* the

growth in late developers is the product of patterns of politics which tend to concentrate in the state both the political will and the bureaucratic competence to establish a developmental momentum in a competitively hostile international environment.

Moreover, for the donors there is an explicit contradiction between the social justice objectives described in the previous section and the economic reform agenda, at least in short term. This conflict may apply at the theoretical level; in the allocation of aid, the conflict is obvious, since the various purposes compete for the (ODA) resources: during the 1980s and early 1990s, budgetary priority has been given, by the major multilateral and bilateral donors, to the economic reform agenda at the expense of the social welfare agenda.

2.3 Political reform: democracy, human rights, 'good governance'

The objectives included in second generation political conditionality are far from new; foreign aid represents a transfer not only of resources and technologies, but of culture and values as well. These values have always been part of the aid baggage – even in the 1960s when such political aspects of aid were played down – and have been, explicitly or implicitly, core issues in the development concept, probably of equal importance to the economic and social issues (economic growth and social justice). As argued elsewhere [*Stokke, 1989abc*], the foreign aid of Western middle powers has its strongest roots in these values.

However, it was not until the end of the 1980s that these issues were brought to the fore of the foreign aid agenda.[15] At the highest level, where the signals to move were first given, the various components of second generation conditionality were intertwined with the objectives of the first generation. Western political leaders, including those with responsibility for foreign aid, expressed the policy aspects

state and the civil society it confronted under the prevailing conditions. 'In case after case, high expectations were followed by profound disillusionment, and the rôle attributed to the African state changed from the prime mover of development to that of its main obstacle' [*ibid.:183*]. For another penetrating analysis of the state in sub-Saharan Africa, which concludes that several of them are seriously lacking in the essentials of statehood, see Jackson and Rosberg [*1986*].
15. Uvin [*1993a:65*] refers to 'two timid' earlier attempts at political conditionality: that of US President Carter in 1977, when he declared that the US would 'reform those policies that accord assistance to repressive governments that violate human rights'; and the French Minister of Development Co-operation, M. Cot, who in 1983 set out to promote morality in his country's policy towards Africa. Encountering the many obstacles of *Realpolitik*, Carter soon retired to greater 'political realism', and Cot lost his job after 15 months in office. See also *supra*, note 6, and *infra*, notes 31, 42 and 63.

21

explicitly.[16] In 1989, the members of the OECD Development

---

16. For a selection of statements, see IDS [*1993*] and Nelson and Eglinton [*1992:15-17*].

The *British* policy position was stated by the Foreign Secretary, Douglas Hurd, in June 1990, arguing that increased political freedom and better governance were essential for economic and social progress in Africa and called for a concerted approach by all major aid donors to improve good government, political pluralism and more open economies, adding that the UK government would also utilise opportunities to support countervailing sources of power and NGOs. One year later, the Minster for Overseas Development, Lynda Chalker, spoke in the same vein, committing Britain to increase its aid targeted to good government (from £28 to £50 million a year).

The *French* policy position was spelled out by the Minister of Co-operation and Development, Jacques Pellier, in statements (in January 1990) arguing that development was not feasible without democracy. France would be solidly on the side of those who made necessary reforms. At a conference of Heads of State of Francophone Africa at La Boule in June 1990, President François Mitterrand confirmed this position, although France would not link aid to specific formal conditions regarding democratic practice.

In 1991, *Germany* produced new guidelines which are presented by Peter Waller [*this volume*]: among the five new criteria for aid, the first three – respect for civil rights, participation of the population in the political process, and the guarantee of the rule of law – related to basic civil and political rights.

In June 1992, *Japan*, traditionally oriented towards economic growth, adopted a special 'Official Development Assistance Charter', emphasising poverty relief, human rights, democracy, environment and reduced military spending.

The policy position of the *Netherlands* was spelled out in an extensive, new white paper in September 1990 [*NMFA, 1991*], *inter alia* emphasising programmes supportive of poverty alleviation, local participation and human rights. A follow-up report three years later [*NMFA, 1993*] adds to this.

In September 1990, the *Nordic* ministers of Development Co-operation, meeting in Molde (Norway), issued a declaration stating that the link between democracy, human rights and sustainable development had become increasingly clear; that the Nordic countries always have had democratic societal development among their main objectives for aid; and that obvious issues in the dialogue with their partner countries would be the prevailing conditions for democracy, respect of human rights and emphasis on popular participation in the development process. In this dialogue, they would convey how important democracy was for development and progress: 'In countries where the democratisation process does not move forward, the donors willingness to provide aid will be influenced' [*Nordic Ministers, 1990*].

The United States linked its foreign aid to democracy and human rights performance in the mid-1970s. At the end of 1990, the US Agency for International Development (USAID) followed this up with its democracy initiative, stating that USAID allocations to individual countries would take account of progress towards democracy.

The European Community included a reference to human rights in the Lomé Convention of 1984; in the 1989 Lomé agreement (Art. 5), development co-operation was explicitly seen as an instrument to promote human rights, although the EC continued to adhere to the principle of non-interference in the internal affairs of the ACP (African, Caribbean and Pacific) countries. However, in the European Council resolution of 28 November 1991, fostering of human rights (civil and political liberties by means of representative democratic rule that is based on respect for human rights along with economic and social rights) was established as a goal for development co-operation.

The policy positions of a few additional European governments are spelled out in

Assistance Committee (DAC) jointly agreed on the main themes for this agenda and these positions were developed further over the following years [*OECD, 1992b, 1993*].[17]

Although providing a clear general direction, such statements do

---

this volume: Belgium (Renard and Reyntjens), Norway (Stokke), and Switzerland (Forster). For the follow up of some of the early policy statements, see also *supra*, note 6 and *infra*, note 42.

17. In the 1989 statement, DAC claimed that 'there is a vital connection, now more widely appreciated, between open, democratic and accountable political systems, individual rights and the effective and equitable operation of economic systems'. It maintained that 'Participatory development implies more democracy, a greater role for local organisations and self-government, respect of human rights including effective and accessible legal systems, competitive markets and dynamic private enterprise'. However, the new emphasis on participatory development did not imply by-passing governments: 'effective development requires strong and competent governments and public services'. This statement established objectives (reconfirmed by the DAC 1990 high-level meeting), but did not invoke conditionality as defined here; however, what has been termed 'positive conditionality' was implied. This was emphasised more strongly in 1991 (OECD Ministerial Council, June), when 'reducing excessive military expenditures' was added as an objective along with 'combating the illicit production, trafficking and consumption of narcotics'; ensuring environmental sustainability was already an established objective. The DAC principles for programme assistance established in 1991 stated that this type of aid and other government-to-government assistance is 'inappropriate' in situations where there are gross violations of internationally recognised human rights. Donors 'need to assure themselves that the recipient country's overall resource and budget allocation priorities are consistent with development aims, paying attention also to expensive prestige projects and large military expenditures.' The DAC 1991 high-level meeting reconfirmed these aid objectives, this time emphasising human resource development and adding that DAC members have become increasingly affirmative in discussions with their developing country partners on the importance of participatory development.

At this stage, conditionality, although still diffuse, is brought into the open: the issues referred to are considered central to their aid relationship 'and very important to their own constituencies. While DAC Members acknowledge the complexities of the issues involved, progress in these areas is bound to become an increasingly important consideration in aid allocations.' The trends towards democratisation in many countries is warmly greeted: DAC members 'will further encourage this process through appropriate development assistance activities and the policy of dialogue, and particularly respect for human rights, representative government accountable to its citizens, and good governance within a framework of law.' Reduction in 'excessive military expenditures' is particularly mentioned in this regard: the growing attention to such spending by the multilateral institutions (World Bank, IMF, UNDP) is welcomed, noting that several DAC members increasingly take the size of and trends in military spending into account when aid is allocated.

In 1993, it is noted that a key cross-cutting concern in these issues is countering the systematic under-representation of the female half of the population in all the processes and institutions concerned. The environmental concerns should also be integrated. The key emphasis was on capacity building, particularly education. The DAC members wished 'to rely to the maximum extent on measures of positive support, but they also wish to be clear about the potential for negative measures affecting the volume and form of their aid, in areas of serious and systematic violations of human rights and brutal reversals from democratisation, or when a complete lack of good governance renders efficient and effective aid impossible' [*OECD, 1993:8-9*].

not go into the nuances and specifics involved, related to norms, strategies to be applied, methods and modalities; nor should this be expected, given the context in which they are made. The statements vary in the way they are phrased and in the emphasis given to various components. Most, however, make reference to democracy, transparency, predictable government according to the rule of law, respect for human rights, accountability and an effective and non-corrupt administration. They are subsumed under the concept of 'good government'.[18]

In this chapter, 'good government' includes the three agendas dealt with next, namely 'good governance', human rights and democracy.[19] The concept may well be broadened, as other agendas – such as military spending – are frequently associated with second generation political conditionality. This agenda will not be included here although it is important to several of the governments focused on [*this volume, chapters on Germany, Norway and Switzerland*].[20] Another

---

18. According to the British government, good government consists of three elements, namely '*Competence*: sound economic policies, effective use of resources, absence of corruption, avoidance of excessive military expenditure. *Legitimacy and accountability*: freedom of expression, political pluralism, broad participation in the development process. *Respect for human rights and the rule of law.*' (Foreign and Commonwealth Office, 1992:para. 35.1, here quoted from Hewitt and Killick [*1993*]).

The British Minister of Overseas Development, in a speech to the Commonwealth Press Union Conference (in Edinburgh, 22 June 1992), was more sweeping (quoted from Moore [*1993a:3*]): 'By good government, I mean the attitude and conduct of those responsible for administration, right down to grass roots level. Even where these are right, the best plan for action and the highest-minded intentions will fail if those who implement them are not equal to the task. So training is vital. Respect for the rights of the individual is indispensable to good government. Mutual trust must be established between those in government and the governed.

This means accountability and transparency in the decision-making process. It means political pluralism with free and fair elections. It means the rule of law and freedom of expression. It means far less spending on military hardware and warmaking and much more on primary schools and healthcare. It means fighting the cancers of graft and nepotism.'

19. This arbitrary definition distinguishes the use of the terms 'good government' and 'good governance' in this chapter; it does not pretend to provide a general definition of the two concepts. For a discussion of the core concepts involved, with the stated objective to develop the concept of governance for use in comparative political analysis, see Hyden [*1992*]. 'Governance' refers to the management of regime relations, that is the rules that set the framework for the conduct of politics; defined in this way, it does not imply, as 'government' does, that real political authority is vested in the formal-legal institutions of the state.

20. In 1991, the IMF included low-level military spending as an objective (since military spending may compete with spending for development purposes); later, multilateral and some bilateral donors adopted the same policy, among others Germany [*Waller, this volume*], Norway [*Stokke, this volume*] and Switzerland [*Forster, this volume*].

Germany and Japan have established guidelines – which have been followed up –

vital agenda concerns environmental objectives, which are likely to become the next central issue related to aid conditionality.[21]

(a) Good governance. From the very beginning, most foreign aid has been channelled through the governing structures on the recipient side. The importance of a functioning government machinery – at central and local levels – for aid to work has been recognised and has affected the allocative decisions of donors. Thus, towards the end of the 1960s, when the Norwegian authorities took the strategic decision to concentrate bilateral aid on English-speaking East Africa rather than West Africa, the perception that public life was less bedevilled by corruption in East Africa was among the factors which tipped the balance. Foreign aid has also been targeted towards such objectives by contributing to institution building and management training.

The new concern with governance came much later. Most donors refer to the same basic policy components when defining 'good governance'. The most systematic effort to explore the agenda and set the objectives has been made by the World Bank. This is not by coincidence; the Bank was in need of an explanation of the quite

---

to this end: cuts in Indian defence spending have been demanded as a condition for the continuation of aid [*Pedersen, 1993:102*].

This condition is not entirely new; in the 1980s, several donors ended or reduced their aid to India because of its nuclear programme.

Although for years, military spending has been contrasted with development needs, no formalised international agreements exist to codify this wisdom and not anything close to a global regime. However, some international agreements may be used as the basis for *ad hoc* decisions by donor governments, for instance – as indicated – the Non-Proliferation Treaty.

For an introduction and discussion of the *problématique* involved, see Nicole Ball [*1992*], who argues that the cumulative weight of over 40 million conflict-related deaths since 1945, arms proliferation, and the diversion of valuable human and financial resources from development have made it increasingly difficult to justify 'business as usual' after 1989. The post-Cold War climate offers an opportunity to develop norms for *all* countries to limit weapon procurement and define an appropriate balance between military and non-military expenditure. As understated by Nicole Ball [*ibid.:1*]: 'Encouraging military reforms in the South gains legitimacy when combined with military reforms in the North.' As noted, the issue has been driven, in particular, by Canada, Germany, Japan and the Nordic countries.

Even in this area, aid conditionality (in this context including military aid) may be supplemented by measures to facilitate a process of scaling down military complexes, which may be a precondition for reductions in military spending. Reforms have a dual objective: enhanced security and enhanced development. Conflict resolution is therefore an integral part of the package.

21. Environmental reforms have been associated already with the second generation aid conditionality agenda by some governments. Contrary to the other agendas, which are basically value-centred and altruistic (reduced military spending might hurt the major producers and exporters as well), the donors' own immediate or long-term self-interests are affected in relation to environmental reforms.

limited successes of the structural adjustment programmes, particularly in Africa, and had, in the late 1980s, come to the conclusion that economic policy reforms, in order to work, had to be bolstered by reforms of the governing system of the countries concerned [*World Bank, 1989; Lancaster, 1993; Waller, 1992*]. In 1991, a task force was established to explore the issues of 'governance' from the Bank's perspective. It defined governance as 'the manner in which power is exercised in the management of a country's economic and social resources for development', and 'good governance' as synonymous with 'sound development management' [*World Bank, 1992:1*].[22]

Although broad and general, the primary concern of this definition is with the public administration aspects, such as effective financial accounting and auditing systems, an appropriate legal framework and open competition for contracts. The emphasis is on accountability, transparency and predictability on the part of politicians and civil servants and on the rule of law. In the World Bank brand, these aspects are conceived of within this more narrow public administration perspective, leaving out aspects that more explicitly belong to the political arena, such as political participation, an open debate and political legitimacy. This may be attributed to considerations related to the mandate of the Bank.[23] The concept might well be broadened to

---

22. Emphasis is given to aspects of government which affect *economic* development, and therefore fall within its mandate, namely the following four areas: 'public sector management, accountability, the legal framework for development, and information and transparency' [*World Bank, 1992:2*]. OECD [*1993:14*] finds it useful to distinguish between the form of political regime, the processes by which authority is exercised in the management of a country's economic and social resources; and the capacity of government to formulate and implement policies and discharge government functions.

Peter Gibbon [*1993:53-54*] argues that the new focus on political conditionality (emphasising human rights and democracy) which emerged in 1989-90 driven by Western governments (in particular, the EC Council of Ministers and the French, British and German governments), confronted the World Bank with several problems, and in particular two: first, it was considered a threat to the viability of economic reforms by 'overloading' governments with other 'difficult' tasks (and besides, the Bank has always been subjectively attached to the idea that a combination of 'enlightened' authoritarian leaders and semi-autonomous technocrats represents the ideal background for successful economic reform); second, the Bank stood the risk of losing its leading role in the aid regime and had to decide on what terms it should take political conditionality on board. Within the Bank, there was strong scepticism about political conditionality, and fear that embracing it could lead to a derogation of the purely technicist basis on which the institution's claim to intellectual/policy leadership was founded. There were, in addition, constitutional constraints. Moreover, 'assuming that political conditionality would also require coordination and therefore a coordinative body, it threatened an undesirable pluralisation of "governance" within the aid regime itself.'

23. For a critical assessment, see Moore [*1993b*]. He maintains that some of the key concepts, particularly 'accountability', are instinctively appealing but provide very limited practical guidance in dealing with the real world; and its treatment of law

include both the public and private sector and the (public) administration as well as the (political) leadership dimensions.[24]

A core question in our context is to what extent the objectives of good governance as set out above and the developmental objectives set for ODA coincide. The features associated with 'good governance' obviously belong to the circumstantial factors which help determine the success or failure of aid. It has also always been a stated objective of foreign aid to improve these features. This coincidence impacts positively on the legitimacy of the policy from the perspective of aid donors.

---

reveals a strong Western and, more especially, American bias. It demonstrates a lack of interest in learning about the kind of governance practised in East Asian countries, which have been economically successful during recent decades. See also Gibbon [1993:54-6]. From a different perspective, Adrian Leftwich [1994:372,381] finds the Bank's prescription for good governance naive because it fails to recognise that good governance is a function of state character and capacity which in turn is a function of politics. 'Neighter sophisticated institutional innovations nor the best-trained or best-motivated public service will be able to withstand the withering effects of corruption or resist the developmentally-enervating pulls of special or favoured interests if the politics and authority of the state do not sustain and protect them.'

The World Bank took up these aspects of 'good governance' at an early stage [World Bank, 1989]. Exploring its concern with the governance issue, Carol Lancaster [1993:9-10] points to the need to explain why its policy of structural adjustment and economic liberalisation, prescribed to African governments and set as conditions for development credits and aid, did not work even when adopted. The Bank's answer was that the policy required a governmental framework which these countries did not have. Corruption, lack of transparency and accountability, and disrespect of the rule of law were among key factors why the prescribed medicine (which was considered to be right) failed to provide the results.

24. Thus, in a patrimonial – or neo-patrimonial – system, efforts to improve the competence of the civil service would, almost by definition, only marginally improve the more fundamental problems of bad governance and this also applies to formal rules and guidelines; the root of the problem is with the governing elite at the political level.

In the conditionality debate, also 'good governance' is interpreted narrowly by some and more broadly by others. As noted by Nelson and Eglinton [1992:12-13], 'narrow interpretations focus on increased honesty and efficiency in the public sector and call for heightened attention to public administration and institutional development. But many development specialists note that public administration projects have a mediocre record, in large part because specific improvements in organization, procedures, and technical and managerial training often have little effect in the absence of deeper changes in the political context and in the incentives shaping staff behavior.

Broader approaches to governance stress institutions, procedures, and attitudes inside and outside of government that promote openness, accountability, and predictability. For instance, public officials can be held accountable to the public for their actions by subordination to elected officials, direct reporting to and guidance from the legislature, review by a semiautonomous auditing and accounting agency, free media, an autonomous judiciary, active interest associations, outspoken university departments or research institutes, and standards of professional conduct established by specialized associations.'

For an effort at developing a concept of governance for use in comparative political analysis in line with this broader approach, and a stimulating discussion which also offers a guided tour through the literature, see Hydén [1992].

27

However, other perspectives make the policy controversial. Multilateral and bilateral aid donors have always been concerned with the effectiveness and efficiency of the administrative system at the recipient side to the extent that they, in some recipient countries, established their own administrations to implement aid-financed activities, bypassing domestic systems. This may have improved efficiency but contributed negatively to development in terms of capacity and competence building in the countries concerned [*Mutahaba, 1990*]. Even against this background of manifest intervention, the 'good governance' policy constitutes a novelty in the relations between sovereign states above all, perhaps, because the interference in *internal* political and administrative structures and processes in developing countries represents such a broad and massive advance. In the words of Martin Doornbos [*this volume*], this package represents a new phase in the state formation processes of the countries concerned; these processes, put under external supervision, bear a qualitative difference from most historic examples of state formation. If imposed from the outside, the effects might well be contrary to the intended ones[25]; aid strategies and forms therefore matters.

(b) *Human rights.* These rights were codified in the Universal Declaration of Human Rights adopted by The United Nations General Assembly in 1948 and in a series of international charters and agreements ratified later.[26] These key documents define human rights over a broad spectrum, including the most fundamental of them all, namely the right to life, freedom from torture, arbitrary arrest and imprisonment, civil and political rights such as freedom of movement, expression, assembly and religion, and economic and social rights, including such rights as employment, shelter, health and education.

Promotion of basic human rights has been an integral part of the justification for and objectives set for aid from an early stage, though

25. Martin Doornbos [*this volume; 1990:188-9*] argues that one effect of the various external initiatives and involvements in promoting 'good governance' might, paradoxically, be to reduce rather than to strengthen Third World governments' capacity for policy-making and implementation as a consequence of their loss of policy initiative. I tend to agree with this analysis. Aid strategies and forms therefore matters; the best strategy is probably to support endogenously driven initiatives towards 'good governance'.

26. The International Declaration of Human Rights (1948) was followed by the International Covenant for Civil and Political Rights and the International Covenant for Economic, Social and Cultural Rights. In addition, other treaties deal with specific categories of people, such as children, women, and the mentally ill, or malpractice, such as torture, discrimination and disappearances. These treaties are ratified by most governments although some have expressed reservations with regard to individual sections.

not always in a strictly formal sense. In the 1970s, they gradually also appeared in a formal sense. One important manifestation is the basic needs strategy – in its various interpretations – which attained almost general approval in the donor community during the second part of the 1970s. Whereas some donor governments, in particular the Nordic and Dutch, have traditionally given most emphasis to economic and social rights, others, particularly the United States since the mid-1970s, have related their aid to civil and political rights.[27]

By the mid-1970s, several donor governments set respect for fundamental human rights as a condition for their bilateral aid.[28] In the case of the US, the reference was to a large extent confined to civil and political rights, and in practice directed towards gross violations of such rights. Some European frontrunners, however, adopted a policy oriented towards social justice as a criterion for the selection of main recipients of bilateral aid (country chapters on the Netherlands, Norway and Sweden in Stokke, ed. [*1984*]). The second generation conditionality, therefore, brought nothing fundamentally new on the agenda in this respect. The novelty in the early 1990s was, above all, a matter of scale and emphasis: the seemingly concerted and strong emphasis which was given to these objectives, particularly to political and civil rights, in the stated policy and the declared determination to follow up, *inter alia* by interfering in processes which previously were considered exclusively internal.

A crucial question, 'to what extent do the objectives pursued through conditionality and the objectives set for aid coincide?', has already been implicitly addressed: several donors have set

---

27. In the Dutch and Scandinavian aid context, 'economic and social rights' were not framed in a human rights context; what is referred to are overall objectives set for the development assistance. This distinction is important; as overall objectives, their main function is to give general direction, not necessarily to provide a 'legal' framework for a human rights regime. Within the latter context, the economic, social and cultural rights (of the universal declaration and covenant) have been defined in less precise terms than for example the civil rights which are codified and related to legal systems domestically and internationally, nor have procedures for their implementation been specified or an international regime for their implementation established. For a discussion of the *problématique* involved, arguing for a minimal threshold approach, see Andreassen *et al.* [*1988*]. For the general theme, see also Tomasevski [*1989*].

28. In 1975, the US Congress passed legislation which established this link [*Nelson and Eglinton, 1992:26-8*]; in 1976, the Norwegian parliament set as a criterion for the choice of new priority countries that recipients should be expected to contribute to the economic, social and civil rights incorporated in the UN Declaration and Convention on Human Rights; in 1976, the Netherlands (with Jan Pronk as the Minister responsible for development co-operation) made compliance with human rights one criterion in the selection of 'concentration countries' for bilateral aid (see country chapters in Stokke (ed.) [*1984*]).

improvement of human rights as an explicit aid objective.[29] From a donor perspective, this makes pursuance of human rights 'legitimate' within the aid setting, even if the broader issue of the relationship between human rights and various forms of development remains unresolved.[30]

In the 1990s, however, the main emphasis has been on civil and political rights. This involves a change of both perspective and priority, away from the welfare agenda and towards the promotion of civil and political rights. Applying conditionality in the pursuit of objectives implies strong commitment and priority; the Western governments have not applied conditionality in order to attain the traditional objectives of aid: improved welfare (economic and social rights).

There is a problem of consistency, too: policy declarations have not always been followed up, particularly when competing interests have been involved. This applies to several donors; it is particularly visible in the case of the US government, which took a leading role in committing itself, in the mid-1970s, to making aid dependent on – and instrumental for – performance of the recipient government in terms of human rights (and democracy).[31] A glaring absence of policy

29. This stance is argued also in the development literature. It is strongly held by Peter P. Waller [*1993*] arguing that reforms in the political domain (human rights, democracy) that run counter to the interest of elites can be pushed through only by outside intervention (aid conditionality would suffice *vis-à-vis* poor countries, in more advanced countries only trade and economic relations offer a leverage).

30. For a strong argumentation for the broader relationship between human rights and development, see Peter P. Waller [*1992; 1993*]; he argues that the link is reciprocal: the use of development aid as a means of enforcing respect for human rights on the one hand and, on the other, the demand for democracy and human rights as a precondition for effective development co-operation. 'These links are so obvious that one is amazed they were not made much earlier. No doubt the reason lies in the constellation that prevailed during the post-war era, and in strategic notions such as the myth of "development dictatorship" ' [*1993:53*]. The editors of the 1994 yearbook on human rights [*Baehr et al., 1994:3*], summing up the 1993 World Conference on Human Rights, are equally convinced: 'there is ... hardly any need to further belabour the intimate relationship between development and human rights. The one cannot be without the other.' For a contrary view, see Leftwich [*1994*].

31. The US government, equating 'good governance' with democracy, which is seen as an end in its own right, is linking its foreign aid to the existence of democratic regimes on the recipient side: it is required in law that aid is cut off to regimes coming to power by overthrowing a democratically elected government. However, this policy has not been followed up consistently: aid has been continued to non-democratic regimes [*Lancaster, 1993a:12,14*]. See also Donnelly [*1992:272*] as quoted by Sørensen [*this volume*].

For a survey of the follow-up of the human rights allocative conditionality, see Nelson and Eglinton [*1992:26-32*], who argue that despite legislation mandating that economic and security aid be withheld from violators of human rights, the US record has at best been inconsistent. This is due both to the struggle between Congress and the executive and the fact that human rights objectives are often subordinated to other

coherence – the follow-up of a stated policy involving global values varies with vested national interests in the specific case – creates, in turn, a legitimacy problem. This legitimacy problem is increased by the historic record of Western powers in the area of human rights (and democracy) both domestically and in their relations with other countries: these inconsistencies tend to weaken the position of Western governments engaged in the human rights drive – even in cases where they are new and without responsibility for past policies.

The issue of the relationship between civil and political rights and economic and social development remains unresolved. I will return to that controversy which, above all, concerns what effects a regime has on social and, in particular, economic growth. This question is increasingly being met by a counter-question: what kind of development should be aimed at? An integration of all human rights in the development concept is embedded in the latter.

(c) Democracy. Promotion of democracy is a more recent objective in a foreign aid context, although not entirely new. Thus, when Sweden first formulated a comprehensive policy for its aid in 1961, promotion of democracy was among the four overall objectives set. It should be added, however, that this particular objective was not actively promoted during the following years [*Stokke, 1978*]. Among the three main objectives of second generation conditionality, it is a latecomer and probably the one surrounded by most ambiguity.

The ambiguity includes the core concept itself. Should the claim for democracy be limited to the formal, procedural aspects, involving an open competition between two or more political parties and free and fair elections?[32] Meeting these criteria is considered sufficient by some donors and tantamount to passing the test.[33] Others tend to pay less attention to the formal criteria; what matters is real democracy,

---

foreign policy concerns. See also *supra*, note 6 and *infra*, notes 42 and 63.

32. Although the aid conditionality policy, in actual practice (which will be described and discussed later), for all practical purposes has taken these manifestations as focal points, most analysts find such a limitation unsatisfactory. Georg Sørensen, for one, disassociates himself from such a limitation, reminding us that democracy is a long-term process which cannot be installed overnight [*1993b:20*]: 'When quick fixes of imposing multi-party systems, for example, are substituted for the long haul of patiently paving the way for a democratic polity the result may be that a thin layer of democratic coating is superimposed upon a system of personal rule without changing the basic features of the old structure. In other words, political conditionality aimed merely at introducing some political competition and basic political rights is not sufficient to secure the basis for a stronger state.'

33. The European Bank for Reconstruction and Development (which directs its activities towards transitional systems in Europe) requires multi-party elections as a precondition for loans.

involving openness and participation, where the emphasis is on a thriving civil society. These constitute core components of the mainstream definition of the concept [*Diamond et al., 1988, Vol. II:xvi*]. The issue might be broadened further, bringing social justice and economic democracy at the micro (and even at the international) level on to the agenda [*Amin, 1993; Gills et al., 1993*].[34] So far, however, this agenda has played only a minor role in the context of second generation conditionality, if it has featured at all. Linking the welfare agenda of the 1970s with the concept would have made a full circle.

A similar controversy as the one referred to above involving the relationship between human rights (in particular civil and political rights) and development applies to the democracy agenda as well: the relationship between democracy, or more generally the governing system, and social and economic development remains unsettled, to the extent that political development of this specific kind is not included in the development concept itself or, in the particular setting of foreign aid, is set as an objective in its own right for development assistance. The development concept is itself controversial and open to quite different definitions and interpretations. As noted, several bilateral donors have for years included political dimensions related to governance into the definition, such as participation by the governed in the decision-making process and free elections, along with civil and political rights discussed above. I will return to this controversy in the following sections.

However, some implications of the increased concern with democracy, as manifest in second generation aid conditionality, should be set out at this stage. Above all, it implies a downgrading of the traditional objectives set for aid, such as those included on the welfare agenda: as noted, conditionality has not been used related to the social justice performance of aid recipient governments. And similar consistency problems appear related to the pursuit of democracy as those identified related to the pursuance of human rights: a poor policy coherence on the part of Western powers (generally speaking, there are exceptions) tends to weaken the legitimacy of the drive and this applies to their historic record, too.

*

The objectives of second generation aid conditionality, briefly identified above, are not the only ones pursued by donor governments *vis-à-vis* Third World governments, nor the only ones pursued with aid as an instrument. They may be ethnocentric, reflecting basic values

---

34. For a further discussion of the concept of democracy and the definitions referred to, see *infra*, Section VII, particularly note 56.

which may be cherished but not always practised fully at home; however, taken at face value they are not geared towards fulfilling the donors' own vested interests, and may sometimes go against these interests. When confronted with the donor's vested interests, therefore, it is far from granted that the more altruistic interests will prevail. This, in turn, may lead to policy dilemmas, contradictions and consistency problems of the kind alluded to above; the policy performance of major and lesser aid donors provides rich evidence.

V. NORMATIVE DILEMMAS

1. Foreign Aid: An Asymmetrical Relationship

The aid relationship itself constitutes the broader framework in which conditionality in general, and economic and political conditionality in particular, should be analysed. Before the normative aspects associated with aid conditionality are discussed, some characteristics of the aid relationship should be identified:

(1) No government can be forced to provide development assistance or to receive it.

Within the confines of a nation state, the tax system is used as a mechanism for raising funds to finance activities deemed necessary by the society and as a mechanism of social and geographical redistribution. Citizens and firms (and other legal entities) have an obligation to contribute. A similar system has not so far been established at a global level, although it has emerged at some (international) regional levels. However, a move in this direction is under way at the global level, manifest, *inter alia*, in commitments to international targets for official development assistance (ODA). This emerging system is, however, a fragile one, as the conduct of several governments has demonstrated: commitments have not always been met and they have frequently been unilaterally reduced or withdrawn.

(2) The aid relationship between donor and recipient is an extremely asymmetric power relationship.

This applies, in particular, to bilateral state-to-state development assistance. However, it is less asymmetric in some relations than in others, depending on the total relationship between the parties involved and the type and context of the foreign aid. Weak, poor and heavily aid-dependent Third World governments are worst-off.

(3) Foreign aid, by definition, represents an intervention in the recipient country.

This applies almost regardless of the aid channel chosen (government, NGO, private sector) or the form of aid. The way aid is channelled, its form and target groups, influences who the beneficiaries (and the losers) will be and, as a result, affects their resources and power position.

These features of foreign aid will not be elaborated, but they serve as an important contextual framework for the discussion. They have important implications for the discussion of conditionality related to aid, both with regard to normative and instrumental aspects.

2. Some Normative Dilemmas

Conditions set by the donor are part of everyday life in aid relations – they are the 'normal' pattern, involving most aid forms. The donor, more often than not, holds strong views with regard to objectives, modalities and even implementation. Other types of conditions with an impact on the real value of ODA transfers to the recipients have also been – and still are – applied: the grant-credit ratio (the grant element of ODA) and procurement tying of aid. The more recent trend, and our main concern, is that conditions have been extended to systemic elements, including the very system of government, the legal system and the administrative system on the recipient side.

First and second generation conditionality, in particular, intervene in the domestic policy of the recipient country and may therefore conflict with norms established for international relations. Quite a few of these norms are also affected by foreign aid in general, although seldom invoked in actual practice, not least because of the asymmetric power relationship between the parties in this particular policy area. Some norms apply more especially to the issue of political conditionality or particular modalities involved in such a context. The purpose of this discussion is to identify some core problem areas involved and to indicate some answers.

At the normative level, political conditionality raises several questions. The most crucial relates to the following:

(1) In international law, *the principle of non-intervention* in the internal affairs of another country has been codified and enjoys wide recognition.

This principle raises several basic questions. Should foreign governments and international organisations abstain from intervention in the internal affairs of other countries in all circumstances? Is intervention justifiable in particular circumscribed situations? If so, which?

The principle of non-intervention, although maintaining broad recognition, has been weakened, and recent developments – including the conditionality debate – have contributed to this process. As observed by Georg Sørensen [*1993a:1*], the linking of aid to demands concerning human rights and (liberal) democracy in recipient countries represents a potentially dramatic change of basic principles in the international system: 'putting human rights first means that respect for individual rights acquires priority over respect for the sovereignty of states. It points to a system ... where universal agreement on basic human rights sets a baseline against which the international community may legitimately intervene in domestic affairs of single states; that is, rights of individuals come before rights of states.'

Much depends on the issues involved and the form that intervention takes. Clearly, issues that involve third parties or international society (including international conventions) are open to international involvement. This includes issues where human rights are involved – although the degree of violation and form of involvement are vaguely defined and give poor guidance in cases where there is a willingness to act. Basically, however, it is up to the government itself to follow up violations of the rights involved.

Georg Sørensen [*this volume*] gives the sovereignty debate an interesting twist, arguing that the double standards and lack of consistency for which the West has been criticised are matched by double standards on the part of aid recipient countries. Self-seeking political elites expect the fruits of sovereignty but are not able or willing to pay its price by providing an effective development regime.[35]

---

35. Jackson and Rosberg [*1986:27-8*] argue in the same vein; juridical statehood in sub-Saharan Africa tends to preserve ex-colonial jurisdictions regardless of their potential for development with the frequent effect that state-building is obstructed. A related consequence is to guarantee the rights of sovereign rulers against foreign intervention, regardless of their internal governing actions or omissions. 'In more than a few countries, sovereign rights have been purchased at the expense of human rights. The new international democracy is often disclosed, somewhat ironically, as a democracy for rulers only.' There are few if any compelling international pressures on governments to engage in state-building, on the contrary: 'in so far as it will not cost them their sovereignty and the significant privileges and perquisites which go with it, they are at liberty to neglect development.' Implicitly, if not explicitly, Jackson and Rosberg find that they should not have it both ways; the analysis leads Jackson and Rosberg to the conclusion that the significance of moral, legal, and political institutions – the superstructure – and the theory behind such phenomena in political science had to be reconsidered. For a warning against massive outside interference in state formation processes, see Martin Doornbos [*1990; this volume*].

The principle of non-intervention is not a sacred one and not without exceptions. The present trend is towards increased eroding of the norm as a result of growing interdependence, the process of regionalisation – even globalisation – of economy and politics, and the technological revolution which has globalised communications.

What of the relevance of the non-intervention principle in the debate on political conditionality? In a formal sense, it may be invoked when development commitments are unilaterally broken (aid reduced, frozen or cut off) by the aid-providing government as a result of the recipient government's refusal to comply with its demand for policy changes. Does this apply to a contractual relationship? Or is there a flaw in the very notion of including commitments to political reforms in a development contract? Formally, it may even be argued that adapting the principle to aid conditionality in general might represent an extension of its domain to a new area.

At lower levels, many more questions may be raised. Two sets deserve to be highlighted:

(2) Prescribing particular solutions involves a *responsibility for the outcome*, not only in cases where the result is a success.

The most basic question in this context is: to what extent is a foreign government willing and able to take responsibility for the short-term and long-term effects of an intervention in a developing country – or *vis-à-vis* the South? This question ultimately applies to any kind of prescriptions by donors related to aid. It becomes especially crucial when prescriptions are not only offered as advice but set as a condition, although, given the aid relationship, the borderline between advice and conditionality may be quite blurred. The brief answer is clear: no donor government (or multilateral agency) has so far taken on full responsibility *vis-à-vis* recipient countries for the effects resulting from their prescriptions. However, another basic question remains: should they? This question can lead to a discussion of basic norms related to both sovereignty and development. In the more narrow context of our discussion above, however, it may be concluded that if the answer of a donor government were 'no', then the legitimacy of an intervention would be affected negatively.

A cluster of connected, more specific questions relate to this *problématique*:

(a) to what extent does a foreign government in the North (or an international agency) *command necessary insights* to prescribe solutions to problems arising from the domestic policy of another country, particularly if the economic, social, cultural – and natural – environments are totally different from its own? And, more specifically,

(b) to what extent can it be relied on that *the recipe recommended will produce the anticipated effects*, namely economic, social, political and cultural development?

The first question serves primarily a rhetorical function in this discussion. Clearly, many governments in the North (and multilateral agencies) have, over the years, accumulated a wealth of information about, and acquired solid insights into, what is taking place in the regions and countries of the South with which they have maintained a multitude of relations. Even so, the geographical and cultural distance makes it difficult to give the issues sufficient attention and to fully appreciate their broader contexts; this, in turn, affects both the ability and willingness of donor governments to take on *responsibility* for domestic policies in the South.

The short answer to the second question is that uncertainty in this regard is deep-rooted. Economists are less confident today than they were in the bold 1950s about which mechanisms and incentives create *economic growth*, although the determination with which the Bretton Woods institutions have pursued the first generation conditionality, particularly during the initial phase, may signal the opposite. The time for the one-ingredient recipe is behind us, and so is the assumption that the effects of a recipe would be the same, regardless of the conditions (environment, culture, economy, political system) prevailing in the society for which it is prescribed. The broader concept of sustainable development complicates the issue still further.

In the context of our discussion, the more specific questions emerging from (b) relate to what extent the objectives set for aid conditionality coincide with the overall developmental objectives set for aid. These have been raised in IV.2. The implicit conclusion, in most cases, is that some coincidence seems to exist. This applies both to the welfare and the 'good governance' agenda. It even applies to important parts of the human rights agenda, particularly to the more peripheral rights as far as the conditionality debate is concerned (economic and social rights and the more recently established right to development).

Some questions relating to the agenda of the second generation conditionality remain unresolved. Amongst these are the following:

37

- What is the relationship between democracy and development? Will democracy, as such, lead to economic and social growth? Will it lead to sustainable development?

In many statements made by Western politicians and aid agencies, bilateral and multilateral, a positive relationship between democracy and development is postulated. This understanding is shared by others, such as the prominent politicians from all over the world who signed the Stockholm initiative [*PMO, 1991*] and reflected in the report of the South Commission [*1990*]. Still, such postulates (leaving aside the *problématique* related to the definition of the concepts) belong to credos or political rhetoric (or both). The relationship between political regime and economic and social development is quite complex and remains unsettled [*Sørensen, 1991, 1993bc and this volume; Healey et al., 1993*].[36]

Within the framework of the established rationale for development co-operation, a positive relationship is required to legitimate the prescription, whether set as a condition for aid or not. However, democracy is included, by some, in the very concept of development. Several donors have established the promotion of democracy as a major objective for their development assistance. However, it is a

36. For a condensed discussion of this *problématique*, adding to the state of the art, see Sørensen [*1993b*]. Identifying autonomy and capacity together with the policy element of statecraft as the core elements of a developmental state which have to be considered in the specific socio-historical framework of the state in question, Sørensen concludes that 'questions such as "does democracy push or retard a developmental state/economic development" are only meaningful in the context of a conceptual specification sensitive to the distinctive features of different types of cases' [*ibid.:28*]. However, he considers 'more real democracy' an asset in a developmental context. This 'must entail a loosening of ties between the regime and elite groups with vested interests in the maintenance of status quo. This appears to amount to a more pronounced role for mass-actors and a less pronounced role for elite groups with vested interests. In other words, democracies sustained by a more solid, popular basis appear to have the best possibilities for pushing changes that can lead to better results in economic development' [*ibid.:30*].

For a different perspective, emphasising the drastic consequences of instability resulting from the overthrow of authoritarian regimes (Somalia, Liberia), see Gills *et al.* [*1993:14*]. This argument is quite familiar with authoritarian African leaders being exposed to demands for democratic reforms, as in the case of Kenya (the alternative to authoritarian rule is chaos and disintegration).

André Gunder Frank [*1993:40*] adds an international – pessimistic and deterministic – dimension to this discourse, observing that bitter experience has shown that 'Second World, socialist national development' in China, the former Soviet Union and Eastern Europe was unable to break out from or overcome the constraints of competition in world economy. 'These countries of the Second World, like those of the Third World, are handicapped by their position in the world international division of labour, quite irrespective of being blessed by political democracy or cursed by its absence or failure.'

different matter actually to make democracy (as defined), or a process towards more democracy, a condition for aid even if the overall aim is the same. Clearly, the concern reflects basic values on the donor side; by the same token, aid becomes an instrument to promote these values in the Third World.

In the case of most major Western donors, particularly the colonial powers, this tradition is rooted in an older foreign policy tradition. When, freely or under duress, they prepared the transition to independence, efforts were made to form constitutional constructs which to a large extent mirrored their own. The United States government has, in the past, used military power to enforce a democratic regime on occupied countries, both in Central America and elsewhere (Germany, Japan, the Philippines). The conditionality policy of today may be rooted in that tradition, too, although the major instrument now is different both in kind (involving economic instead of military power) and in compelling strength.

–   What is the relationship between human rights and development? Do, in particular, civil and political rights lead to economic growth, social justice and sustainable development?

Most statements by Western politicians and aid agencies take for granted a positive relationship between human rights and development, without further analysis or discussion, just as they do between democracy and development. Two factors make it less controversial to use ODA – without and even with conditionality – to promote human rights than to do so to promote democracy:

First, human rights are codified and universally accepted; they are international commitments, although not ratified in full by a number of governments, nor implemented by all, and with the main responsibility for implementation vested at the national level.

Second, human rights are part of the very concept of development, as perceived by most donor governments.[37] This is particularly the

---

37. The concept of development is itself controversial and given a variety of definitions. In the present discussion, it relates to the economic, social, cultural and political objectives identified, which in the aid context varies with the individual donors. For a definition which commands a high degree of international consensus, the UN General Assembly vote adapting the Declaration on the Right to Development (Resolution 41/128,04.12.1986) may be given: '... development is a comprehensive economic, social, cultural and political process, which aims at the constant improvement of the well-being of the entire population and of all individuals on the basis of their active, free and meaningful participation in development and in the fair distribution of benefits resulting therefrom' (Preamble, paragraph 2). This definition come close to universal consensus in a formal sense, since the Declaration was adopted by 147 votes

case with *social* rights. Civil and political rights may be more controversial, given the narrower aid context; a positive relationship
between such rights and 'development' may be required to legitimate
such prescriptions. The UN Declaration on the Right to Development
may, in a formal sense, provide such a legitimation [*Andreassen and
Swinehart, 1992:ix-xi*].

The promotion of human rights has long been included among the
declared objectives set for development assistance by several Western
bilateral donors. However, the emphasis of various donors varies;
while some bilateral donors have given most emphasis to social
rights, others – including the major Western donors – have focused on
civil and political rights. The recent trend, associated with second
generation political conditionality, has brought civil and political
rights to the fore.

Another perspective, the responsibility of an aid-providing government *vis-à-vis* commitments to its own electorate (such as the stated
objectives set for aid), raises a normative issue of equal relevance to
the subject matter. From this perspective, the following question
arises:

(3) To what extent should a donor government which is committed to
     an aid policy aimed at promoting economic and social develop-
     ment, social justice, human rights and democracy, support – or
     continue to provide ODA to – a Third World government regard-
     less of *the policy* pursued in relation to these objectives or its *per-
     formance* judged by these criteria?

The discussion in (2) above focused on the legitimacy of policy prescriptions (with and without conditionality) within the implicit setting
of a development contract between donor and recipient, that is, within
an *international* system; the focus now turns to the 'contract' between
the government and the governed, involving aid policy, within a
national system. Given the particular context of the aid relationship
and the present weakly developed state of the international regime in
relation to aid, it might be argued that this 'contract' within the
national system could be considered of a higher order since it is
legitimised through a transparent and democratic process (even if the
government is sometimes left with generous room for manoeuvre).

The answers to the questions posed above vary. Answers from a
donor perspective may differ from those from a recipient perspective.

---

against one (the United States) with eight governments abstaining. For a less formal
South definition, see *infra*, Section VIII, particularly notes 58 and 59.

It is probable that they also vary within these categories, from one government to another and, within a country, between the government on the one hand and NGOs and other groups on the other.

VI. INSTRUMENTAL ASPECTS: DOES AID CONDITIONALITY WORK?

1. The Core Questions

Instrumental concerns may be just as important as normative ones when a policy is designed or assessed. The core question is, therefore: *does aid conditionality work*, in terms of producing the intended results?

Given the various agendas involved (IV.2), this question needs to be split up and directed towards specific items on these agendas: to what extent is aid conditionality able to facilitate reforms in welfare policy such as increased social justice? How far does it carry economic policy reform, such as those included in the agenda of first generation conditionality – related to structural adjustment programmes? To what extent does aid conditionality lead to improved 'governance', as defined by the World Bank, in terms of accountability, transparency and predictability on the part of politicians and the civil service, the rule of law and an effective, incorrupt public administration? Improved human rights? Does it lead to democratic institutions, broad-based participation, a vital civil society, open discussion and a free and independent press? In short, does aid conditionality produce reforms in aid recipient countries directed towards good government?

Splitting up the general question in this way implies an assumption that aid conditionality may work better for some objectives than for others, and provides an opportunity to explore such possibilities. What are the circumstances which determine whether conditionality works or not? What are the main preconditions for a successful outcome? What modalities are – or are not – effective? These questions, too, are probably best explored within the confines of the more specific agendas already identified.

In addressing these questions, the likelihood of success could be explored from a theoretical point of departure or from past experiences of a similar kind. Clearly they would be best addressed by looking at actual experiences. Since the emphasis here is on second generation aid conditionality, which has been in operation for only a short period, the two approaches will be combined.

2. Aid Conditionality as a Strategy: Potentials and Limitations

What are the potentials and limitations of aid conditionality as a strategy for attaining the objectives identified from an international relations perspective? Under what circumstances may aid work as a lever to make a foreign government undertake policy reforms which it would otherwise not have considered?

Some general observations provide a useful introduction. Through their foreign policy, governments interact in many arenas, and the outcome of interactions in one arena may spill over to affect positions and interactions in others with a different focus. Governments pursue a multiplicity of objectives and the outcome with regard to one may affect the way other objectives are pursued, despite the compartmentalism which characterises most systems.

This implies that each government pursues many – and sometimes conflicting – values and interests at the same time. However important certain values may be, particularly core values of the kind involved here, systemic and private sector interests are also considered significant by governments, and in most systems these are bolstered by well-organised stakeholders. The pursuit of values and norms is not always given priority by governments when conflicting with such interests, whatever their rhetoric implies. Regimes vary in the strength of emphasis they place on ideology and basic values (which they may, of course, use to disguise more selfish political or economic interests), and this extends to the implementation of foreign policy.

What outcome may be expected when the balance of power is the decisive factor in an interaction between a donor and a recipient government which involves the various agendas of aid conditionality? An assessment of the probability for a successful outcome from the perspective of the donor needs to consider the specifics of the particular case. However, some general propositions may be indicated. In the context of a power play, a bilateral donor operating unilaterally has a slim probability of prevailing by threatening the withdrawal of aid (at that level, the credibility of the threat would matter, too) – or even by an actual withdrawal or freezing of aid. However, several factors may have an impact.

(1) The domestic position of the recipient government and its power basis – weak or strong.

The domestic position of a government depends on a wide variety of factors, differing from one type of regime to another. If its prime power basis (and legitimacy) is formed by a monopoly of coercive powers (the military and the police), their continuing loyalty carries more importance than popular support. Other regimes are dependent on popular support and the absence of strong discontent in influential sectors of society such as trade unions, organised business, traditional leaders. The state of the economy affects the position of most governments, even the regime of a repressive system, although such a government may be able to consolidate its position by favouring its social power basis (for instance the officer corps). The government's position also depends on the presence and strength of an alternative leadership, whether (in an authoritarian system) within the power elite itself or (in an electoral system) among the population.

(2) The recipient government's ability to use the occasion of external intervention to strengthen its position domestically, at least in the short run.

Interventions from the outside are seldom welcome, whatever form the regime takes.[38] It is embedded in conditionality that the recipient government is pressed to undertake reforms which are not of its own choice or priority. In addition, conditionality implies superiority: it infringes on sovereignty, insists that the donor(s) knows best, and highlights inequality of power. It should not come as a surprise, therefore, that conditionality is not met with enthusiasm.

However, not every intervention is equally suited to confrontation of the kind anticipated in (2); the degree of interference has to be high and the issue sensitive for the government. In an open confrontation of this kind, which is very likely to involve political conditionality (human rights, democracy), the recipient government may be able to whip up national sentiments and anger against external interference. In this way it may calculate on, and even succeed in, turning a (possible) loss in terms of financial capital (aid) into a gain in terms of its political capital at home. It may even be able, at least temporarily, to turn public attention away from pressing domestic problems.

---

38. The discussion here and previously explicitly relates to state-to-state or international agency-to-state relations; interventions from outside may, of course, be welcomed from individuals, organisations or 'nations' within the country concerned which see their interests served. Even within the stated setting, the statement may be modified: within a government, there may be individuals or fractions who may see their interest served; in such cases pressures from outside may tip the balance. And there may even be cases where the government may, tacitly, welcome conditions set from outside, although accepting them under protest, because popular protests against the hardship caused by the cure then would be directed to an outside enemy and not towards the government. However, the discussion here relates to brinkmanship pursued from outside.

(3) The extent of dependency on aid of the recipient country and, in particular, the importance of the aid at stake, in relation to the total aid package and to the GNP.

This involves two separate aspects which influence the position of the two parties both in terms of their own power and in relations to each other. The extent of aid dependency of the recipient government, in relative and absolute terms, affects its room for manoeuvre. If dependency is high, even marginal reductions in aid may hurt. However, in the absence of a concerted action by donors, significant factors are the proportion of total aid provided by the individual donor and its strategic importance to the recipient (aid from donors is often intertwined). This relationship cannot be considered in isolation; other factors may be expected to influence the balance of power. The government of a large recipient country is likely to be better situated than that of a small one to resist pressure – and to face a loss of aid. Similarly, the government of a large donor country may be in a better position than that of a small one to exert pressure.

(4) The magnitude and relative importance of the bilateral relations.

This affects both parties, although the relative importance may be different. The scope should include the political and economic relationship in its entirety as governments have various interests and concerns, both bilateral and related to international politics in general. This influences a donor government's willingness to apply political conditionality: if relations are broadly based and involve sensitive strategic interests or extensive economic interests related to trade and investment, the donor government's willingness to take action is likely to be reduced; by the same token, added weight is given to any pressure that is applied. However, such considerations do not take place, on either side, in an exclusively bilateral context. Both parties will also be open-eyed to the possibility that other actors may fill the 'vacuum' if a conflict should arise.

(5) The probability that a unilateral action may have a snowball effect.

The perspective has been confined so far to the balance of power prevailing between two governments, a donor and a recipient. This is seldom the case: both parties interact with many other governments, giving rise to formal and informal alignments, both within this particular area of policy and beyond, with implications which need to be considered. However, the influence of different governments varies, depending, above all, on their general position in the international system.

It follows that unilateral action by a major power with the ability to mobilise support stands a better chance of obtaining the intended results than a small or middle power acting unilaterally; similarly, a Third World government with a secure power basis situated in a large country with a relatively large GNP (and consequently, promising market and investment opportunities) stands a better chance of resisting such an intervention than a weak, unstable government of a country that is small, poor and dependent on aid.

(6) An internationally co-ordinated action by donors stands a better chance of success than a unilateral action in terms of attaining the policy reforms pursued.

Internationally co-ordinated action is not easily achieved except in particularly grave situations and in relation to broadly agreed norms and interests. In most situations, competing interests are involved, present and future, actual and potential; moreover, norms and traditions differ among aid donors. However, the scope cannot be limited to aid donors: the possibility that other actors – countries outside the group of donors, and transnationals – will take advantage of a conflict to fill a vacuum, influences the policy analysis on which the actions of most donor governments are based.

Co-ordinated action may be organised by a group of bilateral donors, all bilateral donors, or by multilateral aid agencies. The likelihood of obtaining the desired result grows with increased participation. If important actors – whether or not they are among the aid donors – do not associate themselves with the measures, the power play will be more open, particularly if there is no risk of a proliferation beyond aid conditionality. This will also have an impact on the follow-up.

There is also a distinction to be made between the multilateral institutions: the Bretton Woods institutions are 'owned' by the major Western donor countries and Japan, while the United Nations system is 'owned' by Third World governments as well. It is likely that concerted action is most easily achieved and effectively organised through the former.

These propositions are formulated at a high level of generalisation. Many other factors have an impact on the power play. Analysis should take the specifics of each case into consideration. It is also necessary to distinguish between the degree of intervention and sensitivity of the issues involved. Although these distinctions have been made only occasionally in the above discussion, the context makes it clear that the analysis primarily applies when brinkmanship is employed, in situations involving a high degree of political interference or issues which are sensitive for the recipient government. It should be emphasised that where this applies, the effectiveness of this type of brinkmanship is limited: a government, particularly one that is authoritarian and repressive, cannot be expected to agree to conditions which will inevitably lead to its own liquidation.

3. Some Experiences of Applied Aid Conditionality

To what extent are these propositions confirmed or weakened in the light of actual experience of the implementation of second generation aid conditionality? What additional insights of relevance to our core question are gained from the experience so far: does conditionality work?

It makes sense to distinguish between various agendas and the more specific objectives within these agendas (VI.1). A distinction should also be made in assessing success in promoting policy reform on the recipient side and the success of those reforms *vis-à-vis* the objectives set – these may not necessarily coincide.

The focus is on comparatively recent experiences with reference to second generation political conditionality. However, there have not been many cases where brinkmanship has been involved; in those where it has, the recipient regime has been of an authoritarian, often repressive, nature. This discussion concentrates on a few examples which are analysed in greater detail in separate component studies included in this volume: the Indonesian case with particular reference to the Netherlands, the Kenyan case with particular reference to Germany, and the cases of Burundi, Rwanda and Zaïre, with particular reference to Belgium.

Two observations should be made at this stage. The first is that, so far, second generation aid conditionality has been confined to a very large extent to declaratory policy. The other applies to the practicality of making the preferred distinctions: most cases of brinkmanship involve several of the main items on the agenda, often intertwined – violations of human rights, abuses against democracy, and other aspects included on the 'good governance' agenda. Although isolated events are focused on, more often than not the crux of the problem is the policy at an aggregate level. Analysis of the more specific items on the agenda is therefore difficult.

3.1 The case of Indonesia: when conditionality backfired

The case of Indonesia provides a testing ground for several of the propositions offered in the previous section, particularly those pointing at the limitations of the strategy to promote 'good government' when it is undertaken unilaterally.[39] What are the main lessons to be drawn from this case?

The November 1991 massacre of more than 90 unarmed civilian demonstrators in East Timor, annexed by Indonesia in 1976, led to international condemnations and resulted in the suspension of aid programmes by a few bilateral donors (including Denmark and the Netherlands) while others (such as Canada) suspended ongoing discussions on future aid. A snowball effect seemed imminent: major aid donors (such as Australia, Japan and the US) added demands for a full investigation to their condemnations. For Indonesia, an aid package worth about US$ five billion – about one-fifth of government income in the 1991-92 budget – was at stake.

The Indonesian government adopted a strategy of containment, part of which was an attempt to translate financial loss into political capital at home (proposition (2)). The Dutch government, which took the leading role, was the former colonial power in Indonesia. The transition to independence – and, in particular, relations during the first decades after independence – had been somewhat traumatic. When confronted with the reactions, the Indonesian government portrayed criticisms of the East Timor incident as an imperialist intervention.

These condemnations were combined with a quick investigation in order to fend off criticism. This led to the removal (by early retirement) of two generals with responsibility for military affairs in East Timor, disciplinary action (in the form of mild sentences) against 17 low-ranking military personnel and the withdrawal of the battalion involved from East Timor. This may be contrasted with the treatment of the civil rights demonstrators: a number of them received long sentences, of between nine years and life imprisonment.

A successful diplomatic offensive vis-à-vis the major donor government (Japan) prevented concerted action by the aid providers; the Japanese government expressed satisfaction with the way the Indonesian government had tackled the situation. Most other Western governments then followed suit, with one outstanding exception: the Dutch government linked future aid to improvements in Indonesia's

---

39. The description here draws extensively on Nico S. Nordholt [this volume] and Mark Robinson [1993a;1994].

human rights performance (*ex ante* allocative conditionality). It was at this point that the Indonesian government found the time ripe for an offensive, singling out the Dutch government. It called for an end to all Dutch aid – the Netherlands was given one month to phase out its aid activities. It also dissolved the 14-member aid consortium, chaired by the Netherlands, and succeeded in making the World Bank set up a new consortium which excluded the Netherlands.

What are the main lessons to be drawn? I tend to agree with Mark Robinson [*1993a:62*] who concludes that an individual donor government acting unilaterally is unable to exert significant influence on a country's human rights performance by means of aid conditionality, especially when the volume of aid is small in relative terms (proposition (3)). The direct loss to the Indonesian government in financial terms involved a yearly amount of some US$ 90 million; in relative terms, Dutch ODA amounted to less than two per cent of Indonesia's total foreign aid.

Considerations of trade and diplomacy, on the part of major donors, weighed heavily against such an intervention and probably inhibited a snowball effect (propositions (4) and (5)). This was specially the case for the main regional donors: both Australia and Japan had important immediate and long-term economic interests at stake related to Indonesia's large and fast-growing economy.

However, the Netherlands also had immediate and long-term economic interests at stake. The really interesting question, therefore, is to ask what factors led the Dutch government to employ brinkmanship and thus give priority to norms (the pursuance of human rights); however, this performance weakens proposition (4). Those factors are vividly described and analysed by Nico Schulte Nordholt [*this volume*].

3.2 The case of Kenya: when conditionality works although its main objectives remain unattained

The case of Kenya offers additional insight. For years, the regime of President Arap Moi had showed little sensitivity towards demands, particularly those from within, of the kind included in the second generation conditionality agenda. The poor performance *vis-à-vis* these criteria hardly affected generous aid transfers from Western donors and multilateral aid agencies. That changed in the late 1980s, when certain donors started to question violations of human rights. In 1990, an incident[40] gave the regime an opportunity to demonstrate

---

40. A Kenyan politician with refugee status in Norway was arrested by Kenyan authorities and imprisoned. When the case came to court, the Norwegian ambassador

strength by breaking off diplomatic relations with Norway, a minor aid donor. Norway responded by ending its bilateral state-to-state aid to Kenya, one of the first countries with which Norway established long-term development cooperation. From the Norwegian side, this outcome was unintended and was not the result of human rights conditionality [*Stokke, this volume*]. There was almost no immediate snowball effect.

In the autumn of 1991, however, a further change took place. The US Ambassador to Kenya emerged as an open critic of the system and Germany played a prominent role, described by Peter Waller [*this volume*]. At its meeting in Paris in November, the consultative group for Kenya, which included all major aid donors, decided to suspend quick-dispersing aid until the Kenyan government had re-established a multi-party system, reduced corruption and implemented economic reforms. Within days, this concerted pressure led to systemic reform: President Moi announced that the constitution confirming Kenya as a one-party state should be amended and free elections held.

A multi-party system emerged. The elections took place at the end of December 1992; however, a divided opposition – and technical arrangements favouring the ruling party – allowed power to remain in the grip of the old regime. Even so, the political scene changed, although it remains to be seen whether there will be long-term effects for politics, development and human rights in Kenya with the intro-duction of a multi-party Parliament which includes a strong opposi-tion. The prospect for these reforms remains bleak.

Although fundamental policy reforms were not attained within the areas identified, or at best these were marginal, concerted pressure from the major donors produced systemic reform in Kenya. What made the donors act? And what made the regime give in to the pressure? Several factors coincided. In the new international situation, Kenya lost its strategic position previously so important to the Western powers. The regime had earned a bad reputation, both for its human rights performance and for its corrupt practice. This was matched by an arrogant display of power. Another feature important for the outcome was that two major powers took a lead role in co-ordinating the pressure – the United States and Germany. When the Cold War ended, they had no important strategic or economic interests which might be hurt as a consequence of brinkmanship; in contrast, important British economic interests were at stake, and the

---

to Kenya attended personally. The case raised a storm of protests in the Norwegian media. The Kenyan government considered the ambassador's presence an unfriendly act and an interference into Kenya's internal affairs [*Stokke, this volume*].

UK government kept a low profile, in common with the French who had political reasons associated with more indirect economic interests in Africa.

The authoritarian, repressive regime in Kenya was confronted with concerted action by the major aid providers which gave it almost no chance of playing off one party against the other, with even the World Bank lining up with its critics. Although it compares well with its neighbours, Kenya is a poor country according to most criteria and highly dependent on foreign aid: almost 90 per cent of its development budget was financed by aid. A large proportion of this was immediately at stake – some US$ 350 million from a total of one billion [*Waller, this volume*] – with the very real possibility of a snowball effect.

Although the regime was in control of the coercive powers, a loss of foreign aid, and especially the foreign currency involved, might affect even this, in view of Kenya's multi-ethnic setting and the mounting social unrest which was nourished as much by economic hardship as by human rights violations, corruption and self-enrichment by the governing elite. Even confronted with the possibility of losing its power to a mounting, visible and apparently united opposition, the regime probably had no option but to give in. It is likely that even in its own analysis, the prospect of long-term survival appeared even bleaker for the alternative option; drastically reduced aid flows might result in mounting social unrest and even to a disintegration of its control of administrative and coercive powers.

It transpires from this analysis that the relative success of the brinkmanship, exerted by way of aid conditionality, resulted from the presence and strength of the internal political forces opting for political reform; in such a situation, concerted pressure by the main aid providers was able to tip the balance.

3.3 The cases of Zaïre, Burundi and Rwanda: Belgium's experience

Belgium's experience in applying various kinds of political conditionality *vis-à-vis* its former colonies – Zaïre, Rwanda and Burundi – provides additional insights. Past relations, in each case, have an impact on more recent relations. The specifics of the three cases are described and analysed in the chapter by Renard and Reyntjens [*this volume*].

Rich mineral resources complicated the transfer to independence in Zaïre; subsequent relations between Zaïre and Belgium have been ambivalent, with several ups and downs. To the extent that aid conditionality was applied before 1990, the objectives pursued reflected traditional interests of a kind other than those associated with second generation political conditionality. In 1990, this changed, mainly for reasons related to domestic politics in Belgium but also because of the changes taking place internationally and in the region, which affected the aid debate as well. In the new situation, the authoritarian, repressive regime of President Mobutu lost its importance to the United States as a strategic ally; the remaining attractions of this corrupt regime were few, the economy was in disarray and the system in an advanced stage of disintegration. In previous years, President Mobutu, confident of continuing Belgian interest in the potentials of Zaïre, had himself applied brinkmanship in his relations with the Belgian government: he had repeatedly set conditions, including some involving aid, for maintaining good relations. The effects of this 'inverted' conditionality can be anticipated: when compensations are not sufficiently high or secure, humiliations tend to backfire.

In 1990, several processes converged, affecting the Belgian position. One of the government parties (Flemish Socialists) had emphasised the human rights issue for some time, with particular reference to Zaïre. As a result, commitment to human rights was integrated into a new aid agreement with Zaïre. When the security forces, only a couple of months later, killed a number of students at the Lubumbashi University campus, the Belgian government invoked this agreement and called for an international inquiry into the incident; this was refused. In response, the Belgian government froze agreed loans and suspended further commitments for 1990. Mobutu retaliated by ordering Belgian aid personnel to leave the country, closing down Belgian consulates, and carrying out other acts of harassment. This led to the withdrawal of all bilateral Belgian aid.[41]

What is the explanation for this turn of events? What were the effects and the main lessons? The main conclusion is that, in this case, allocative conditionality did not succeed. It is the change in Belgian policy which attracts particular attention. Clearly, the incident took place at a stage when Zaïre had lost much of its attractiveness in

---

41. Belgium was not alone; the European Community and the US also suspended aid to Zaïre. For an assessment of the US support to the Mobutu government, see Lancaster [1993b:54] who argues that this aid 'was not intended primarily to promote development but rather to bolster an inept and corrupt government that had been supportive of the U.S. policies. It was long feared that without U.S.support, Zaïre (large, strategically located, and rich in natural resources) might disintegrate or be taken over by a government friendly to Moscow. By strengthening Mobutu's regime, the United States may have inadvertently prolonged the economic disaster Mobutu brought to his people.'

Belgian circles which previously had strong vested interests in maintaining relations; interest had cooled both within the administration and in Belgian business. From the perspective of President Mobutu, Belgium was the most important source of foreign aid; however, the aid was not vital in relative terms, amounting to 2.6 per cent of GNP. Moreover, an increasing portion of it was provided in a way which made it less attractive for a corrupt regime emphasising self-enrichment rather than development: it was not easily available and tended to support activities and target groups which the regime did not favour and which might even be perceived as a threat. To Mobutu, the turn of events could appear to provide a means of ridding himself of a potential problem.

The case throws light on a policy dilemma which appears when a recipient regime which is authoritarian and self-seeking has a long-standing and deep engagement with the donor, where both business and NGOs are interested in maintaining relations. Allocative conditionality aimed at pursuing objectives associated with second generation conditionality may countervail opportunities to pursue these objectives by other means. This contradiction, Renard and Reyntjens argue, also exists with regard to the objectives of first and second generation conditionality, respectively: the refusal of the Belgian government to resume aid outside the government-to-government sphere until the Zaïrian government conceded economic reform in line with IMF/World Bank conditions, prevented Belgium from pursuing objectives associated with second generation conditionality by giving support to important actors within civil society who might have promoted democracy and by measures to relieve poverty.

In the cases of *Burundi* and *Rwanda*, the core problem relates to ethnic division. This was not unaffected by the Belgian colonial administration which relied on the minority group (Tutsi), thereby changing the power balance *vis-à-vis* the majority group (Hutu), with particular implications for the participation in the 'modern' economy and for social mobility through education. The grave violations of human rights which took place after independence, with widespread killings involving the security forces, may be perceived from the perspective of ethnic conflict. Until 1990, such incidents were associated mainly with Burundi where the minority elite was in control of political and coercive powers.

Gross violations of human rights, in 1983-87 and again in 1988, affected the aid flow to Burundi and prompted Belgium to threaten other sanctions and call for an international enquiry. Other major donors followed suit (USA, Canada, Germany and Switzerland).

These threats went home: a programme of national reconciliation was initiated and driven from the top (by President Buyoya). Belgium and a few other donors bolstered the process with additional aid. At the end of 1991, with the referendum on a pluralist constitution imminent, a new wave of violence took place, involving the armed forces and resulting in a heavy death toll. The progress towards democracy continued, however, and the free and fair elections in mid-1993 brought the opposition to power with a solid majority vote. A military coup took place in late October, again involving many deaths including that of the newly-elected President, and once more changed the situation for the worse. Belgium and other main donors suspended aid immediately.

Nevertheless, the Burundian case proves that employing brinkmanship in relation to aid may succeed, but that other forces may be even stronger in a society where a minority elite is confronted with the risk of losing its control of economic and political power, and of coercive power as well. It also demonstrates the important role an individual can take in directing events, particularly in the short term: the democratisation process was driven by the convictions of the man at the head of the administration, though he was probably acting not entirely without the hope of a popular reward.

Belgium's relations with Rwanda have traditionally been much more intimate than those prevailing with Zaïre and Burundi. In 1990, a predominantly ethnic conflict entered a new phase when Tutsi refugees invaded Rwanda from neighbouring countries, resulting in gross violations of human rights on both sides. Belgium showed a greater understanding *vis-à-vis* the Rwandan government than it had earlier shown towards Zaïre and Burundi. However, it did intervene (along with other donors). In March 1993, an international enquiry reported gross human rights violations. The Rwandan government admitted that the complaints were justified and promised to improve the situation. Although sanctions loomed in the background and were decisive in determining the outcome, the Belgian government, as in Burundi earlier, was quick to provide additional aid in order to enable the Rwandan government to follow up its pledges. The aid was targeted towards improvements in areas pertinent to the main objectives on the agenda for second generation conditionality, so-called positive measures. This took place before the catastrophe that exploded in early April 1994.

*

However, further examples deserve attention, although the policy of

Western powers has not always been consistent.[42] In particular, there is the case of Malawi, where concerted action was taken by the major bilateral aid donors. This provides experiences that supplement the lessons drawn from the Kenyan case, which illuminated the limitation of using aid as an instrument to produce political reform within an

---

42. There are many other examples of individual donors who, within the framework of second generation conditionality, have terminated, frozen or cut foreign aid (see *supra*, note 16). The British government has cut off aid (other than humanitarian) to the Sudan, Somalia and Burma. The French government has suspended aid to Zaïre. In recent years, the US government has suspended its aid (other than humanitarian) to Myanmar, the Sudan and Zaïre because of human rights violations, and to Haiti after a military coup in September 1991 removed an elected government.

The latter case is quite illustrative: for a long time the military government in Haiti was able to resist the pressure from its neighbouring government, the world's only remaining superpower, which has taken a leading role in the formulation and implementation of the agenda for second generation aid conditionality, with particular emphasis on democracy and human rights. Moreover, the US government was not alone. Every member of the Organization of American States agreed to suspend all but humanitarian aid and to impose a trade embargo. Many European aid donors, including the EC and France, suspended their aid (except for humanitarian aid) as well.

In all these cases, the justification for the intervention has been persistent violations of human rights: the measures were in defence of civil and individual rights and democracy.

There have been further examples of concerted action, in addition to the Kenyan case, involving both multilateral agencies and major donors. An example is the intervention of the World Bank *vis-à-vis* the regime in the Republic of Congo in 1989, which also had a signal effect for bilateral donors.

The Council of Ministers of the European Community has adopted strong political conditionality since 1989 and followed up, during the 1990s, by reducing or cutting ODA (except for humanitarian aid) to about 20 countries, including Liberia, Myanmar, Somalia, the Sudan and Zaïre. Commissions have been appointed by the EC to look into human rights violations in several of the countries to which it provides foreign aid.

However, as noted by Mark Robinson [*this volume*], even in countries where elections have taken place, incumbent rulers have remained in power (Ghana, Kenya); where they have resulted in victory for the opposition (Zambia, Benin), very little democratisation has taken place beyond a purely formal process of transferring power from one government to another.

The policy of Western powers has not always been consistent, not *vis-à-vis* all Third World countries nor over time towards the same country (even the same government). Thus, according to Gills *et al.* [*1993:15*] France reverted its policy by mid-1992. Initially France favoured national conferences to be convened in order to establish new multi-party systems in Francophone countries (indicating that progress towards democratisation would influence France's aid policy), although the pressure was less forthright in countries where France felt that it had vital national interests involved (such as the Ivory Coast and Togo) than in others (Madagascar). According to the authors, this reconsideration came as 'a reaction to the instability already created by previous national conferences, including increased tribal conflict and military unrest, leading to the prospect of ungovernability. The remaining repressive regimes in former French colonies in West and Central Africa were thereby given a signal that repression of the democratic opposition might be seen as preferable to the risk of instability.' See also *supra*, notes 6 and 31, and *infra*, note 63.

authoritarian, repressive system. Confronted with pressure from bilateral donors, the one-party government responded by calling a referendum to decide whether the country should revert to a multi-party system of government. Ultimately, it resulted in multi-party elections taking place (May 1994).

The outcomes of these cases do not provide sufficient evidence either to prove or disprove the propositions set out in VI.2: in the analysis one is (marginally) weakened and several others strengthened. Some kind of concerted international action emerges as almost an essential, although not necessarily sufficient, precondition if aid conditionality is to be successful *vis-à-vis* authoritarian, repressive regimes. There may be exceptions, particularly involving governments of countries that are small, poor and highly aid-dependent. However, those regimes, motivated by a desire for self-enrichment rather than for development, seem to be able to resist even concerted donor pressure.

These cases have been selected on the basis that brinkmanship has been applied and they may not tell the full story: pressure for policy reform is often more discreet, as Samuel Mushi indicates in his analysis of the Scandinavian-Tanzanian aid relationship [*this volume*]. There is not necessarily a correlation between brinkmanship and effectiveness: a 'soft', discreet approach, in the context of mutual trust, may sometimes be more effective.[43] However, a dialogue of this kind may not come within our definition of the concept of conditionality. More important, applying brinkmanship may carry heavy costs; in most cases there is a possibility that it will deflect the possibility of policy dialogue, undermine the recipient authorities' sense of responsibility for the actions taken and might even discredit the reforms. Experience over almost a decade and a half of first generation conditionality provides additional insights of relevance to our analysis.

---

43. John P. Lewis, former President of DAC, relates two cases which may illuminate the point [*Lewis, 1993:16-17*]. The first refers to a proposed World Bank SAL without tranches to Indonesia. Asked by the Board of Executive Directors how the management proposed to enforce the policy conditions, the answer, according to Lewis, was that 'the Indonesian government, with which the Bank characteristically has had quite constructive and amiable relations, had, after discussions with the Bank, already taken the reform steps that the SAL stipulated that it should take.' The other example is older: 'In the mid-1960s, the author and others in the U.S. Agency for International Development (USAID) mission to India were involved in a great deal of interactive dialogue with the government, especially its agricultural ministry, about agricultural reform. USAID nonproject loans were triggered by India's adoption of reforms that the dialogue apparently had helped bring about. But at the same time, President Lyndon Johnson was "short-tethering" food aid to India to provide *ex ante* leverage in behalf of the same reforms.' Lewis's basic argument is that sometimes soft and hard modes of policy conditionality can work in tandem.

4. Some Preconditions for Effective Aid Conditionality: An Exploratory Agenda

If the tentative conclusion above is correct, what preconditions are necessary to achieve concerted international action in pursuit of the various objectives associated with second generation aid conditionality? And what are the prospects for generating these preconditions? I will address these questions from both a long-term and a short-term perspective.

4.1 The long-term perspective of an international regime for 'good government': a utopian vision?

The alternative to the present practice in which individual donor governments act, on their own or jointly with others, more or less on an *ad hoc* basis, is an international regime pursuing objectives associated with second generation aid conditionality. Is there a probability that an international regime[44] of this kind, with aid conditionality as the prime tool, may be generated before the end of this century? Which of the present international institutions is best suited to administer the instrument? And what are the main modalities?

Different types of regime may be contemplated. Even a group of *donors* may establish an international regime of the kind, provided they agree on a common set of norms, elaborate objectives and implementation procedures for the pursuit of such objectives as human rights, democracy and 'good governance', involving, *inter alia*, sound public sector management, accountability, the rule of law and transparency, with ODA as the main instrument. The aid from this group would be ended, suspended or reduced if the defined expectations

---

44. An international regime is characterised by a system of norms, objectives and rules, formalised through some sort of international agreement between most actors in the policy area; there are procedures for the implementation of these rules, including negotiation, mediation and conflict resolution; and there are institutions responsible for policy decisions, monitoring and enforcement of the rules set. For a mainstream definition, see Krasner [*1982:185*]: 'International regimes are defined as principles, norms, rules and decision-making procedures around which actor expectations converge in a given issue-area.' This definition has survived although heavily attacked for being too vague. A new consensus was established in 1991 [*Young, 1991*]: 'We agreed to begin with a universe of cases including all arrangements that meet the explicit rules test. This would be followed by an effort to identify that subset of the initial universe meeting the explicit rules test and also achieving prescriptive status in the sense that actors refer regularly to the rules both in characterizing their own behaviour and in commenting on the behaviour of others. Beyond this, analysts should seek to pinpoint a smaller subset of arrangements that meet the first two tests and that give rise to a measure of rule-consistent behaviour as well.' As summed up by Keohane [*1993:28*], '... regimes can be identified by the existence of explicit rules that are referred to in an affirmative manner by governments, even if they are not necessarily scrupulously observed.'

(conditions) were not met; 'positive conditionality' would be another lever, offering increased aid to governments which improve their performance in this regard. In addition to the conditionality mechanism, the group might also use 'positive measures' to attain the objectives set.

However, this discussion will focus on global regimes which have a mandate to pursue objectives associated with second generation conditionality even if the mandate may be wider (or limited to only a few of these objectives) and the instruments at their disposal not confined to aid conditionality. Although this broadens the scope, the *problématique* is probably better illuminated from such a perspective.

There are lessons to be drawn from the experiences of first generation conditionality. In assessing its achievements, a distinction should be made between performance in creating an effective regime for the pursuance of certain objectives and performance in meeting the specific objectives set, that is, the effectiveness of the measures imposed on recipients. In terms of the former, it has been surprisingly effective; its success in terms of obtaining the stated (and implicit) objectives set has been more mixed.[45]

First generation conditionality was up against heavy odds: the objectives were controversial and highly political, although framed in 'technical' terms; and the medicine prescribed was bitter and painful, in particular for the poorest groups, but even for domestic business interests, too, and this had repercussions for the governments. Several factors combine to provide an explanation for the regime success, against these odds, in producing the intended reforms:

(1) There was a well established international regime (institutions, rules and modalities) for tackling the main problem, identified as the balance-of-payments crisis, and this regime was applied in the new context.

(2) Although highly political and controversial, the problem was framed in a technical language and was depoliticised.

(3) Vital interests (strategic and economic) in the North would not be negatively affected by the measures proposed; on the contrary, the measures were intended to save the international financial system and to ensure that extensive debts to private financial

---

45. The greatest successes, on both criteria, have been where there was least need for brinkmanship – involving regimes with a policy stance very similar to the IMF/World Bank prescription, as illustrated in the case of Turkey [*Morrissey, this volume*]. In other cases, the results, particularly *vis-à-vis* the second criterion, have been less convincing [*Mosely et al., 1991*].

institutions in the North were serviced and paid back. Because of this,

(4) the main powers of the North succeeded in rallying additional support for the policy in the World Bank and within the OECD. The warnings, typically, came from the United Nations system where Third World influence is more entrenched than in the Bretton Woods institutions; here, structural adjustment with a human face was advocated [*Cornia et al., 1987*].

The study by Oliver Morrissey [*this volume*] focusing on Turkey, which comes close to a 'success story', gives additional insight to these macro-level observations. During the 1980s, Turkey made substantial progress in placing its economy on a more solid footing. This success entailed a distributional cost, and both labour – facing a consistent decline in real wages – and agriculture emerged as losers. The gainers were the exporters and importers, and the public enterprises which were largely sheltered from the effects of adjustment.

Regime factors in Turkey were decisive in achieving this policy: these included military rule during the first crucial years of implementation; a trained leadership committed to reforms of the type aimed for by first generation aid conditionality; and power was concentrated in a small elite and there was a weak opposition. As Morrissey observes, it is not surprising that a military regime could impose reforms with negative distributional effects for labour and agriculture; what is remarkable is that the main architect of this policy was able to lead his party to a democratic victory only one year after leaving the military administration. The general conclusion is that new, strong governments, including military regimes, are able to withstand opposition to reforms better than old governments tarnished with the failures of the past. However, a most important observation is that the World Bank refrained from direct interference, involving brinkmanship, in Turkish politics.

The situation with second generation aid conditionality is very different:

(1) A well-established, international regime ready to push forward and administer the policy is missing.
(2) The agenda is highly political, and explicitly so, although the World Bank brand ('good governance') is given a 'technical' framework.
(3) Economic interests in the North are at risk of being harmed, in the short run, unless universal action is taken – and concerted

action involving the good government agenda is not easily achieved. However, there are possible economic gains (for the North), especially if 'good governance' reforms are attained – such as increased transparency, predictability and the rule of law. The normative aspects involved (human rights, democracy), although generally valued, are gains of a general nature belonging to the common goods and escape the traditional measures of economic gains. Moreover, the 'good governance' dividend appears long-term and elusive when weighed against more immediate, specific losses.

(4) In terms of the normative aspects, particularly human rights, a high degree of consensus exists within the aid-providing community. This also applies to the 'good governance' objectives.

The first criterion, concerning the regime, is the most crucial. From this perspective, the possibility of success for second generation conditionality seems bleaker than for the first. Which regimes can accommodate the various objectives involved? And what prospects are there for such regimes to be given additional powers in order to serve these needs better (using aid conditionality either as the sole instrument or as one tool among others) or for new institutions to be created for these purposes? There are several potential regimes to take on additional responsibility but most are poorly equipped to perform the particular tasks involved. There is no existing international regime which covers all objectives associated with second generation aid conditionality. Since several of the objectives involved are interrelated, this represents a serious set-back.

Among these objectives, *human rights* are best situated from a regime perspective. A set of norms has been established internationally (through UN declarations and conventions, including the recent one on the right to development). Equally important, institutions to survey and monitor human rights worldwide have also been established. The Geneva-based United Nations Commission on Human Rights (UNCHR) is of particular importance in this regard. However, it has been noted already that the powers of the United Nations system in general and UNCHR in particular are circumscribed and somewhat feeble; the onus is on member governments to report, monitor and implement human rights, although the trend is towards greater involvement from the international community. These institutions contribute to regime development through policy prescriptions (norms and recommendations regarding implementation) but the system for enforcement is so weakly developed as to be almost non-existent.

For certain sections of the human rights agenda, there are other, more specialised international regimes, such as the International Labour Organisation (ILO) which is concerned with social rights. The United Nations Development Programme (UNDP) has recently taken on a role in monitoring core aspects of human rights; its alternative human development index covers relevant areas.[46] Several non-governmental organisations are also active within this field, particularly Amnesty International, with its independent network and reporting system. In many cases, and particularly with regard to authoritarian, repressive governments whose gross violations of human rights make them rank high among targets for aid conditionality, Amnesty International may be more effective than the multilateral system in terms of monitoring and documentation.

For effective implementation of aid conditionality, universally agreed norms and a system for documentation and monitoring represent a *sine qua non*; these components of the international regime are assets as far as human rights are concerned, although neither the norms nor the documentation and monitoring systems are currently adjusted to the particular needs of aid conditionality.[47] For the system to work on these criteria, general rights are not sufficient: they need to be translated into specific prescriptions. There needs to be a consensus (or decisions) on the kinds of violations or processes that will release the aid conditionality mechanism.

Within the multilateral system, there seems to be a long way to go.

---

46. This index includes indicators that cover, in particular, the traditional agenda for development assistance, namely economic and social development (social and economic rights). Peter P. Waller [*1993:54; 1992:25-27*] makes an interesting observation from the perspective of the aid debate in the 1990s: the UNDP previously refused to make aid an instrument in enforcing civil and political human rights; according to Waller, this strict division of the two domains runs counter to the United Nations Charter and was maintained by a powerful block of authoritarian Third World regimes and socialist countries. The events of the late 1980s turned the UNDP towards a new track.

47. Major attempts at developing human rights indicators are made by Humana [*1986*] and by the UNDP (the Human Freedom Index). For a critique of the early efforts of the UNDP, particularly involving the Political Freedom Index, see Tomasevski [*1991*], who found it surprising that 'a book that had not passed peer review [Humana's book] has been adopted as a model. Indeed Humana's book was rejected by those involved in human rights research, East and West, North and South' [*ibid.:13*]. The data compiled by Amnesty International (annual reports and special reports) and Human Rights Internet provide basis for a monitoring of the human rights performance. Also the annual country reports on human rights practices of the US Ministry of Foreign Affairs, initiated in the mid-1970s, provide a source of systematic information of this kind (limited to civil and political rights). More recently, the annual review of the human right performance of selected developing countries, compiled by the human rights institutes in Canada, Denmark, Finland, the Netherlands, Norway and Sweden adds to these efforts, extending the perspective also to include economic, social and cultural rights.

The mechanism is administered *ad hoc* by individual donors or a group of donor governments, occasionally even in a multilateral setting (consultative groups) and so far it has been used only when spectacular and grave violations of human rights have occurred. Despite this threshold, the prospect for building a multilateral regime should not be abandoned. An existing framework might be given additional authority and adapted to the task or, more realistically, a new framework established; for instance, this could take place under the Office of the UN Secretary-General, relying on existing UN institutions for documentation and monitoring. However, in limiting the mechanism to particularly grave violations, important structural human rights violations – less spectacular, but of equal or even greater importance from a development perspective – are allowed to evade reaction from the international community.

In terms of other objectives associated with second generation aid conditionality (democracy, 'good governance'), no international regimes of a similar kind exist. The most fundamental components are missing. Thus, although there may be wide consensus on certain fundamental norms, these universal norms are not codified in so far as they are not included as human rights. No multilateral institution has been set up to monitor and implement these norms, and there are no enforcement mechanisms – that is, unless the violations are of the kind which invokes the enforcement clauses of the UN Security Council. This applies to democracy in particular but also to 'good governance' as defined by the World Bank.

However, no determinism is involved and an existing international regime can adapt to – or be adapted to – pressing needs as perceived from within and/or outside the institution. The role of the World Bank with regard to 'good governance' illustrates the point: it has been instrumental in placing the theme firmly on the agenda and it has made systematic contributions in exploring the normative basis for this form of regime. It has gone further: the agenda explored was restricted to the area where the Bank itself would be able to step in as the operative institution. As an international regime this represents only the first, stumbling steps. Nevertheless, in view of its position as norm-setter and its financial resources with their multiplying effects, such first steps are not unimportant.

The 'good governance' agenda invites some additional observations on the effectiveness with which second generation aid conditionality may be operated. The relative effectiveness – from a regime perspective – of first generation conditionality has, *inter alia*, been explained by some 'technical' characteristics: the instrument was most effective when the objectives were few, the means employed also few and the criteria on which the performance was measured both few and simple [*Lewis, 1993:20-21*].[48] For second generation aid conditionality, particularly with regard to the 'good governance' agenda, the context is totally different.

International regimes which cover key items on the good government agenda exist already and their mandates might be extended to areas not yet covered. Currently, there is no single regime that covers the whole agenda, and those that cover part of it are weak with regard to follow-up and enforcement. At this stage it may therefore be premature to discuss where, in the multilateral system, responsibility for the implementation of aid conditionality should be placed. Is the best solution to develop further the fragmented regimes which already exist or would it be better – and possible – to create a new regime? The best starting point in terms of participation is the United Nations, the multilateral system in which donors and recipients are represented most equally. From the point of view of efficiency, or even of effectiveness, however, this is probably not the best choice. Nevertheless, in the long-term, the project depends on the involvement of both the North and the South in order to be effective; it follows that the responsibility and the institutional machinery are best situated with the United Nations. Moreover, this course is in line with the recommendations of the Stockholm initiative on global security and governance [*PMO, 1991:32-5,45*].[49]

4.2 The short-term perspective: aid conditionality effective only vis-à-vis weak, aid-dependent governments?

In a more short-term perspective, what are the prospects that aid conditionality will work? What are the chances for concerted action? Not

---

48. Lewis [*idem*] contrasts the IMF's traditional conditioning with the World Bank's SALs and SECALs. These have an array of policy conditions, an average of 56 per loan in recent years, and Lewis argues [*ibid.:43,47*] against the proliferation of targets: the more policy targets – and the more conditions – that any given loan carries, the weaker the enforcement of any one condition tends to be.

49. The Stockholm initiative, building on the work of the international commissions of the 1980s chaired by Willy Brandt, Olof Palme and Gro Harlem Brundtland, respectively, strongly emphasised the need for global governance. The statement recognised democracy and human rights as truly universal values which had their origins and history in societies of all continents and which were essential to the prospect of development. It emphasised strengthening the UN role in monitoring countries' performance in terms of international conventions and declarations concerning human rights and democracy. However, it also proposed strengthening independent international institutions (such as Amnesty International and the International Commission of Jurists) offering to monitor countries' observance of democratic rules and principles, in particular during elections, respecting the constitutional order of each country.

all effects of a policy are always transparent or easily documented. It is quite possible that the main effects of second generation political conditionality will emerge as a result of the *declared* policy rather than from its actual implementation. The warnings from major donors have been loud and clear. In addition, it is likely that the cases where brinkmanship has been applied have had a significant signal effect. However, action matters more than rhetoric: the more silent allocative practice will strengthen or weaken these signals. For many Third World governments, foreign aid is important. They may therefore be sensitive to consistent signals indicating changed criteria for the distribution of aid. They may prefer to follow a strategy of early adaptation rather than confrontation. Indirect effects may in this way outweigh the effects of open brinkmanship and should not be excluded when judging the success or failure of the policy.

Nevertheless, concerted action (brinkmanship) by Western donors involving second generation political conditionality has taken place in the recent past and cannot be ruled out in the immediate future. In the absence of a comprehensive multilateral regime, it is likely to be undertaken on an *ad hoc* basis by individual donor governments or as a coordinated action by several donors. It is less certain whether such a policy will be pursued in the form of discreet diplomacy or with full transparency. Which approach would be the more effective is also open to discussion. However, it is easy for 'dialogues' involving conditionality to be disclosed even when the parties intended them to be discreet; the temptation to leak to the media will always be present for a donor government needing to justify its policy *vis-à-vis* its electorate. Donor consultation, even co-ordination, is already taking place on these issues; but if it is to be effective, it is necessary to agree on the basic concepts, mechanisms and modalities.

This strategy has several limitations. What are the circumstances which make it work – and what makes it ineffective? For example it is limited by the type of issues for which it is adapted and also by the effectiveness of the instrument. The instrument is somewhat crude, and therefore not always applicable. Its use presupposes a dramatic situation, as the cases above indicate. In the absence of an international regime, where the objectives and more specific rules and procedures would constitute an integral part, some limitations of this kind may be indicated.

Grave violations of *human rights* – involving loss of human lives or other atrocities – trigger allocative conditionality; however, this is not automatic. Violations that are less spectacular yet systematic tend to be left aside. Major human rights violations seldom appear in

63

isolation; when aid conditionality is invoked by such an incident, it may be applied in order to obtain policy reform within a broader spectrum, including systemic reforms. In principle, allocative conditionality may be used towards all countries with unelected regimes; in practice it will probably not function like that, although donor guidelines to this end involving future aid may be envisaged. The probability is that the instrument will be process-oriented: it will be used less in relation to established authoritarian regimes (including military regimes) than when a democratically elected regime is toppled by a coup and replaced by an authoritarian one (for instance a military regime). In addition, when an incident involving the *democracy* agenda triggers aid conditionality, it may be directed towards a broader spectrum of policy reforms, particularly those involving human rights.

For reasons indicated above, especially the multitude of particular objectives involved and the lack of precise criteria on which performance may be evaluated, aid conditionality is not well suited as an instrument for the '*good governance*' agenda – with the exception, already noted, of particular spectacular cases involving gross political corruption. Although the scope for aid conditionality is limited, the areas where it might be applied are far from unimportant. The crucial question is to what extent it works within these areas. This highlights another limitation already identified, namely the type of regime involved: an authoritarian regime may be inclined to avoid pressure for reforms by paying lip-service to the reforms or by reform gestures with little real content.[50] Moreover, a repressive regime may be resistant to the indirect pressure of a declared policy for reasons of sheer self-preservation; the probability is that it will also resist the implementation of aid conditionality, even when there is concerted action, as several of our cases indicate. In a situation where groups within the ruling elite seek policy reform of the kind identified, there is a greater chance of success: they may be able to use the pressure from outside to strengthen their position and thereby tip the balance. However, in the context of the kind of system under discussion (authoritarian and repressive regimes), the opposite result should also be anticipated:

---

50. Nelson and Eglinton argue [*1992:37*], 'where governments are not committed to reforms but badly need external finance, and where donors feel under some obligation to provide funds, the process of conditionality can degenerate into a charade. Without ownership, extensive use of conditions is likely to produce elaborate games of superficial or partial compliance, failure to adopt key supplementary measures to make the reforms effective, or a trail of reform efforts launched and abandoned. These games are worse than frustrating; they destroy the credibility of the reform process within the country concerned, and they obstruct dialogue and persuasion between the government and external donors or creditors.'

brinkmanship from outside may discredit their case and reduce their ability to pursue reform.

Aid conditionality is not a particularly hard-hitting weapon, except in the cases of a few extremely aid-dependent countries.[51] In these cases, however, it may have contributed to creating opportunities for a change of regime, although not necessarily to a fundamental change of policy.[52] Peter Waller's conclusion, based on German experiences [*this volume*], is that conditionality may be successful in heavily aid-dependent countries where economic and strategic interests are minimal. For most authoritarian and repressive regimes, where the need for political reforms of the kind included on the good government agenda is most acute, aid conditionality would be of little avail. Little will be achieved if an intervention towards an authoritarian, repressive regime stops short of toppling the governing structure. There are few, if any, indications that international society would contemplate such an action, regardless of the degree of human rights violations: this was demonstrated for decades *vis-à-vis* the apartheid regime of South Africa. If pressured from the outside to undertake reforms which a government strongly resents, the authorities, even while paying lip-service to the demands, will find ways and means to avoid delivering in terms of actual policy. On the contrary, this form of external intervention may, in the worst case scenario, negatively affect the intended objectives by weakening the possibility of a change to take place from within the ruling elite.

The discussion has so far centred around the *probability* that aid conditionality will work. A more fundamental question would be: *if* it works, would it work *vis-à-vis* the overall development objectives set for aid? There will certainly be more than one view on this issue.

---

51. For many developing countries, official development finance (ODF) – in 1991 amounting to US$ 70.4 billion (of which ODA US$ 54 billion) – represents a major resource inflow. Total net resource flows, including export credits and private flows, amounted to US$ 127.2 billion [*OECD, 1992:78*]. While some Third World countries are highly dependent on continued aid (and even small cuts may hurt), for others aid is marginal, representing only a tiny proportion of the country's GNP or the government's budget. This affects how hard-hitting the aid conditionality instrument will be in each individual case.

52. Mark Robinson notes [*1993b:87-9*] that by the time of the fall of the Berlin wall, 38 of the 45 states in sub-Saharan Africa were governed by authoritarian regimes; 18 months later, half of these were committed to multi-party elections or had held elections. Although this development is attributed to other major determinants – a combination of internal and external, with emphasis on the former – aid conditionality is attributed a role (in addition to the disappearance of support, military and economic, to the authoritarian regimes from the major Western *cum* former colonial powers, particularly in Francophone Africa). For assessments of the relative weight attributed to aid conditionality, see Robinson [*ibid.:92-7*].

Martin Doornbos [*this volume*] gives a timely warning that one paradoxical effect of the various external initiatives promoting 'good governance', is that Third World governments' capacity for policy-making and implementation is reduced rather than strengthened, for a variety of reasons.[53] The cost of enhancing external accountability might be a progressive erosion of policy-making capacity.

To sum up, there is little likelihood that political conditionality will work except in the limited areas already indicated. It follows that additional or alternative strategies should be explored and these will be considered next. The discussion will again take as its point of departure the objectives included in the good government agenda. The more fundamental question – whether these objectives should be given highest priority in the particular setting of North-South development co-operation – will remain unaddressed.

VII. ALTERNATIVE STRATEGIES

Alternative strategies in pursuit of the objectives associated with second generation conditionality were indicated when the concept was defined (Section III). Whereas the concept in our definition was confined to the stick, others have included the carrot.[54] There is a logic for including the carrot, in that it adds a positive dimension (reward of good performance) to the negative one (denial of aid resulting from bad performance) by implying that a recipient government is confronted with a double 'offer': if you are not making policy reforms relevant to the good government agenda, we will freeze, reduce or stop our foreign aid; if you are undertaking the reforms recommended, we will increase our aid (or aid directed specifically to ensure these reforms). It has been noted already that this was how the Belgian government implemented its aid conditionality *vis-à-vis* Burundi and Rwanda.

Applied *ex post*, however, this extended version of conditionality might involve a complex interaction, with drastic reductions in ODA

---

53. In this discourse, the role of the state is crucial. Autonomous institutions for improved management, externally induced, may undermine local government capacity – and central government co-ordination. This may apply when aid is channelled through NGOs. See also Mutahaba [*1990*] on this point. Donor co-ordination increasingly sets the limits and targets for national policy-making. The implicit ethnocentricity of the approach is also pin-pointed: the question, according to Doornbos, is whether general standards of 'good governance' are acceptable to all actors involved, given the variation in cultural factors from one setting to another.
54. See *supra*, Section III, particularly note 8.

transfers one year, as a consequence of bad performance *vis-à-vis* the good government criteria, followed by large increases as a reward for good performance. Belgium, and Germany in the case of Zambia [*Waller, this volume*], demonstrate that this is possible, but it presupposes a high degree of flexibility within aid agencies. Such flexibility is seldom found, particularly within systems operating long-term strategies in terms of planning and commitment.

Alternative strategies have to go beyond the confines of the logic of aid conditionality, even the extended version. The fundamental question is: what factors produce good government as defined earlier? This question cannot be addressed in isolation from the social, cultural, economic and political setting of each particular society, nor from its historical context; these framework conditions vary from one society to another.[55] Furthermore, what function may ODA serve in promoting processes towards these objectives? The latter question relates to the form of co-operation, the aid channel, target groups, the form of aid and its content; it is only within the confines of a few dimensions at the macro level, such as the balance-of-payments situation of a recipient, that it is meaningful to talk about foreign aid without reference to these factors.

The discussion here will, by necessity, be exploratory, both with regard to the factors leading to good government – that is, democracy, human rights and 'good governance', each of which, although inter-related, has a separate agenda – and in considering how best to use development assistance in order to promote and improve the various aspects of good government.

The vast and growing literature on democratic regimes reveals that the very value set as an objective for the conditionality policy – *democracy* in its many variations – is itself an instrument which may be used for many purposes depending on who is pulling the strings. Like conditionality, democracy becomes meaningful only in a particular

---

55. The study of democracy as a system of government has long traditions with roots back to the Greek philosophers. In the late 1950s and early 1960s, the 'wind of change' swept over Africa and other parts of the Third World: Western colonial powers moved out, leaving behind independent states with democratic constructs modelled on the outgoing European (or North-American) imperial power. This process attracted the interest of social scientists analysing political systems from a comparative perspective and using the tools of quantitative methods: comparative studies of democracy and development (or 'modernization', a term which involves even stronger value connotations, with ethnocentrism in addition when extended from the North to the South) had an added component from the South. These early studies provide a vast amount of data and insights on which we can draw even today. Among the classic works from this period are Almond and Coleman [*1960*], Almond and Verba [*1963*], Rokkan [*1970*] (limited to European systems), Binder *et al.* [*1971*], and Dahl [*1971*].

setting; unlike conditionality, it is operated from within the society concerned, affecting power relations, values and distribution of resources. Established interests groups are affected, for better or worse, and their attitude towards the instrument is not entirely unaffected by the outcome, as powerful elites have often demonstrated when democratic rule has threatened their privileges.

The concept of democracy is defined – and used and misused – in many different ways [*Sørensen, this volume*]. Even within the confines of the conditionality agenda, it is given different meanings: in a limited sense, it merely involves formal free and fair elections and a multi-party system. One interpretation, emphasising liberal elements, foresees a limited role of the state *vis-à-vis* individuals and the market. Others emphasise pluralism and participation as essential, going beyond the requirement of formal elections. Further interpretations couple the concept with other values in so far as they are intrinsic to the definition: for instance, parliamentary democracy might be conceived as a partial democracy unless these other claims are fulfilled. The claims apply to other objectives associated with the conditionality agenda. These aims include the full spectrum of human rights from the economic and social ones, which may involve economic democracy at various levels as well as social justice, to civil and political rights, and the right to development.[56]

---

56. In a major comparative study on democracy in developing countries, resulting in a four-volume work [*Diamond, Linz and Lipset, eds., 1988-90, I-IV*], the editors argue for a definition that separates the political system from the economic and social system to which it is joined, insisting that economic and social democracy should be separated from the question of governmental structure. The 'classical' definition suggested on this basis, is the following [*ibid., II:xvi, III:xvi*]: 'a system of government that meets three essential conditions: meaningful and extensive *competition* among individuals and organized groups (especially political parties) for all effective positions of government power, at regular intervals and excluding the use of force; a highly inclusive level of *political participation* in the selection of leaders and policies, at least through regular and free elections, such that no major (adult) social group is excluded; and a level of *civil and political liberties* – freedom of expression, freedom of the press, freedom to form and join organizations – sufficient to ensure the integrity of political competition and participation.' The authors admit (in line with Robert Dahl's concept – *polyarchy* [*Dahl,1971*]) that, confronted with the real world, the definition presents a number of problems because systems which broadly satisfy the criteria nevertheless do so to different degrees.

The editors of another comparative study [*Gills et al., 1993*] find a definition of democracy which excludes the economic and social reality from the political totally unsatisfactory, missing the first and most important task of democratic regimes, namely social reform: 'in the absence of progressive social reform the term "democracy" is largely devoid of meaningful content' and may serve as a euphemism for sophisticated modern forms of neo-authoritarianism. 'Without *combining* political democracy and social reform, one could argue that democracy itself is undermined in the medium to long term.' With particular reference to the current debate, the editors conclude [*ibid.:4*] that the studies undertaken provided 'little evidence to support the

There exists no single concept of democracy even in the Western tradition; there are several. In this particular context the core question is how to promote democracy, whether it is given a 'classical' or a more extensive definition, by means of foreign aid. A strategy to this end will have to adapt to many different realities: the particular historical tradition matters as do other factors such as the legitimacy of the regime and its effectiveness, social and cultural conditions related to class structure, ethnicity and religion, and the extent to which state structures are adapted to such realities. Constitutional framework conditions are important for a democracy to function, but so is the civil society outside the social structures identified in the classical definition of democracy (political parties) in addition to those identified. Civil and political liberties, and independent, free and vital mass media constitute important framework conditions for a thriving civil society.

Given the marginal importance of aid's role in most Third World countries (though some outstanding exceptions have been identified) in fulfilling the original agenda, namely to promote economic and social development, too much should not be expected from the new. The more fundamental systemic reforms, involving constitutional matters such as checks and balances of state powers and the institutional arrangements might be omitted from the discussion; bringing the focus on to processes and structures at a lower level. Apart from the framework conditions, contributions to facilitate the vitality of the civil society is the most obvious area where foreign aid may play a role in fostering democracy. However, at the risk of stating the obvious, foreign aid can play only a supportive role in self-generated processes; a vital civil society cannot be created from outside!

Even within these confines, there is considerable room for 'democracy-building' foreign aid. This can be provided within the traditional framework, that is, channelled through the authorities at the

---

widespread assumption that formal electoral democratisation alone would bring about a lasting progressive breakthrough in these societies or that it is capable of solving their fundamental social and especially economic problems. What should more accurately be called "elite democracies" in effect coexist with tacit military dictatorships. Social reform agendas that could have established the basis for broader popular participation and greater social justice have been abandoned. Human rights violations continue virtually unabated. The new regimes are more readily manipulated by external forces such as the International Monetary Fund (IMF) or via bilateral political and economic pressures, particularly from the United States. Economic policies often mandate austerity for the majority without, in most cases, bringing about significant economic growth. Progressive movements find it virtually impossible to implement an agenda for reform when powerful domestic and international groups opposing such change, not least the military, remain in place.' See also *supra*, sections IV.2.3 and V.2.

recipient side (state-to-state aid) and earmarked for a wide variety of purposes and target groups; it may be directed towards specific institutions (and include framework conditions), processes, target groups or purposes which are assumed to have a direct or indirect influence in assisting greater popular participation both in government at various levels and in democratic institutions. Education, for instance – both at basic and higher levels – is considered a necessary (but not necessarily a sufficient) precondition for participation and democratic rule, although the links may be indirect and difficult to trace; in many authoritarian systems, universities and other institutions of higher learning have constituted the only open space for the formulation of policy alternatives to the government.

Aid targeted towards democracy may also be provided outside government institutions, either to the private sector or the myriad non-governmental organisations and institutions that are part of civil society. Not all are of equal importance in facilitating the democratic process; within an autocratic setting, certain NGOs may benefit from – and strengthen – the system. NGOs explicitly aiming at changing the system may have to operate within tight and circumscribed confines. Foreign aid to these organisations is problematic to organise. In many autocratic systems there is still room to support organisations with the potential to transform the system – such as trade unions (even when they function as part of the ruling system, as illustrated recently in Zambia) and other professional organisations and human rights movements. The mass media institutions within the private sector are considered of particular importance in this context; these may be supported in many different ways, including institution-building and professional training.

However, the capacity of NGOs to absorb political funds is limited; as noted by Mark Robinson [*this volume*], it would be unrealistic of donors to expect that this capacity can be vastly increased without becoming counter-productive. In a transition to democracy, technical assistance may be provided for the government pursuing democratic reform in terms of the logistics of democracy, including the elections, and giving legitimacy to the outcome by offering observers to follow an election process.

Pursuit of *human rights*, particularly civil and political rights, through foreign aid confronts many of the same constraints as those already identified that pall democracy; various preconditions for democratic rule are also prerequisites for various human rights or for their capacity to function. Pursuit of these rights, of course, needs to be adapted to the particular rights involved.

The targeted aid may be channelled through the recipient regime or, in the case of a bilateral donor, through multilateral or international (non-governmental) channels. It may also be channelled directly to organisations with system-transforming programmes. Aid targeted for these purposes includes aid directed towards processes leading to improved human rights – civil, political, economic and social – including institution-building within particular strategic areas and improvements in the framework conditions. The more specific targets and target groups vary considerably. Even humanitarian aid (in terms of support for refugees, legal aid for victims of repressive regimes, etc.) is included.

Aid targeted for these purposes constitutes an important part of a human-rights-oriented aid strategy; however, as emphasised by Waller [*1992:28*], it is of equally importance to ensure that activities within the general aid package do not *violate* human rights.

This applies to the '*good governance*' agenda as well, although it is probable that aid in pursuit of its various objectives will have to be directed to a greater extent through the governing structures and will therefore be more vulnerable in cases where an authoritarian or repressive government is deeply involved in corrupt economic or political practice. Foreign aid is likely to have little of its intended impact under such circumstances; it may actually fuel corruption even if the regime may pay lip-service to the values in question. To be effective the various forms of aid from outside have to be fed into a reform process initiated by the recipient authorities themselves.

VIII. SOME CONCLUDING OBSERVATIONS

Second generation political conditionality, to a greater extent even than the first, confronts several unresolved problems. One of these is a complex question of legitimacy which partly tags on to a problem of consistency within a setting characterised by asymmetric power relations. There is also an instrumental problem, since the strategy seems to produce the intended results only in exceptional cases. These aspects will be briefly addressed before turning to the conclusion: the need for additional – supplementary or alternative – strategies in order to attain the objectives sought.

Core aspects of the complex *legitimacy problem* were discussed in Section V. The principle of non-intervention in the internal affairs of other sovereign states, although eroded, constitutes a problem which arises, in particular, *vis-à-vis* the demand for systemic reform

71

(democracy). The problem is less pronounced with regard to demands involving improvement in a country's human rights performance due to its international commitments, when the government itself has responsibility to implement these commitments. Although a matter of degree, this problem of legitimacy is not restricted to second generation aid conditionality; ultimately it applies to all foreign aid.

The principle of non-intervention does not recognise a competing legitimacy, namely that of the concerned regime *vis-à-vis* the governed.[57] It does not distinguish between a regime which bases its position on the control of coercive powers and one founded on popular consent. With growing recognition, from various perspectives, of the value of some form of participation by the governed in decisions which affect their fortunes, a competing legitimacy has a bearing on our *problématique*. The increased international prominence of the human rights agenda serves both as a facilitator and an indicator in this regard. Authoritarian, repressive, self-seeking regimes – in the post-Cold War world order – are no longer considered a treasured conservation target.

Apart from the legitimacy of the recipient government (although this, too, has an impact), the characteristics of the aid relationship make it necessary to balance one type of legitimacy against another. A donor government may have to choose between the legitimacy of its policy *vis-à-vis* it own electorate and its legitimacy *vis-à-vis* a contested principle of non-intervention. This dilemma does not make an intervention legitimate; it does, however, make it legitimate for a donor government to abstain from providing aid to a recipient system where the framework conditions are not in place for aid to work according to the objectives and guidelines set.

This also applies to the more 'technical' conditions set by the World Bank 'good governance' agenda. As argued by Geoffrey Hawthorn [*1993:29*], states in their role as donors, and *a fortiori* the international institutions whose *raison d'être* is to be donors, exist solely and explicitly to improve the standard of living or well-being of the citizens of other states, that is, to ensure that the social rights of

---

57. This legitimacy is imbedded, *inter alia*, in the traditions of the French and American revolutions and further developed in the Universal Declaration of Human Rights, as noted. In international law, however, it is weakly – if at all – developed. Thus, the main criterion for recognition is traditionally the government's effective control of a territory (country) and whether it takes responsibility for the foreign commitments (including debts) of its predecessor. For a discussion on the contradiction involved, from the perspective of international law, see Asbjørn Eide [*1992:3,13-20*]. Uvin [*1993a:68*], however, postulates that it is unlikely that sovereignty will become subservient to human rights in the foreseeable future.

these citizens and those civil and political rights without which these social rights as claimable rights would be incomplete, are extended and observed.

In this discussion, Western liberal democracies have been identified as the champions of 'good government' both in the wider sense referred to above and in the more narrow sense of 'good governance' as defined by the World Bank. The setting implicitly suggests that this heroic fight is fought against predominant norms prevailing in the South and Third World regimes at large. This is by no means a true picture. It is, however, true that aid conditionality as such has been met with reluctance in the South – and this is natural for regimes which have been exposed to both first and second generation conditionality. It should come as no surprise that authoritarian and repressive regimes of various kinds, whether the power of their patrimonial (or neo-patrimonial) elites has a military, one-party or even a multi-party basis, vehemently resent outside interference which threatens their position. In addition, reluctance in the South against the new drive from the North is rooted in past experiences of colonialism and neo-imperialism, and stimulated by what is conceived as mixed motives and inconsistent practice in the context both of the North and the Western powers in their relationships with individual regimes in the South. The resentment may to some extent be culturally based; however, it may be interpreted as a protest against interference and dominance from the North rather than a rebuff of the values involved.

Nevertheless, others have welcomed the objectives associated with second generation conditionality. Not surprisingly, suppressed opposition or minority groups within countries with a repressive government, and political refugees who have had to flee from these countries, have appealed to Western governments, mostly in vain, to follow up their stated policy in support of human rights and democratic reform [*Robinson, 1993a; Wamwere, 1989*]. More importantly, representative voices from the South have championed the very norms which are part and parcel of the good government agenda, although an ocean may exist between the declared intentions and actual practice of many of the governments concerned as well as great variations in their genuine willingness or ability to deliver. The South Commission, defining development[58] and its preconditions, includes basic human

---

58. According to the South Commission [*1990: 10-11*], '... development is a process which enables human beings to realize their potential, build self-confidence, and lead lives of dignity and fulfilment. It is a process which frees peoples from the fear of want and exploitation. It is a movement away from political, economic, or social oppression. Through development, political independence acquires its true significance. And it is a process of growth, a movement essentially springing from within

rights in their full breadth and places emphasis on popular participation, democratic institutions and the possibility of changing government through peaceful means, and on transparency, the rule of law, and other values associated with the 'good governance' agenda. The Commission identified the following among the main challenges for the South: 'to strengthen democratic institutions so that its people may live in freedom and chart their own path to development in harmony with their culture and values.'[59] Similar views have been expressed by the Heads of State and Government of the Organisation of African Unity [*OAU, 1990:3-4*].[60]

Confronted with the demands from the North included in the agenda both of first and second generation aid conditionality, these forces in the South have been brought on the defensive rather than strengthened. The demands represent an implicit, and often explicit,

---

the society that is developing. ... The base for a nation's development must be its own resources, both human and material, fully used to meet its own needs. ... Development is based on self-reliance and is self-directed; ... True development has to be people-centred.'

59. The South Commission [*1990: 10-14, 23, 277, 287 (quotation p. 23)*]. Summing up [*ibid.:13-14*], the Commission insists that 'development presupposes a democratic structure of government, together with its supporting individual freedoms of speech, organization, and publication, as well as a system of justice which protects all the people from actions inconsistent with just laws that are known and publicly accepted.'

60. In the declaration, the Assembly recognised that in order to facilitate a process of socio-economic transformation and integration according to the Lagos Plan of Action and Africa's Priority Programme for Economic Recovery, 'it is necessary to promote popular participation of our peoples in the processes of government and development. A political environment which guarantees human rights and the observance of the rule of law, would assure high standards of probity and accountability particularly on the part of those who hold public office. In addition, popular-based political processes would ensure the involvement of all including in particular women and youth in development efforts. We accordingly recommit ourselves to the further democratisation of our societies and to the consolidation of democratic institutions in our countries. We reaffirm the right of our countries to determine, in all sovereignty, their system of democracy on the basis of their socio-cultural values, taking into account the realities of each of our countries and the necessity to ensure development and satisfy the basic needs of our peoples.'

For other representative voices of the South, see also the Joint Communiqué issued by the Heads of State and Government of the Group of Fifteen after the Third Summit Meeting in Dakar in November 1992 [*Group of Fifteen, 1993:4*], stating, *inter alia*, that 'We are committed to the promotion of democracy, at both the national and international levels, pluralism, the rule of law and human rights in all their multidimensional aspects – civil, political, economic, social and cultural – on the basis of the full respect for national sovereignty, territorial integrity and non-intervention. The violation or abuse of human rights of individuals or peoples should not be condoned under any circumstances. It is also important to stress that development is a key factor for the sustainability of democratic processes, the respect and promotion of human rights, and global peace and security. The interdependence of Democracy, Human Rights and Development should be one of the main issues of consideration of the World Conference on Human Rights to be held in Vienna in 1993.'

general criticism of governments, systems – even peoples and cultures – inhabiting countries and regions in the Third World. They signal the superiority of the North: first of all moral superiority, but also superiority with regard to insights into what would be in the best interest of the South. Implicitly, the North claims ownership of the values involved; the ownership is taken away from the South.

This is reinforced by the particular setting of foreign aid, involving an asymmetric power relationship. The analysis of the South Commission emphasises this aspect.[61] The broader North-South perspective adds an extra dimension. If the notion of universal respect for basic human rights is the main determinant of political conditionality, it makes sense to ask, with Georg Sørensen [*1993a:4*], if not the donors in fact preside over an international system which in several ways is counter-productive in terms of extending basic human rights to the roughly four billions of the globe's inhabitants living in developing countries.[62] This recognition may well have wider implications for their foreign policy.

The bluntness of the instrument creates an additional problem for the North; it is not unimportant that aid conditionality is not, or cannot be, used with equal confidence *vis-à-vis* all regimes, regardless of their power position and economic attractiveness to the North. A problem of consistency becomes apparent; hypocrisy is a nearby conclusion. History brings similar consistency problems to the fore, particularly in relation to the governments which are driving second generation conditionality. Several have been colonial powers, and in a number of the cases cited (Indonesia, Zaïre, Burundi and Rwanda), it was the former colonial power who was responsible for imposing the pressure. Although the regime pressing for human rights and democracy is new, the past creates a problem of credibility or may be exploited to this end.

---

61. The South Commission [*1990:3*] attributes the widening disparities between North and South not merely to differences in economic progress, but also to an enlargement of North's power *vis-à-vis* the rest of the world. 'The leading countries of the North now more readily use that power in pursuit of their objectives. The "gunboat" diplomacy of the nineteenth century still has its economic and political counterpart in the closing years of the twentieth. The fate of the South is increasingly dictated by the perceptions and policies of governments in the North, of the multilateral institutions which a few of those governments control, and of the network of private institutions that are increasingly prominent. Domination has been reinforced where partnership was needed and hoped for by the South.'
62. From a different angle, Martin Doornbos [*this volume*] argues in the same vein. The responsibility for an 'enabling environment' is placed with the developing countries concerned, ignoring the co-responsibility of international donor organisations for the prevailing situation. To what extent, asks Doornbos, does a global 'enabling environment' obtain for 'good governance' and what conditions should receive most attention in this context?

This applies to the recent past as well: authoritarian, repressive regimes, reliable allies in the Cold War, received generous aid from the major Western powers which strengthened their domestic power position.[63] Southern Africa is just one example where history provides ample evidence of these policies: regimes and terrorist organisations, oppressing fundamental human rights and democracy for years, have been bolstered by today's crusaders of these lofty values. The defensive position taken in the South *vis-à-vis* second generation aid conditionality – and even towards other forms of aid geared towards policy reform – may be attributed to a significant extent to inconsistencies of this kind.

These inconsistencies in the past and present policy of Western powers, whether driven by strategic or economic interests or by considerations of effectiveness, clearly affect the legitimacy of second generation aid conditionality negatively. However, the most crucial legitimacy problem of this kind currently relates to an inconsistent practice of aid conditionality, the lack of policy coherence, although past performance adds to it. If this is true, the question arises: should aid conditionality be applied in order to promote the objectives identified ('good government') where it might work, that is, *vis-à-vis* weak, aid-dependent governments, and at the same time not be applied *vis-à-vis* other governments, where the chance to succeed is deemed small or the costs high, although similar policies are pursued by the aid-recipient governments, for instance systematic violations of human rights – reducing or ending aid to Kenya while continuing or extending aid to China?[64]

---

63. Examples are legion, involving most major powers. The US administration decided to resume aid to Peru at a time when disappearances and police violence increased. President Carter, with a human rights profile, in his first year cut security assistance to a number of Latin American countries (Argentina, Bolivia, El Salvador, Guatemala, Haiti, Nicaragua, Paraguay, Uruguay), for which he was strongly criticised by Ronald Reagan during the following presidential election. However, he was also criticised for inconsistencies: human rights violations in the Philippines, South Korea, Iran and Zaïre went seemingly unnoticed for geopolitical reasons. President Reagan's profile was different, which lead to continuous conflicts with Congress, illustrated, *inter alia*, by the conflict over foreign aid to El Salvador [*Nelson and Eglinton, 1992:28*]. For other examples, see Uvin [*1993b:17*]. Although stating that 'the protection of human rights require no justification', Natraj [*1992:9-10*], for one, drives home the double standard argument with reference to such inconsistencies on the part of major governments in the North. The argument is extended to social human rights: admitting that the record of many developing countries is not too impressive, he argues that the violation or non-protection of some of these rights is directly related to the pervasive poverty in the South; this constraint does not apply in some affluent countries in the North where such rights are violated. See also *supra*, notes 6, 15, 31 and 42.

64. For an argumentation for applying aid conditionality where it works although an inconsistency (lack of coherence in the policy) might be involved, see Peter P. Waller [*1993:72-73*].

A consistency problem of a different kind exists between first and second generation aid conditionality. Both generations share the same parentage. To a very large extent they are presented by their major proponents, as elements of a consistent policy [*World Bank, 1992*]. This is a dubious postulate. A vast literature dealing with the effects of structural adjustment programmes seems to be in broad agreement, though with dissenting voices, that the effects with regard to social justice and welfare have been negative, at least in the short run [*Cornia et al., 1987; Harrigan and Mosley, 1992; Jolly, 1991; Mosley et al., 1991*]; Gouda Abdel-Khalek and Karima Korayem [*this volume*] reach a similar conclusion based on the Egyptian experience. Some of the remedies prescribed have created, in the short run, economic and social hardship, particularly for the most deprived social groups. Such effects run contrary to social justice, a major objective of second generation aid conditionality (improvement of economic and social human rights). They cause social discontent and political unrest, with destructive effects for the promotion and maintenance of another main objective of the second generation, namely democratic rule.

An even more fundamental question that arises, relates both to the claim of consistency and the concept of democracy: how far does the term democratic rule apply to a system where the major issues are removed from the agenda and the decisions are taken by outside bodies with no responsibility *vis-à-vis* the governed? This question certainly has a wider bearing than the issues discussed here; however, it also applies in the present context. To what extent may the governing system of a poor, debt-ridden and aid-dependent African country be termed democratic, even if the government has emerged from free and fair elections with several parties competing, when overall economic policy is decided from outside? This is the situation of several governments which have accepted the structural adjustment conditions set by the main multilateral and bilateral aid donors although, in a strictly formal sense, the governments concerned have agreed to the conditions. Also domestic, non-elected structures may exert a similar influence, particularly the military, who – because of the control of coercive powers – may set the political framework conditions and from the sideline pull the strings even when important current decisions are taken.

Instrumental considerations do not add credibility to aid conditionality as a lever in promoting the second generation agenda. No single established regime exists with a set of universal rules, procedures, and with institutions and criteria for evaluation and enforcement; moreover, competing interests, particularly economic interests, make *ad hoc* international co-operation difficult to achieve, except *vis-à-vis* small, aid-dependent authoritarian regimes. When applied, the success has been quite mixed even in cases involving regimes of the latter category. More technical aspects add to the complexity: the agenda includes a large number of objectives and several of them are not easily operationalised. The mechanism is far from tuned to the various particulars involved.

A logical conclusion from this evidence is that second generation aid conditionality emerges as a shaky project: it is problematic from a normative perspective and scores low from an instrumental perspective. Still, this conclusion may be premature in omitting, as it does, the possible indirect effects of the signals given, provided the main donors follow up their rhetoric in their future aid allocations. If this is done in a less spectacular way than through brinkmanship, aid flows to authoritarian and repressive regimes from bilateral donors will silently drain away. The country studies bring evidence that some donor countries prepare the ground for *ex post* allocative conditionality; this applies, in particular, to Germany [*Waller, this volume*]. When large aid donors actively orient their aid along such lines (and not using the mechanism to justify reductions in their total ODA allocations), it may affect the direction of the ODA flow and possibly also the political behaviour of some aid-dependent governments.

The probability of these indirect effects to appear depends on the credibility of the rhetoric and the perceptions of the losses involved. In the domestic political arena of a donor country, values and interests are competing; it cannot be taken for granted that values associated with second generation conditionality will come out as the winner, particularly if there are competing economic interests at stake. For a variety of reasons it would be difficult for the multilateral system, within the present written and unwritten rules, to operate a silent withdrawal of new aid commitments to recipient regimes of the types identified; the difficulties would be greater for the United Nations system than for the Bretton Woods institutions. Knowing this, may induce recipient governments at risk to adopt a wait and see attitude; however, political signals are not restricted to public rhetoric alone.

Withdrawal might produce policy reforms from within the system in the short or long term. However, it may have other effects, too; Renard and Reyntjens [*this volume*] note that in the case of Zaïre, the complete withdrawal of Belgian aid had negative effects both for the alternative leadership and for high priority developmental objectives such as poverty alleviation, and these might have been avoided if direct state-to-state aid only had been cut off. The implication of a withdrawal appears to be that any opportunity that might exist to exert influence and repair damages is lost: the oppressed are left to themselves and, as Mark Robinson argues [*this volume*], the poorest people can be adversely affected. Both Renard and Reyntjens and Robinson argue for the insulation of poverty-oriented projects when governments apply aid conditionality.[65]

This discussion applies, in the first place, to the effectiveness of aid conditionality *vis-à-vis* unwilling, authoritarian governments related to the objectives of the second generation. One conclusion that seems to be emerging from several of the component studies is that the policy is most effective when objectives are more or less similar on both sides – illustrated earlier in the case of Turkey in relation to first generation aid conditionality – where foreign aid supports reforms which the government itself wants to carry out [*this volume: Clay; Morrissey; Waller*].[66] The question which then arises is whether or not this should be considered a result of aid conditionality.

In some countries, circumstantial conditions are such that any government – be it authoritarian or democratic, willing or unwilling to comply with the conditions set – would be unable to deliver the results. This applies to the objectives associated with both first and second generation aid conditionality. The recipient government may agree to undertake reforms knowing that it will be unable to deliver or that the reforms will not work; the donor agencies would be equally well placed to draw the same conclusion. This applies to several

---

65. Robinson [*this volume*] argues that in countries such as Haiti, Burma (Myanmar), the Sudan and Iraq, the poor have suffered because the NGOs cannot operate with impunity. Uvin [*1993a:78*] argues that during the last years of the Duvalier regime, Canada, France and Switzerland maintained aid to Haiti through their NGOs for these reasons, creating a strong organisation of civil society, a sense of pride in millions of people, which created the basis for the election of Father Aristide. For similar assessments of Canadian aid to Haiti, see Rudner [*1991*]. The Swiss government has used a similar argumentation for not making aid dependent on respect of human rights [*Forster, this volume*]. After the coup against the democratically elected president (Astride) in 1990, the Swiss government saw no possibility of co-operating with the Haitian state, but wanted to grab every opportunity to support educational programmes which supported the least privileged sectors of the population, according to Forster [*ibid.*].

The Belgian government has proposed to the European Community that donors should avoid penalising the population when ODA is cut off: basic health care, education, decentralised and integrated rural development and emergency and humanitarian aid should not normally be halted [*Renard and Reyntjens, this volume*].

66. Nelson and Eglinton [*1992:48-9*] conclude in the same vein: real influence is likely to be greatest where reform-minded elements in the recipient government are neither very weak or very strong. 'Where they are very weak, conditioned aid is not likely to produce real or sustained reforms, though if the aid is badly needed the government may go through the motions of compliance. At the other extreme, if the reform elements within the government are very strong, conditions are largely superfluous.'

governments in the Third World and is not restricted to countries ridden by civil war or which find themselves in an advanced process of social and political disintegration (Liberia and the Sudan are extreme examples); it is also illustrated in the case of Russia in the turbulent transition that country is presently going through [*Zhukov, this volume*].[67] It places a dilemma firmly on the donors: in these cases, should the conditionality mechanism be applied – even if it means pulling out? On the other hand, if it is not enforced consistently the credibility of conditionality as an instrument is weakened and thereby its effectiveness.

In the pursuit of the objectives included in the agenda of the second generation what alternatives to aid conditionality are to be found? Within a development co-operation framework, the idea of a *development contract* between donor and recipient authorities has been brought forward in order to combine conflicting principles – the principle of non-intervention with the principle that agreements which have been freely entered into should be jointly binding. The idea has been proposed at a high level of generalisation, emphasising the main principles on which this contract should be based rather than entering into the substance in any detail. In its original form the construct aimed at reform of development co-operation based on traditional developmental objectives. It was presented as an alternative approach to that of first generation aid conditionality.[68] However, it can also be used in the pursuit of both traditional developmental objectives and objectives associated with first and second generation aid conditionality. In common with conditionality, it serves as a means to pursue a variety of objectives and is not an objective in its own right.

The concept is rooted in traditional forms of development co-operation; support for specific projects and programmes has always been based in formal agreements, and the more extensive and long-term country programmes between certain bilateral donors and the recipient government have similarly been mutually agreed and formalised. However, the concept of a development contract aims at still broader frameworks of development co-operation which need not be

---

67. There are other examples of situations which allow for difficult choices involving the agenda for second generation political conditionality: ethnic conflicts being the most obvious cases in point.
68. The concept was introduced, in very rudimentary terms, by Thorvald Stoltenberg, then Norway's Minister of Foreign Affairs, at the 25th Anniversary of the OECD Development Centre in Paris in February 1989 [*Stoltenberg, 1989:241-2*]. It was explored later by Arve Ofstad and Arne Tostensen of the Chr. Michelsen Institute, Bergen, in collaboration with Tom Vraalsen, previously Norway's ambassador to the UN and at the time of writing the Minister of Foreign Affairs [*Ofstad et al., 1991*], and Louis Emmerij, former president of the OECD Development Centre [*Emmerij, 1993*].

restricted to one donor and one recipient but may involve several parties, including the multilateral agencies.

The main features of the proposed form of development contract include a formalised agreement between partners intended to be equal based on mutual benefits and mutually binding obligations. It should provide a more stable and predictable external environment for the implementation of major economic and political reforms, providing more long-term commitments and obligations on both sides. Commitments by the recipient government should not be restricted to policy reforms but should include the creation of conditions for social progress and 'good governance'. Commitments by the donor parties should not be limited to foreign aid and debt relief, and should include on a reciprocal basis trade policy, access to markets, investments and other matters affecting development opportunities of the South. A fundamental prerequisite is that the national authorities themselves of the countries concerned should elaborate the reform programmes included in the contract; these should not be imposed from outside. The concept can be extended for groups of Third World countries to co-operate and enter jointly into development contracts rather than on an individual country-by-country basis, thereby strengthening their bargaining position and making the asymmetric power relationship less pronounced. An international framework for the initiation, monitoring and arbitration of development contracts is also part and parcel of the concept [Ofstad et al., 1991; Emmerij, 1993].

The concept remains at the design stage. It has not been tested out as a practical device, in a bilateral or regional setting, nor has it been confronted with theoretical scrutiny, even by its initiators. A development contract needs to be substantive. This involves one set of challenges. Given its broad framework, involving several parties, there needs to be a broad consensus both with regard to development objectives and how to achieve these objectives. The perspective, by necessity, will be broader still and include related objectives, since the contract presupposes mutuality of interest. Although development and poverty alleviation in the South are of interest to the North, more vested interests would have to be included in addition to normative ones. Issues related to environmental challenges, drug trade, refugees and migration may serve as examples. This involves many controversial issues already on the international agenda.

The various aspects necessary for the mechanism to function need further exploration. The regime factors previously discussed apply in this context too: these involve jointly agreed objectives, strategy, operationalised criteria for success and failure, a system for monitoring and evaluation, and procedures for handling defaults of the contract; there should be a machinery for appeal and arbitration, and also for enforcement. A core problem is very likely to be the reaction of the parties to the contract when binding obligations, for a variety of reasons, are not followed up on one side. Meeting this challenge needs technical solutions: the formulation of specified obligations with indicators that are easily measured and monitored, and specified procedures. Even more important, it needs political determination to follow the rules. These decisions will not be taken in a political vacuum; they will be influenced by other considerations related to values and the type of more profane interests previously indicated.

The alternatives referred to previously – so-called positive conditionality and aid targeted directly on processes, groups and institutions which are promoting the objectives pursued – seem to stand a better chance of working than aid conditionality in its various forms. The country studies show that most donors orient their bilateral aid in this direction [*Renard and Reyntjens, Waller, Stokke, Forster, this volume*]. Foreign aid with this direction supports processes and forces in the society which work towards good government. The mechanisms at hand cover a broad spectrum, from policy dialogue with the government (which receives financial support) to technical assistance within strategic sectors and alternative channels for aid, including NGOs. The strategy is based on a recognition of the fact that reforms have to emerge from within.

Good government can be enforced from outside only in exceptional cases. History reveals a few of these exceptions, West Germany and Japan after World War II. Even more hard-hitting mechanisms than aid conditionality, such as international economic sanctions, may fail to do the trick *vis-à-vis* repressive governments, as South Africa demonstrated for decades; even military sanctions may fail, as the regime of Saddam Hussain in Iraq confirms. And a decision by the international community (the UN Security Council) on binding sanctions is neither easily reached nor easily implemented.

The proposition above parallels the wider argument that self-sustained development cannot be created or driven from outside. External incentives and support (international agencies, individual governments, NGOs) may stimulate processes, groups and institutions in the countries concerned that are working towards the objectives established above. However, if it is not attuned to endogenous processes, intervention may even be detrimental to those objectives. The same applies to pressures from outside intending to create good government.

REFERENCES

Abdel-Khalek, Gouda and Karima Korayem, 1994, 'Conditionality, Structural Adjustment and Development: The Case of Egypt', this volume.
Almond, Gabriel A. and James S. Coleman, eds., 1960, *The Politics of Developing Areas*, Princeton: Princeton University Press.
Almond, Gabriel A. and Sidney Verba, 1963, *The Civic Culture*, Princeton: Princeton University Press.
Amin, Samir, 1993, 'The Issue of Democracy in the Contemporary Third World', in Gills *et al.*, eds., 1993.
Andreassen, Bård-Anders, Tor Skålnes, Alan Smith and Hugo Stokke, 1988, 'Assessing Human Rights Performance in Developing Countries: The Case for a Minimal Threshold Approach', *Human Rights in Developing Countries 1987/88*, Copenhagen: Akademisk Forlag.
Andreassen, Bård-Anders and Theresa Swinehart, 1992, 'Promoting Human Rights in Poor Countries: The New Political Conditionality of Aid Policies', *Human Rights in Developing Countries Yearbook 1991*, Oslo: Scandinavian University Press.
Arefieva, Elena B., 1990, 'Soviet *Perestroika* and the New Aid Policy', Paper presented at the VI EADI General Conference in Oslo, June 1990.
Baehr, Peter, Hilde Hey, Jacqueline Smith and Theresa Swinehart, eds., 1994, *Human Rights in Developing Countries Yearbook 1994*, Deventer: Kluwer Law and Taxation Publishers.
Ball, Nicole, 1992, *Pressing for Peace: Can Aid Induce Reform?*, Washington, D.C.: Overseas Development Council.
Barya, John-Jean B., 1992, 'The new political conditionality of aid: an independent view from Africa', Paper presented at a conference on 'The New Political Conditionalities of Aid' organised 23-24 April 1992 in Vienna by EADI, *IDS Bulletin*, Vol. 24, No. 1 1993, Brighton: IDS.
Berlage, Lodewijk and Olav Stokke, eds., *Evaluating Development Assistance: Approaches and Methods*, London: Frank Cass.
Binder, Leonard, James S. Coleman, Joseph La Paloma, Lucian Pye, Sidney Verba and Myron Weiner, 1971, *Crises and Sequences in Political Development*, Princeton: Princeton University Press.
Clay, Edward, 1994, 'Conditionality and Programme Food Aid: From the Marshall Plan to Structural Adjustment', this volume.
Cornia, Giovanni Andrea, Richard Jolly and Frances Stewart, eds., 1987, *Adjustment with a Human Face*, Volume 1: *Protecting the Vulnerable and Promoting Growth*, A Study by UNICEF, Oxford: Oxford University Press.
Dahl, Robert A., 1971, *Polyarchy: Participation and Opposition*, New Haven: Yale University Press.
Diamond, Larry, Juan J. Linz and Seymour Martin Lipset, eds., 1988-90, *Democracy in Developing Countries*, Vol. I: *Persistence, Failure, and Renewal*, Vol. II: *Africa*, Vol. III: *Asia*, Vol. IV: *Latin America*, Boulder: Lynne Rienner Publishers.
Donnelly, J., 1992, 'Human Rights in the New World Order', *World Policy Journal*, Vol. IX, No. 2.
Doornbos, Martin, 1990, 'The African State in Academic Debate: Retrospect and Prospect', *The Journal of Modern African Studies*, Vol. 28, No. 2, Cambridge: Cambridge University Press.
Doornbos, Martin, 1994, 'State Formation Processes under External Supervision: Reflections on "Good Governance" ', this volume.
Duncan, A. and P. Mosley, 1985, 'Aid Effectiveness: Kenya Case Study', Study commissioned by the Task Force on Concessional Flows (unpublished part of the Cassen report), Oxford and Bath.
Edgren, Gus, 1984, 'Conditionality in Aid', in Stokke, ed., 1984, Vol. 2.
Eide, Asbjørn, 1992, 'National Sovereignty and International Efforts to Realize

Human Rights', in Asbjørn Eide and Bernt Hagtvet, eds., *Human Rights in Perspective. A Global Assessment*, London: Basil Blackwell.

Emmerij, Louis, 1993, 'International Relations in the 1990s', Paper prepared for the VII General Conference of EADI, Berlin 15-18 September, 1993.

Fahy, John C., 1984, 'IMF conditionality: a critical assessment', *OPEC Review*, Autumn 1984, Vienna.

Foreign and Commonwealth Office, UK, 1992, *The Government's Expenditure Plans, 1992/93 to 1994/95*, London: Her Majesty's Stationery Office.

Forster, Jacques, 1984, 'Swiss Aid: Policy and Performance', in Stokke, ed., 1984.

Forster, Jacques, 1994, 'Conditionality in Swiss Development Assistance', this volume.

Frank, André Gunder, 1993, 'Marketing Democracy in an Undemocratic Market', in Gills *et al.*, eds., 1993.

Gibbon, Peter, 1993, 'The World Bank and the New Politics of Aid', *The European Journal of Development Research*, Vol. 5, No. 1, London: Frank Cass.

Gills, Barry, Joel Rocamora and Richard Wilson, 1993, 'Low Intensity Democracy', in Gills *et al.*, eds., 1993.

Gills, Barry, Joel Rocamora and Richard Wilson, eds., 1993, *Low Intensity Democracy*, London: Pluto Press.

Griffin, Keith, 1991, 'Foreign Aid after the Cold War', *Development and Change*, 1991:4, London: Sage Publications.

Group of Fifteen, 1993, *The Summit Level Group of Developing Countries*, Issue No. 3, Geneva: Technical Support Facility.

Harrigan, Jane and Paul Mosley, 1992, 'Evaluating the World Bank Structural Adjustment Lending', in Berlage and Stokke, eds., 1992.

Hawthorn, Geoffrey, 1993, 'How to ask for good government', *IDS Bulletin*, Vol. 24, No. 2, Brighton: Institute of Development Studies, Sussex.

Healey, John, Richard Ketley and Mark Robinson, 1993, 'Will political reform bring about improved management in sub-Saharan Africa?', *IDS Bulletin*, Vol. 24, No. 2, Brighton: Institute of Development Studies, Sussex.

Hewitt, Adrian P. and Tony Killick, 1993, 'Bilateral Aid Conditionality and Policy Leverage', Paper presented at the VII EADI General Conference in Berlin 15-18 September 1993.

Humana, C., 1986, *World Human Rights Guide*, New York: Facts on File.

Hydén, Göran, 1992, 'Governance and the Study of Politics', in Göran Hydén and Michael Bratton, eds., *Governance and Politics in Africa*, Boulder and London: Lynne Rienner Publisher.

IDS, 1993, 'The Emergence of the "Good Government" Agenda: Some Milestones', *IDS Bulletin*, Vol. 24, No. 1, Brighton: Institute of Development Studies, Sussex.

Jackson, Robert H. and Carl G. Rosberg, 1986, 'Sovereignty and Underdevelopment: Juridical Statehood in the African Crisis', *The Journal of Modern African Studies*, Vol. 24, No. 1, Cambridge: Cambridge University Press.

Jepma, Catrinus J., 1993, 'OECD-Wide Untying', Paper presented at the EADI VII General Conference, Berlin, 15-18 September 1993.

Jolly, Richard, 1991, 'Adjustment with a Human Face: A UNICEF Record and Perspective on the 1980s', *World Development*, Vol. 19, No. 12, December.

Keohane, Robert O., 1993, 'The analysis of International Regimes: Towards a European-American Research Programme', in Volker Rittberger, ed., *Regimes in International Relations*, Oxford: Clarendon Press.

Krasner, Stephen D., 1982, 'Structural Causes and Regime Consequences: Regimes as Intervening Variables', *International Organization*, Vol. 36, No. 2.

Lancaster, Carol, 1993a, 'Governance and Development: The Views from Washington', *IDS Bulletin*, Vol. 24, No. 1, Brighton: Institute of Development Studies, Sussex.

Lancaster, Carol, 1993b, *United States and Aid to Africa: Into the Twenty-First Century*, Washington, D.C.: Overseas Development Council.

Leftwich, Adrian, 1994, 'Governance, the State and the Politics of Development', *Development and Change*, Vol.25, Oxford: Blackwell Publishers.

Lewis, John P., 1993, *Pro-Poor Aid Conditionality*, Washington, D.C.: Overseas Development Council.

Love, Alexander R., 1992, 'Remarks by Alexander R. Love, Chairman, Development Assistance Committee, Organisation for Economic Co-operation and Development, to the Norwegian Institute of International Affairs', Seminar 15 September 1992 (mimeo).

Moore, Mick, 1993a, 'Introduction', *IDS Bulletin*, Vol. 24, No. 1, Brighton: Institute of Development Studies, Sussex.

Moore, Mick, 1993b, 'Declining to learn from the East? The World Bank on "Governance and Development" ', *IDS Bulletin*, Vol. 24, No. 1, Brighton: Institute of Development Studies, Sussex.

Morrissey, Oliver, 1994, 'Conditionality and Compliance: The Sustainability of Adjustment in Turkey', this volume.

Mosley, Paul, Jane Harrigan and John Toye, 1991, *Aid and Power. The World Bank and Policy Based Lending*, Volumes 1 and 2, New York: Routledge Chapman and Hall.

Mushi, Samuel S., 1994, 'Determinants and Limitations of Aid Conditionality: Some Examples from Nordic-Tanzanian Co-operation', this volume.

Mutahaba, Gelase, 1990, 'Foreign Assistance and Local Capacity-Building: The Case of Swedish Aid to Tanzania's Rural Water Supply', *The European Journal of Development Research*, Vol. 1, No. 1, London: Frank Cass.

Myrdal, Gunnar, 1969, *Asian Drama: An Inquiry into the Poverty of Nations*, New York: Twentieth Century Fund and Pantheon Books.

Natraj, V.K., 1992, 'External Aid and the Imperatives of Development', Paper presented at a conference on 'The New Political Conditionalities of Aid' organised 23-24 April 1992 in Vienna by EADI (mimeo).

Nelson, Joan M. with Stephanie J. Eglinton, 1992, *Encouraging Democracy: What Role for Aid?*, Washington, D.C.: Overseas Development Council.

NMFA, 1991, *A World of Difference: A New Framework for Development Co-operation in the 1990s*, The Hague: Ministry of Foreign Affairs.

NMFA, 1993, *A world of dispute*, The Hague: Ministry of Foreign Affairs.

Nordholt, Nico G. Schulte, 1994, 'Aid and Conditionality: the Case of Dutch-Indonesian Relationships', this volume.

Nordic Ministers, 1990, Communiqué of the Nordic Ministers of Development Co-operation, Molde, Norway, 10-11 September, 1990.

OAU, 1990, Declaration of the Assembly of Heads of State and Government of the Organization of African Unity on the political and socio-economic situation in Africa and the fundamental changes taking place in the world, 11 July 1990, Addis Ababa: OAU.

OECD, 1992a, *Development Co-operation, 1992 Report*, Paris: OECD.

OECD, 1992b, DAC and OECD Public Policy Statements on Participatory Development/Good Governance, Paris: DAC (OCDE/GD(92)67).

OECD, 1993, DAC Orientations on Participatory Development and Good Governance, Paris: OECD (OCDE/GD (93)191).

Ofstad, Arve, Arne Tostensen and Tom Vraalsen, 1991, 'Towards a "Development Contract" ', Paper presented at a meeting of the North-South Roundtable, Ottawa, June 1991.

Pearson, Lester B., 1969, *Partners in Development. Report of the Commission on International Development*, New York: Praeger.

Pedersen, Jørgen Dige, 1993, 'The Complexities of Conditionality: The Case of India', *The European Journal of Development Research*, Vol. 5, No. 1, London: Frank Cass.

Pharo, Helge Ø., 1977, 'Norge og den tredje verden' (Norway and the Third World), in T. Berg and H.Ø. Pharo, eds., *Vekst og Velstand*, Oslo: Universitetsforlaget.

Pharo, Helge Ø., 1986, *Hjelp til selvhjelp. Det indisk-norske fiskeriprosjektets historie 1952-72* (Help to self-help. The history of the Indian-Norwegian Fishery Project, 1952-72), Oslo: NUPI.

PMO, 1991, *Common Responsibility in the 1990s*, The Stockholm Initiative on Global Security and Governance, April 22 1991, Stockholm: Prime Minister's Office.

Pratt, Cranford, ed., 1989, *Internationalism under Strain*, Toronto: Toronto University Press.

Renard, Robrecht and Filip Reyntjens, 1994, 'Aid and Conditionality: The Case of Belgium, with Particular Reference to the Policy *vis-à-vis* Burundi, Rwanda and Zaïre', this volume.

Riddell, Roger C., 1986, 'The Ethics of Foreign Aid', *Development Policy Review*, Vol. 4, London, Beverly Hills and New Delhi: SAGE.

Robinson, Mark, 1993a, 'Will Political Conditionality Work?', *IDS Bulletin*, Vol. 24, No. 1, Brighton: Institute of Development Studies, Sussex.

Robinson, Mark, 1993b, 'Aid, Democracy and Political Conditionality in Sub-Saharan Africa', *The European Journal of Development Research*, Vol. 5, No. 1, London: Frank Cass.

Robinson, Mark, 1994, 'Political Conditionality: Strategic Implications for NGOs', this volume.

Rokkan, Stein, with Angus Campbell, Per Torsvik and Henry Valen, 1970, *Citizens, Elections, Parties: Approaches to the Comparative Study of the Processes of Development*, Oslo: Universitetsforlaget.

Rudner, M., 1991, 'Canada's Official Development Assistance Strategy: Process, Goals and Priorities', *Canadian Journal of Development Studies*, Vol. XII, No. 1.

Serageldin, Ismail and Rashid Faruqee, 'Conditionality in World Bank Adjustment Lending: A Review of the Sub-Saharan Experience', Paper presented to a workshop on Aid and Conditionality, organised by the EADI Working Group on Aid Policy and Performance in Berlin 13-15 September 1993.

South Commission, 1990, *The Challenge to the South. The Report of the South Commission*, Oxford: Oxford University Press.

Stokke, Olav, 1978, *Sveriges utvecklingsbistånd och biståndspolitik* (Sweden's Development Assistance and Aid Policy), Uppsala: Scandinavian Institute of African Studies.

Stokke, Olav, 1984a, 'European Aid Policies: Some Emerging Trends', in Stokke, ed., 1984, Volume 1.

Stokke, Olav, 1984b, 'Norwegian Aid: Policy and Performance', in Stokke, ed., 1984, Volume 1.

Stokke, Olav, ed., 1984, *European Development Assistance*, Volume 1, *Policies and Performance*, Volume 2, *Third World Perspectives on Policies and Performance*, EADI Book Series No. 4, Tilburg: EADI.

Stokke, Olav, 1989a, 'The Determinants of Aid Policies: General Introduction', in Stokke, ed., 1989.

Stokke, Olav, 1989b, 'The Determinants of Norwegian Aid Policy', in Stokke, ed., 1989.

Stokke, Olav, 1989c, 'The Determinants of Aid Policies: Some Propositions Emerging from a Comparative Analysis', in Stokke, ed., 1989.

Stokke, Olav, ed., 1989, *Western Middle Powers and Global Poverty. The Determinants of the Aid Policies of Canada, Denmark, the Netherlands, Norway and Sweden*, Uppsala: Scandinavian Institute of African Studies.

Stokke, Olav, 1991, 'Policies, Performance, Trends and Challenges in Aid Evaluation', in Stokke, ed., *Evaluating Development Assistance: Policies and Performance*, London: Frank Cass, EADI Book Series 12.

Stokke, Olav, 1994, 'Aid and Political Conditionality: The Case of Norway', this volume.

Stoltenberg, Thorvald, 1989, 'Towards a World Development Strategy', in Louis

Emmerij, ed., *One World or Several?*, Paris: OECD.
Sørensen, Georg, 1991, *Democracy, Dictatorship and Development*, London: Macmillan.
Sørensen, Georg, 1993a, 'Introduction', *The European Journal of Development Research*, Vol. 5, No. 1, London: Frank Cass.
Sørensen, Georg, 1993b, 'Democracy, Authoritarianism and State Strength', *The European Journal of Development Research*, Vol. 5, No. 1, London: Frank Cass.
Sørensen, Georg, 1993c, *Democracy and Democratisation*, Boulder, CO: Westview.
Sørensen, Georg, 1994, 'Conditionality, Democracy and Development', this volume.
Tetzlaff, Rainer, ed., 1993, *Human Rights and Development*, Bonn: Eine Welt.
Tomasevski, Katarina, 1989, *Development Aid and Human Rights*, London: Pinter Publishers.
Tomasevski, Katarina, 1992, 'A Critique of the UNDP Political Freedom Index 1991', *Human Rights in Developing Countries Yearbook 1991*, Oslo: Scandinavian University Press.
UNDP, 1990, *Human Development Report 1990*, New York/Oxford: Oxford University Press.
UNDP, 1991, *Human Development Report 1991*, New York/Oxford: Oxford University Press.
UNDP, 1992, *Human Development Report 1992*, New York/Oxford: Oxford University Press.
Uvin, Peter, 1993a, ' "Do as I Say, Not as I Do": The limits of Political Conditionality', *The European Journal of Development Research*, Vol. 5, No. 1, London: Frank Cass.
Uvin, Peter, 1993b, 'Political Conditionality as a Regime and as a Policy Instrument: Nature and Probable Effectiveness', Paper prepared for the workshop of the EADI Working Group on Aid in Berlin 13-15 September 1993.
Waller, Peter P., 1992, 'After East-West Detente: Towards a Human Rights Orientation in North-South Development Cooperation?', *Development*, 1992:1, Rome: SID.
Waller, Peter P., 1993, 'Human Rights Orientation in Development Co-operation', in Rainer Tetzlaff, ed., 1993.
Waller, Peter P., 1994, 'Aid and Conditionality: The Case of Germany, with Particular Reference to Kenya', this volume.
Wamwere, Koigi wa, 1989, *Kenya – selvstyre uten frihet* (Kenya: independence without freedom), Oslo: Pax.
World Bank, 1989, *Sub-Saharan Africa: From Crisis to Sustainable Growth*, Washington, D.C.: World Bank.
World Bank, 1991, *Assistance Strategies to Reduce Poverty*, A World Bank Policy Paper, Washington, D.C.: The World Bank.
World Bank, 1992, *Governance and Development*, Washington, D.C.: World Bank.
World Bank, 1994a, *The World Bank and the Poorest Countries. Support for Development in the 1990s*, Washington, D.C.: The World Bank.
World Bank, 1994b, *Poverty Reduction and The World Bank. Progress in Fiscal 1993*, Washington, D.C.: The World Bank.
Young, Oran, 1991, Report on the 'Regime Summit', held at Dartmouth College in November 1991, Hanover: Institute of Arctic Studies.
Zhukov, Stanislav, 1994, 'Aid Dialogue between Russia and the West: Upward the Learning Curve', this volume.

2

Aid and Conditionality: The Case of Belgium, with Particular Reference to Burundi, Rwanda and Zaïre

ROBRECHT RENARD AND FILIP REYNTJENS

I. INTRODUCTION

The recent emphasis on conditionality seems to suggest that in earlier periods development aid was given with no strings attached. Nothing could be further from the truth. In fact, it is more correct to say that aid has always been subject to a battery of conditions. What has changed, therefore, is not the principle of conditionality as such, but the nature of this conditionality. This applies as much to Belgium as to any other donor country.

The geopolitical and military reasons, for instance, which have motivated and to some extent shaped Belgian development aid in the past – notably in its support of President Mobutu's regime in Zaïre despite this country's appalling development record – may be considered a particular type of *political conditionality*. The end of the cold war, and the pursuance of macro-economic conditionality in the 1980s led Belgium, like other donors, into a new type of political conditionality, more benign than the previous one, and associated with 'soft' values like human rights, democracy and good governance. The 'new' political conditionality will be discussed in Section III.

Independent of these considerations conditions have always been imposed by the Belgian Administration for Development Co-operation (BADC) with a view to fostering economic development. Whereas in the 1960s and 1970s such *economic conditionality* was micro-oriented the 1980s saw a flurry of new types of aid which were macro-oriented. Old and new economic conditionality is the subject matter of Section II.

In Section IV a more detailed case study is provided of the most dramatic instance of the new conditionality at work: the halting in 1990 of all development aid to Zaïre, indiscriminately applied to all major categories of aid except some emergency assistance.

Multilateral aid will not be dealt with in this chapter, although in recent years BADC has increasingly supported structural adjustment programmes sponsored by the World Bank, especially through the programmes for structural adjustment and the Special Programme of Assistance (SPA) for Africa. The reason for not dwelling on multilateral aid is that Belgium – by inclination and because of its size – is neither willing nor able to exert significant influence on the conditionality clauses imposed at this level. Despite the occasional grudging remarks of experienced field personnel about the high-handed approach of the Bretton Woods institutions and their lack of understanding of the local political, socio-cultural and even economic context, BADC lacked and continues to lack the macro-economic expertise to challenge the Bretton Woods institutions. At the level of government, Belgian decision-makers were quick to grasp that the so-called policy 'dialogue' more often than not meant one-sided imposition of politically sensitive and socially costly economic reforms, an exercise they have happily left to the multilateral agencies to undertake. Belgium therefore participated in multilateral aid efforts, consistently but not more generously than the circumstances called for, and not much needs to be said about it.

This chapter will pay particular attention to Zaïre, Rwanda and Burundi. From 1985 to 1989, the last year before relations were suspended with Zaïre, these three countries accounted for 53.1 per cent of Belgian bilateral Official Development Assistance (ODA).[1] These are also the three countries in relation to which Belgium carries some weight at the international level and for which, as a consequence, policy formulation and implementation by Belgium has some broader relevance.[2]

---

1. Zaïre received 37.8 per cent, Rwanda 8.9 per cent and Burundi 6.5 per cent. After the severing of relations with Zaïre in 1990, volumes of aid spent on Rwanda and especially on Burundi went up substantially.
2. This may be illustrated by the following DAC statistics. In the period 1986-1988 Belgium was the most important bilateral donor both in Zaïre and in Rwanda, and the second donor, after France, in Burundi. It provided almost 40 per cent of all bilateral aid from DAC countries to Zaïre, and more than 20 per cent of such aid to Rwanda and to Burundi. Yet in the same period Belgium provided only 1.4 per cent of total DAC bilateral aid to all countries, thus occupying only the 13th place overall. Therefore it is only in the three countries discussed here that Belgian aid is significant enough to make a serious difference. Even so the importance of Belgian aid should not be overestimated. The above figures exclude, for instance, multilateral donors from the picture, and they have been important providers of funds to all three countries. The figures for 1986-1988 are further put in perspective if one realises that

II. THE 'NEW' ECONOMIC CONDITIONALITY

Micro-economic Conditionality

In this section we will be concerned with conditionality as applied by BADC in 'direct', i.e. government-to-government, bilateral ODA which for the time being we will separate from conditionality as applied to 'indirect' bilateral aid through Belgian universities and non-governmental organisations (NGOs). This will be examined in Section IV in the case study on Zaïre. We also exclude other departments, of which the only important one is the Ministry of Finance. One brief comment may be in order about the latter. Bilateral ODA provided by the Ministry of Finance, in collaboration with the Department of Foreign Trade, concerns tied soft loans which are meant to serve both the objective of fostering development in the recipient country and that of stimulating Belgian exports. Since the end of the 1980s the Ministry of Finance has added the condition that such loans should serve investment projects which meet with the approval of the World Bank. This is a considerable improvement over previous practice which did not go beyond paying lip service to the development objective and led to a number of investments of doubtful quality being funded.

The 'new' macro-economic conditionality can best be understood in contrast with the 'old' micro-economic conditionality. The comparison is the more useful since the old conditionality has not

---

Belgian aid, as a share of recipient GNP, was 2.6 per cent for Zaïre, 1.4 per cent for Rwanda, and 1.6 per cent for Burundi. Further information is contained in Table 1.

Table 1.
Belgian ODA to Zaïre, Rwanda and Burundi, 1985-1989 annual averages

	Zaïre	Rwanda	Burundi
ODA (million Belgian francs)	4960.30	1182.30	835.80
ODA (million US $)	117.10	28.00	19.10
of which :			
official technical cooperation (including Belgian schools)	45.77	50.64	61.46
NGOs	6.72	12.95	3.81
indirect technical co-operation	4.52	4.51	9.46
soft loans in support of Belgian exports	11.23	0.00	7.18
other	31.75	31.91	18.10
total	100.00	100.00	100.00
ODA to country as % of total bilateral ODA	37.95	9.04	6.39

Source: BADC [1991].

90

disappeared. Micro-economic conditionality is typified by project funding, where BADC links the provision of aid resources to a particular development project, described in every detail prior to approval and the subject of an agreement which sets out the responsibilities of recipient and donor. Not only is the decision to accept or reject a project a form of micro-economic conditionality. So too is the interruption of funding when the project runs into problems such as bad management or corruption. The donor thus in effect steers the resources he is providing to particular applications which are to his liking. With aid generally tied to purchases in Belgium, and BADC often in charge of implementation, the imposition of micro-economic conditionality is almost automatic.

By sector of destination, the major category of Belgian bilateral ODA is technical assistance. It is superior in size to investment projects, sector aid or programme assistance. From the point of view of the micro versus macro distinction it unmistakably belongs to the former type. In fact, BADC exerts considerable influence over the input of foreign, that is Belgian personnel, which typically it has itself recruited. The same occurs in the case of scholarships or trainee programmes which bring students of recipient countries to Belgium for training. In both cases BADC steers the micro-economic allocation of resources.

Macro-economic Conditionality

By contrast macro-economic conditionality is concerned with bringing about changes at the macro-economic or sectoral level. Government-to-government aid is used to 'bribe' the recipient government to follow policies which meet with the approval of the donor. In exchange for such policy changes resources are provided in ways which are deemed attractive to the recipient. The clearest case is where the recipient government is granted freely useable foreign exchange. The donor in this case is not so much interested in steering the specific resource allocation of his aid. In fact he may never know to what particular use his money is being put. The satisfaction he gets is that the recipient is, for example, reforming his trade policy, liberalising prices in agriculture or privatising certain public firms. He is especially reassured by the fact that the allocation of resources, including the aid he is providing, is thereby improved.

At BADC macro-conditionality is most visibly associated with balance-of-payments support and debt relief, interventions whose importance grew rapidly during the 1980s. They were originally handled by the department of financial aid within BADC. The reform of BADC in 1991 abolished the financial department and such aid is now handled by the regional desks. In the Memorandum to DAC for the year 1990 bilateral programme assistance subject to macro-conditions is for the first time separated out in the statistical tables. It comes to a total of US$ 52.5 million of which 36.6 million is in direct support of structural adjustment programmes. This amounts to some 12 per cent of BADC bilateral aid and some ten per cent of total bilateral aid in that year, a situation comparable to that found in many other DAC countries [*DAC, 1992: table 30*].

Significance of the 'New' Macro-economic Conditionality

This macro-economic conditionality for development purposes is in the case of Belgium essentially a new phenomenon which began in the 1980s. But how significant is it? Donors' talk about macro-conditionality may in reality be just a lot of noise without any effective sanction. In this case it is unlikely to have a noticeable effect on the recipient. To make any difference, conditionality must imply that the donor will if necessary withhold resources. The decision can consist of not granting new resources, or cutting off already committed resources. Decisions to cut off aid are more dramatic and severe forms of conditionality and often more painful for the recipient. One would expect the donor also to take positive action by granting extra resources when a recipient government carries out difficult but courageous macro-economic reforms.

Belgium holds institutionalised bilateral talks about development co-operation with some 20 recipient countries, typically every one to three years. Since the end of the 1980s Belgian delegations have increasingly put discussions of the macro and sectoral policies of the recipient country on the agenda. Usually the briefing document prepared for the Belgian delegation is based not on an independent in-depth assessment of the situation by BADC, but on a synthesis of the positions developed by others. Much is learned from the consultations held at the level of the EU between the Commission and member states on individual recipient countries, and of course from documents of the International Monetary Fund (IMF) and the World Bank. The exceptions are the three former African possessions, in respect of which some macro-economic expertise is available within BADC to complement those other sources of information. When differences with the Bretton Woods institutions have emerged, they have not up to now concerned the basic underlying principles of the proposed policy reforms, but specifics such as timing or details of certain sectoral reform programmes. In summary the attitude of Belgium is to stick to the general lines of donor co-ordination, with at most an occasional difference on the detailed implementation of certain measures.

Such exchanges on macro-economic and sectoral policies during bilateral talks, increasingly important in the second half of the 1980s, serve several purposes. One is to allow Belgium to signal to what point it is aligning itself with the World Bank and other donors. At the same time the recipient government gets the chance to put its positions forward, often convincingly answering the criticism from the donor community. The outcome is that both parties are better informed about each other's positions. Also, such discussion serves as a good introduction to the subsequent detailed discussion on projects and programmes submitted for Belgian funding.

When, as is the case for many African recipients of Belgian aid, a Policy Framework Paper exists which sets out the agreement with the World Bank and the IMF, it will often be referred to during bilateral talks. One test now routinely applied is to check whether projects proposed for funding are on the list of priority projects retained by the World Bank, and whether they are consistent with the sectoral reform programmes being proposed. In this way macro-conditionality is having direct consequences, in the form of the refusal to accept projects and programmes which do not meet the standards of the World Bank.

It is to be noted that for the most part the old type of micro-economic conditionality is not hereby abandoned. It is just front-loaded with macro-economic conditions. This is not necessarily to be regarded as a bad evolution. The new conditionality brings in its awake a *de facto* coordination between Belgian aid policies and those of the Bretton Woods institutions and in this way with the rest of the donor community. It also brings more macro-economic logic into aid-allocation decisions which for the rest continue to be steered in a micro-economic way by BADC. Nevertheless particular types of micro-macro combinations may pose problems because they are difficult to monitor, cause bureaucratic delay, or are simply excessive.

As already mentioned, a small but increasing share of BADC bilateral aid takes the form of balance-of-payments support, debt forgiveness and related modalities, which share an emphasis on quick disbursement in return for macro-economic reform. Even here BADC insists on micro-conditionality. Usually this is performed by linking such aid to the use of counterpart funds. Balance-of-payments support for instance may be provided in the form of import support programmes for the productive sectors of the economy. Foreign exchange provided by BADC is thus sold to economic operators from the private or the public sector. By imposing sometimes elaborate restrictions on the type of activities eligible for import support, and by approving individual contracts which are often tied to purchases in Belgium, BADC exerts considerable micro-economic control. The use of the local currency proceeds from sales of foreign exchange by the recipient government is then subject to a second round of BADC control through counterpart funds. In the case of debt-relief measures, BADC developed an ingenious method of gaining control at the micro level. When debt relief is granted, the foreign exchange resources consist of the debt-service payment which is no longer required. As a consequence it is difficult to pinpoint the specific resources which a particular donor has contributed and over which he may wish to extend his bureaucratic control. Yet BADC has devised a way of doing exactly this. It requests the recipient government to pay into a counterpart fund an agreed fraction of the local currency equivalent of the debt which has been cancelled. In this way BADC field staff are put in a position where they can control the corresponding part of the recipient government's budget.

It is suggested here that rather than representing a well thought-through and balanced approach to conditionality, this procedure illustrates a scepticism towards mere macro-conditionality. The view is widely held at BADC that the best guarantee of proper use of development aid is the maximum extension of donor control over resource use. If macro-economic conditionality is necessary, it will be added on top. Whether such elaborate ploys to gain micro-economic control over resources already earmarked for and subject to macro-conditions serve any useful purpose is, however, questionable. The imposition of counterpart funds on debt-relief operations in particular may be inconsistent with the effort to impose some orthodoxy on the recipient's monetary policies and public finance. Since the beginning of the 1990s a policy shift has occurred[3] whereby in principle the recipient government must take full charge of both project identification and implementation. The role of BADC, apart from making up its mind about whether or not to fund, is essentially that of control and evaluation. This new policy is presently being applied to both Rwanda and Burundi, but its extension to other recipients is anticipated.

Before ending this section we should ask why the new macro-economic conditionality practised by BADC is so limited to the Bretton Woods type of economic reform. The question is not without foundation. As noticed, technical assistance is the single most important sector category of Belgian bilateral aid. And it is now

---

3. This new policy is labelled 'co-gestion' which, literally translated, means joint management.

widely agreed in the international donor community that much technical assistance fails to have an impact because of a lack of macro-economic coherence in the use of human resources by the recipient governments and a corresponding lack of co-ordination on the part of the donor community. Some efforts at macro-coherence in the field of human resource use have been proposed by United Nations Development Programme (UNDP) in the so-called National Technical Co-operation Assessment and Programmes (NATCAP) exercises. Transposed to our discussion of micro- and macro-conditionality this suggests that donors ought to complement and sometimes simply replace their micro-conditions for technical assistance with suitable macro-conditions. The fact that there is no effort on the Belgian side to do this suggests that its acceptance of the new conditionality in other sectors has been externally driven.

III. SECOND GENERATION (POLITICAL) CONDITIONALITY

Past Practice

In the field of second generation (political) conditionality there has been a remarkable evolution in Belgium. In the recent past there was no policy on the linking of development co-operation with recipient country performance in the fields of human rights and democracy. Thus a policy document on Africa published by the Ministry of Foreign Affairs in 1983 devotes only a summary, vague and non-committal section on human rights issues [*Ministerie van Buitenlandse Zaken, 1983: 82-83*]. As late as in 1988, one of us wrote that 'the discussion (on political conditionality) in Belgium has hardly started' [*Reyntjens, 1988: 144*]. However, in line with international developments a considerable evolution has taken place during the last couple of years.[4] A number of signs bear witness to this.

In recent years dozens of parliamentary questions on the human rights situation in many countries have been addressed to the Ministers of Foreign Affairs and of Development Co-operation. Very often MPs will also challenge the government's bilateral relations with the countries in question, should human rights violations continue or should no action be taken against the perpetrators. In recent years ministerial statements have included respect for human rights and support for democratisation processes as 'essential priorities' of Belgian foreign policy. Finally an attempt has been made to translate

---

4. For an assessment by a senior diplomat of what has been achieved in Belgium so far, and a plea for more, see Stevens [*1993: 269-273*].

these new concerns institutionally: in May 1990 a member's bill was tabled in Parliament with a view to linking human rights performance with bilateral ODA. Although it has not figured high on the parliamentary agenda, this bill has finally become law in early 1994.

The fact that until recently there was no stated coherent policy on the relationship between development co-operation and human rights/ democracy does not mean that considerations in line with conditionality concerns have been absent from the bilateral practice of Belgium with her Central African partners.

This is particularly clear with regard to *Burundi*, a country where ethnic strife has claimed the lives of well over 100,000 people, most of whom have been the victims of massacres committed by the armed forces. While it has remained implicit and not subject to policy formulations, the linking is clearly visible in practice. Thus the massive killings of Hutu in 1972 was termed 'genocide' by Prime Minister Eyskens, and it resulted in the termination of military assistance and a temporary decrease in other ODA. Again in 1983-87, when human rights (and religious freedom in particular) were grossly violated, the ODA flow diminished and Burundi was threatened with more sanctions. When in the aftermath of the military coup of September 1987 the human rights situation improved markedly, there was a new thaw in bilateral relations. However, in August 1988 many thousands of people were again killed by the armed forces. The Belgian Minister of Foreign Affairs insisted on an international inquiry and threatened sanctions. In an unprecedented move, dozens of civil servants working for BADC signed a letter to the Minister of Development Co-operation asking 'the Belgian government to formulate a principled condemnation of these massacres and to announce measures of re-orientation of our assistance, so that it benefits the entire Burundian population'. The threat, which also emanated from other donors (particularly the USA, Canada, Germany and Switzerland), did not go unheeded: as from September 1988, Burundi's President Buyoya embarked on a courageous programme of ethnic reconciliation. Not only did sanctions become unnecessary, but Buyoya was in fact encouraged to carry on with his reforms by a marked increase in bilateral ODA. When announcing a further package of aid in 1991, the then Minister of Development Co-operation Geens placed it in the context of 'political support for the attempts at democratisation and national reconciliation'.

Not much needs to be said about *Rwanda*, which has been

considered a 'problem-free' country[5] until October 1990; the more recent past will be dealt with later.

Zaïre is quite another matter. Since the independence of the former colony in 1960, Belgian-Zaïrean relations have been very unstable; periods of intense crisis have alternated with moments of relative harmony. However, up to the end of the 1980s it is not so much human rights/democracy issues which have conditioned bilateral relations, but political problems. As a matter of fact, even at times when diplomatic relations between the two countries were frozen, aid has continued to flow. As we have already noted, human rights/democracy concerns have not had a major impact on ODA allocation; relations between the two countries have generally been determined by strictly political and economic factors.

This was to change dramatically at the end of 1989.

A Cautious Conditionality Policy

At the end of another protracted crisis between Belgium and Zaïre, a 'peace accord' was signed in Rabat in July 1989. It was followed by the painful negotiation of new co-operation agreements, which were eventually signed in March 1990. For our purposes the most important new factor is the inclusion of the 'reaffirmation' by both countries of their attachment to fundamental human rights and to the principles of the UN Charter. The commitment is included merely in the preamble and formulated in a general and vague way; even so, a long battle was waged over its inclusion, not only between Belgium and Zaïre, but within the Belgian government as well. One of the coalition partners, the Flemish Socialist Party (SP), had insisted since December 1989 that the failure to include a reference to human rights would result in a cabinet crisis. In fact, over the years the SP had become a very vocal critic of the Mobutu regime, and it was obvious that the party considered the negotiation of the new conventions as a good opportunity to further its policy with regard to the Zaïrean leadership.

However, no one expected that the human rights clause would so soon play a major role in bilateral relations. After a number of students were killed by security forces at the Lubumbashi University campus in early May 1990, scarcely two months after the 'normalisation' between the two countries, Belgium asked that an international independent inquiry be conducted into these events. Invoking the reference to human rights in the bilateral agreement and faced with

---

5.   'Trouble-free' is a highly relative concept, which could be reasonably used only in comparison with Burundi and Zaïre.

the refusal of the Zaïrean authorities to accept what the latter called an 'ultimatum', the Belgian government decided on 25 May to postpone the meeting of the bilateral co-operation commission, to freeze loans agreed in 1989 and to suspend further commitments for 1990. In retaliation Zaïre ordered the Belgian co-operation staff to leave the country and closed some Belgian consulates; in addition some other measures were taken, including a curb on Sabena flights. This meant in effect the end of bilateral co-operation, including indirect aid and the activities of NGOs.

The May 1990 incident is interesting in that Belgium was forced to apply radically a conditionality policy for which it was not really ready. Although the human rights clause in the preamble to the March 1990 agreement has been the basis for Belgium's measures, in fact the real cause was once again more political: the Belgian government in general and the Flemish Socialists in particular[6] had become increasingly reluctant to 'do business' with the Mobutu regime. The disengagement from Zaïre did actually start long before the latest crisis, both in business and political circles.

Nevertheless, this incremental move must be seen in relation to a definite change of thinking on conditionality. It is no coincidence that also in May 1990 a draft bill on the linking of development co-operation and human rights performance was tabled in the Belgian Parliament, nor that the initiative came from Mr. Vanvelthoven, a Flemish Socialist MP. This bill, which has to become law in early 1994, aims at 'assessing' development co-operation policy in terms of the human rights performance of recipient countries. This text imposes a dual responsibility on the government. On the one hand, it must table a policy paper on general principles within three months of the coming into force of the Act. On the other hand, it must submit an annual report on the human rights record of countries linked to Belgium by a general co-operation agreement (currently about 20); these reports are to be accompanied by 'specific' policy conclusions, but the text does not define the meaning of 'specific'.

Both the Zaïre incident and the draft bill can be seen as the symbols of the start of a new policy, which has increasingly institutionalised concerns based on second generation conditionality.

The New Belgian Policy

We shall discuss successively the formulation of the new policy, its salient features and actual practice over the past few years.

---

6. It is relevant to point out that today the portfolios of both Foreign Affairs and Development Co-operation are held by Flemish Socialists.

(a) Formulation of a new policy. At the end of 1990 the Minister of Development Co-operation published a policy paper on the relationship between development assistance and human rights [*Ministerie van Ontwikkelingssamenwerking, s.d.*]. Coming after the Zaïre crisis which, as we saw earlier, was dealt with in a rather intuitive way, this was a first attempt at creating a frame of reference. The paper insists that 'human rights are a legitimate component of international development policy [which] can contribute to a positive influence on the human rights policy of [recipient] countries. (...) Donors have the right to promote the universal values of democracy, both because of their inherent importance and because of their instrumental value in the development process'. However, the text warns that sanctions are appropriate only 'when all possibilities of positive influencing by way of a policy dialogue' have been exhausted: 'The complete suspension or termination of ODA must be a last option, considered only after the use of other measures, which allow for a flexible approach geared at particular sectors addressed to the basic needs of the most vulnerable groups of the population'. Clearly the approach was cautious, and favoured the use of positive measures, an element which will become constant. However, although the paper contained no operational directives, this was the first time a policy formulation at cabinet level explicitly adhered to the principle of political conditionality.

Later statements became increasingly precise. A policy document by the present administration [*Staatssecretaris voor Ontwikkelingssamenwerking, 1992*] summarises the 'range' of measures available. 'Positive' measures include the funding of programmes directly aimed at human rights improvement and the strengthening of civil society. As far as sanctions (called 'negative measures') are concerned, the document advocates a diversified and phased approach based on the type of human rights violations and the authorities or persons responsible.

(b) Salient features. The formulation of the new Belgian policy of conditionality shows a number of characteristics.

The first is the *broadening of thinking*. While conditionality was traditionally associated with the weapon of sanctions, there is now an emphasis on the need to consider positive actions as well. Even in the area of sanctions, a wider array is considered: it integrates diplomatic action and other measures available in the field of bilateral relations. The broadening of scope is to some extent inspired by European Union thinking in this field, a point which leads us to the second characteristic.

A second feature is the *integration in a broader EU context*. Belgium aims at defining her co-operation policy in the context of a resolution taken in the Council of Co-operation Ministers on 28 November 1991. This resolution insists on the importance of a positive approach, directed at encouraging respect for human rights and the emergence of a democratic system of government. However, it also recognises the need under certain circumstances to resort to restrictive measures on the basis of objective criteria. Apart from her traditional EU-minded approach, underlying this tendency is the fact that Belgium does not want 'to go it alone': increasingly, the most effective channel for action is seen as the forum constituted by the European Political Co-operation (EPC). This is not altogether surprising when one realises that even in relation to the three main recipient partners, Belgium's ODA in itself is not crucial in macro-economic terms.[7]

A third characteristic is the *increased level of conceptualisation*. The proposal to be put to her European partners constitutes a summary of present Belgian thinking in this field. Under the heading of *positive measures*, the proposal addresses the issues of democratisation and human rights. Initiatives to promote democratisation processes include the funding of negotiation process, particularly in cases of military confrontation, support for the media, trade unions, and civil society, and assistance in the organisation of elections. With regard to this last element the proposal suggests that interventions should remain limited as 'donors focus too much on the day of the elections, and too little on the global process leading to a representative parliament and government'. Initiatives in favour of human rights include support for the improvement of the judicial system and for human rights associations, judicial and medical relief for political prisoners and their families, and training efforts in the fields of human rights and humanitarian law. On the side of *restrictive measures*, the proposal advocates a diversified approach based on the type of violations and the authorities or persons responsible. Moreover, measures should be applied in successive phases: diplomatic efforts, the threat of sanctions or the inclusion of conditions when new programmes are negotiated, the delaying of implementation, the re-orientation of ODA through other non-governmental or multilateral channels, and only ultimately the suspension or termination of certain ODA flows. With respect to this last phase, the proposal insists on the need to avoid penalising the population: thus basic health care, education,

---

7. See note 2.

decentralised and integrated rural development and emergency and humanitarian aid should not normally be halted.

(c) Actual practice. Since Belgium embarked on an explicit policy of conditionality in the wake of the May 1990 Lubumbashi events, policy-makers have faced several human rights crises in the three Central African countries under survey. Zaïre has been a constant democratisation/human rights concern; since October 1990, Rwanda has been experiencing a low-level civil war and recurring human rights violations; and Burundi has faced major human rights crises in November 1991 and October 1993. Enough material, one would think, to shape Belgian practice and implementation of aid conditionality.

As far as *Zaïre* is concerned, we have already noted that the strong Belgian reaction after the Lubumbashi massacre resulted in the suspension of ODA. However, some selective forms of aid have continued or have been resumed; these include a substantial amount of emergency aid and some limited funding of the democratisation process. With bilateral co-operation virtually halted, little remains in Belgian hands to exert pressure on the Mobutu regime, with which relations were *de facto* severed. The only partner recognised by Belgium is the government that emanated from the National Conference and its successor, the High Council of the Republic. It is through these institutions that democratisation support is channelled; for its part, emergency aid is indirect and uses NGO channels.

While the hard-line approach followed by Belgium has undoubtedly influenced Zaïre's other main partners (the USA and France in particular) in their decision to take a strong stand, Belgium cannot be said to be taking the lead on how the world should relate to Zaïre. Quite the contrary: as will be detailed more fully in Section IV, Belgium has made resumption of her development assistance, including indirect aid, contingent on an agreement between Zaïre and the World Bank/IMF, thus in fact leaving the decision to the Bretton Woods institutions.

The attitude towards *Rwanda* has been much gentler. However, since that country was invaded by a rebel force of Rwandan refugees from Uganda, human rights have been under considerable strain: thousands of people – mainly Tutsi – were detained in harsh conditions during the first months following the outbreak of the war, and between October 1990 and early 1993 as many as 2000 civilians were killed, mostly by the armed forces and local semi-official militias. And yet the Belgian attitude up to the catastrophy of 1994 remained distinctly more lenient than it has been in the case of Zaïre.

This strikingly different approach has several causes. In the past, relations with Rwanda have been virtually flawless and the country was considered a 'model' in terms of decent management, stability and even human rights; as a consequence, the ties with a country seen as respectable were diverse and profound, and NGOs in particular have found the working conditions particularly favourable. A second aspect is that Rwanda was the victim of an invasion by a force which the Belgian 'Rwanda experts', both in the Foreign Office and in the NGO world, did not believe constituted a viable alternative to the incumbent regime, even though it was recognised that the latter was showing signs of exhaustion. Finally, there was a widespread feeling that sanctions – particularly in the form of withdrawal of personnel – might result in even worse human rights violations. Of course these arguments have not convinced everyone, and the opposition (in particular the Francophone Liberals) have frequently alleged that Belgium was applying a double standard in comparison with Zaïre.

Yet Belgian human rights/democracy interventions in Rwanda have been frequent. Pressure by donors was instrumental in the release of thousands of political detainees in March-April 1991, in the formation of a broad-based coalition government in April 1992 and in monitoring recurrent human rights abuses over recent years. After having made representations to the Rwandan authorities on several occasions, the Belgian government was forced to take a stand when an international commission of inquiry drew a dramatic picture of the human rights situation in a report published in March 1993.[8] The possibility of sanctions was raised, but the Belgian government announced that it would first await an official Rwandan reaction to the report. When on 7 April 1993 the Rwandan government responded, by and large admitting the claims and announcing measures to improve the situation, the Belgian government reacted with relief. While stressing that it was to remain very watchful and that it expected genuine improvements in the human rights situation, the government announced 'positive measures' – relief for the hundreds of thousands of displaced persons and support for the rule of law, the judiciary, the peace negotiations, the democratisation process

---

8. This episode also highlighted another aspect of policy-making, which must be mentioned in passing. This concerns the relationship between the ministries of Foreign Affairs and of Development Co-operation, whose views often differ. Thus, when in late 1992 the Minister of Development Co-operation wanted Belgium to promote an EPC initiative for the sending of an international commission of inquiry into the human rights situation in Rwanda, this was blocked by the Foreign Ministry. In particular the diplomats at the Foreign Ministry eschew the implementation of conditionality policies because of their negative nature.

and the demobilisation of the military who were to become redundant once a peace accord came into effect.

A few words on *Burundi* conclude this section. As already stated, both the Belgian government and the NGO community have supported the reconciliation/democratisation process initiated by President Buyoya after the August 1988 massacres. As Burundi was preparing for a referendum on a pluralist constitution, violence once again broke out in November 1991. The armed forces killed many innocent civilians, mainly Hutu (independent estimates put the death toll at between 1000 and 3000). Although Belgium expressed concern and asked for an investigation and the punishment of those responsible, the Burundian authorities were less than forthcoming. However, given obvious progress in the area of democratisation and in consideration of the fragile position of President Buyoya in the face of Tutsi hardliners, the issue was not pressed. Clearly, Belgium decided to wait for the electoral moments of truth. The proof of the pudding was to be in the eating: the presidential and parliamentary elections held in June 1993 were free and fair, with the opposition candidate Melchior Ndadaye winning the presidency with 65% of the votes and his party FRODEBU gaining 70% of the parliamentary vote. This remarkably smooth transition seemed to vindicate the policy pursued by the international community, until on 21 October a military *coup d'état* was staged with disastrous consequences. President Ndadaye and other high officials were killed and widespread violence erupted all over the country; tens of thousands were killed either by the army or in intercommunal strife. As did other donors, Belgium immediately suspended her co-operation. As the *coup* collapsed after a few days, co-operation was soon resumed, but the Belgian government announced that it would be re-oriented, putting more emphasis on the strengthening of civil society and the advancement of the rural population.

IV. THE MICRO-MACRO MUDDLE : A CASE STUDY OF ZAÏRE

The analysis in this section concentrates on the way in which indirect aid through the NGOs and the universities was caught in the cross-fire between Mobutu and the Belgian government. It will be argued that the halting of all such aid to Zaïre, officially justified as a case of macro-economic and political conditionality, was a mistake from a development perspective. The episode illustrates the pitfalls of complex and overlapping conditionalities.

The first thing to notice is that the decision, taken in the middle of

1990, to stop all aid, was the consequence of the request by President Mobutu that Belgium should withdraw all its aid and technical assistance personnel, including some 180 NGO personnel financially supported by BADC. Belgium duly recalled aid personnel and put an end to all its projects and programmes, official and other. Dozens of NGOs and several Belgian universities had to abandon development projects and research and training activities which they were running with BADC funds in collaboration with local partner institutions. A large number of personnel and important funds of 'indirect' aid were thus frozen. In 1988, the last year of normal operations in Zaïre, the total amount of indirect aid to the country through the NGOs and universities amounted to US$ 11.7 million which is more than the total ODA Belgium devoted in that year to any single country except the four main recipients. From that point in time up to the moment of writing official funding of indirect aid to Zaïre has not resumed. The exception is emergency aid, mainly medical aid, which has continued to flow. In fact this increased greatly compared with the period preceding the crisis, but without making up for the high amount of indirect aid previously extended to Zaïre.

The immediate reason for the measure was the fact that President Mobutu had asked for it. This was regarded as an example of the diplomatic bluff poker Mobutu was so adept at playing. Only, this time the Belgian government decided to out-bluff him. In the past Mobutu had usually gained considerable advantage from diplomatic incidents of this kind, with measures taken against Belgian interests, such as the withdrawal of landing rights to the Belgian airline Sabena, the refusal of visas to Belgians wanting to visit Zaïre, or the 'threat' of refusing further Belgian aid. The last time this had happened was just a year earlier, in the middle of 1989, when a similar conflict, and mediation by the king of Morocco, had led the same Belgian government to grant Zaïre a generous debt reduction, a deal which had been very badly received by the Belgian public.[9]

The fact that Mobutu had this time explicitly included the NGOs, and thus indirect aid, in his measures against Belgium, in retaliation against Belgian demands for an international commission of inquiry into the Lubumbashi university campus massacre, need not have forced the Belgian government to stop such aid. In fact, as a good poker player the Belgian government could have decided that on the contrary it would expand it. Indirect aid is decided in Brussels, after negotiations between BADC and Belgian NGOs or universities, and is

---

9. On this latest conflict, see De Villers [*1990*].

not subject to routine communication to, let alone approval by, the recipient government. If safety was an issue, NGO and university field personnel could be temporarily withdrawn, while the funding of the local partner institutions was continued. Such a use of indirect aid in cases of conflict with the recipient government had been used with considerable success in the 1980s in Latin America. Belgium participated in such operations, giving generous subsidies to – amongst others – Belgian NGOs working in General Pinochet's Chile.

The decision of the Belgian government to end all indirect aid to Zaïre, notwithstanding strong criticism from the NGOs, was not necessary. It was the outcome of its free choice. A discussion of the many factors which played a role in the decision are beyond the scope of this paper [*Renard, 1993: 36-45*]. We are interested here in only one important aspect of the debate, the fact that the government argued that the measure was the natural outcome of applying conditionality clauses. In the circumstances it was widely regarded as the correct line of action to take. This was not only the opinion of the government, but also of most Members of Parliament, the media and the general public. In fact there was widespread support for the new conditionality as applied to Zaïre, and the protests by NGOs and to a lesser extent by members of the academic profession were interpreted by many as efforts to protect their self-interests.

The arguments given by the Belgian government to justify its policy stand on Zaïre changed as the internal political events in that country unfolded. Some months after the halting of Belgian aid, a government was formed by Prime Minister Tshisekedi, one of Mobutu's staunchest adversaries, supported by the political opposition forces and civil society, united in the *National Conference* and only reluctantly accepted by Mobutu himself. The Tshisekedi government never gained control of the affairs of state, certainly not of the affairs that really mattered, such as the army, the security forces, monetary policy or revenue collection from the lucrative diamond and gold business. To make the chaos complete, in the spring of 1993 Mobutu installed his own government headed by a former ally of Tshisekedi, Mr. Birindwa. The Tshisekedi government has been officially recognised by Belgium, and the president of the *National Conference* (later the *High Council of the Republic*), Archbishop Monsengwo, has been treated with special attention on his occasional visits to Belgium.

Early on in 1992 the Tshisekedi government had lifted the ban on indirect aid, and was asking the Belgian government to help it in any way possible to get rid of Mobutu. Yet the Belgian government continued to block the resumption of NGO aid for almost a year. In February 1993 restricted NGO funding, but no university funding was at last awarded to Zaïre, but it would take many more months before even this limited co-funding with the NGOs would be back on the rails. The major argument repeated over and again by the Ministers of Foreign Affairs and of Development Co-operation was that any resumption of aid would interfere with IMF and World Bank conditionality. Belgian aid could only be resumed when there was an agreement between Zaïre and the Bretton Woods institutions on a thorough economic recovery programme. With the government of Tshisekedi not really in charge, and the country slipping further into institutional chaos, the chance of this happening in any forseeable future was considered negligible. Until such time the resumption of aid, with the exception of relief aid, made no sense according to this official position, and all Belgium could do was to apply constant diplomatic pressure on Mobutu to step down or at least to release the control of government.

The episode illustrates two features of Belgian development policy since the end of the 1980s: the eagerness to use the new conditionality, of both the macro-economic and the political variety, but also the tendency for the new conditionality to get mixed up uncomfortably with other types of conditionality. The two successive Belgian governments that have handled the Zaïrean crisis since mid-1990 have consistently followed the same line. Their tough stand against Mobutu illustrates how the new conditionality is changing the rules of the game of international relations for corrupt African leaders. Yet at the same time the halting of indirect aid to Zaïre was a serious mistake in the eyes of the authors. First, it was a case of sanctions directed at the wrong partner, as Mobutu did not suffer from such measures. On the contrary, the halting of indirect aid has deprived the broad opposition coalition, in which academics, the Catholic church and local NGOs play a powerful role, of important financial and other support. Second, it is not true to state, as the Belgian government did, that indirect aid makes no sense without an IMF or World Bank reform programme. However useful and necessary such a programme may be for the future of Zaïre, much indirect aid works at another, often complementary level. Projects to empower local people in their relations with political authority, self-help projects in the urban informal sector, public health projects with a strong participatory component, vocational programmes, or social science research by Zaïrean academics, all contribute to strengthening the forces of change as well as helping ordinary people to survive in very difficult times.

V. CONCLUDING REMARKS

The end of the 1980s witnessed a considerable change in the way conditionality was handled in Belgian development aid policies. This may seem surprising, as Belgium had not been a pioneer in this area before. As a matter of fact, before 1990 even on the principle of political conditionality there was nothing resembling a consensus. This has dramatically changed in recent years. External political events and new perceptions regarding aid effectiveness have created an awareness of the need for a conditionality policy which is now shared in government, parliament and the Belgian development co-operation community generally. This changed perception presented Belgian policy-makers with a Pandora's Box labelled 'new conditionality'. Abruptly opened as a consequence of turbulent events in the three former colonial possessions in Central Africa, it let out policy options and responsibilities more quickly than government and administration were able to handle. The application in actual policy-making, however incomplete or hesitant it may have been, is having far-reaching consequences for relations with the countries concerned.

The fact that Zaïre, Rwanda and Burundi are former possessions may well have made a difference, but it is not always easy to say in which direction. On the one hand it could be argued that relations are more emotional with those countries than with others, laden with nostalgia for some, with guilt feelings for others, with hurt pride for still others, thus increasing the political significance of the events and making it more difficult to take a tough stand. Yet, on the other hand the colonial period is fading rapidly into history. Fewer and fewer politicians have a personal knowledge of any of the three countries. And it is well known by observers of the political scene that a significant part of Belgian public opinion has limited patriotic feelings. For them the so-called 'privileged relationship' with the three countries may well be something of a forced marriage. This would suggest that it would be easier to take a tough position with those countries than with others. Whatever the case may be, there can be no doubt that the outcome of the conditionality debate in Belgium was strongly influenced by tactical struggles within and between political parties and other internal events that are not necessarily related to the fundamental issues at stake.

In the economic field, the strong lead taken by the Bretton Woods institutions in macro-economic conditionality made things relatively easy. Belgium did not offer to do more than was expected from her as a small donor, but that it did without complaining. The old conditionality, micro-economic in nature, was never questioned during this change. Indeed BADC staff continued to tie projects round carefully with bureaucratic and technical strings, thus exerting considerable control over the allocation of aid resources. We cautiously welcome the changes which have occurred. On the positive side, macro-economic conditionality makes a lot of sense. Looked at from the point of view of Belgian aid policies, there is now a *de facto* international co-ordination of aid whose value should not be underestimated. Also positive is that conditionality is now more applied at the level where it matters most, that of macro-economic and sectoral policy-making in the recipient country. One may regret the absence of even more of this type of conditionality with respect to technical assistance, which remains the largest form of Belgian bilateral aid.

As regards political conditionality, the ongoing attempts to formulate and implement a more coherent policy linking development to recipient human rights/democracy performance must be welcomed. While negative conditionality measures are part of that policy, an increasing stress is laid on the opportunities offered by forms of positive action. Moreover, decisions in this field are taken after a cost-benefit analysis, which is still intuitive and implicit, but nevertheless real. The attitude towards the Rwandan dilemma is a case in point. Finally, faced with the limited impact of single-donor measures, the EPC is set to play an increasing role in Belgian policy as a forum for effective implementation. Needless to say, this embedding in a larger supranational context also offers the advantage of avoiding upsetting bilateral partners in a region where other European donors – France in particular – tend to increase their influence at the expense of Belgium.

Yet not everything in the picture is rosy. To give the example of an obvious point not discussed in this chapter, the quality of the conditionality prescribed by the Bretton Woods institutions is not wholly unquestioned. It may be much better than having no macro-conditionality or donor co-ordination at all, yet it is clear that there are some weaknesses in the analytical framework, procedures and specific country applications. At the level of BADC, we have some reservations about the way in which macro-economic and micro-economic conditionalities are combined. In principle this need not pose problems, in the sense that both can be compatible and complementary to one another. Underlying this chapter is the view that the donor is entitled to impose benign conditions which foster development objectives. In practice, the superimposition of conditionalities may become too much and lead to excessive and useless administrative control which defeats the purpose, or leads to internal contradictions.

It is fair to say that old and new conditionalities do not always live harmoniously side by side in Belgian policy.

Our final comment is that any positive reactions to daring new policy initiatives are tempered by the sobering observation that the period of new conditionalities has coincided with a stark reduction in ODA spending, which as a share of Belgian GNP fell from 0.46 per cent in 1989 to 0.39 per cent in 1992. At first sight this would lend strength to the assumption that it is easier to apply negative sanctions than to introduce positive measures in the new family of conditionalities. There are some signs which lend support to this interpretation, such as the needless halting of all indirect aid to Zaïre. However, it may well be that the fall in ODA spending is not linked to conditionality policies at all but to sheer budgetary constraints. As in many other donor countries, considerations of this domestic nature are more helpful in explaining declining aid flows than any form of 'new' conditionality.

REFERENCES

BADC, 1991, *Concentration de l'Aide Publique au Développement accordée par la Belgique*, Brussels.
DAC, 1992, *Development Co-operation Report 1992*, Paris: OECD.
De Villers, G., 1990, 'Belgique-Zaïre: le grand affrontement', *Cahiers du CEDAF*, No. 1-2.
Ministerie van Buitenlandse Zaken, 1983, *Het Belgisch Afrika-Beleid*, Brussels.
Ministerie van Ontwikkelingssamenwerking, 1983, Reflectienota over ontwikkelings-samenwerking en mensenrechten, Brussels.
Renard, R., 1993, 'De Belgische hulp als wapen tegen Mobutu', *Socialistische Stand-punten*, Vol. 40, April.
Reyntjens, F., 1988, 'The growing role of human rights in development co-operation', in Van Den Bulcke, D. (ed.), *Recent Trends in International Co-operation*, Antwerp: College for Developing Countries.
Staatssecretaris voor Ontwikkelingssamenwerking, 1992, *Van kwantiteit naar kwali-teit*, Brussels, May.
Stevens, W.J., 1993, ' "Zachte waarden" in internationale samenwerking', *Internatio-nale Spectator*, Vol. 47, May.

3

Aid and Conditionality: The Case of Germany, with Particular Reference to Kenya

PETER P. WALLER

I. INTRODUCTION

Political conditionality in connection with development aid is now widely practised by major Western donor countries. Its application means that the amount of aid allocated to a recipient country is linked to respect for human rights and progress towards democracy in that country. Whereas in the early phase of its application the controversy was mainly about its legitimacy – interference in the internal affairs of sovereign nations – the focus has now shifted to questions such as 'does political conditionality really work?' and 'are there better alternatives to conditionality, like the so-called positive measures?' [*Uvin, 1993, Robinson, 1993a*].

There are a number of constraints on effective political conditionality such as the marginal role of aid in many of the larger developing countries, priority economic interests on the donor side as well as the possibility of evading political conditionality through 'cosmetic changes' or the playing off of one donor against the other on the recipient side [*Uvin, 1993: 68 ff.*]. What has been mostly neglected so far is that there may exist a number of other constraints on the donor side, namely lack of a clear concept of political conditionality, inadequate implementation of the concept within the donor administration and lack of public support for political conditionality. These aspects will be analysed in relation to the situation in Germany.

The central question arising out of the debate can be put as follows: is political conditionality, despite all the constraints, a useful complement to other measures to encourage political reforms in some developing countries [*Nelson and Eglinton, 1992: 4*] or does it tend to be ineffective and even counterproductive and therefore should it be discarded in favour of other approaches, notably 'positive measures' which encourage the creation of an enabling environment for democracy and respect of human rights? [*Uvin, 1993: 76*].

In the following study, based mainly on the experience of the German-Kenyan relationship, it will be argued that political conditionality can be effective if certain preconditions referring to the various constraints are met and if other approaches are applied. It is suggested that there are three main approaches through which development aid can contribute to the promotion of democracy and human rights [*Waller, 1992: 27ff.*]:

– positive measures to support human rights and democracy;
– reform-orientation of development aid;
– political conditionality linked to development aid.

The first approach is the direct one: development aid support is given to projects and programmes, which specifically promote human rights and democracy such as the monitoring of free elections, legal training, assistance to human rights groups, etc. The second approach is an indirect one: the composition of the ongoing development aid is geared towards the support of political reforms. In a country with an authoritarian regime aid is shifted to non-governmental organisations, thus strengthening civil society and reducing direct support for the government. Aid instruments such as budget aid, structural aid or commodity aid, which strengthen the position of the government, would not be implemented in such cases but would be made available to reform-oriented countries. The third approach, conditionality, is also an indirect one, because the total amount of development aid is used to support economic and political reforms. This can be done in two ways, either by reducing the amount of aid if respect for human rights and democracy decreases (negative conditionality) or through increased aid disbursements to a country where human rights and democracy are improving (positive conditionality).

So, in principle, there are alternative forms of political conditionality. The question is: can these be implemented separately or are they mutually dependent on each other? The experience of German development aid can supply a tentative answer to these questions. First the basis for political conditionality on the donor side, and then the experience of implementation in the recipient countries, will be analysed.

II. POLITICAL CONDITIONALITY: THE DONOR SIDE

The Emerging Political Conditionality of German Aid

When Germany became an aid donor in the early 1960s, the first attempt at political conditionality was to connect diplomatic relations and development aid with the non-recognition of the German Democratic Republic (GDR). This was not at all successful, and the Federal Republic had to accept that the GDR, as a member of the United Nations, was recognised diplomatically by all nations. Thus conditionality that runs counter to worldwide trends cannot be implemented even by a fairly strong economic power and an important aid donor.

A second attempt, which was much more in line with international trends began in the early 1980s when development aid was linked to human rights and democracy. In 1982 the federal parliament (Bundestag) stated in a unanimous resolution: 'In its development cooperation the Federal Republic of Germany regards the implementation of human rights as an essential goal of the federal government. ...those countries should be especially supported, which try to establish democratic structures... In states where despotism, intimidation and physical threat characterise the relationship between the governing and the governed, only those projects can be supported which benefit directly the oppressed population' [*Deutscher Bundestag, 1982: 2*].

Although, two years later, the Bundestag again unanimously adopted guidelines for the federal government, stating that the goal for development co-operation should be to guarantee the dignity of human life (securing basic needs) and to contribute to a higher level of civil and political rights in developing countries, the Ministry for Economic Co-operation and Development did not really respond to these resolutions and to a large extent left human rights policies to the Foreign Office.

It was only five years later, when political reforms in countries with structural adjustment processes seemed to be unavoidable and especially after the collapse of the socialist states in Eastern Europe that political conditionality and 'help through intervention' were discussed in Germany [*Waller, 1989; Wissenschaftlicher Beirat, 1992*]. Finally, in October 1991, the Minister for Economic Co-operation and Development, Carl-Dieter Spranger, publicly announced five criteria for German development co-operation: respect for human rights, popular participation in the political process, observation of the rule of law, a market-friendly approach to economic development and the recipient government's commitment to development [*van de Sand and Mohs, 1991: 4-5*]. The first three criteria constitute a clear policy of political conditionality based on respect for human rights and an orientation towards democracy.

The Administration of the Political Conditionality

After announcing the new criteria the Minister for Economic Co-operation and Development made one of his two deputy ministers the human rights coordinator. In a series of meetings the ambassadors of developing countries were informed about the new criteria and the human rights orientation of German development policy. The co-ordination of the human rights orientation within the ministry was entrusted to the existing development policy section (Referat 200: Grundsatzfragen), and no separate human rights section was created. This can be interpreted positively, since the development policy section has a very central function within the ministry and so far has been very much engaged in the internal implementation of a policy oriented towards human rights. On the other hand the development policy section has many other tasks and thus only limited manpower for human rights implementation is available.

In order to ensure that the criteria were applied in the country aid allocations, the development policy section developed a checklist of indicators. In relation to the first three criteria it was ensured that all indicators were based on internationally codified UN human rights such as freedom from torture, equality before the law and freedom of assembly, so that no recipient country could object that it was being subjugated to German standards. In this checklist there is also a clear distinction in terms of assessment between the current status of respect for human rights in a given country and the tendency towards improving human rights performance, the latter being considered more important.

The introduction of human rights criteria for country allocations also led to increased support for human rights and democracy projects, the so-called 'positive measures'. The major political parties in particular, but also church organisations and other NGOs, have a long tradition of projects to strengthen the civil society of developing countries through support for trade unions, chambers of commerce, human rights groups, etc. In 1992 the Ministry for Economic Co-operation and Development spent DM 405 million on positive measures through political foundations (mainly the Friedrich Ebert Foundation, Konrad Adenauer Foundation and Friedrich Naumann Foundation) and church organisations. The ministry now also engages directly in such positive measures as strengthening of the legal system, demobilisation and re-integration of soldiers (Mozambique,

Uganda, Ethiopia, Nicaragua), decentralisation and community development. The Foreign Office is converting a fund which was formerly
used for military aid and training of policemen into a source for positive measures such as support for free elections, consultancy services
for parliaments and seminars on democratic constitutions [*Adelmann,
1992*].

The major administrative instrument for the implementation of a
human rights orientation is the country concept (*Länderkonzept*).
There has been a major effort to draw up such concepts for about 40
countries. In addition to offering an economic analysis these address
social and political conditions and are designed explicitly to refer to
trends that relate to the five criteria. The country concepts are the basis for decisions in relation to country allocations and for government-
to-government consultations.

A recent assessment of these concepts by the policy section of the
ministry revealed that the implementation of the new criteria within
the administration is quite a complicated process and will take some
time. However, it is hoped that a series of internal training workshops
will improve the quality of the country concepts.

Support for Political Conditionality Amongst the German Public

The response of the German public to the new criteria for development aid was very positive. The parliamentary opposition stated only
that they would monitor implementation and even the most critical
NGOs did not reject the criteria but criticised the double standards
applied in their implementation. Even with the 'ordinary voter' not
very interested in Third World affairs, the new policy was quite popular because of the message that no taxpayer's money should be given
to dictators who oppress their own people or to corrupt regimes which
use development money for their private purposes. There was no criticism by the private sector of the general policy guidelines; however,
the various vested interests of the business community were very relevant at the implementation stage in certain economically important
countries (see the case of China below).

There is a very intensive discussion going on among NGOs, especially Amnesty International, about their position in relation to the new
conditionality [*Deile, 1992*]. Some major demands are as follows:

–   the promotion of human rights cannot be limited to development
    co-operation but must be a major goal of German policy includ-
    ing economic, security and foreign policy (the problem of policy
    coherence);

- respect for human rights must be equally demanded from all countries, be they small or large, economically important or not (the problem of double standards);
- government decisions concerning changes in development co-operation with individual countries must be transparent to the public so that they can be discussed and criticised by human rights groups;
- all human rights, civil and political as well as social and economic, must be treated as equally important.

The five criteria for conditionality of the Ministry of Economic Co-operation and Development were criticised on the grounds that it was not clear if they were all of equal ranking. A priority for a market-friendly economic system combined with less insistence on respect of human rigths would not be acceptable. Although NGOs declared their willingness to co-operate with the ministry in supplying necessary information they were also aware of the danger of losing their independence, especially in relation to recipient countries, if they were directly associated with conditionality. They made it clear that they would exercise the right to criticise specific government decisions about the application of conditionality to a particular country. On the other hand they also made it clear that they would not support a general rejection of conditionality by the governments of developing countries, since there were many demands from partner NGOs within these countries for strict political conditionality to be applied to their own governments.

III. POLITICAL CONDITIONALITY: THE RECIPIENT SIDE

The Implementation of German Aid Conditionality

In the first budget of the Ministry for Economic Co-operation and Development after the introduction of the new criteria, a remarkable shift in country aid allocations was evident, whereas in the past there had been only very minor variations from year to year. These changes concerned three groups of countries:

(1) Repressive regimes. With a first group of countries (Haiti, Malawi, Togo, Zaïre) development co-operation was stopped because of very severe human rights violations and a complete obstruction of the development process. Withholding aid was not realistically expected to lead to reforms in the short term, but at least the appearance of propping up repressive regimes was avoided [*Nelson and Eglinton, 1992: 49*].

(2) Authoritarian regimes. A second group of countries such as China, Indonesia and Kenya saw their allocations substantially reduced because of human rights violations and suppression of the process towards democracy, although their development orientation was not questioned. Here a 'negative' political conditionality was supposed to lead to political reforms in the respective countries. The possibilities and limits of this approach will be analysed in the two case studies of China and Kenya (there was another group of countries, such as India and Pakistan, which also had a reduction of aid although they were considered to be democracies. The reason was that their arms spending was considered excessive).

(3) Fragile reformers. A third group of countries benefited from a 'positive' conditionality and had their aid allocations substantially increased. These countries, including Benin, El Salvador, Ethiopia, Namibia, Nepal and Zambia, had either just ended a civil war and were moving towards more democratic regimes or had successfully organised democratic elections and had improved their human rights record. Here conditionality is not intended to pressurise a government towards policy change but to support a country that has already gone through a policy change in its course, because it may have great difficulty in sustaining this course without increased assistance. It is, however, understood that this support is given under the condition that the government does not fall back into its former authoritarian practices, with increased human rights violations, etc.

There were some exceptions to these rules. There was, for example, no reduction of aid to *Turkey*, a country where heavy human rights violations continue and where arms spending is very high. In this particular case strategic and commercial interests, as well as the fact that many Turks live in Germany, were the reason for not applying a political conditionality which would certainly have strained German-Turkish relations.

Another very interesting case that shows the limits of applying conditionality in development cooperation is *China*. After the Tiananmen Square massacre in June 1989 the German Bundestag decided unanimously that development co-operation should be stopped with the exception of projects 'that directly benefit the population'. On 30 October 1990 the Bundestag, with the majority of the coalition parties, voted for a limited resumption of development co-operation, adding projects 'for the protection of the environment and projects which contribute to the reform of the Chinese economy'. This change was justified on the grounds that environmental protection was necessary and that China had taken a constructive position during the Iraq conflict.

In November 1991 Minister C.H. Spranger refused to sign a special financial arrangement for a contract for container ships which were to be built in an east German shipyard, because none of the exceptions of the Bundestag resolution would apply. After continued criticism from members of the coalition, mainly reflecting massive economic interests, in June 1992 the majority in the Bundestag cancelled its resolution of October 1990, enabling the government to finance the shipbuilding contract on preferential terms. The arguments were that although respect for civil and political rights was very poor the improvement of economic and social rights was impressive, that economic reforms would eventually lead to improvements in the human rights situation, that China was of high security interest and that other countries were ready to capture the big export contract. Although the ministry did reduce its aid allocation to China by DM 40 million, major improvements in the human rights situation could not be observed.

A positive example of development co-operation oriented towards human rights and democracy is the case of aid to *Zambia*. During the 1980s there was a heavy German commitment to support the Zambian trade union movement through one of Germany's political foundations. During the democratisation process in Zambia the trade union movement turned out to be the only effective political force able to contest the governing party and consequently in the first free elections in October 1991 the union leader Frank Chiluba was elected president. Germany had substantially reduced its aid allocations to the former single-party government but it quickly reacted to the new situation. Only 100 days after the elections it unblocked its funds and even increased its allocation to DM 95 million as 'start-up help' ('Starthilfe'). Without the clear directives provided by the new aid criteria the reaction would have been much less pronounced. This policy reorientation was in line with that of most of Zambia's other donors who also reacted very quickly and supported the democratisation process with masssive financial support.

A Case Study of Aid to Kenya

(1) Macro-conditionality and constitutional change. Until the late 1980s Kenya was considered a successful case of economic and social development combined with political stability. It was one of the favoured aid recipients of multilateral and bilateral donors in general and of Germany in particular. After an abortive military coup in 1982 President Daniel Arap Moi established a more and more repressive and corrupt one-party regime, entrenching the power of the Kenyan

African National Union (KANU). The human rights record rapidly deteriorated. Inspired by events in Eastern Europe more and more people became dissatisfied with their government. In the summer of 1990 widespread anti-government demonstrations and rioting occurred, which were very brutally cracked down on by the regime. The Nordic countries warned President Moi that aid disbursements could be jeopardised if he continued to ignore calls for more democracy. In November 1990 Kenya severed diplomatic relations with Norway and new aid commitments were suspended after the arrest of a political refugee formerly resident in Norway [*Robinson, 1993a: 63*].

In August 1991 prominent public personalities formed the Foundation for the Restoration of Democracy (FORD). A rally staged by FORD in Nairobi was attended by several Western diplomats including the German ambassador, which did not prevent the government from brutally dispersing the crowd of several thousand people. In the following months, at the initiative of the American and the German ambassadors, donor country representatives organised an informal circle of 'serious-minded donors', which tried to pressurise President Moi into carrying out political reforms. The British, who because of their historic role could have been the leading Western donor, did not take the initiative, because they favoured a softer approach. They were influenced by the fact that most of the foreigners living in Kenya were British citizens and that most of the capital invested in Kenya was British. Germany, on the other hand, has only minor investments in Kenya (100 million DM) and whereas its trade relations with Kenya are very important for the latter they are of only marginal importance to Germany [*Bass, 1993: 48*].

When there was no positive reaction from the Kenyan government all the Western aid donors, with the exception of France, decided at a Kenya Consultative Group meeting in Paris on 25 November 1991, to suspend any quick disbursing aid until the multi-party system was re-established, corruption was reduced and economic reforms implemented. With the inclusion of the World Bank this meant a reduction of total aid from about one billion to 650 million dollars. Since about 90 per cent of the Kenyan development budget is financed through development aid, the reduction of foreign currency by about 350 million dollars was certainly a major blow to the government.

Within a few days President Moi announced that article 2a of the constitution declaring Kenya a one-party state would be abolished and free elections held. In December 1992 these elections took place and were monitored by many foreign observers. Although they could not be considered really fair, the voting results seemed to represent the will of the people. Because of a divided opposition, President Moi was able stay in power with only 33.4 per cent of the vote. In the parliamentary elections KANU received only 23 per cent of the total vote but took 100 out of the 188 seats. This was mainly due to the extremely different sizes of the constituencies. In outlying rural areas like the North Eastern Province – a KANU stronghold – it took only 18,378 votes to secure a seat in parliament whereas in Nairobi – a stronghold of the opposition – it took 109,152 votes [*Mair, 1993: 106*]. So although the overwhelming majority of the people voted for the opposition, a change of power could not take place.

The major problem, however, is that the regime is still completely hostile to any reform in the direction of more democracy, less corruption and a more liberal economy. Every single reform step has to be achieved through a combination of pressure from below (the internal opposition) and above (foreign donors). This is why there is no rejection of political conditionality by members of the opposition, NGO personnel or intellectuals. On the contrary, rather than rallying around the established powers [*Uvin, 1993: 72*] intellectuals in Kenya emphatically urge foreign donors not to reduce their pressure on the government to implement reforms.

Compared to the pre-1991 situation there can be no doubt that the human rights situation has improved considerably and that the major reason for this improvement has been the political conditionality applied by Western aid donors. This marked change is certainly not merely cosmetic [*Uvin, 1993: 73*] and it is very unlikely that it could be reversed. On the other hand, there has been no change of power, and Kenya is still *de facto* an authoritarian one-party state because the regime refuses to implement the necessary legal changes and political reforms which would lead to a multi-party democracy as advocated by the opposition and the majority of the population. How can foreign aid donors, who in a first phase helped to achieve constitutional change and fairly free elections, continue to support the reform process in a second phase?

In the summer of 1993, after having postponed bilateral aid negotiations with Kenya for over a year, the German government started consultations again with the clear indication that it wanted the process towards a pluralistic democracy to be continued and fundamental human rights including the freedom of the press to be respected.[1] On

1.   Opening Statement by His Excellency the German Ambassador Bern Mützelburg on the occasion of the Kenyan-German Government Consultation 16/17 June, 1993 in Nairobi.

the basis of a new *Länderkonzept* Germany was to pursue a strategy consisting of three elements: macro-conditionality, project aid oriented towards reform, and direct positive measures [*BMZ, 1993*].

Because of the stagnation in the reform process Germany did not resume quick disbursing aid but did not further reduce its aid allocation either. Since macro-conditionality had already been used with success in the first phase its use in the second phase could only be quite limited. Its major impact derived from the clear indication that if the reform process was substantially reversed, then a reduction in aid or even its suspension was possible. This gave the opposition and other democratic forces an important shield of protection. In order to encourage the democratisation process a positive conditionality was indicated: a substantial increase in aid allocations to Kenya would be made if progress with reforms were achieved.

(2) Reform-orientation of project aid. In the case of Kenya ongoing and new project aid was analysed in relation to its direct or indirect contribution to the reform process. There are two major objectives in this exercise: to strengthen civil society in its resistance to government dominance and to prevent development aid from becoming a source of government corruption. Three strategies were identified to achieve these objectives: shifting projects from central government departments to regional and local authorities (decentralisation), channelling funds through NGOs and changing the composition of aid [*Gsänger and Waller, 1993: 18 ff*].

Decentralisation was already being indirectly supported through German capital aid for a number of water supply projects for middle-sized cities. Because of the extreme dependance of Kenyan municipalities on central government (the Ministry for Local Administration) the implementing agency (Kreditanstalt für Wiederaufbau) insisted on the creation of independent communal organisations for the management of the water supply of the municipalities concerned. Since these capital aid projects represent a substantial part of German project aid the Kenyan government accepted these demands for greater independence on the part of local administrations although this was against its own political interests. This approach could be called 'project conditionality'.

After the elections many of the municipalities came under the rule of opposition parties, which led to increased resistance and obstruction from the central government. A test case for conditionality will be another German capital aid project, support for a new central market for Nairobi, because the city council of the Kenyan capital city is in the hands of the opposition. Without political pressure at the highest level this project does not seem to have a chance.

Channelling more funds through NGOs such as churches, chambers of commerce, trade unions and self-help groups was already a trend of German development aid in the 1980s. It was certainly strengthening civil society in Kenya but was not free of conflicts. First of all the KANU regime managed to bring many civil organisations, such as women's organisations, trade unions, farmers' unions and chambers of commerce, under its absolute control. Supporting these 'NGOs' was hardly contributing to a democratisation process. In fact a number of German projects with these organisations were terminated in the late 1980s. It was mainly after the formal abolition of the one-party state that these organisations started to drift away from KANU control and play their role as real non-governmental organisations. Moreover, many other independent organisations, such as political parties, could only be founded after the constitutional change, for which political conditionality had been important. Thus, supporting NGOs through development aid could not be seen as an alternative to political conditionality because without political conditionality the government would not have allowed NGOs to operate.

The last years had seen a tremendous increase in the development activities of the NGO sector which in 1992 mobilised US$ 135 million, or about 15 per cent of total aid to Kenya for that year. No wonder that an authoritarian regime like the Kenyan one was not happy about this development and tried to regulate and control these NGOs through the NGO Act of 1991, which forced them to register and to inform the government about their financial transactions. The NGOs organised themselves in a network and protested against the strangulation by the government. It was only through the pressure of foreign donors (who got their own NGOs exempted from the law), that a compromise was reached with the government, which was acceptable to the NGOs [*Gsänger and Waller, 1993: 19*].

A special aspect of co-operation with NGOs is that it can avoid government corruption. The first financial aid project with a NGO was the Mathare Slum Upgrading Project. The counterpart is the Roman Catholic archdiocese of Nairobi, considered to be an 'island of integrity' in a sea of corruption.

Changes in the composition of aid. As a consequence of the deteriorating efficiency of the Kenyan administration there was in the early 1990s a tendency towards a concentration of German aid in certain sectors while others, such as the energy sector, were completely left out because of the well-known inefficiency and pervasive corruption in the responsible ministry. Sectoral concentration of projects was thought to give the German aid agencies increased bargaining power *vis-à-vis* the Kenyan ministry and to allow better co-ordination of activities through sectoral programme co-ordinators.

Another change occurred in terms of the types of aid provided. Commodity aid was abandoned after massive attempts at corruption had been experienced in connection with a big loan for fertilizer procurement for the Ministry of Agiculture. Nor was a rural development fund seen as an appropriate aid programme after misuse of funds on a huge scale was discovered in a Danish project. This is a very disappointing state of affairs from a development point of view, since a rural development fund is a very progressive aid instrument allowing maximum participation by the population. In a situation of all-pervasive corruption, however, progressive instruments are not feasible.

(3) Positive measures in support of human rights and democracy. While indirect support was given to the democatic process through the reform-orientation of ongoing development projects, there was also strong direct support of the political reforms through 'positive measures'. These were mainly aimed at strengthening the formal political and legal system, decentralising the administration and building up the independent organisations of civil society.

Strengthening the formal political and legal system. In contrast to other donors Germany has not been in the forefront in this area. One of the political foundations has strongly supported the opposition parties in drawing up an election manifesto. Another political foundation has tried to support the newly elected parliament but was turned down by its president who belongs to the ruling KANU party and probably acted on 'higher orders'. This shows that an autocratic regime knows quite well that strengthening democracy is not in its interests and has many tricks in hand to obstruct 'positive measures'. Since it is not possible to apply pressure through the use of macro-conditionality for every project idea that is turned down by the government, the German political foundations are really applying a 'niche strategy', that is searching for partner organisations in the democratisation process with whom they can collaborate without interference from the government.

Decentralisation of the administration. In the case of the water supply projects mentioned above, conditionality was able to help strengthen local authorities in an indirect way. There is also a technical assistance project, the Small Towns Development Project, which directly supports decentralisation. Especially since the elections of December 1992, when many local councils passed into the hands of the opposition, and now that many new opposition politicians have the chance to practise politics for the first time, the Ministry of Local Government which controls the finances of the communes has been keen to weaken power of local authorities. The Small Towns Development Project, on the other hand, aims to strengthen these. It provides advisory services and training in areas such as investment, urban planning and financial management, assists them in establishing or updating valuation rolls and streamlining their fees and charges in order to increase the revenue base of the communes.

Strengthening of civil society. In contrast to many other African countries Kenya has an already fairly differentiated civil society. There are many small groups and long-established institutions, such as the churches, the Kenya Law Society and the Kenya Human Rights Commission, which directly support human rights and democracy. These groups are supported by German counterparts and the local branches of the German political foundations. A very endangered part of civil society is the free press, which is still harassed by the government [*Gsänger and Waller, 1993: 34*]. A number of donors including Germany are planning the foundation of a Media Trust to support the critical press.

To sum up, the German experience of using positive measures in the case of Kenya is one of implementing them within a context of conflict with the authoritarian government which is well aware of the fact that progress in democratisation is not in its interests. Therefore these measures can only be executed if they are closely linked with other development assistance in which the government has a definite interest.

IV. GERMANY AS AN AID RECIPIENT UNDER SEVERE CONDITIONALITY: THE MARSHALL PLAN

Before drawing conclusions about Germany as an aid donor we should also look at the experiences of Germany as an aid recipient who was exposed to severe conditionality during the Marshall Plan period after World War II. Contrary to general belief it was not so much the amount of money transferred to the Western European countries which made this exercise 'history's most successful structural adjustment programme', but rather the strict conditionality attached to it. Between 1948 and 1951, US$ 13.2 billion were transferred from the United States to West Europe, a sum which amounted to only 2.5 per cent of the combined national incomes of the recipient countries [*De Long and Eichengreen, 1992: 11*].

Each recipient had to sign a bilateral pact with the United States in which they agreed to balance government budgets, restore financial stability and stabilise exchange rates at realistic levels. In addition, for every dollar of Marshall Plan aid received, the recipient country was required to place a matching amount of domestic currency in a counterpart fund to be used only for purposes approved by the US government.

There was no direct political conditionality applied, but it was clear that the US government was trying to achieve three major political goals:

–   to establish the Federal Republic as a separate state;
–   to integrate the Federal Republic into the West; and
–   to steer development towards Western-type democracy and a
    market economy [*Knapp, 1990: 59*].

It is of course true that there were strong forces inside Germany which themselves wanted to achieve these goals but there were certainly also strong groups which opposed them. It should not be forgotten that 'post World War II Europe was far from laissez faire, government ownership of utilities and heavy industry was substantial' [*De Long and Eichengreen, 1992: 38*] and the attraction of socialism as an alternative was still very strong. The Marshall Plan tipped the balance in favour of Western integration and the free market economy (a social market economy in the case of Germany) and can thus be considered as a successful example of positive conditionality.

The success of economic conditionality can also be measured through a comparison between the different recipient countries. Although Germany received much less money than Great Britain or France its economy grew much faster than that of the other two. Great Britain received US$ 3.2 billion, France 2.7 billion and Germany 1.4 billion. However, average growth rates of real GNP during the 1948-1951 period were 12 per cent for Germany, 6 per cent for France and 2.5 per cent for Great Britain [*De Long and Eichengreen, 1992: 8 and 11*]. There were a number of reasons for the different economic performances but it seems clear that economic conditionality worked best in countries where the US had the strongest influence, such as Germany, far less well in countries such as France and Great Britain, which were in a strong fiscal position and could resist the American conditionality much more effectively than Germany could.

Although there are important differences between Marshall Plan aid to a war-damaged industrial country like Germany and aid to developing countries, the experience of Germany both as an aid recipient and as a donor seems to underline two points of general importance: positive conditionality works if it is accepted by strong internal forces and helps to 'tip the balance' and it works the better the more dependent a country is on the aid received and the donor involved.

V. CONCLUSIONS

The major experience with human rights conditionality in German development co-operation is that this policy can be implemented with a good measure of success in countries which depend heavily on foreign aid and where economic and strategic interests are minimal. There is little chance for success in economically important or strategically interesting countries. This has led to severe criticism by the German public, which has accused the government of 'double standards' [*Nuscheler, 1992*]. As a consequence greater 'coherence' of all policies towards developing countries is demanded, which means that development policy should have a higher priority than economic or security interests.

This demand, however, would have to be based on strong political support amongst the German public and in important interest groups. Although development aspects have in general increased in importance since the disappearance of the East-West conflict other interests, such as preservation of jobs or the economic development of Eastern Germany, have a much higher priority and will have for quite some time to come.

The basic question then, is: should one accept 'double standards' in relation to political conditionality and try to slowly increase the number of countries where development orientation has highest priority or should one postpone in a more purist way the application of a human rights oriented conditionality even in those small countries where it is implementable and wait until such time that human rights conditionality can be successfully introduced in all countries? Since such a policy would be at the cost of potential improvement of human rights and democracy in many countries the answer that human rights and development oriented NGOs in Germany give is to support the political conditionality where it is sincerely applied and to use the 'double standards' argument as political pressure to increase the application of political conditionality in as many countries as possible.

A second experience refers to the the necessity of a mix of approaches to achieve progress towards democracy and respect for human rights. Political conditionality – negative or positive – reform-orientation of aid and positive measures in support of democracy and human rights are not alternatives but are mutually dependent on each other. There are governments which support the process towards democracy and respect for human rights. They will be very interested in positive measures but since they are still fragile economically they should also be supported by positive conditionaliy in terms of more aid to help them economically. Governments which are not supportive of reforms towards democracy and human rights will not be supportive of positive measures either and can only be pushed into a reform process through the application of all three approaches.

Finally there is the question of the sustainability of political conditionality especially in the face of the deteriorating economic situation in many donor countries. Judging from the German experience there seem to be two trends. In relation to economically important developing countries a certain retreat in the application of political conditionality can be observed because of economic interests. In relation to economically weak partners, however, the public pressure not to spend money on undemocratic and repressive regimes has even increased, not least because of the scarcity of funds for urgent internal social problems. In view of the fact that the worldwide deterioration of the environment, the fear of international migration, and the growing international engagement in peace-keeping, will make development co-operation more rather than less important in the future it can be safely predicted that this co-operation will continue to be linked to conditionality. Since democracy and respect for human rights are the most important factors to prevent mass migrations and political conflicts, political conditionality is in the interest of donor countries as well as of the majority of the people in developing countries.

REFERENCES

Adelmann, K., 1992, 'Demokratisierungshilfe – neues Arbeitsfeld der deutschen Entwicklungspolitik', *Entwicklung und Zusammenarbeit*, No. 4, Frankfurt am Main.
Auswärtiges Amt, 1992, *Menschenrechtsbericht der Bundesregierung*. Bonn.
Bass, H.-H., 1993, 'Kenia 1991-1992', in Bass, H.-H. *et al.*, 'Menschenrechtskonditionalität in der Entwicklungspolitik. Drei Länderstudien', *epd Dokumentation*, No. 34, Frankfurt am Main.

THE CASE OF GERMANY

Brandt, H.-J., 1988, 'Human Rights, Legal Services and Development: Theory and Practice', in *Law, Human Rights and Legal Services: A Neglected Field of Development Co-operation*, Sankt Augustin, Germany, Friedrich Naumann Stiftung.
BMZ (Bundesministerium für wirtschaftliche Zusammenarbeit und Entwicklung), 1993, *Länderkonzept Kenia*, Bonn, 23 September 1993.
Deile, Volkmar, 1992, 'Entwicklungspolitik und Menschenrechte', *ai-Info*, May.
De Long, J. and B. Eichengreen, 1992, 'The Marshall Plan: History's Most Successful Structural Adjustment Programme', *CEPR Discussion Paper* No. 634, London.
Deutscher Bundestag, 1982, *Drucksache 9/1344*.
Eichengreen, B. and M. Uzan, 1992, 'The Marshall Plan: Economic Effects and Implications for Eastern Europe and the former USSR', *CEPR Discussion Paper* No. 638, London.
Erdmann, G., 1992, 'Demokratisierung in Afrika und Menschenrechtskonditionalität der Entwicklungshilfe: Neue alte Aufgaben für NRO', *WEED-Arbeitsmaterial 1/92*, Bonn.
Erdmann, G., 1993, 'Menschenrechtskonditionalität in der Entwicklungspolitik. Drei Länderstudien, Kenia, Peru, Sri Lanka, Einführung', *epd Dokumentation*, No. 34, Frankfurt am Main.
Gsänger, H. and P.P. Waller, 1993, *Perspektiven der deutschen Entwicklungszusammenarbeit mit der Republik Kenia*, Berlin, Deutsches Institut für Entwicklungspolitik.
Heinz, W.S., 1989, 'The Federal Republic of Germany: Human Rights and Development', in Forsyth, D. (ed.), *Human Rights and Development*, London.
Heinz, W.S., 1992, 'Deutsche Entwicklungspolitik, Politische Konditionalität und Durchsetzung der Menschenrechte', *epd Dokumentation*, No. 22, Frankfurt am Main.
Holtz, U., 1984, 'Menschenrechte im Bundestag', *Entwicklung und Zusammenarbeit*, No. 3.
Humana, C., 1992, *World Human Rights Guide*, New York and Oxford: Oxford University Press, Third Edition.
Knapp, M., 1990, 'Deutschland und der Marshallplan: Zum Verhältnis zwischen politischer und ökonomischer Stabilisierung in der amerikanischen Deutschlandpolitik nach 1945', in Schröder, H.-J. (ed.), *Marshallplan und westdeutscher Wiederaufstieg, Positionen – Kontroversen*, Stuttgart: Steiner Verlag.
Lancaster, C., 1993, 'Governance and Development: the Views from Washington', *IDS Bulletin*, Vol. 24, No. 1.
Mair, S., 1993, *Kenias Weg in die Mehrparteiendemokratie. Ursachen, Akteure und Interessen*, Ebenhausen: Stiftung Wissenschaft und Politik.
Nelson, J.M. and S.J. Eglinton, 1992, *Encouraging Democracy. What Role for Conditioned Aid?*, Washington, D.C.: Overseas Development Council.
Nuscheler, F., 1992, 'Menschenrechtliche Doppelstandards in der Entwicklungspolitik', in Haungs, P. *et al.* (eds.), *Civitas*, Paderborn.
Robinson, M., 1993a, 'Will Political Conditionality Work?', *IDS Bulletin*, Vol. 24, No. 1.
Robinson, M., 1993b, 'Aid, Democracy and Political Conditionality in Sub-Saharan Africa', *The European Journal of Development Research* (EJDR), Vol. 5, No. 1.
Stucken, R., 1964, *Deutsche Geld- und Kreditpolitik 1914-1963*, Tübingen.
Uvin, P., 1993, ' "Do as I say, Not as I do": The limits of political conditionality', *The European Journal of Development Research* (EJDR), Vol. 5, No. 1.
van de Sand, K. und R. Mohs, 1991, 'Neue politische Kriterien des BMZ', *Entwicklung und Zusammenarbeit*.
Waller, P.P., 1989, 'Hilfe durch Einmischung. Entwicklungshilfe muß politischer werden', *Die Zeit*, No. 47.
Waller, P.P., 1992, 'After East-West Detente: Towards a Human Rights Orientation in North-South Development Cooperation?', *Development*, Vol. 34, No. 1.

Wissenschaftlicher Beirat beim BMZ, 1992, 'Grundsätze für die Entwicklungszusammenarbeit in den 90er Jahren: Notwendige Rahmenbedingungen', *BMZ-Material*, Bonn.

Wissing, T., 1992, 'Die gegenwärtige Diskussion über Kriterien bei der Vergabe staatlicher Entwicklungshilfe' (unpublished thesis), Bonn.

4

Aid and Conditionality: The Case of Dutch-Indonesian Relationships

NICO G. SCHULTE NORDHOLT

The fiercely nationalistic tone which characterised President Suharto's decision of 25 March 1992, to terminate Dutch-Indonesian aid relationships contained echoes of the defiant *'Go to hell with your aid'* with which Sukarno, the flamboyant first President of the Indonesian Republic, broke off relationships with the capitalistic Western world in 1963. However, Sukarno's definition of his position in 1963 was highly emotional and impulsive, while Suharto's 1992 strategy was well-considered and well-timed. Sukarno's nationalistic course contributed to his downfall in 1965. In contrast, Suharto's tug-of-war with the former colonial ruler of Indonesia consolidated both his national and his international position.

Suharto's decision was a painful confrontation of Dutch policy. The respect of human rights as a permanent condition of its foreign policy and development aid since 1979 was attacked without considering the possibility of voluntary termination by a recipient. Initially, therefore, the Dutch response to such an unforeseen event was amazement, bewilderment, and sometimes even indignation. Above all, this case undermined the strong Dutch conviction that a coupling of human rights to development aid is necessary and indeed justifiable. After almost two years there has been no fundamental debate about the tenability of such a political link. Positions concerning this issue were included in the 1994 election programmes of the major political parties, but they were formulated in strikingly vague and general terms.

Dutch policy was modified, however, including immediate action to secure commercial relations with Indonesia. Within two months of Suharto's decision, Mrs van Rooy, the Dutch State-Secretary for International Economic Affairs, left for Jakarta where she was personally received by the President. Dutch exports to Indonesia increased by 70 per cent in the first five months of 1993, while imports increased by 25 per cent during the same period. The salesman has outwitted the parson!

This chapter considers the causes that led to the break between Indonesia and the Netherlands and, more importantly, the consequences for both countries. An analysis is offered of the implications of a foreign policy in which development aid is made conditional on the respect of human rights, taking as its starting point the event which caused the break in aid relationship between Indonesia and the Netherlands: the slaughter by Indonesian troops in Dili, capital of East Timor, on 12 November 1991. The analysis distinguishes three levels: the international and national, which have general relevance, and the individual level. The case of Dili demonstrates the crucial importance of the roles and the mutual relationship between President Suharto and the Dutch Minister for Development Co-operation, Jan Pronk.

Section I briefly describes the most important characteristics of Indonesian political-economic developments under President Suharto, with special reference to the conditions which the international donor community imposed on Indonesia before the Dili massacre of November 1991. Section II includes a survey of discussions on Dutch foreign policy which have been held in the Netherlands since 1979, when development aid was officially made conditional on the respect of human rights. In Section III the Dili case and the reactions this incident provoked in the international community are discussed in relation to factors in Indonesia which eventually led to Suharto's decision of 25 March 1992. And Section IV offers a description and analysis of the consequences of the break in aid relationship between Indonesia and the Netherlands.

I. MAIN POLITICAL-ECONOMIC CHARACTERISTICS OF SUHARTO'S NEW ORDER: MARCH 1966 – NOVEMBER 1991

On 11 March 1966, Major-General Suharto obtained full authorisation from President Sukarno to restore 'peace and order'. In the preceding months a power-vacuum had arisen following an attempted coup which had caused the violent death of six generals. In one of Suharto's careful political-military manoeuvres, he immediately defined Sukarno's written instruction as *SUPER SEMAR*, an acronym for *Surat perintah sebelas Maret* (warrant of 11 March), which, in

Javanese culture, also refers – in a superlative sense – to the God *Semar* from the *wayang*-stories. This symbolic reference was an attempt by Suharto to procure for himself a cultural legitimation for a transfer of power without a constitutional basis. Although at that time his political position was by no means secure, the action had a further symbolic significance. Seventeen years previously, on 1 March 1949, as Lieutenant-Colonel, Suharto's regiment had raised the Indonesian flag for six hours in Yogyakarta, capital of the Republic then occupied by the Dutch. With a great sense of international publicity, especially with respect to the USA, arrangements were made to ensure that foreign journalists could report this surprise attack. This military operation contributed to the Indonesian army claim that, more than the civil diplomats involved, it was responsible for exerting pressure on the Western world (and particularly on the USA) which forced the Dutch to enter into negotiations with the Indonesians. Later the same year, the Netherlands finally recognised Indonesia's sovereignty, which Sukarno and Hatta had proclaimed on 17 August 1945.

Suharto also demonstrated his sense of history and awareness of the symbolic significance of a particular date in his method of announcing his refusal to accept further Dutch aid. During the war of independence, a truce was signed in the mountain village of Linggardjati in West Java. This treaty, agreed to under international pressure and signed by Indonesian civil politicians, was regarded by the military as humiliating. Suharto chose to publicly insult the former colonial power on the very same date 45 years later, apparently still wanting revenge. However, as Section III demonstrates, he acted only after he had ensured ample compensation by other donors for the financial aid he would refuse from the Netherlands.

After Suharto had obtained Sukarno's official warrant to restore 'peace and order' in March 1966, he proceeded gradually but energetically. He declared everything even remotely politically to the left, forbidden. It is now generally estimated that in the following three years, this resulted in the death of 500,000 people. More than 100,000 women and men were imprisoned, of whom 10,000 men were interned in concentration camps on the island of Buru in the Moluccas. The Western world, especially the USA, applauded the anti-communist attitude of the new regime. Consequently, the massive slaughters were considered rather as a bloody *finale* to the social tensions which had arisen during the preceding years, presumably instigated by communist agitators. In 1965, the USA had already sunk deep into the Vietnamese morass and therefore needed support, in return for which a country would be generously rewarded and their actions mildly judged.

131

The Indonesian archipelago is situated between two oceans, linked by two deep-sea channels through which it is possible for nuclear submarines to move undetected by radar. Its geopolitical location proved to be of crucial importance to Western hegemony. In 1975, this very factor was one of the most important arguments for Australia and the USA in sanctioning the annexation of East Timor by Indonesia. This former Portuguese colony, after all, threatened to embark on a communist course – a development which might lead to a second Cuba. After the fall of Saigon, this had be avoided under all circumstances: in those days, the domino theory still had wide-spread support. In addition, the Western world wanted to remain in control of this area because of the discovery of a huge oilfield in the Timor Sea between Australia and Timor in August 1975. The two factors of Indonesia's geopolitical location and its natural resources led the West, from 1975 up to 1989, to systematically ignore or minimise the massacre of 200,000 East Timorese (one-third of the total population of this part of the island!) through wars and famine [*Taylor, 1991*].

In November 1991, a five-minute BBC feature about a brutal shooting at a cemetery in Dili precipitated worldwide indignation jeopardising further financial support for the Indonesian economy and threatening the political future of the President. However, quickly and cunningly Suharto took advantage of the international indignation by blaming certain forces of competition to himself within the army, and emerged victorious from this political disaster having consolidated his position. This raises some fascinating but as yet unanswered questions: who permitted the filming of a military intervention at that particular moment? And how was it possible to fly the film out of the island in order to be broadcast all over the world the very same day?

These questions are considered again in Section III. The Dili massacre had direct implications for the President's ambitions for a sixth term of office. Having completed the first 25 years of economic development, Suharto needed to map out a course for the second long-term development plan and to secure the economic interests of his family empire.

Indonesia's economic achievements under Suharto received international praise and respect. From 1966, he systematically dragged Indonesia out of the economic chaos caused by Sukarno's Guided Democracy and Economy. Suharto achieved this politically by constructing a corporate state based on a new legislation: the New Order brought all professional categories under state control. The government party, GOLKAR, operated with the army, ABRI, acting as a threatening truncheon in the background, and the state ideology,

Pancasila, functioning as a form of intellectual shackles. This combination offered the state sufficient means to exert control effectively and in this way, Suharto was able to ensure the political stability which Western political scientists of developing countries such as Samuel Huntington [*1968*] considered a prerequisite for a stable economic growth. In complete defiance of Western ideologies, the policy denied the people's right to a free press and free organisations, yet such challenges did not inhibit the West in financing Indonesia. Moreover, however nationalistic he may have been, Suharto fully understood that without Western aid he could not resolve Indonesia's economic chaos.

A small group of young economists, educated in the USA and therefore dubbed the 'Berkeley Mafia', received full authorisation from Suharto to initiate an economic development plan. One of their first strategies was to establish an international consortium: the Inter-Governmental Group on Indonesia (IGGI) whose most influential member was the World Bank. However, with a masterful diplomatic insight Indonesia requested the Netherlands as chairman of this consortium, on the grounds of its reputed greater familiarity with their country.

In 1958, following the complete break in diplomatic relations due to the Dutch refusal to recognise Indonesia's sovereign power over West New Guinea/Irian Jaya, this request by the new regime in Jakarta flattered and appeased the Dutch government. Indonesia was motivated by at least two factors: it feared over-dominance by the truly great economic powers, the USA and Japan, still a rising nation at that time; as a smaller European power, the Netherlands was considered an adequate buffer state [*Uddink, 1992*]. In addition, Jakarta, with a keen insight into Dutch relations and interests, anticipated that this position of honour would force the Netherlands into a diplomatic squeeze. As former coloniser, the Dutch would feel obliged to rank Indonesian interests above its own, possibly critical, views or insights. During the 25 years that IGGI has been active, this calculation proved to be more or less correct. With the exception of the period 1973-77, when Jan Pronk first became Minister for Development Co-operation, the Dutch chairmanship of IGGI was regarded without suspicion by Indonesia. This stance changed only after 1989 when geopolitical relationships changed dramatically, the World Bank adopted a more political-economic policy, and the Netherlands threatened to use the EC as a platform for its critical development policy. In 1992, coinciding with the refusal of Dutch aid, IGGI was replaced by a consortium even more neutral: the Consultative Group on Indonesia (CGI), presided over by the World Bank.

Formally, IGGI had been nothing more than a pledging forum: the countries and international organisations involved, on the basis of World Bank analyses, were able to present their intended financial support for the coming budget year. However, during the annual two-day assembly, the Indonesian delegation was the object of frequent criticism in the lobbies, especially in relation to violations of human rights.

There was a significant development in 1976 when the USA elected a new president, Democrat Jimmy Carter, whose foreign policy gave a high priority to human rights. Jan Pronk, then chairman, immediately took the opportunity to intensify the political pressure within IGGI on Indonesia's human rights policy, focusing on the fate of political prisoners on the island of Buru.

As a member of a Left-Centre Cabinet, Pronk had to subscribe to the widely supported Dutch policy of financial aid to the Suharto government. However, as an exponent of the then left wing of a Social-Democrat party, the PVDA, he was directly confronted with a most powerful rank and file that had aligned itself with the slogan '*not a penny for Suharto*'. This movement regarded IGGI as an instrument of capitalist imperialism and it was generally agreed that the Netherlands should withdraw from the consortium or at least resign the chairmanship. In emphasising the critical positions he had adopted as chairman of IGGI, Pronk hoped to meet the political demands of his supporters. He was opposed within the Cabinet by a Centre-Right member of his own party, the Minister for Foreign Affairs, Max van der Stoel. Contrary to his famous, open and highly critical attitude towards the Greek colonels' regime, van der Stoel firmly believed in silent diplomacy with Indonesia, particularly in relation to its violation of human rights.

Against this background, the political debate concerning the primacy of human rights as part of foreign policy or development aid was brought explosively into the open in the Netherlands. Important conclusions can be drawn from P. Baneke's [*1983*] thorough study of this debate in relation to Indonesia, particularly with respect to the outcome of the Dili massacre.

Van der Stoel's attitude (evidently in contrast to his own viewpoint) paradoxically gave Pronk greater political freedom to express himself critically with respect to Jakarta. As long as Pronk presented himself as a critical 'lone wolf' within the Dutch Cabinet, Jakarta believed there was no cause for alarm. A final intervention by Foreign Affairs, *in casu* van der Stoel, was bargained for by Indonesia to sanction their development aid. This calculation proved correct for the government of 1973-1977 but appeared less certain during a possible second period. In both The Hague and Jakarta it was an open secret that Pronk had prepared a policy document arguing strongly for a discontinuance, or at least phasing out, of Dutch aid to Indonesia. Pronk, however, was not included in the 1977 Cabinet and did not re-enter the government until 1989. On resuming his former post, Jakarta was painfully reminded of Pronk's threatening, although unpublished policy document. Moreover, by 1992 it was apparent to the Indonesian government that Pronk's criticism was backed up by Hans van den Broek, then Minister for Foreign Affairs. Consequently, Suharto began to take immediate measures to isolate the Netherlands diplomatically on the one hand, and to secure financial compensation from other sources on the other.

Indonesia's economic and international position was much stronger in 1992, encouraging Suharto to believe he could succeed in such political manoeuvring. Undoubtedly, he would have liked to do the same in 1976, but was forced to accept Pronk's criticism quietly: in the 1970s, the Dutch Minister for Development Co-operation was backed by President Carter, whilst in 1992 the Republican Bush was in power.

Indonesia's economy had grown rapidly and beyond all expectations during the initial phase of the New Order. Apart from substantial IGGI aid (during the First Five Year Plan, 1969-1974, it formed 75 per cent of the Indonesian development budget), this was due mainly to the unforeseen rise in oil prices after OPEC was established in October 1973. In the mid 1970s, however, two factors endangered this continued rapid growth. Firstly, a lack of rainfall led to shortages in the production of rice, threatening an inflationary spiral. In order to prevent this, the Indonesian government resorted to large-scale rice imports, thus increasing their dependence on American food aid. Moreover, Jimmy Carter attached explicit conditions concerning the respect of human rights and the consolidation of democracy. Secondly, Indonesia's dependence on the international aid it received through IGGI was magnified by a gigantic US $10 billion debt of the state company Pertamina [*Robison, 1986*]. In 1975 it suddenly became apparent that this company, under the management of the dynamic director Ibnu Sutowo, could no longer meet the planned repayments. The debt, a non-governmental loan, had increased within a few years. The government's guaranteed annual discharge of this gigantic debt ensured that Indonesia did not lose its credit with IGGI, but the consortium was now able to impose more stringent conditions. This strengthened the control of the Western-orientated technocrats, the so-called 'Berkeley Mafia', over the management of Pertamina. In this way, the World Bank hoped to check Ibnu Sutowo's plans for nationalistic industrialisation using Pertamina funds.

This nationalistic, protection-orientated industrialisation policy was clearly supported by Suharto, whose family had increasing material interests in companies financed by Pertamina funds. Suharto would only submit himself to the will of Western donors whilst strictly necessary: in 1978, with oil prices rising and the Pertamina affair almost forgotten, he appointed Prof Dr Ing Habibie as the new Minister for Research and Technology. Dr Habibie immediately gained a reputation as a strong promoter of the introduction of new advanced technology, with the aim of establishing Indonesia as one of the great industrial powers of South-East Asia by the start of the next century. He was given full control over ten strategic industries, including telecommunication and aviation, and provided with extensive funds which were mostly not included in the official state budget. The appointment of Habibie introduced a second major political-economic trend within the range of action of the New Order: the development of a strong, nationalistic industry based on Indonesian technological expertise. Promoters of this policy are dubbed 'technological nationalists', and their opinion is at right angles to the standpoint of the 'Berkeley Mafia', also known as the 'technocratic globalists' [*Schulte Nordholt, 1991*].

From the First Five Year Plan (1969-1974) onwards, these 'globalists' were able to rely on the support of Western donors organised in IGGI. Their strategy was to exploit Indonesia's comparatively advantageous economic position to improve its position in the world market. A large amount of foreign capital was required in order to exploit its two major assets: a super-abundance of cheap manpower and copious natural resources. The availability of the finance was dependent on favourable circumstances, such as an adequate infrastructure, a stable monetary policy, and, above all, political stability. The government was supposed to meet these demands, a developing role in line with the modernisation theory designed by the World Bank/IGGI during the latter half of the 1960s. US-educated Indonesian economists and important military strategists were familiar with this modernisation theory, so there was no question of conditionality between the World Bank/IGGI and the 'technocratic globalists' in relation to this issue. On the contrary, their ideas were virtually identical.

During the 1960s, central planning of economic growth was commonly regarded as the ultimate policy instrument. Consequently, the role and position of the state were consolidated, especially with respect to its executive bureaucrats. Theorists such as Rostow regarded this as a necessary but merely temporary phenomenon persisting only while a private entrepreneurial class was lacking in Indonesian society. However, the New Order's corporative form of government was based on a state ideology, the *Pancasila*, which does not tolerate opposition: the development model was interpreted in a way that made the state *the sole agent of change*, implying that there would not and should not be any social power which might weaken its position or that of its leaders. This political monopoly, gradually acquired since 1966, enabled the Indonesian government to pursue its economic goals with virtually no external supervision. The most substantial state revenues, such as international aid through IGGI and the ever increasing oil profits, appeared to surge into the Treasury from above. Because these revenues were not derived from tax levying within the Indonesian community, the government was able to imply that it was not accountable to the people for spending the proceeds. IGGI, it is true, supported the Indonesian economy on the condition that the government would legitimate itself through national elections, but in reality this was nothing more than an official expectation. The Indonesian legislation introduced by the New Order, backed if necessary by the army's grip of iron, guaranteed that this international expectation could be amply fulfilled, as illustrated by quinquennial results of the polls.

However, the New Order recognised the need for an adequate social-economic policy aimed at improving the living standards of large social groups, as a prerequisite to its own legitimation within Indonesian society. The government's Second Five Year Plan (1974-1979) introduced the so-called *Instruksi Presiden, INPRES* programmes, financed in part by the World Bank/IGGI and intended to distribute the social-economic growth more equally among the different islands of the vast archipelago. For the greater part, the New Order has succeeded in this. Drake's excellent study [*1989*] gives primary credit to these programmes for the national integration of Indonesia's highly heterogeneous population. Moreover, they contributed to the World Bank calculation in 1990 that the percentage of Indonesians living below the poverty line decreased from 40 per cent in 1979 to 17 per cent in 1987.

The second source of state revenues, oil, was used partly to finance 'political loyalty': special social-economic programmes were offered as a reward to certain strategic social groups or regions, especially during the months preceding national elections. However, the bulk of the income was deployed in the realisation of Habibie's dream: a great technological leap forward. One of the negative side-effects of this form of state expenditure was an alarming growth in the 'high cost economy', with a consequent proportional swelling of corruption.

With the state revenues secured, and actually increased, Suharto was able to silence his critics and gain the political support of the most prominent social groups within the Indonesian community. In addition to the two principal movements of 'technocratic globalists' and the 'technological nationalists', each with a powerful rank and file in the army and among urban intellectuals, Suharto also had widespread support amongst the multitude of small, mostly Islamic, entrepreneurs. Closely related to the latter was a nationalistic movement with sharply defined, populistic rules and values, an inheritance from the Independence Movement which was particularly cherished and supported by sections of the army. Despite their severe criticism of growing corruption and dissipation, these small entrepreneurs hoped to share in Indonesia's economic growth, if not during the Third Five Year Plan, then during the Fourth (1984-1989).

However, from 1983 the world recession finally, and seriously, hit Indonesia, resulting in the abrupt and dramatic fall in oil prices in January 1986 (from US $34/barrel to US $9/barrel in one month), and forcing the New Order to revise its economic policy. During the mid 1980s, Indonesia acted on the view promoted by the World Bank of a 'withdrawal of the State' in favour of 'strengthening market-forces in the development process'. As regular as clockwork, every six months, a new package of policy measures were issued aiming to deregulate the Indonesian economy, a neutral term preferred within Indonesia's strong, nationalistic climate to the politically loaded term 'privatisation'. The 'high cost economy' was to be curtailed by a number of debureaucratisation measures, whilst the central government devolution of many development tasks from central government to lower administrative levels, such as the districts, was announced as 'decentralisation'. The Indonesian press dubbed these three different forms of policy measures *Paket-De*: *de*regulation, *de*-bureaucratisation, and *de*centralisation.

A joint Dutch-Indonesian research project into the backgrounds and consequences of these measures notes that the change of direction in politics and economics was not the result of a confrontation between the international donor community, led by the World Bank, and the Indonesian government. There was, however, an eventual clash between the two contrasting viewpoints on development *within* the New Order, from which the 'technocratic globalists' initially appeared to emerge victorious. Although this was in part due to World Bank/IGGI support for the introduction of restructuring policies, their role could be only indirect. Their emphasis on the importance of deregulation and de-bureaucratisation to economic growth allowed potential private investors from Western countries to contribute untroubled by restrictive measures. Western donors primarily regarded decentralisation measures as a prerequisite of the essential economic and political democratisation process of developing countries, to which priority was given by the World Bank in 1989 [*World Bank, 1989*]. This policy had the direct consequence of undermining the monopolistic position of a few highly influential families.

However, in addition to its Western donors, Indonesia was financially supported by Japan and 'the Four Asian Tigers'. Their support was closely connected both to the economic interests of the 'technological nationalists' and in particular, to the interests of large family concerns. This led to considerable delays in the restructuring of Indonesian economy, tolerated to some extent by the 'globalists', who recognised that abrupt economic changes can cause social chaos.

Indonesia's political-economic situation since 1985 can therefore roughly be summarised thus: the 'technocratic globalists', whose influence correlates closely to the fall or rise of oil prices, are widely and openly supported by the World Bank/IGGI but silently opposed by Asian financiers.

Deregulation and de-bureaucratisation led to major challenges to the comfortable positions and economic interests of the strategic pillars of Suharto's New Order: civil servants/military-cum-entrepreneurs, import and export licensees, mostly moneyed Chinese capitalists were all affected, and, moreover, the group of small, mostly Islamic entrepreneurs were confronted, through the *Paket-De*, with international competition and saw their hopes of personal enrichment vanish into thin air. These measures also caused confusion in the army, the ultimate and central power body of the New Order. Alhough there was acknowledgement by some important groups within the army of the necessity to curtail a 'high cost economy', *Paket-De* directly and indirectly affected the material interests of the military [*Robison, 1988*]. Nonetheless, many of the military were strongly influenced by the arguments of Habibie's 'technological-nationalistic' school.

However, the stability of the New Order was threatened not so much by the clash of viewpoints concerning the direction of Indonesian development (for which a compromise needed only temporisation), but by problems in the implementation process itself. Each package of measures contained many exceptions which, on close inspection, appeared time and time again to have been added in order to secure the economic interests of companies belonging to politically powerful family concerns. These systematic exceptions were a thorn in the side of those actually hit by deregulation measures, who included (military) employers and employees in privatised companies, and the mass of small entrepreneurs. The numerous exemptions also interfered with the promotion of the economic restructuring policy. Moreover, the large family concerns applied many privatisation measures entirely for their own benefit. In contrast to the intended economic democratisation process, the deregulation and de-bureaucratisation policy thus created an even higher concentration of economic power.

Consequently, the latter half of the 1980s witnessed the rise of a broadly organised protest movement, openly supported by some important army officials, including the Minister for Armed Forces, General Benny Murdani. This movement was directed against a continuation of Suharto's term of office: although his political leadership was generally undisputed, the intertwinement of his family's economic interests and those of the state had become unacceptable.

It was within the context of this political-economic arena that Jan Pronk became, in 1989, Dutch Minister for Development Co-operation and Chairman of IGGI for the second time. His policy during the two following years was characterised by ambiguity: praise for the economic achievements of the New Order was combined with criticism of its protectionism and violations of human rights. However, the praise simply endorsed his kindred economic spirits within the group of 'technocratic globalists', which included some fellow students from Rotterdam, pupils of Tinbergen, whilst his criticism associated him with those Indonesians who were against a continuation of Suharto's term of office.

In an early challenge to Pronk in 1990, Suharto threatened to execute four political prisoners who had been waiting the death penalty for 20 years. Acting from a humanitarian standpoint, and without the knowledge of the Minister for Foreign Affairs, Hans van den Broek, Pronk withdrew 27 million guilders of development aid. Van den Broek criticised this decision and referred to the primacy of Foreign Affairs where this policy issue was concerned. Jakarta initially regarded this as confirmation that political relations within the Dutch Cabinet were similar to those during Pronk's first period in office, 1973-1977, when Minister Max van der Stoel kept Jan Pronk's critical attitude in check. However, the four prisoners in question were not executed and, perhaps encouraged by this success, Pronk continued to adopt an openly critical attitude towards political developments in Indonesia. On his biannual visits to Indonesia, in his capacity as chairman of IGGI, and as Dutch Minister for Development Co-operation, Pronk took every opportunity to meet groups and individuals of the opposition in a most ostentatious manner. He also expressed open sympathy with a group of Indonesian dissidents on hunger strike in Amsterdam. During a press conference in Jakarta, in June 1991, he declared that 'without political deregulation measures, economic deregulation would be pointless'. This critical remark, made only a year before Indonesia's national elections in 1992, was interpreted within the political-economic arena of Jakarta, as nothing less than opposition to a continuation of Suharto's term of office. Moreover, President Suharto felt himself personally offended by Pronk's fierce criticism of the way the Indonesian family planning programme was implemented: in general the programme was regarded as very succesful and earned Suharto a UNESCO Award in 1989.

Suharto, meanwhile, through his Minister for Information, Harmoko, ensured that Pronk's attitude and actions were presented as negatively as possible in the Indonesian press. The daily national *Kompas* illustrated that his influence included newspapers not directly controlled by the Indonesian government: it published a photograph of Pronk, dressed in a khaki safari-suit and an Australian bush hat, taken from such an angle that he appeared to be towering over a small and seemingly scared Javanese woman.

Due to his public stance, Pronk became a player in Jakarta's political-economic arena, but in contrast to his great opponent Suharto, he was unable to follow the laws of the game. To his dismay, Pronk's attitude towards Indonesia offered Suharto the opportunity to stigmatise him on 25 March 1992, in front of the whole world, as the prototype of a colonial inspector.

In the weeks following this Indonesian incident, the Dutch political arena took advantage of Pronk's negative image. Pronk's political opponents, the Liberal VVD, but also MPs belonging to the coalition party CDA (Christian-Democrats), tried to place exclusive responsibility on Pronk for the break between the Netherlands and Indonesia. The following shows that in political terms this was not the full story and therefore incorrect.

II. THE DUTCH DEBATE ON CONDITIONALITY OF HUMAN RIGHTS, AID AND FOREIGN POLICY

The parliamentary debate of 6 April 1992, which arose from Suharto's decision to refuse Dutch development aid, resulted in a clash: De Hoop Scheffer, MP of the majority party CDA, demanded, symbolically speaking, the head of Jan Pronk (PVDA), in order to present it as a peace offering to President Suharto. De Hoop Scheffer was supported by Frans Weisglas, representing the largest opposition party, the Conservative VVD.

It was, however, significant that the debate took place in the absent of the regular VVD spokesperson on matters concerning development aid, Erica Terpstra, who had always whole-heartedly supported Pronk's policy concerning human rights in Indonesia. In using a different, antagonistic official representative, VVD took the opportunity to ferment discord between the two coalition parties. A CDA and VVD combined parliamentary majority could force Pronk's resignation. Foreign Minister van den Broek, however, prevented this (and in doing so probably averted a cabinet crisis) by supporting his unfortunate colleague during the debate. He had a moral obligation to do so. He was signatory to the Dutch government's official reaction in January 1992 which openly questioned the results of the official Indonesian investigation into the brutal military action at Dili.

The then Indonesian ambassador, Bintoro Tjokroamidjojo, subsequently revealed that it was precisely the signing of this reaction which had caused serious doubts in Jakarta that van den Broek would be able and willing to neutralise Pronk's critical attitude [*De Volkskrant, 12 June 1993*]. The concluding sentence retained a proviso that made the continuance of aid conditional on Indonesia's proper completion of the judicial process in this matter. Pronk, who had to maintain his critical stance towards the Dili tragedy due to pressure from a majority of Parliament, including CDA and VVD, had added this proviso to the original text written by the Department of Foreign Affairs.

The political decision of CDA and VVD to change their view so drastically between January and April 1992, that is *after* Suharto's decision, was downright opportunistic: while betraying a profound aversion to Pronk, it is irrelevant to the *fundamental* question about the political applicability and tenability of a principle that renders human rights, development aid, and foreign affairs mutually conditional. Two years later, this debate has still not taken place.

During the 1970s, however, this issue was debated in the Dutch

Parliament intensively and thoroughly, resulting in a very progressive memorandum on 'Human Rights in Foreign Policy'. Until 1991, only Canada and Norway had adopted an equally progressive stance in terms of human rights and foreign policy. This memorandum describes human rights, or basic rights, as 'those elementary rights considered as indispensable for the development of the individual'. This description conflicts inherently with the Indonesian *Pancasila*, the state ideology in which the fundamental rights of the individual are given a lower priority than communal rights and collectivism. These so-called collective rights include the socio-economic and cultural. The government, however, determines who belongs to the 'community' and whose 'collective' rights should prevail.

These contrasting perspectives (the individual versus the community, or classic civil rights versus socio-economic rights of the community) actually reflect the discrepancy between systems based on Western capitalism and those which are centrally planned. Since 1989, South-East Asian countries, in particular, no doubt supported by the People's Republic of China, have tried to break away from the grip of the North and its emphasis on individual civil rights within the concept of human rights. During the 1993 International Conference on Human Rights in Vienna, the apparent incompatibility between these different perspectives was resolved. In the newly formulated Declaration on Human Rights, classic civil and socio-economic rights are placed beside cultural rights and regarded as universal, indivisible, interdependent and interrelated.

Partly due to pressure from private human rights organisations, such as Amnesty International and the Dutch Lawyers' Committee for Human Rights (NJCM), the Dutch Ministry of Foreign Affairs appointed in 1983 an Advisory Board for Human Rights, to give advice, sometimes unsolicited, to the Minister. The 1979 memorandum emphasised human rights as an essential part of Dutch foreign policy, but not, however, its predominant aim. This led Foreign Affairs to exclude certain issues, and to inconsistencies in policy due to differing priorities of the various divisions of the Ministry. In addition to this Advisory Board, a special committee was responsible for co-ordinating the human rights policy within a Ministry that included 40 divisions.

The Advisory Board drew up criteria in order to answer the reproach that the Netherlands applied different standards to the conditionality of human rights. In particular among political parties of the left, heated debates centred around the fact that, after the massacre of 15 members of the opposition in December 1982, the Netherlands ceased development aid to the former colony of Surinam; yet it continued to support Indonesia, a country that violated human rights more often and on a much larger scale.

The Social-Democrats (PVDA) had supported the decision of the Centre-Right government to discontinue development aid to Surinam. At this time still in opposition, prominent members were influenced by smaller, political parties to the left and well-informed NGOs, such as the Indonesia Committee, to similarly publicly denounce violations of human rights in Indonesia and to question further development aid.

The government, denying any inconsistencies in its policy, argued that the respective situations in the two countries were incomparable: a development *treaty* between the two governments allowed the Netherlands to exert pressure on Surinam to implement agreed political commitments. Moreover, the extent of the financial help to Surinam, which was far more substantial than the development aid granted to Indonesia, potentially provided greater political leverage as an instrument to correct Surinam's internal policy. Despite chairmanship of the important donor consortium, IGGI, Dutch material inputs contributed only two per cent at most to Indonesia's annual international income, and, according to the Dutch government, the withdrawal of aid would have little effect on Indonesia's economy. It should be remembered, however, that the Indonesian economy was strategically far more valuable and important to the Dutch economy than that of Surinam. It is hardly surprising, then, that Professor Baehr, as a seasoned chairman of the Advisory Board, said that the Netherlands indeed measured by two standards [*Baehr, 1991*].

International criticism against violations of human rights in Indonesia began to make greater impact after INGI, a broad platform of Indonesian and Western NGOs, was founded in 1985. Its aim was to scrutinise the IGGI/World Bank policy with respect to Indonesia. Attracting the most severe criticism was the so-called *transmigration programme*: this was part of the Third Five Year Plan (1984-89) which the Indonesian government, with World Bank support, attempted to provide a better future for five million poor Javanese on the Outer Islands. The coercive nature of this programme resulted in abuse and it was then pilloried by international non-governmental networks, such as INGI, so effectively that even the World Bank was forced to reconsider its involvement.

Another major abuse at this time (the mid 1980s) was the phenomenon of mysterious killings, commonly referred to by the Indonesian acronym *PETRUS, penembak misterius*. A reign of terror was created by the shooting of thousands of criminals, proven or not, with the bodies left by the side of the road. These massacres occured during a period of increased dependency on international aid for the Indonesian economy, due to a fall in oil prices: Government sensitivity to criticism from the donor community was subsequently magnified.

In January 1984, Hans van den Broek of the newly elected Centre-Right cabinet in the Netherlands visited Jakarta for the first time as Minister for Foreign Affairs. To everyone's surprise, he publicly denounced the '*PETRUS* slaughters'. However, the Indonesian government officially denied any direct involvement in this systematical form of extrajudicial crime fighting, maintaining that these killings were merely internal reckonings between gangsters and mobs. In an official memorandum of 1990, denying the existence of systematic violations of human rights in Indonesia, van den Broek referred to his public intervention of 1984 as an example of his commitment to and concern with human rights. Significantly, this memorandum omits all reference to Suharto's claim of full responsibility for the '*PETRUS* slaughters'. His autobiography, published in 1989, reveals that he regarded the killings as imperative to deal with the increasing criminality in Indonesia by what he himself called 'shock therapy' [*Suharto et al., 1989*]. The President's public statement furnishes clear proof of systematic violations of human rights on a large scale for which the Indonesian government carries full responsibility.

It is precisely this issue, since the 1979 memorandum, that had formed the basis of Dutch foreign policy in which violations of human rights are regarded as a political justification for the discontinuance of development aid: during the 1980s, Dutch debates on the nature and extent of human rights violations in Indonesia centred around whether these should be an accusation of 'systematic and large-scale violations of human rights for which the Government is accountable'. Despite the systematic denials of the Ministry of Foreign Affairs, critics, including many parliamentarians (and members of PVDA), remained doubtful.

It is interesting to note the dramatic events in East Timor were virtually ignored within Dutch politics. Attention focused instead on the disastrous fate of Papuans in Irian Jaya (formerly West New Guinea) who had been victimised by the above-mentioned transmigration programmes. Mrs. Eegje Schoo (VVD), as Minister for Development Cooperation, even went to Jakarta on their behalf to make a diplomatic intervention.

The Dutch government shielded themselves behind a neutral stance in the Jakarta-Lisbon conflict over East Timor, ostensibly to meet Portugal's diplomatic request that the Netherlands service its interests in Jakarta following their termination of diplomatic relationships due to the Indonesian annexation of East Timor. Not even Parliament could force the government into a different position. This was due partly to ineffective lobbying by international non-governmental organisations in relation to human rights violations in East Timor: reliable information was very difficult to obtain from Indonesia's firmly closed, 27th Province. Moreover, as John Taylor indicates in his standard work on this 'Forgotten War', until 1989 there was little enthusiasm in the West to publish material about East Timor. With the additional reluctance of Indonesian NGOs to express themselves publicly on this issue, it became very difficult for international lobby networks, such as INGI, to mobilise Dutch politics.

It is possible to detect a slight change in the official stance of the Indonesian government since 1989. Indonesian civil diplomats, especially Ali Alatas, Minister for Foreign Affairs, have tried to find a political solution to the still unresolved conflict in East Timor.

The next section discusses recent developments in East Timor, focusing on the Dili case which led to the diplomatic break between Indonesia and the Netherlands.

III. THE DILI CASE, 12 NOVEMBER 1991, AND ITS AFTERMATH

President Suharto's autobiography opens with an account of the presentation of the FAO prize, received in the presence of a few 'great men', for his merits in the field of Indonesian food production. The autobiography makes it clear that Suharto aspires to equal, if not surpass, the fame of his predecessor, Sukarno. Economic success had already earned Suharto a substantial international reputation, but he realised that he could not hold a candle to his illustrious predecessor as far as international politics were concerned. Sukarno's reputation was due partly to his role as co-organiser of the great Asia-Africa conference in Bandung, 1955, where the so-called Non-Aligned Movement had presented itself upon the world political stage as a middle course between the capitalist Western World and the socialist Eastern Bloc.

Suharto, therefore, made no secret of his wish, towards the end of his presidency, to be chairman of the Non-Aligned Movement. His Minister for Foreign Affairs, Ali Alatas, was unable to realise Suharto's ambition in 1989, largely due to fierce anti-Indonesian campaigns conducted by a few former Portuguese colonies, that violently opposed Suharto's nomination after the annexation of East Timor. In order to stand a reasonable chance of success in 1991, Suharto realised that he must find a political solution to this problem. Ali Alatas was given full authority to achieve this, displeasing certain groups within the army: they feared that an accommodating attitude towards East Timor might stimulate and invigorate other separatist movements in the vast archipelago, including the eastern province of Irian Jaya and in the north-western province of Aceh, thus undermining the political dogma of the Unitary State.

Ali Alatas's attempts to reach a political agreement with Portugal aimed at decreasing the isolation of East Timor and simultaneously demonstrating the wonderful progress the province had made under Indonesian rule. However, to the extreme dismay of civil diplomats in Jakarta, East Timorese youth took a very different view of the consequences of Indonesian interference in East Timor. The opportunity of a visit by the American ambassador and Pope John-Paul to East Timor in 1990 was used to protest against Indonesian rule in the presence of many foreign reporters. This was interpreted by the military authorities as a clear pretext for violent intervention and further reason to oppose the open-door policy of Ali Alatas.

Nevertheless, Ali Alatas had scored some success. His compliant attitude towards Portugal had secured Suharto the coveted chairmanship of the Non-Aligned Movement. Furthermore, he had arranged for a Portuguese parliamentary delegation to pay an official visit to East Timor, paving the way for a political solution. At the last minute, however, this visit was cancelled after military authorities objected to the presence of a Portuguese journalist.

The East Timorese resistance movement, FRETELIN, made full use of the attention of the world press, already in Dili to cover the visit of this delegation, by organising a mass demonstration by East Timorese youth. On the date originally scheduled for the delegation's arrival this took place. Although the demonstration fell short of massive, two East Timorese were killed in a violent confrontation with the notorious Battalion-802 of the Presidential Guard, which had been flown in from Jakarta to maintain order during the expected visit of the Portuguese delegation. These troops were directly under the command of their commander-in-chief, who happened to be Suharto's brother-in-law: the territorial military commander in Dili had no direct authority over them. On November 13, this battalion suddenly left East Timor. One day earlier, a protest march commemorating one of these victims culminated at the cemetery of Santa Cruz. While 3000, mostly young, demonstrators assembled at the cemetery, trucks arrived with military personnel who began to shoot into the crowd without warning. As a short BBC film shows, the demonstrators panicked. According to both independent observers and church sources in Dili, between 150 and 200 people were shot dead.

Alarmed by the international criticism which erupted after the release of the BBC film, the immediate response of the commander-in- chief, General Try Sutrisno, was defensive. He bluntly denied the extent of the blood bath: according to his statement, only 19 people were killed and 91 wounded during the massacre. Moreover, he blamed the demonstrators for the wholesale slaughter, claiming that their aggression provoked the military, who, Sutrisno stated, had acted purely in self-defence. The military staff in Jakarta appeared to have been surprised by these events and seemed not to fully realise the consequences of the release of the BBC film. The army had always previously managed to conceal from the world press its brutal interventions – not only in East Timor, but also in other provinces including Irian Jaya (1983-1984), Tanjung Priok (1984), South-Lampong (1989) and Aceh (1989-1991). The BBC film proved, for the first time, that the army employed brute force to silence demonstrators.

Donor governments could not accept such a defensive reply from the military: criticism from their own public led to demands for further investigations. The 'technocratic globalists' warned Suharto that this time donors might really decide to discontinue financial aid. Even the Japanese Parliament threatened to make financial aid conditional on the results of a further investigation.

Suharto reacted to this critical situation with his usual speed and competence. On the eve of his departure for Mexico and Africa as new Chairman of the Non-Aligned Movement, he authorised an official investigatory committee to make a thorough inquiry into the 12 November events in Dili. In his constitutional capacity as High Commander-in-Chief and acting over the head of the army, this assignment included a specific instruction to determine the exact number of victims. Within one month this committee presented a report which was surprisingly critical by Indonesian standards and that belied the statements of the military commander. Figures were given of 91 people killed and 50 missing, implicitly confirming the larger numbers of victims reported by foreign journalists and in statements by the East Timorese church. Moreover, the local commander was held largely responsible for the violent intervention of the military. Whilst there had been provocation from the demonstrators, the military response had been excessive and consequently, the report admitted, not in accordance with instructions applicable to such situations.

148

On the basis of this investigation, Suharto took, by Indonesian standards, strong measures: two generals were removed from their command and retired; seventeen low-ranked military personnel were prosecuted, although their eventual term of imprisonment was very short. Many East Timorese received more severe sentences for provocation and disturbancing the peace.

Suharto's retirement of the two generals formally responsible for military operations in this region diminished the domestic image of the Military Command; especially that of General Try Sutrisno who had so publicly played down the massacre in Dili.

On closer inspection Suharto appeared to have achieved more than one success in a single blow. He had clearly demonstrated to his most influential opponent, the Catholic general and Minister for Defence Benny Murdani, his supremacy in command as President, with the capacity to determine the careers of others. Moreover, both generals who were removed belonged to the group of confidants of Murdani and the 'Christian Clan' within the army: their punishment allowed Suharto to reassure the Islamic majority in Indonesia that the suspected 'Christianisation' of the Military Staff was not true. Finally, by punishing merely territorial commanders, the Presidential Guard and Suharto's own confidants avoided blame.

The surprisingly critical investigatory report, and the unexpected punitive measures taken against high-ranked officers, also paved the way for Suharto's international comeback, having regained the trust of his most important donors: Japan, the USA, and the World Bank. The removal of the threat to continued financial aid and the possibility of a subsequent economic recession invigorating internal criticism, strengthened Suharto's ambition for a sixth term of office.

A few smaller donors, however, including the Netherlands, and above all international non-governmental organisations such as Amnesty International, maintained that this investigation was not independent: though surprisingly quick and outspoken, certain crucial questions remained unanswered. The identity of the military unit involved in the action was not established, and more importantly, the possible role of Battalion-802 had not been considered, despite widespread rumours within East Timor.

Provocation by demonstrators during the walk between the church and the cemetery did not explain why soldiers, arriving in trucks and themselves not directly provoked, started to shoot at least one hour later and a few kilometres away. The report makes no mention of a great number of corpses which were witnessed being transported away on the same trucks: it merely records about 50 people missing.

Another extraordinary aspect is that the military, who had wide experience in putting their violent scenes out of bounds to the press and their cameras, shot openly at a cornered crowd in front of foreign journalists. The massacre even included an Australian journalist, which was certain to lead to sharp international criticism.

If the report is right in suggesting that provocation and inadequate control were to blame, it is all the more significant that the military made no attempt to hinder relevant news services with one of their usual 'reflex actions'. Expected censorship was forestalled so that a film could be flown out of the country on the same day. This inevitably raises the question as to who would benefit from international criticism. Confronted with these horrible pictures, it was inevitable that the international world would assume a critical attitude towards Indonesia.

As long as a free and independent investigation is not possible, that is under present Indonesian conditions, this question cannot be answered conclusively; despite speculation both in Jakarta and beyond. For the time being there remains but one certainty: President Suharto has taken advantage of the reactions at home and abroad to act quickly and adequately in his own interest.

In the commotion, Suharto even managed to seize the political initiative to shake off the nosy, troublesome 'Colonial Inspector' Jan Pronk. A thorough analysis of the Dutch political process demonstrates that this possibility had never even been considered [*Droogenbroeck, 1993*]. The oversight is typical of the way Dutch foreign policy operated during the preceding years, making development aid conditional on human rights: as a donor, the Dutch Parliament regarded itself as solely responsible for determining development aid; it assigned to the Ministry of Foreign Affairs the political primacy to assess the most important criterion for discontinuation: that is, large-scale violations of human rights. This primacy was once again emphasised by Minister van den Broek in a memorandum in September 1990, commenting explicitly on human rights in Indonesia.

However, the 1979 memorandum had already stated 'violations of human rights may not automatically be followed with a discontinuance of development aid'. In reality, such a sanction would punish precisely those who are victimised by their own government: in denying them necessary aid, they would be penalised twice. For this reason the government agreed that such a decision would be considered only as an 'extreme and exceptional' example. The 1991 policy document, *A World of Difference* (the basis of Minister Pronk's policy for the 1990s) formulated the conditionality of human rights in a more positive and constructive way.

During the period of the Centre-Left cabinet in which both van den Broek (CDA) and Pronk (PVDA) served, Parliament reached a consensus both on the nature and scope of violations of human rights and on the impressive economic success within Indonesia. In practice, discussion centred on development aid to Indonesia and whether to change the nature of the aid relationship.

The new party *Groen-Links* (Green-Left), formed in the 1970s from various smaller groups to the left, had adopted a very critical attitude and pleaded for drastic reduction or even discontinuation of development aid. The Social-Democratic government party PVDA, during Pronk's term of office, had also become more critical and applauded Pronk's decision in 1990 to suspend 27 million guilder donor aid in response to Suharto's threat of the four executions.

During the mid 1980s, concern grew in the smaller Christian parties about the position of Christian minorities in East Indonesia as a consequence of the notorious transmigration programmes. Moreover, the largest government party, the Centre-Christian CDA, participated in the more critical stance toward developments in Indonesia: this was due partly to the alarming information about East Timor, which resurged after 1989 mostly and increasingly through Catholic channels (especially Pax Christi); but there was also a general CDA tendency towards a shifting of development aid to Eastern Europe, on the basis that Indonesia's economic success would create financial space.

Disapproval mounted in the two largest opposition parties, the Left-Liberal D'66 and right-wing-Conservative VVD, generated largely by the combination of human rights violations and environmental degradation in Indonesia. The more critical attitude of both CDA and VVD is explained partly by their traditionally close contact with international commerce: industrialists favour a policy of deregulation rather than the technological-nationalistic policy which protects and reinforces Suharto's family imperium. Until November 1991, Pronk was able to declare in Jakarta that a coupling of economic and political deregulations was necessary, thereby explicitly implying a gradual phasing out of development aid, with the tacit consent of industrialists.

In contrast to his own policy document, *A World of Difference*, in which he pleads for a 'positive conditionality' by representing development aid as a reward for democratisation processes, Pronk's attitude towards Indonesia was consistent with his approach during the 1970s: both implicitly and explicitly he threatened a reduction, if not total withdrawal, of development aid [*Indonesia's Experiences under the New Order: 262 and 263*].

The Minister for Foreign Affairs, in contrast, remained, until November 1991, isolated in his interpretation of Indonesia's violations of human rights as 'in themselves serious, but nevertheless isolated events'.

The breadth of Pronk's parliamentary support became most evident during the visit of a multi-party parliamentary delegation to Indonesia in August 1991, focusing on the notorious provinces of Irian Jaya and Aceh. The delegation unanimously believed that, despite impressive economic achievements, these provinces were subject to a systematic and gross violation of human rights. The abuses were ascribed partly to the way in which both the army and justice had been used as tools to uphold the New Order as a political-economic system. Before Parliament could discuss the critical report which followed this visit, the events in Dili on 12 November produced proof for a suspension or withdrawal of aid to Indonesia.

Pronk forestalled a possibly over-negative parliamentary reaction (this time *after* consultation with Minister van den Broek) by suspending the remaining aid of 27 million guilder to Indonesia for the year 1992. Accepting this critical reaction, Parliament further insisted upon an independent, international investigation arguing that until all the facts of the Dili case come into the open, there could be no discussion on the continuation of development aid.

The Netherlands was not alone in its critical reaction: after the Dili tragedy Denmark and Canada announced an immediate suspension of part of their aid for Indonesia. The American Congress, and even the Japanese Parliament, reinforced demands for a thorough inquiry into the actual cause of events, although neither country specified the nature of such an inquiry.

Suharto's speedy response to this international criticism has already been noted. The unexpectedly critical report of the investigatory committee he set up was accepted by all foreign donor governments. Nevertheless, certain countries insisted upon the visit of a UN representative who could verify the observations of the Indonesian report.

According to the first, non-official reaction of the Dutch government, it considered the results of the Indonesian report as a positive development but still believed an independent investigation conducted by the UN was necessary. The subsequent official government reaction of 20 January 1992 followed its positive remarks on the Indonesian report by announcing that the Netherlands was willing to resume aid. The statement was, however, accompanied by a critical clause: the Netherlands presumed that Indonesia would come to an agreement with the UN Secretary General, but 'if these negotiations do not produce satisfying results, the Netherlands will turn to its European partners to discuss the ensuing consequences'. In hindsight, this proviso was the time bomb which would shortly destroy Dutch-Indonesian aid affairs.

It has been noted already that this proviso instigated by Pronk (in the belief that it reflected the critical attitude of a vast majority in Parliament) but officially signed by the Minister for Foreign Affairs, signified to Indonesia that it could no longer count on van den Broek's intervening, helpful role. Moreover, the reference to European partners implied a far greater threat to the Indonesian economy than just the discontinuation of Dutch aid. The danger was all the more real, because in November 1991 the European Community with Pronk himself acting as chairman had accepted a resolution agreeing to a common line of conduct if a gross violation of human rights were in question.

Recognising the need for time to neutralise the critical reaction of the Netherlands as effectively as possible, Jakarta swiftly announced on 22 January because of 'a few technical problems', a temporary waive of further negotiations about the allocation of new Dutch aid. In the mean time, a diplomatic counter-offensive was developed, aimed at isolating the Netherlands from its fellow donors. Chance would have it that the new Dutch ambassador in Jakarta, van Royen, had not yet presented his letters of accreditation. Jakarta postponed this ceremony while securing the support of its most important donors: the World Bank, the USA and Japan. Unaccredited, van Royen could not, according to diplomatic rules, function officially and was unable to gain access to important, informal information from diplomatic circles. The Indonesian Ministry of Foreign Affairs had, moreover, advised him not to leave the premises of the embassy to avoid risk of increasing the President's annoyance, resulting in further postponement of the ceremony. As long as van Royen was not in office, financial negotiations between Indonesia and the Netherlands could not take place.

The Indonesian Minister for Foreign Affairs, Ali Alatas, used the time to travel around the world. During his visits to Tokyo and Washington, he gained support for the Indonesian plan to replace IGGI with the *Consultative Group on Indonesia, CGI*, under the chairmanship of the World Bank and with the exclusion of the Netherlands. Pronk's attitude appeared to draw insufficient support. Moreover, Tokyo guaranteed a $ 91.3 million grant, compensating for the loss of Dutch aid which was only about 1.7 per cent of the total amount Indonesia received from the international community.

Despite rumours already circulating early February in Jakarta, The Hague was taken unpleasantly by surprise when on 13 February President Suharto flouted diplomatic custom by using van Royen's ceremony publicly to attack the Netherlands. The Dutch attitude was regarded as 'colonial', as illustrated by their persistent interference in Indonesia's interior affairs; while the conditionality linking human rights to economic aid was interpreted as typically 'Western': thus Suharto laid down the law for eight minutes on prime-time TV. The style and formulation of his fierce nationalistic speech was reminiscent of his predecessor Sukarno when accepting the letters of the then American Ambassador Green (by chance a relative of van Royen) in 1963.

Ali Alatas, travelling in Europe, immediately followed up this painful incident by a visit to The Hague. Suharto's aggressive and provocative act reinforced his individual warnings to both van den Broek and Pronk (to whom he spoke separately) against any combined action with their European partners: 'In that case, the President might become even more furious so that he (Ali Alatas, NGSN) could not make himself answerable for the consequences with respect to Dutch economic interests'. The alarm this raised in Dutch industrial circles was reflected in the instruction of Dutch embassies throughout Europe not to provoke President Suharto. The widespread alert carried a single message: Suharto intends to reconsider his relations with the Netherlands. For the very first time, Dutch diplomats realised that The Hague no longer determined the decision-making process: the political process was created and dictated by Jakarta.

Pronk made remarkably little of the concern and commotion expressed by the diplomats: while following Ali Alatas's advice, he nevertheless continued to make preparations for his annual trip to Indonesia as Minister of Development Co-operation. Under pressure from Parliament, in which now only the CDA party (apparently at the instigation of Minister van den Broek) urged for caution, Pronk refused to cancel his visit to Aceh – against strong advice from the embassy in Jakarta. Seen in this light, it is hardly surprising that Pronk was so dumbfounded when Suharto renounced further Dutch aid on 25 March 1992.

Apparently, Pronk had underestimated Suharto's political wit. This can, at least in part, be ascribed to Pronk's character and personality. Widely reputed to be highly intelligent and capable, he confronts problems with an exhaustive analysis. However, this precise quality tends to make him blind and deaf to the advice of others, or at least likely to be selective in choosing his sources. During an extensive radio inter-

view a few months later Pronk reflected on the break between Indonesia and the Netherlands and concluded that his only error was, perhaps, insisting on adding his notorious clause to the government statement in January 1992. Apart from this, he believed he had acted in
conformity with the political demands of a majority in Parliament. He
even cited his good, political, personal, and close relationships with
some Indonesian ministers. The statement indicates a gross underesti-
mation of the character of the presidential cabinet of the New Order,
in which President Suharto has the final say, in all areas, including
that of foreign policy.

Having lost his duel with Suharto, Pronk was stung by those who
had given parliamentary support until 25 March, only to abandon and
attack him afterwards, assigning to him responsibility for the break
between Indonesia and the Netherlands. He was also disappointed in
his partners in ICGI and the EC. Above all, he later revealed personal
grief that his fellow ministers, including members of his own party,
filed to Jakarta to make amends. He has not, however, resigned: on
the contrary, he has fought aggressively and defended himself fiercely
in parliamentary debate to counter the accusations of both the opposition, VVD, and the coalition partner, CDA. His attitude and political
isolation with respect to Indonesia has obstructed an easy solution.
The consequences of this political choice will be discussed in the next
section.

IV. CONSEQUENCES OF THE DECISION OF 25 MARCH 1992

It is important to consider the extent to which the poor and the powerless within Indonesian society were affected by the break in aid relations between the Netherlands and Indonesia. Until there is specific
and evaluative recearch on this matter, no concrete answer can be
given. However, an analysis of the scope and nature of cancelled programmes can give a rough indication of groups which were hit in the
first instance. It is also important to assess the negative influence on
relations between both countries, which, two years after the events,
will be an easier exercise than the first.

After initial uncertainty, it rapidly became clear that Suharto's decision particularly affected bilateral aid: programmes conducted by
the Directorate-General of International Co-operation (D-GIC) of the
Ministry of Foreign Affairs, which were, in other words, financed
from Pronk's budget.

Jakarta stated specifically that by rejecting development aid, trade relations might flourish and result in improved political and cultural relations between both countries. However, his fiercely nationalistic tone induced the Indonesian bureaucracy, more strongly committed to the President's word than to a given law, to ostracise practically everything even associated with the Dutch government. There was initial confusion on both sides as to how Suharto's rejection should be interpreted and the likely consequences.

However, a visit by Indonesia's then Minister of Trade, Siregar, to the Netherlands as a token of reassurance for the private sector, was subsequently returned by the Dutch State-Secretary of Trade, Yvonne van Rooy, and a meeting with Suharto took even place. One year after the events, the private sector on both sides appeared to have profited. The export of Indonesian products increased by 25 per cent, although this may not imply an equal growth in Indonesian-Dutch trade transactions, because the calculation included transit cargo in Rotterdam's harbour intended for Germany. Dutch exports to Indonesia increased by 70 per cent during the same period. Of course, both governments cite this growth as proof of improved mutual relations. However, the proportion in relation to the total of Dutch trade turns out to be very small. Subsequently, Dutch industrial circles are less positive about economic relations with Indonesia, and during Yvonne van Rooy's re-visit to Indonesia, in November 1993, a slight irritation was noticeable when she publicly observed that insufficient economic deregulation had been implemented too slowly [*NRC/Handelsblad, 1993*].

Indonesia's more 'open' attitude towards the Dutch private, commercial sector did not apply to the private non-profit sector, especially NGOs. Jakarta was aware that the most important Dutch NGO donors are subsidised by the budget of the D-GIC through the so-called Co-Financing Programme of Minister Pronk. Initial uncertainty as to whether the activities of this NGO sector would be affected by Suharto's rejection became clear within a few weeks: all Dutch bilateral government and NGO programmes, if co-financed by Pronk's budget, would be stopped on 25 April 1992. Explicit permission for continuance could be given only if the Indonesian government, or other donors, were willing to finance the project in question.

Relations between Dutch NGO donors and Indonesian NGO recipients are determined primarily by capital expenditure and rarely include direct support with Dutch personnel. This allowed most organisations to use the short 'grace period' until 25 April to ensure the remittance of 'surplus capital' for one or two years to avoid cancelling current programmes. In the long run, measures were taken for financial exchange to take place through sister organisations in other countries. In many cases, this new situation was also used as an opportunity to cease ineffective aid donations, although it is difficult to indicate the scope because of the reluctance of the NGO organisations involved to give further information. A simple quantitative assessment of the discontinued projects will not say anything about the negative consequences for the target groups in question if ill-running projects were involved.

In a qualitative sense, on the other hand, the 25 March decision has, in the short run (one to two years) had conclusively negative effects. A clear intention of rejecting development aid for the Suharto government was to harm the more politically critical NGOs in a material sense without the necessity of a direct ban. It should be remembered that most NGOs were organised within the international network of the largely Dutch-financed INGI. Political intimidation of unpatriotic behaviour, interpreted as continued co-operation with the Netherlands, meant certain Indonesian NGOs faced serious opposition by local authorities. In some cases this led to a temporary halt in activities, with a subsequent resumption in a different form.

Suharto's rejection had subsequently greater material consequences for the 111 projects financed directly by D-GIC, which involved roughly US $90 million, than for those funded through Dutch NGO channels which totalled only about US $15 million in 1991.

No more than 36 projects were continued with Indonesian or other donor funds. D-GIC, one year after the event, was unable to provide specific information about the status of many projects; nor was the financial scope known of the projects granted permission to continue [*Wijck, 1993*]. A verbal explanation from an official provides the only basis to indicate the nature of projects that have been cancelled and continued. Those surviving include only one of the 11 projects concerned with rural development; six of the 15 drinking-water and sanitation projects; three of the five projects concerned with women and development, and one of the three health care/family planning projects. The figures indicate that Suharto's rejection has had negative effects on the poor and powerless. As opposed to this, 12 of the 26 projects concerned with transport and communication, while three of the five projects aimed at macro-economic aid, have been continued. To a few consultancy agencies, this offered some solace at least. The area of research and education has been severely affected: 18 of the 24 projects were cancelled, threatening institutional knowledge built up on both sides over the previous two decades. That suggests a danger that the discontinuation of research and educational projects could lead to the disastrous ignorance and lack of mutual understanding that existed during the 1950s and 1960s, when the Irian Jaya question seriously damaged Dutch-Indonesian relations.

During reciprocal visits between the Dutch and Indonesian Ministers of Education and Culture (Minister Fuad Hassan) and of Research and Technology (Minister Habibie) in 1992, new aid programmes were agreed, although at the end of 1993, their financing appeared to be stretched and insufficient. 15 million guilder available for education and research before the break had been reduced to a mere 5 million guilder by 1994. Despite repeated suggestions from many sources, including Indonesian partners, Minister Pronk refused to channel funds to 'third parties', such as to the Dutch Ministry of Education and Culture or private foundations, in order to expand education programmes in Indonesia.

From a macro-economic perspective, however, Suharto's decision did not have any negative results. By taking the initiative, he was able to take the necessary precautions in time. The transformation of IGGI into CGI did not result in a reduction of annual donor aid: on the contrary, in 1992 and 1993 Indonesia exceeded its request, receiving more than US $5 billion.

With the World Bank now formally chairman, Indonesia might appear even more vulnerable to the pressure of the international donor community. However, these international organisations cannot make public statements with a political purport, such as Pronk's 1991 observations about the necessity of political deregulation. Besides, Suharto can resist the indirect pressure of the World Bank, by playing off Japanese and other Asian interest against those of the Western world. This is, for example, apparent in his repeated defiance of the Clinton administration on labour rights by his refusal to grant the unions freedom of organisation.

As Chairman of the Non-Aligned Movement, Suharto appears to believe himself sufficiently prestigious to continue this political game for the time being. However, his strongest cards remain the increasing, economic developments and relative political stability which make the Indonesian market too interesting for Western companies to risk provoking a more powerful, nationalistic course. With this in mind, the echo of the 25 March decision still resounds loudly enough through the capitals of the Western world.

Suharto actually consolidated his domestic position during 1992 and 1993: another GOLKAR electoral victory was achieved, with relatively slight loss despite the clear dissociation of the army from the government party. The army even supported the 'semi-opposition' party PDI in the background. With his power base remaining untouched, in March 1993 he was able to procure a sixth term as president as the only candidate. The politically interesting debate concerned the choice of vice-president. Born in 1921, his possible death in office should be seriously taken into account in considering a potential successor for 1998. A vice-president is the constitutional successor with up to five years to increase and consolidate his power base: political circles in Jakarta had no doubt that Suharto's choice would safeguard his family's rule.

Professor Dr Ing Habibie, the driving force behind the expansion of an indigenous, high technology industry, seemed to be a suitable candidate. It is an open secret that his development model has the political support of the President, whose family has vast commercial interests in the strategic industries which are controlled by Habibie. While the formation of his sixth cabinet in April 1993 indeed illustrates political support for this development strategy [*Bastin et al.*], the vice-presidency was given to the army's Chief of Staff. General Try Sutrisno had been Suharto's personal adjutant for years, so could be counted a member of the inner circle. At the same time, Suharto's selection appears to have aimed at a reconciliation with the army, having offended them during the aftermath of the Dili tragedy by dismissing the two generals on the basis of a critical report written by the official investigatory committee.

However, Suharto's powerful position in the sycophantic political arena of the New Order depended on securing himself against the influence of his potential rivals in the army. This was neutralised by the appointment of a military man as vice-president, with the simultaneous loss to the army of many former positions in the new cabinet. Moreover, in the months succeeding his re-election, Suharto practically transformed the army staff. In doing so, he undermined the power of his only real rival within the army, former General Benny Murdani. Over and above that, Suharto ensured the appointment of a civilian as the new chairman of the government party: his confidant and former Minister of Information, Harmoko. This post is of great strategic importance as a 'kingmaker' in the selection process of a possible successor to Suharto in 1998. Lastly, Suharto arranged the election of three of his children to important administrative positions (including that of treasurer!) in GOLKAR.

Despite all these precautionary measures to maintain political stability, the internal, political-economic situation of the New Order remains turbulent and unpredictable below the surface, leading to renewed public debate on the question of Suharto's succession during the first months of 1994. Publications about his alleged role in the

September 1965 coup are now condoned by certain military figures, and there is open press criticism of the Suharto imperium. Growing labour unrest, manifesting itself in numerous strikes, threatens to undermine Indonesia's international economic relations. It is directly connected with the USA awarding Indonesia the status of 'most favoured trading partner'. In addition, Indonesia's reaction to the Dili tragedy continues to raise international concern and suspicion, even in March 1994. The European Union, under Greek chairmanship, responds to repeated news of human rights violations in East Timor by pressing for a special UN mission to ascertain the facts of the Dili case and its aftermath.

Since 25 March 1992, the Netherlands has had no significant role in this international-political arena. From this perspective, Suharto has succeeded in teaching The Hague a lesson. In relation to Indonesia, Dutch politics operates only through international channels, with no definite public stand. This is all the more significant since the Minister for Foreign Affairs, Hans van den Broek – a supporter of 'silent diplomacy' until forced by Pronk to adopt a different position – became a Commissioner of the European Union in January 1993. He was replaced by Professor Pieter Kooijmans, who was present in Dili on the day of the massacre as a special rapporteur on torture for the UN. Nobody in The Hague doubts his sincerity in relation to human rights and his critical stance on their violation. Nevertheless, he has also opted for a 'low-profile' attitude with respect to Indonesia. Pronk no longer has the political power to attack or change this policy, having lost the ability to secure a parliamentary majority due to the complete change of position made by CDA and VVD after 25 March 1992.

A fundamental debate on matters of human rights within foreign policy has yet to start. Such a debate, however, will be postponed until a newly formed cabinet, based on the national elections of May 1994, will have formulated a new memorandum.

REFERENCES

Baehr, P.R., 1991, 'Het Nederlandse mensenrechtenbeleid' (The Dutch Human Rights Policy], in *Mensenrechten in Indonesië: Perspectieven voor verandering?* (Human Rights in Indonesia: Perspectives for Change?) Den Haag: De Bijstand (Congresverslag INDOC).

Baneke, P., 1983, *Nederland en de Indonesische gevangen: Een studie naar de effectiviteit van Nederlandse bemoeienis met mensenrechten* (The Netherlands and Indonesian Prisoners: A Study on the Effectivity of Dutch Concern with Human Rights), Amsterdam: Wiarda Beckman Stichting (Buitenlandse-politieke Notities 3).

Bastin, J., L. Schmitt and N.G. Schulte Nordholt, 1993, 'Soeharto's zesde kabinet: mogelijkheden voor 'take-off'?' (Suharto's Sixth Cabinet: possibilities for 'take-off'), *Internationale Spectator*, Vol. 47, July/Aug.

Dirkse, J.P., F. Hüsken and M. Rutten, 1993, *Development and Social Welfare: Indonesia's Experiences Under the New Order*, Leiden: KITLV Press.

Drake, C., 1989, *National Integration in Indonesia: Patterns and Policies*, Honolulu: University of Hawaii Press.

Droogenbroeck, R.J.M. van, 1993, *Mensenrechtenbeleid en soevereiniteit; een onderzoek naar de Indonesische weigering van Nederlands ontwikkelingsgeld* (Human Rights Policy and Sovereignty: a Study on the Indonesian Refusal of Dutch Development Aid), unpublished MA Thesis, Enschede: University of Twente.

Huntington, S.P., 1968, *Political Order in Changing Societies*, New Haven: Yale University Press.

NRC/Handelsblad (Daily), 1993, Interview with State-Secretary Y. van Rooy, 23 November.

Robison, R., 1986, *Indonesia: The rise of capital*, Sydney: Allen & Unwin.

Robison, R., 1988, 'Authoritarian States, Capital-owning Classes and the Politics of Newly Industrializing Countries: The Case of Indonesia', *World Politics*, Vol. 41.

Schulte Nordholt, N.G., 1991, *Indonesië* (Indonesia), Amsterdam: KIT-uitgeverij (Landenreeks).

Suharto, Ramadhan K.H. and G. Dwipayana, 1989, *Pikiran, ucapan dan tindakan saya*, (My Thoughts, Words and Deeds), Jakarta: Citra Lamtoro Persada (Dutch translation: *Mijn gedachten, woorden en daden*, by Rookmaker and van der Helm, Franeker: van Wijnen, 1991).

Taylor, J., 1991, *Indonesia's Forgotten War: The Hidden History of East Timor*, London: ZED-Press.

Tjokroamidjojo, B., 1993, 'Eigenlijk zijn we de beste vrienden, maar als gelijken' [Actually, we are the best friends, but as equals], *De Volkskrant* (Daily), 12 June.

Udink, B.J., 1992, 'Armenhulp voor een oud-kolonie' (Charity for a Former Colony), *De Volkskrant* (Daily), 11 April.

Wijck, M.A. van der, 1993, *Indonesië en Nederlandse ontwikkelingshulp. De gevolgen van het verwerpen van Nederlands ontwikkelingsgeld* (Indonesia and Dutch Development Aid. The Consequences of the Refusal of Dutch Development Aid), unpublished paper, Enschede: University of Twente.

World Bank, 1989, *World Development Report 1989*, Oxford: Oxford University Press.

5

Aid and Political Conditionality: The Case of Norway

OLAV STOKKE

I. INTRODUCTION

North-South relations changed dramatically during the 1980s and early 1990s. Foreign aid was increasingly made conditional, its provision being dependent on policy reforms. The major difference in the new conditionality was a massive advance in scope and emphasis. Whereas previously conditions had their primary justification in the effectiveness and efficiency of aid within the limited confines of a project or a programme (in addition to concerns related to the donor's self-interest, involving tied aid), the new generations conditionality entered the domestic political arena of the recipient at a higher level, more directly and with fewer inhibitions. The first generation, on its rails in the late 1970s, was initiated and driven by the International Monetary Fund (IMF) and the World Bank, and was aimed at economic policy reform. The second generation, starting in the late 1980s, aimed at political reform involving both systemic and substantive aspects.

The background to these new advances is outlined elsewhere [*Stokke, this volume*]. The deep-rooted economic crisis evolving in the late 1970s, which crippled the economy of so many Third World countries, triggered first generation conditionality. The main justification was that the recipient governments, in order to obtain aid, had to

Note of acknowledgements. An early draft was presented at a workshop of the EADI Working Group on Aid Policy and Performance in Berlin in mid-September 1993. I am grateful to participants, particularly Oliver Morrissey, Robrecht Renard and Mark Robinson, for their comments. I am indebted to Tore Linné Eriksen, colleague at NUPI, Helge Kjekshus, Special Advisor on human rights in the Ministry of Foreign Affairs and presently a colleague at NUPI, and Nils Vogt, formerly Director-General of NORAD and presently its human rights advisor, for comments on a later draft. Needless to state, I am alone responsible.

put their economy in order. The cure prescribed followed a common pattern which involved, *inter alia*, tightened budgets and devaluation of the currency; however, the main thrust was highly political, involving market liberalisation and a reduced role for the state in the economy. The revolutionary events in Eastern and Central Europe triggered the second generation conditionality; after the disintegration of the Eastern bloc and its core power, major Western powers were searching for a new justification for their development assistance. However, there was also a need to explain why the cure prescribed for the economic crisis (first generation) failed to produce the expected results, particularly in Africa. Much of the blame was placed at the doorsteps of the state; economic policy reforms, in order to work, had to be followed up by administrative and political reforms in terms of good governance, participation, democracy and human rights in the countries concerned.

Most forms of foreign aid represent an interference in the internal affairs of recipient countries – resources and skills transferred from outside tend to strengthen certain interests and weaken others. Nevertheless, the new conditionality represents a novelty not so much in terms of principle as due to its magnitude. For several small and middle powers, it also represents a shift of policy involving basic principles. Interventions of this kind represent a less dramatic change of policy for the major powers whose aid policy has been driven by strategic interests [*Griffin, 1991; Love, 1992; Lancaster, 1993*] and can probably be best analysed within a realist paradigm, than for several small and middle powers whose aid policy has primarily been driven by solidarity concerns and therefore can best be analysed within the paradigm of humane internationalism [*Stokke, 1989a*].

Second generation conditionality involves several agendas. A variety of objectives are pursued: improvements in human-rights performance, involving economic, social, political and civil rights as well as the right to development; improvements in the governing process, involving participation and democracy; and improvements in the administrative system and practice – 'good governance' in the language of the World Bank [*1992*]. Other objectives include the transfer of public spending from military to civilian purposes and a concern for environmental issues.

The pursuit of these objectives by means of aid conditionality implies that the recipient has to commit itself to improvements in order to obtain aid (*ex ante* conditionality) or that future aid is made dependent on past performance (*ex post* conditionality). This definition implies a *denial* of aid to governments that are not meeting certain standards or who demonstrate a negative trend. However, the objectives may also be attained through so-called 'positive conditionality', that is by rewarding – with increased aid – good performance (*ex post*) or by making commitments to do so (*ex ante*). Another means of pursuing the aims is by targeting aid to institutions, groups or activities considered likely to fulfil the objectives set ('positive measures').[1]

The case of Norway is interesting because of the contradictions involved in its policy: On the on hand, it has traditionally maintained a high profile, in its stated policy, with regard to the core issues involved in the conditionality debate (promotion of social justice, human rights, democracy). Poverty alleviation is given prominence among the stated objectives. On the other hand, it has insisted that bilateral aid should be genuinely recipient-oriented, predominantly for utilitarian reasons (of effectiveness and sustainability) but also in order not to interfere in the policy of recipients. This position is not unique; in contrast to major powers whose justification for aid is different and who have traditionally taken a different line with regard to interference, several Western small and middle powers, particularly the so-called like-minded, share the contradiction, although the balance may vary.

In this chapter, the evolving conditionality policy of Norway, as stated and implemented, will be described with particular reference to second generation conditionality. The aid policy of a small country is shaped by domestic interests and values in interaction with recipients; however, in a setting characterised by complex interaction among donors, the policies of other donors are also significant. To what extent was Norwegian aid policy, as stated and implemented, influenced by changes in international environments towards the end of the 1980s, particularly by the new emphasis placed on 'good government' by the Bretton Woods institutions and the main Western powers? Was the response one of resistance or adaptation?

In addressing the task set, the declared policy will be explored with particular reference to the main features of second generation conditionality (objectives and strategies). The analysis will focus on continuity and change, with particular emphasis on trends since the late 1980s, involving both objectives and means to attain these objectives. Some of the established guidelines constitute major manifestations of the conditionality policy. They also serve as indicators: the

---

1. There are several definitions of the concept; all include the stick ('negative conditionality'), some add the carrot ('positive conditionality'), a few even include 'positive measures'. See Stokke [*this volume*], particularly section III and note 8.

strength of particular policy features may, over time, be measured according to the support they carry in the stated policy and the follow-up. This applies, in particular, to the criteria set for the selection of main recipients of bilateral aid (poor countries with a government pursuing a development-oriented policy that includes social justice, and respects human rights). Other guidelines are expressions of a countervailing policy as far as the strategy is concerned and may serve as indicators of the strength of the resistance to the conditionality mechanism over time. As indicated, this applies, in particular, to the guideline prescribing recipient orientation of aid.

The choice of strategy is of crucial importance: to what extent has the conditionality mechanism been involved? This question can be most directly addressed by exploring the way aid has been implemented over time, involving the guidelines referred to. At the stated level, the relative weight attached, by the government and Parliament, to each of the three identified approaches (the stick, the carrot and 'positive measures') will be indicative. In this context the 'positive measures', in particular, constitute an alternative to conditionality; attention will be directed towards possible changes during recent years.

The general problem posed will, accordingly, be approached by addressing the following set of questions:

(i) To what extent do Norwegian aid objectives coincide with those of second generation conditionality? To what extent were they adjusted, given added emphasis or a stronger follow-up during the late 1980s and early 1990s?

(ii) To what extent were the guidelines associated with second generation conditionality strengthened or weakened in the stated policy of the late 1980s and early 1990s? To what extent have they been followed up?

(iii) To what extent were the countervailing guidelines strengthened or weakened in the stated policy of the late 1980s and early 1990s? To what extent were they followed up?

It follows that the emphasis will be on the bilateral aid policy. One policy guideline prescribes that aid allocations should be equally divided between multilateral and bilateral aid; however, during recent years about 60 per cent of total aid has been channelled bilaterally. Although influence on the use of multilateral aid is not totally absent, the implication is that about 40 per cent of Norwegian aid is excluded from conditions set by Norwegian authorities.

Since 1961, Norwegian policy has been formalised in a series of government white papers which in turn have been adopted by Parliament. The most recent was presented to Parliament in May 1992 and considered in the spring of 1993. The motives for providing aid are stated, overall objectives set, strategies discussed and guidelines for implementation elaborated [*Stokke, 1984, 1989b, 1992b,c*]. These documents provide the main source of the *stated* policy on conditionality. They give insights in implemented policy, too. For the implementation, I have relied on a multitude of additional primary and secondary sources (identified in the list of references) and a few interviews with principal aid administrators[2], particulary related to the follow-up of the stated policy in the 1990s.

In Section II, the foundations of the aid policy, the justifications and objectives, will be briefly explored in order to establish whether there is a coincidence between the overall objectives set for Norwegian aid and those of second generation conditionality, with particular reference to changes in emphasis and orientation during the 1980s and early 1990s. The strategies selected for attaining these objectives constitute the real test. In Section III, the criteria for the selection of main recipients of bilateral aid will be identified and the follow-up will be outlined and discussed. In Section IV, the guideline which prescribes that aid should be recipient-oriented, provided in accordance with the priorities set by the authorities at the recipient side and integrated in their plans will be addressed. This policy norm, involving non-interference at the policy level, contradicts conditionality. It also complicates the pursuit of the objectives set by the donor. The way this dilemma has been tackled over time at the level of declared policy will further illuminate the *problématique*. In Section V, the major features of policy evolving in the 1990s will be described in some detail and analysed. Emphasis here will be on the stated policy; however, efforts will be made to assess also the follow-up, thus approaching the main question posed: the impact from outside on Norwegian aid policy during these crucial years. The main features of the policy will be summed up in the concluding Section VI, assessing how the dilemmas involved have been tackled on the levels of rhetoric and implementation.

---

2.   Interviews with Helge Kjekshus, Special Advisor, human rights, Ministry of Foreign Affairs (MFA); Asbjørn Løvbræk, Advisor, human rights, MFA; Olav Myklebust, Ambassador, formerly Director-General, MFA, in charge of bilateral cooperation; and Nils Vogt, formerly Director-General and presently Advisor, human rights, Norwegian Agency for International Development (NORAD).

II. MOTIVES AND OBJECTIVES SET FOR NORWEGIAN AID

Predominantly Altruistic Motives

The stated motives are basically altruistic, with the main emphasis on the moral obligation to help fellow human beings in distress, based on universal brotherhood and solidarity. In addition, political motives have been expressed at a high level of generalisation, mainly centred around international common goods such as peace and stability. As the Labour government stated in 1975 [*Report No. 94*], it was in the best interests of industrial countries to promote better development in the Third World. 'A society burdened with great social and economic inequalities is an unstable and unsafe society, and ... a world where great inequalities exist between the nations is an unsafe world.' Economic self-interest, primarily related to the promotion of exports, has been part of the motives for aid, too, but clearly a secondary one [*Stokke, 1989b:169-72*].

Objectives: Developmental Concerns Come First

The overall objective set for aid, in 1962, was to promote economic, social and cultural development. Ten years later, income distribution was added and a long-term goal sketched [*Report No. 29*]: 'Cooperation not involving direct aid, but rather based on mutual exchanges of goods and services between the countries and increased cultural and political intercourse and co-operation with the people in the partner countries.' In 1984 [*Report No. 36*], the government reaffirmed that

> the overriding goal for the development assistance activities shall also in the future be to assist in creating lasting improvements in the economic, social and political conditions of the people in developing countries. Development assistance shall be used in a way that maximises its development effects for the poor sections of the people. Aid shall in the first place be directed to the poorest developing countries and be provided in a form that creates as little dependence on continued aid as possible.

Two further dimensions were added in 1984, although they may be traced back to previous key documents and policy manifestations: democratic development within nations and liberation from external economic dependence.

Three years later, the government confirmed this overall objective and placed particular emphasis on the following five objectives [*Report No. 34*]: responsibility in the administration of natural resources and the environment; economic growth; improvements in the conditions of the poorest, in particular women; support of social, economic and political human rights; and the promotion of peace between nations and regions [*Stokke, 1989b:173*].

Norwegian aid may be analysed most usefully within the paradigm of humane internationalism [*Stokke, 1989a*]. Its primary justification has been neither strategic interests related to security nor economic gain for Norway; the stated development objectives may, to a large extent, be taken at face value as the main justification. As argued elsewhere [*Stokke, 1989b*], aid has been driven by the same forces that promoted and maintained the welfare state at home; it is anchored in the same political values, particularly cross-border social justice. Other values have been cherished, too; among them the right to independence and self-determination. This value was also built into the aid policy, involving both form and substance, and it is reflected, *inter alia*, in the guideline prescribing recipient-orientation of aid. However, in the context of aid, one policy guideline may contradict another and cherished values may be in conflict with each other, too. This is highlighted in the conditionality *problématique*: thus, social justice is not always best pursued by a strict adherence to the principle of recipient-orientation of aid, given that the real world includes the neo-patrimonial state run by self-seeking elites [*Sørensen, 1993: 15-17*].

Entrenched in the overall objectives set for Norway's development co-operation are the very norms which form the core objectives for political conditionality: namely, the promotion of *social, economic and political human rights and democracy*. There is a high coincidence between the two sets of objectives, although the emphasis on social and economic human rights and social justice is significantly more pronounced in the overall objectives set for Norway's aid. These objectives were self-generated and established years before the second generation conditionality of the late 1980s and early 1990s.

It is the responsibility of the aid administration, particularly the implementing agency (NORAD), to pursue these objectives. The crucial question concerns the ways and means: have they been pursued by setting policy reform on the recipient side as a condition for aid?

III. CRITERIA FOR THE SELECTION OF NEW BILATERAL PARTNERS IN DEVELOPMENT

Between 1970 and 1972, it was decided that Norway's bilateral aid (with the exception of a few specified activities) should be concentrated geographically on a limited number of recipient countries. Long-term development co-operation which covered a broad spectrum of activities was established, based on country programmes with a revolving 4-year planning horizon (programme countries).[3] According to the 1972 criteria [*Report No. 29*], to qualify for inclusion, a country had to be poor (among the LLDCs), with a government committed to pursuing a development-oriented and *socially just policy*.[4] In 1976, Parliament added a new criterion: recipients of Norwegian aid were expected to observe the *human rights* as laid down in the UN Declaration and Convention [*Recommendation No. 192*].

These guidelines interpret and give substance to the overall objectives set for aid. However, in our context the crucial questions are whether the criteria can be interpreted as political conditionality the way this is defined, to what extent they have been used for such a purpose and, if so, to what extent they have been followed up over time.

The guideline prescribing geographical concentration of bilateral aid had as its main rationale to ensure aid effectiveness. This also applies to the criteria for the selection of new programme countries: the effectiveness (in terms of achieving overall objectives) and the sustainability of aid were supposed to increase when channelled through a recipient system whose policies pursued similar objectives. Indirectly, therefore, they strengthened the objectives set in the stated policy, including human rights; these objectives coincided with those of second generation conditionality. They may therefore serve as indicators for analysing how genuine the stated objectives are and how well the implemented policy coincides with the stated.

---

3. The term programme countries is used here although it is a latecomer. 'Partners in development' or 'main partner countries' were the terms in common use; other terms were 'main recipients' and 'priority countries'.
4. In 1987, Parliament included among the objectives the social justice criterion, involving the poorest development countries and target groups within countries: the principle of poverty-oriented aid [*Recommendation No. 186*]. The Committee emphasised the importance of the socio-economic structures of the recipient country and the extent to which the administration pursued a policy geared towards social justice and development. It found, however, that where projects were directed directly towards the target groups, ODA might be provided even to countries which did not qualify as programme countries according to the criteria set.

This criterion obtained broad public support, which has been reflected in the public opinion polls for years [*Stokke, 1989b:note 44*].

Within the confines of Norwegian domestic politics (guiding unilateral domestic decisions) they fit into a conditionality frame. Given this narrow framework, the important questions are the following: to what extent have the criteria been used for this purpose? Given a context of conflicting guidelines, to what extent have they been followed up? To what extent have they influenced the distribution of aid?

It is safe to conclude that these criteria have played only a marginal role. In the stated policy, a 'safety clause' was added: in the event of a system transformation which is considered by Norway to have adversely affected the direction of policy, aid should be oriented towards sectors and activities likely to obtain effects in accordance with the overall objectives set for aid regardless of the policy orientation of the recipient government. Their immediate impact was limited for a variety of reasons. They explicitly applied only to the inclusion of *new* programme countries, and were not supposed to affect those already included. Their scope was therefore limited: only Mozambique and Sri Lanka were included during the following two decades.[5] Moreover, the selection of the two new countries (in 1977) was more based on concerns related to domestic Norwegian politics (balancing 'socialist' Mozambique with 'market-oriented' Sri Lanka) than on an analysis of how well the two political systems scored *vis-à-vis* the criteria set [*Stokke, 1988:49-54*].

Another guideline made the exclusion of existing recipients even more difficult: development co-operation should be based on a *long-term commitment*. In a setting where conflict arises between different guidelines which are not explicitly ranked, the implementation reveals their relative strength. To what extent have the criteria, and the main rationale on which they were based, been followed up?

During the late 1970s and 1980s, efforts were made in Parliament to extend the criteria established for the selection of new programme countries so that they would apply to the existing. In view of the rationale on which they rested this was to be expected. Certain

---

5.   At the end of 1991, the following countries were included: in sub-Saharan Africa, Botswana, Mozambique, Tanzania and Zambia; in Asia, Bangladesh, India, Pakistan and Sri Lanka. In addition, three regions were identified: southern Africa (SADCC), Sahel (including Ethiopia and the Sudan) and Central America (in particular Nicaragua). The 1992 White Paper established some changes: a few additional countries with which development co-operation had been pursued for several years were included (Namibia, Nicaragua, Zimbabwe, with Uganda on the waiting list), while aid to two of the original programme countries, India and Pakistan, was to be phased out by the end of 1995. The planning period was reduced from four to three years. In Parliament, a majority was also in favour of phasing out aid to Botswana after majority rule had been established in South Africa [*Recommendation No. 195, 1993*].

political parties proposed in Parliament to include certain new programme countries and to exclude others on the basis of their past performance. Performance *vis-à-vis* the social justice criterion provoked calls for the removal of certain countries (Kenya and Pakistan). Later, performance with regard to human rights, particularly civil rights, was invoked with reference to grave violations (in particular, Pakistan, Kenya, Mozambique and Sri Lanka). However, in all these cases, governments with varying party bases have resisted the proposals, rebuffing them with large majorities in Parliament [*Stokke, 1988, 1989b, 1991*].

This indicates that the overall objectives were not given a particularly strong emphasis. However, the evidence may be overstated: the indicator, after all, represents a strategy (albeit the main strategy) to attain the objectives and does not necessarily tell the full story. It does convey that the strategy has not been given high priority.

A crucial question in our context, however, is whether the efforts in Parliament to remove some of the programme countries on the basis of poor performance *vis-à-vis* the criteria amount to what has been termed *ex post* conditionality. This would presuppose that the possibility of such a reaction had been communicated to the governments of the programme countries in a direct way. Until the 1990s, such a policy has been under-communicated, if at all.

Within the confines of Norwegian politics, the mechanism might still apply, in a more gradualist way, if performance had an impact on the level of the transfers (a poor performance leading to reduced annual allocations). Even on this criterion, the conclusion is negative: no rapid adjustments have been made as a result of changes of regime on the recipient side which signalled a negative performance *vis-à-vis* the norms established. However, traces of so-called positive conditionality may be found: the special status of Tanzania during the 1970s and 1980s in terms of high and increasing ODA allocations cannot be explained without reference to the confidence which the political system, and President Nyerere in particular, enjoyed on the Norwegian side, particularly in relation to the social justice criterion. This confidence was based not so much on performance as on declared policy intentions, and no *ex ante* conditions were involved.

There is no case where aid relations have been terminated as a result of the recipient government's policy or performance, no matter how poor its record (several Norwegian programme countries have been heavily criticised in the annual reports of Amnesty International). However, there are two instances where aid has been terminated: in the case of Uganda in 1972, and of Kenya in 1990.[6] In neither case was this a response to the recipient governments' policy or performance *vis-à-vis* the norms involved (social justice, human rights, democracy). In the extreme situation created by the terror regime of Idi Amin in Uganda, the decision was based primarily on practical considerations related to the continued implementation of aid, including a concern for the safety of aid personnel.

In the more recent case involving Kenya, the government's human rights record was only indirectly involved: Norway's state-to-state aid to Kenya (but not all aid) was terminated as a result of the Kenyan government's unilateral decision to break off diplomatic relations with Norway in October 1990. The termination was not a response to the government's human rights record; some time before, Norwegian authorities in Kenya had even turned a blind eye to severe violations of human rights.

The crisis was triggered by the arrest, amid accusations of kidnapping outside Kenyan territory, of Koigi wa Wamwere, a Kenyan opposition politician (and author) who was living in Norway where he had been granted political asylum. It led to a storm in Norway's press with renewed calls to cut off aid to the Kenyan regime; in 1987, outspoken and critical media reports induced President Moi to cancel a planned visit to Scandinavia. The presence of the Norwegian ambassador in court at the opening of the trial of Wamwere enraged the Kenyan government: Norway was accused of interference in the internal affairs of Kenya and diplomatic ties were cut.

However, the issue of human rights had been raised at an earlier stage, both by Norwegian media and in Parliament, with demands that state-to-state aid to Kenya should be terminated both because its government's policy failed to contribute to social justice, instead favouring an elite, and because the government violated basic human rights. Wamwere [*1989:160*] had himself nurtured such claims.[7] The human rights situation in Kenya had also become an issue at the

---

6. In two other cases, involving Cuba and Vietnam, development co-operation was terminated in the mid-1970s for political reasons; in the case of Vietnam, human rights violations were invoked. In both, as Hugo Stokke [*1985:19*] has noted, military presence in other countries was part of the reason. However, neither of these countries was included among the programme countries.

7. Wamwere's description of the reactions of Norwegian authorities in the wake of President Moi's cancelled state visit to Norway in 1987, if correct, calls for special attention [*Wamwere, 1989:155ff*]. President Moi had already at this stage threatened to turn down Norwegian aid and break off diplomatic relations. According to Wamwere, this led the aid agency (NORAD) and the Ministry of Development Co-operation to discard him as a consultant and others were advised to do the same if interested in continued support.

official level. It was raised, in general terms, in the annual negotiations with the Kenyan authorities on the country programme in the autumn of 1988. Concern was also expressed in government policy documents[8]; even before diplomatic relations were cut off by Kenya, these concerns had led to minor cuts in aid allocations.[9] In addition, state-to-state aid had been increasingly targeted.[10] Nevertheless, the aid was not channelled so as to bypass the state by providing a larger share through non-governmental organisations. Moreover, the government had no intention of ending aid to Kenya [*Stokke, 1991:49-51*].[11]

During the 1980s, human rights issues were raised in a few instances during the annual dialogue on the country programme and on other occasions involving other governments. There are a few instances where, for these reasons, aid has been frozen at a level already established, marginally reduced and/or redistributed.

---

8.   The government, reporting to Parliament towards the end of 1990 after Kenya had broken diplomatic ties [*Proposition No. 17:5*], maintained that the situation in Kenya had taken a negative turn with regard both to democracy and human rights. 'Norway has pursued an active dialogue with the Kenyan authorities on these issues in connection with the Norwegian development assistance; the Kenyan side has agreed to this.' The deterioration during the first half of 1990 induced the Nordic countries, on Norway's initiative, to present a joint *démarche* to the Kenyan authorities in which concern was expressed. This, in turn, had been followed up by the major donor countries and placed the Kenyan government under diplomatic pressure but [till then, towards the end of 1990] to no avail, according to the government.
9.   In mid-1990, about US$ 7 million (NOK 30 million), committed within the country programme, was frozen and later withdrawn. This was justified by delays in the implementation of agreed plans. In the government's budget proposal for 1991 [*Proposition No. 1*], which was approved 21 September (one month before diplomatic ties were broken), aid to Kenya was set at the new level (a reduction of NOK 30 million – i.e. about 15 per cent – compared with the previous budget). This cut was explicitly justified with reference to the unsettled political situation and a concern for human rights.
10.   This was explicitly stated in Proposition No. 1 [*1990:115*].
11.   In his MA thesis, Magne Lunde explores the Norwegian policy *vis-à-vis* Kenya basing his conclusions primarily on interviews and contributions in the press by the main Norwegian actors [*Lunde, 1991:127-60*]. Although Lunde is critical of the way the Norwegian political authorities tackled the crisis, his data seem to confirm that they did not intend a total termination of aid because of Kenya's human rights record. For example, the massacre which took place in 1988 was overlooked; the human rights situation was raised, probably for the first time, though not as a prominent issue, during the annual negotiations on aid in the autumn of 1988 [*ibid.:132*]. The first direct reaction in financial terms came in mid-1990, justified with implementation delays. However, during the previous years, Norway had targeted its state-to-state aid more strongly than previously. However, alternative channels for the aid – such as NGOs – were not sought, nor did Norway reduce the (nominal) level of aid. Lunde is critical of the way the Norwegian policy was co-ordinated and communicated *vis-à-vis* the Kenyan authorities. This he attributes to the difference in perception of the human rights situation in Kenya between the Norwegian representation in Nairobi and the Ministry of Foreign Affairs in Oslo, weakly operationalised guidelines, and poor diplomatic craftsmanship.

However, justification was seldom explicit; consequently, if conditionality was involved at all, it was in a discreet and tacit form. In a few cases, there were changes in the composition of the aid package: state-to-state programme aid was replaced with targeted aid, and a redistribution resulted in the provision of less aid to the recipient state and more directed through other channels, including NGOs. This was the case with aid to Pakistan and Sri Lanka.

The Sri Lankan case illuminates important characteristics of the policy during this period, in particular the self-imposed restraint of the Norwegian government in following up criteria for the selection of new programme countries. It also illustrates some of the broader dilemmas confronting donors. The civil war *cum* ethnic conflict in Sri Lanka led to gross violations of human rights. This led Norway, in 1983, to renegotiate the country programme; funds previously earmarked as state-to-state assistance were redistributed in the form of humanitarian aid directed towards concerns in the Tamil north. The human rights situation was raised at a political level through the involvement, on the Norwegian side, of the State Secretary of the Ministry of Development Co-operation [*Sæter, 1984:5*].[12]

In April 1985, aid to Sri Lanka was made subject to the following guidelines:

- programmes not directly affected by the conflict were to continue;
- programmes benefiting victims of the conflict, most of whom were Tamils, were to be given increased emphasis;
- commodity aid was to be reduced; and
- no commitments for new activities were to be made.

Later that year an independent report described the human rights situation in Sri Lanka in terms which made continued aid difficult to reconcile with the strategy established in the 1984 White Paper.[13]

---

12. Odd Jostein Sæter, then State Secretary of the Ministry for Development Co-operation, commenting on the general problem involved, namely whether to cut aid relations with countries which violate human rights, points out that the poverty criterion and the human rights criterion may be conflicting and argues for a gradualist approach except in extreme cases: if aid projects are stopped, it is often the suppressed and poor who will suffer [*idem*]. The tolerance threshold with regard to human rights violations differs between the press and some politicians, with a low threshold, and the Ministry of Foreign Affairs, with a high threshold. For a review and discussion after the first human rights yearbook had been published, see Hugo Stokke [*1985:17-20*].
13. Summing up, the report [*Andreassen et al., 1985:195*] found the human rights violations 'grave (including political murder, "disappearances" and torture); they are

174

Two years later, an extensive country study by an independent group, commissioned by the Ministry of Development Co-operation [Sørbø et al., 1987] concluded that the situation in Sri Lanka had deteriorated rather than improved by January 1987, and that the government of Sri Lanka was considered

> (a) to be implicated in causing – by errors of commission as well as omission – the ethnic conflict to have escalated to its present level; (b) to bear considerable responsibility for the brutality with which the conflict is being pursued; and (c) to have so far apparently not been fully committed to negotiation [ibid.:166].

The group discussed options for future aid under different scenarios; it found that although aid was considered unjustified according to human rights criteria, it was recommended that only some components of the aid programme should be terminated immediately and the final decision postponed, subject to future developments in Sri Lanka. Two arguments were put forward in support of this recommendation: the first pointed to the unstable political and military situation, and moves towards a negotiated settlement by the government; and the second emphasised the high quality of the Norwegian aid programme which included assistance to groups directly affected by the armed conflict and which benefited population groups generally given very high priority for Norway's aid (the poor, women and children).

Other instances involve Bangladesh (1986) and Zambia (1991).[14] When the government decided to phase out traditional aid to Pakistan and India and give emphasis to other forms of co-operation (inter alia, commercial co-operation involving mixed credits), the official

---

extensive (thousands are killed, tens of thousands have lost their houses and homes, and the social conditions of hundreds of thousands have drastically deteriorated); they are systematical (targeted against the Tamil minority), and they are long-lasting (more or less continuing since the 1970s). Extensive documentation is also available which shows that central and local authorities have often tolerated the terror, have sometimes assisted in the violations and in several cases directly carried out grave violations of human rights.' The emphases (not added) refer to the general criteria set by the government where a termination of the aid relations might be considered. See also subsequent reports for similar assessments [Skålnes and Egeland, eds., 1986; Andreassen and Eide, eds., 1988; Nowak and Swinehart, eds., 1989].
14. In the case of Zambia, one of the Norwegian programme countries, Norway participated actively in the pressure for economic reforms which was being co-ordinated by the Consultative Group in Paris during 1991, when elections were due. In March, the government of Zambia agreed to reforms and harvested praise among the Group followed by increased aid. In June, however, the Group found that President Kaunda was failing to observe the conditions set. Norway responded actively: a letter signed by the Prime Minister withdrew commitments of additional aid.

justification cited the intention to concentrate aid on Africa. However, the real motives were more mixed, and included issues on the agenda for second generation conditionality.[15]

The main conclusion is that the Norwegian government, by and large, has kept a low profile *vis-à-vis* the governments of programme countries on these issues. Based on policy implementation until the early 1990s, it may be concluded that the guideline prescribing long-term aid relations has been predominant *vis-à-vis* criteria for the selection of programme countries. In its general rhetoric, in contrast, the profile has been high. This conclusion is not confined to issues involving democracy and other political and civil human rights: it applies to the social justice criterion as well [*Stokke, 1989b:194-96*]. In 1993, Parliament reconfirmed the criteria and gave them added emphasis: if one or more of the preconditions changed, it might be necessary for Norway to terminate co-operation [*Recommendation No. 195:43*].[16]

It remains to be seen how this rhetoric will be followed up in the 1990s. In the meantime, their importance has been reduced by another trend: the country programmes have increasingly been given less weight in terms of their relative share of bilateral aid; aid is increasingly being provided within regional frameworks.

---

15. Pakistan has never been a major recipient of Norwegian bilateral aid; it was included among the programme countries above all to balance (politically in the region) the inclusion of India where Norwegian bilateral development co-operation was established in the early 1950s. Criticism of continued aid to Pakistan based on its poor record on the criteria relating to social justice, human rights and democracy, mounted during the 1980s, and led to government adjustments to the aid package, moving away from programme aid towards targeted aid. However, the role of Pakistan as host country for Afghan refugees made it difficult for the government to terminate its status as a programme country. In the late 1980s this changed. Terminating India's special status became more difficult, particularly because the then Minister of Development Co-operation, Tom Vraalsen, had offered, in a newspaper interview, an additional explanations to the official one: namely India's position as a nuclear power and its excessive military spending. These arguments were not unfamiliar; right-wing MPs have used them in their argument for discontinuing aid to India.

16. Parliament noted that the guideline prescribing recipient responsibility made it difficult to provide meaningful aid if the priorities of the recipient country itself were quite different from those governing Norway's aid. What makes this emphasis particularly interesting is the extra snap delivered by the Conservatives [*Recommendation No. 195:44*]: the criteria had been there for years, but had not been followed up. Norway should make aid increasingly dependent on requirements to be met by the recipients in order to make it work according to its intentions: 'questions concerning distribution, military expenditures, a development-oriented policy, the determination to develop according to the principles of sustainable development, over-expenditure of public funds, limitations in public interference in the market and development of democracy and participation are important issues for dialogue with the recipient countries. How such demands should be put, and what consequences lack of agreement would have, should be clarified.'

IV. RECIPIENT ORIENTATION OF AID

A second guideline, with a direct bearing on the conditionality issue, was adopted in 1972 and prescribes that Norwegian aid should be based on the priorities and development plans of the recipient government. This guideline has been repeatedly reaffirmed – and was given prominence in Norwegian aid policy many years after others had abandoned it.[17] The implication, as interpreted in the 1970s and early 1980s, was that the initiative should rest with the authorities on the recipient side; the increasing decentralisation of the Norwegian aid administration, strengthening the mandate and capacity of the NORAD offices in the programme countries, which took place at that stage, may be interpreted in the same vein. Until the early 1980s, Norwegian aid authorities never interfered in the way programme countries used their own incomes.

This guideline represents, for obvious reasons, a stumbling block for a donor government determined to press for objectives set for the aid, except in so far as they correspond with the objectives and priorities of the recipient government. The criteria for the selection of partners in development were established in order to avoid such conflicts; in real life, this is not easy to attain, particularly when the countries are chosen first and the criteria for selection set afterwards. The way the guideline has been implemented therefore serves as a good parameter for assessing the balance struck by the government in relation to the dilemmas involved, with particular reference to aid conditionality.

Modifications in the mid-1980s: The Social Justice Imperative

The conflict was brought into the open in 1984, and is reflected in the modifications included in the 1984 White Paper on aid [*Report No. 36*] aimed at overcoming the dilemma: reaffirming that aid should be recipient-oriented, it added that objectives and priorities set for Norway's aid should be given equal weight to those of the recipient countries; agreements should be reached by continuous and genuine dialogue and negotiations. Norway's aid was not to be provided

---

17. In 1984, Gus Edgren, Assistant Director-General of SIDA and later State Secretary (Deputy Minister) for Development Co-operation in the Swedish Ministry of Foreign Affairs, referred to the first half of the 1970s as the 'flower-power-period' of Swedish aid, with particular reference to the strict implementation of the principle of recipient-oriented aid. Authorities on the recipient side who were experienced in dealing with donor agencies on aid issues, simply did not believe that this position was more than rhetorical – time was needed to convince them that it was intended seriously, according to Edgren [*1984*].

automatically in accordance with the preferences and plans of the recipient side; in certain situations, Norway might offer assistance outside the country programme in fields which were not given priority by the recipient government. NGOs were considered a useful channel for this type of aid. Environmental issues and aid oriented towards women were given as examples of appropriate areas.

In 1987, Parliament agreed to the modification proposed by the government. The justification given by Parliament's Committee on Foreign Affairs [*Recommendation No. 186*] illustrates the inherent dilemma. According to the Committee, some of the assumptions on which the guideline prescribing recipient-oriented aid was based proved unreliable, including the most basic: namely, that the governments of the main recipient countries pursue development-oriented policies, aimed at social justice. In addition, the capacity and competence of the poorest countries to formulate plans and priorities – and to follow them up – were weakly developed. Donors might therefore be faced with requests for aid that were not feasible according to the criteria established for their ODA. Moreover, structural aspects of the aid relationship had a negative impact: the negotiation partner was usually the Ministry of Finance or Planning, which could be expected to give higher priority to concerns related to the country's external economic relations than to the needs of its poor and neglected groups. The guideline, therefore, should not hinder Norwegian authorities from championing the interests of weak groups in consultations concerning aid [*ibid.:31*]:

> The need for development assistance as far as ethnic minorities, women, peasants in the periphery, family planning, protection of the environment and ensuring human rights for minorities are concerned, may, as experienced, easily be neglected and should deliberately be given priority from the donor side in the consultations.[18]

---

18. These formulations give the reasons why the doctrine was modified. The Committee also circumscribed the modification [*ibid.:31*]: it stated explicitly that it should not be implemented with the purpose of promoting the donor country's political and economic interests. The Committee also voiced concern about the recent trend of the Norwegian aid administration in circumventing the usual national and local administrations on the recipient side by running projects directly through administrative systems (staffed by Norwegians) set up for the specific task under the pretext of effectiveness and the need to meet established time schedules. According to the Committee, Norway's future aid should be provided more consistently according to a long-term perspective and should be instrumental in developing the capacity of the recipients themselves to implement and maintain development projects.

The balance, at the level of declared policy, clearly represents a greater willingness to intervene directly, albeit outside the country programme and with extra resources. However, the new formula indicated a strong will to press for objectives which were given high priority by the Norwegian authorities, with signal effects also for those in charge of the country programmes, thereby weakening the guideline as previously interpreted. This, in turn, affected both the bilateral dialogue and the dialogue – mainly within the consultative groups – in international fora, where macro-economic issues, press freedom and governance entered the agenda in the mid-1980s, along with calls for greater insight. From the late 1980s the discussion extended to include the concern for human rights. In cases where distributional performance was particularly poor, criticism of those aspects too was sounded in negotiations on the country programmes.

Twin concerns of 1992: Recipient Orientation Combined with Recipient Responsibility

A further advance, at the level of *declared* policy, was initiated by the aid agency: in 1990, NORAD made an effort to operationalise the objectives and guidelines set for Norwegian aid [*NORAD, 1990*]. The outcome largely reconfirmed the pre-1984 principle of recipient orientation, which was further elaborated and extended: a new concept, *recipient responsibility*, was formulated. In a slightly modified form this concept, and the rationale on which it was based, was elevated to government policy in the 1992 White Paper [*Report No. 51*]. The main modality proposed was a mutually agreed and binding *development contract* between donor and recipient.

The justification provided for the *recipient orientation* of aid is simple [*ibid.:219-20*]. It is based on a *normative* stance: every country is responsible for its own development. 'Aid neither can nor should replace a country's policy; the role of aid is to support the recipient country's own development efforts. It is not the task of Norwegian aid to repair or counteract a country's own priorities.' It follows that in those cases where the authorities of the recipient country pursue a policy which runs contrary to major objectives set for Norwegian aid, development co-operation has to be reassessed. However, the White Paper prescribed that reaction should be determined on a case-to-case basis.

Since the early 1970s, the justification has included a *utilitarian* stance: aid should be based on the development plans and priorities of the recipient countries. This is considered a prerequisite if aid is to have lasting effects and for its role in promoting self-help. Without such an integration, the activities are likely to stop as soon as foreign aid is terminated. In 1992, the government added that another important function of recipient orientation was to avoid alienating recipients on issues affecting their own living conditions and development; this applies to central and local authorities as well as to the more direct beneficiaries.

In 1992, an *international law* justification was made explicit: the guideline reflects a wish to respect the sovereignty of other countries and a recognition of their responsibility to form their own policy. It also represents a recognition of the fact that a recipient country's choice of policy, its culture and values constitute framework conditions that have decisive impact on development activities.

However, the dilemma which a few years earlier had led to the modification of the guideline prescribing recipient orientation of aid had not disappeared into thin air. The resolution out offered in the 1992 White Paper was the supplementary guideline of *recipient responsibility*. The two guidelines were interlinked. Although the justification for the first may be considered in its own right, in a policy context it rests on the guideline of recipient responsibility; this also applies to the second.

The justifications given for the guideline prescribing recipient responsibility are therefore significant. Based on those given for the recipient orientation, with regard both to the normative and utilitarian aspects, the emphasis is on the latter: the prime concern is to address the dilemma at the level of aid implementation, with particular reference to the 'solutions' sought increasingly by aid agencies in the 1980s and early 1990s, particularly *vis-à-vis* poor, aid-dependent countries.

Two interdependent dilemmas can be identified. First, the administrative systems in most of the programme countries, particularly those most dependent on aid, were weakened as a result of years of severe economic crisis. Their capacity to plan, implement and follow-up development activities was reduced; at the same time they were confronted with the task of integrating in their plans, implementation and follow-up offers of assistance from a wide range of bilateral and multilateral aid agencies, all with specific objectives, guidelines and conditions attached, which added to their 'normal' burdens. Second, confronted with this reality, the aid agencies, who were exposed in the 1980s to increased domestic pressures to show results [*Stokke, 1992a*], often established their own parallel administrative systems to plan, implement and survey aid in order to ensure outcomes which corresponded with their own objectives and which were carried out within the time schedule set. Although, as a result, the immediate objectives were met, this practice led the authorities on the recipient side to perceive aid activities as not their own concern and responsibility; this left the aid agencies with an additional responsibility to follow up, which in turn resulted in accelerating aid dependency even with regard to planning and implementation.

The combined guidelines of recipient orientation of aid and recipient responsibility were perceived as a way out of the dilemma. The policy and priorities of the recipient country were seen as framework conditions of greatest importance for aid. In terms of direct state-to-state co-operation on aid[19], dialogue on overall policy and priorities between donor and recipient was thus of great importance. Donors had to take the consequences of the conclusions.[20] The government stated its intention to place greater emphasis on the general policy orientation of the recipient governments when assessing the amount and direction of future aid. Implementing the guideline of recipient responsibility, therefore, affects both policy dialogue with the recipient country and the actual form and implementation of aid.

Following up the policy guideline does not, however, take place in a political vacuum. In practice many other considerations will influence the decision on how to react. The guideline also plays down the separate responsibility of the donor for the outcome. This responsibility, in turn, makes a strict implementation both difficult and uncertain [*Stokke, 1991*].

---

19. The guideline was not confined to state-to-state aid relations. NGOs should also plan to transfer the implementation of their activities to local partners. The NGOs also had a responsibility to ensure that any of their activities financed by Norway's ODA was in line with the development strategy of the recipient country [*Report No. 51:223*].

20. The consequences are fairly similar to those already indicated, but stated anew [*ibid.:221*]: 'Aid aimed at long-term improvements for the people in the recipient country presupposes that the recipient country itself actively contributes in creating favourable conditions for economic growth, and that it has a fair policy of distribution. In a situation where the recipient country follows a policy that runs contrary to the overall objectives set for Norwegian aid for a development-oriented policy, a fair social distribution or respect of human rights, and shows no political will to change, then development assistance channelled through the authorities of the recipient country may work contrary to its purpose. Continued economic aid through the authorities may hinder a change of policy in a more development-oriented direction and delay important political and democratic reforms.'

V. A POLICY TO PROMOTE GOOD GOVERNMENT: CONTENT, STRATEGY, MODALITIES AND IMPLEMENTATION

The 1992 government White Paper covered a wide area; this section will discuss in greater detail aspects relating to the second generation conditionality agenda in order to explore continuity and change. Some aspects were new; others had been included at an earlier stage. This includes the human rights issue, first placed firmly on the agenda in the 1984 White Paper [*Report No. 36:117-19*], where a strategy was outlined for the pursuit of human rights by way of aid.[21]

The Content: Reflecting the International Agenda

The government explicitly related the substance of its policy aimed at good government to the discussion of 'good governance' taking place in the United Nations and the World Bank [*Report No. 51:221-24*]. The various elements of the concept were elaborated upon: these include a responsible and transparent administration, predictable government guided by the rules of law, respect for human rights and room for opposition, and a government that was responsible in elections for its policy *vis-à-vis* the governed.

The policy did not, according to the White Paper, aim at introducing democracy of the kind known in the West; each culture had to find for itself the most appropriate form of government. However, some general requirements of effective government, considered of great importance for a positive development process and an effective development co-operation, might still apply. The requirements which were listed may shed additional light on important aspects of the policy:

(1) *Transparency* in decision-making processes is considered necessary in order to allow citizens to criticise the way resources are utilised; transparency is also necessary to give donors a chance to assess whether aid has been used effectively, and not led to a reallocation of the country's own resources for purposes – such as military expenditure – which are less conducive to development. The main concern is that aid should be used effectively for its agreed purposes.

(2) The relative proportion of *military expenditure* in the budget is considered a relevant theme both in the international development

---

21. The presentation and discussion in this section is based on the 1992 White Paper. These issues have been discussed within the OECD setting since the late 1980s [*Stokke, this volume*] and Norwegian policies have been influenced through this source, too. Norway has accepted the OECD guidelines [*OECD, 1992,1993*].

dialogue and when Norwegian aid is to be distributed. It is, however, acknowledged that it might be difficult to arrive at an internationally agreed level for such expenditure that is universally applicable, regardless of the security context of individual countries.

(3) *Predictable government* according to the rule of law is seen as an important precondition for attracting investment, and likely to have an impact on the effectiveness of aid. This should be incorporated into the international development dialogue concerning a rational use of resources for development purposes.

(4) Human rights are considered norms that are internationally accepted by all members of the United Nations. Respect for basic human rights is considered a precondition for the attainment of the overall objectives set for Norwegian aid. In giving either state-to-state aid or multilateral aid, donors have to relate to the authorities of the recipient country. The crucial question, therefore, is whether these authorities pursue a policy that corresponds to the preferences of the people. When assessing the level and orientation of state-to-state aid, the government will place emphasis on whether the recipient country is *developing in a democratic direction and showing respect for human rights.*[22]

The Strategy: Emphasis on the Multilateral Approach

A dual *strategy* is identified: First, the government will pursue 'good government' objectives in the *bilateral dialogue* with the programme countries (on an annual basis, in relation to a revolving three-year country programme). Second, and receiving most emphasis, an *international dialogue* on these issues is anticipated. It is acknowledged that if the donors pursue individually their particular and possibly contradictory demands and conditions, the situation is likely to become intolerable for the recipients. Active participation in appropriate international fora is seen as the most constructive approach. The Consultative Group of donors and recipients led by the World Bank and the Global Coalition for Africa were identified as examples.

The 1992 White Paper formalised a policy change that, at the level of implemented policy, was under way in the late 1980s, with particular reference to the policy *vis-à-vis* Tanzania, for years the largest recipient of bilateral Norwegian aid. Confronted with IMF/World Bank

---

22. These concerns are reflected in the joint communiqué from the meeting of the Nordic Ministers of Development Co-operation, Oslo, 9-10 November 1992. The Nordic countries supported the democratisation process through development co-operation and posed explicit demands to their partners in this regard: 'in countries where the democratisation process is not progressing, the willingness of donors to provide aid will be influenced' [*Report No. 9, 1993:115-16*].

demands of economic policy reform (structural adjustment), the Tanzanian government had been able, to some extent, to play on the unconditional support from the Nordic countries. In the second half of the 1980s, their governments, including Norway, fell in line.

The change of policy *vis-à-vis* Tanzania related to first generation conditionality. The strategies outlined in the 1992 White Paper involved both the first and second generation. A core feature in the policy change is the attitude to intervention in the domestic policy of a partner country. The attitude towards international co-ordination may therefore serve as another indicator of continuity and change as far as the stated policy is concerned. In the 1992 White Paper, international co-ordination, and a joint stand on internationally agreed policies, was established as a norm [*ibid.:44,49,56,197*].[23] The 1984 White Paper, in contrast, despite abandoning the 1972 position of non-interference in the *policy* of recipient countries, demonstrated reluctance towards the demands for increased donor co-ordination of aid which came, in particular, from the OECD's Development Assistance Committee, suggesting dialogue and conditionality as instruments to obtain changes in the economic policy of developing countries. Although in favour of a dialogue on the policies within those *sectors* in which individual donors concentrated their aid, Norway was critical of a dialogue that involved conditions affecting the *major lines* of the recipient country's economic and social policy [*Report No. 36:39*].[24]

The 1992 White Paper therefore represents, at the level of stated policy, a substantial change in degree, with reference to objectives associated with both first and second generation conditionality. There was little recognition of the *problématique* which related to consistency of objectives between the first and second generation, involving

---

23. It is stated [*ibid.:56*] that the government would work hard to obtain acceptance of Norwegian policy positions on the multilateral organisations' aid policy and performance – this also applied to the IMF/World Bank structural adjustment programmes (which had generated a somewhat critical government response, in particular regarding their social profile). However, it was considered important that agreements in international fora were followed up in Norway's bilateral aid relations.

24. The 1984 White Paper [*Report No. 36:39-40*] presented arguments for and against co-ordination and conditionality. Among the arguments *against* were the concerns both for the sovereignty of the recipient country and for the loss of freedom to manoeuvre on the part of the donor. For Norway, 'an important problematic is that co-ordination of aid may easily be dominated by the large, bilateral aid donors, which often pursue an aid policy which differs from the Norwegian one. There may also exist more than one opinion about some of the prescriptions of the large multilateral organisations for some recipient countries.' These are vague formulations, perhaps, but the conclusion was more clear: 'Norwegian development co-operation will first of all pursue the objectives and guidelines established for Norwegian aid.'

both social justice and democracy [*Stokke, this volume*]. The dilemma was, however, addressed indirectly: the answer seems to be nothing less than reform (driven from inside the organisation) of the World Bank structural adjustment programmes with respect to their social effects [*Report No. 51:115,197-8*]![25]

In the stated policy, emphasis has always been placed on *supportive* actions. The 1984 White Paper [*Report No. 36:117-19*], addressing the relationship between development and human rights, with particular reference to political and civil rights and the promotion of democracy,[26] stressed the importance of avoiding an unacceptable form of intervention in the political life of a country. The aid administration should, however, be prepared to supply special aid to ensure the democratic process in countries which asked for this kind of assistance. The form of aid should vary according to the countries and regions in question: in southern Africa, the best contribution would be humanitarian aid to victims of South Africa's apartheid policy and political and material support of the liberation movements; in Central America the answer would be to support the current democratisation process. The strategy included strengthening civil society in the countries concerned: associations of jurists, churches, trade unions and humanitarian organisations should be supported in addition to local initiatives to promote internationally accepted human rights through information, education and research.

The strategy prescribed in 1984 was to use development assistance for specific purposes that could ensure human rights; aid should not be perceived as an instrument for 'rewarding' some governments and 'punishing' others. Human-rights objectives should be pursued primarily through co-operation, taking, as the point of departure, the social and cultural conditions pertaining in each country. The government found, however, that in certain contexts the question of a redistribution, reduction or even the termination of aid might be raised:

---

25. Helge Kjekshus [*1992*], noting that part of Norwegian aid since 1984-85 had been aligned with the IMF/World Bank strategies and conditionalities, maintains that Norway 'has (in close collaboration with other Nordic states) exercised critical and constructive influence vis-a-vis these institutions. In particular, attention has been called to the negative socio-political consequences that invariably seem to have followed from harsh adjustment conditions and to what seems to be undue political interference caused through the adjustment conditions. While agreeing in principle that adjustments are necessary, our attitude has been critical to form and content of the programmes.'

26. It was emphasised that the international convention on economic, social and cultural rights and the international convention on civil and political rights were of equal importance and that a mutual dependency existed between the rights embedded in the two conventions.

when the responsible authorities of a country assist in, tolerate or directly administer violations of human rights; when these violations are systematic and lasting and the authorities do not make efforts to prevent and prosecute those responsible for the violations; and when the violations are gross and extensive [*ibid.:118*].

In this respect, there is a high degree of continuity in the stated policy between 1984 and 1992. In the 1992 White Paper, the government stressed that the greater emphasis on national framework conditions and the development policy of the recipient governments did not imply willingness to use aid as a lever in order to influence the policy of poor countries. Experience shows that little of positive value emerges from enforced demands. However, it was considered an obligation to assess continuously whether the conditions for effective aid prevail. The assessment includes both overall policy issues and more particular preconditions for aid within specific areas. Redistribution, a possible reduction or termination of aid channelled through the authorities of a recipient country, might be considered when a change takes place in important preconditions. Humanitarian aid or aid channelled through NGOs might then appear as alternatives to direct state-to-state aid [*Report No. 51, 1992:222*]. Conditionality, both in terms of denial and reward, was explicitly part of the strategy.[27]

The Modality: Dialogue and a Jointly Agreed and Binding Development Contract

The main modality proposed was a mutually agreed and binding *development contract* between the donor and recipient governments. The concept was first proposed by Thorvald Stoltenberg, then Norway's Minister of Foreign Affairs, at the 25th Anniversary of the OECD Development Centre [*Stoltenberg, 1989*]. It was further explored in a paper presented at a meeting of the North-South Round Table in Ottawa two years later, initiated by the subsequent Minister of Foreign Affairs, Tom Vraalsen, who was also one of the authors [*Ofstad et al., 1991*]. It found its way into the NORAD strategy for the 1990s [*NORAD, 1990*] and the 1992 White Paper.

---

27. According to the White Paper [*ibid.:214-15*], the emphasis was on positive measures in support of democracy and human rights by way of bilateral and multi-lateral aid. However, a positive development in a country might lead to increased aid and a negative development might get the opposite effect. In 1993, Parliament agreed: a positive development *vis-à-vis* democracy and human rights might open up for increased aid while a negative trend would result in reduced state-to-state aid: it may be redirected, reduced or terminated. Assessments had to be made on a case-by-case basis to decide whether aid should be ended or directed towards human rights organisations, trade unions, and other organisations through non-governmental channels [*Recommendation No 195:43*].

The discussion on future bilateral relations between Norway and the recipient governments was closely attuned to the framework provided by this concept. However, the concept is not confined to the aid relationship between a single donor country and recipient; on the contrary: it foresees development contracts established between several parties both on the donor and recipient side on a regional basis or even on a political, between like-minded governments at both sides. Although couched in legal terms, and conceived ultimately as binding, the process leading towards it matters as much as the contract itself.

The development contract should be based on a joint perception of mutual benefits; the donor countries commit themselves to long-term economic co-operation with one or more developing country in exchange for commitments to, for instance, economic or political reforms or environmental activities agreed by the two parties. For the developing countries, this might ensure transfers of resources for a certain period; the interests of the donors might include stable access to important raw material, a reduction of threats to the environment, or the attainment of political objectives.

The government envisaged that agreements of this kind might be worked out under the auspices of international organisations, after developing further present arrangements such as the Round Table conferences organised by the UNDP and the Consultative Group organised by the World Bank. A crucial concern would be to ensure a just partnership and a central role for the developing countries involved. The SADCC-Nordic agreement was offered as an illustration.[28]

In applying this to Norway's bilateral aid relations, it is repeatedly emphasised that aid by itself cannot produce development; it can merely assist activities and processes driven by the developing countries themselves: it is the responsibility of the authorities and institutions of the recipient country to plan and implement development activities. For Norway, as an aid provider, the challenge is to identify partners, types and forms of aid which make it possible actually to follow up the guideline of recipient responsibility.

In the process leading to development co-operation and its implementation, discussions and dialogue between the authorities on both sides concerning the framework and basic preconditions emerged as the key mechanism: the objectives had to be adapted to the recipient's

---

28. Reference was also made to the 1992 UNDP Human Development Report, which proposes an agreement on human development: this implies assistance to promote economic and social development in exchange for assistance in fighting narcotics trade, pollution and pressure for immigration. This approach is developed in Kaul [*1993*].

prevailing situation and agreed in an open dialogue. The two parties had to reach an understanding with regard to the conditions, on which the objectives were based, and where responsibility rested if these were not met; in addition, the consequences that would ensue from a failure to meet conditions need to be stated in clear terms. A basic prerequisite for effective and successful aid, according to the government, is that the recipient country fully shares the aims set for the co-operation.

When the concept was first presented and its implementation indicated [*NORAD, 1990*], the consequences of a recipient country failing to meet the agreed commitments were stated in candid terms. Critics warned of certain undesirable consequences of strict practice: a suspension of long-term aid relations might reduce the effects of aid already invested and negatively affect the target groups (such as the poor, women or children). Given the nature of those included in the group of programme countries (mostly LLDCs) and the crisis almost all of them had found themselves in since the early 1980s, this might, within a brief time span, drastically affect the very foundation of Norwegian aid policy: namely, its poverty orientation [*Stokke, 1991*].

The government, whilst maintaining the core concept, addressed these objections by modifying the prescriptions for the follow-up: it suggested a flexible response. It was acknowledged that an early implementation of the principle *vis-à-vis* countries with a seriously weakened administrative system might have effects contrary to those intended in terms both of attaining objectives and ensuring the effectiveness of aid. If necessary, recipient governments finding themselves in this situation should be offered assistance in order to strengthen their administrative competence and capacity. However, access to control the use of financial transfers was stated as an absolute condition. The White Paper also emphasised that the recipient country had a responsibility to fight corruption.

The core dilemma confronting the government is transparent throughout the White Paper: how to combine pursuance of Norwegian aid objectives with a policy of non-intervention. At the level of *stated* policy, the government makes no modification: it insists on the pursuance by means of development assistance of the objectives included in the concept of good government; insistence is stronger than ever and the policy is spelled out in operational terms in greater detail than before. At the same time, it continues to insist on its non-intervention stance: the way out of the dilemma is to seek partners with a common desire to pursue objectives similar to those of Norwegian aid policy.

Adopting this strategy would imply a revival of the policy formu-

lated 30 years ago, manifested in the criteria for the selection of programme countries. As noted above, that policy has yet to be followed
up. Far from diminishing, problems of follow-up increase when aid
relations have been cultivated for years (more than 30 years for most
programme countries). The probability is, therefore, that the dilemma
will remain – at the level of implemented policy – in future years as
well.

Policy Implementation: Where the Real Trouble Starts

To what extent has the declared policy been followed up? It may be
premature to address this question since the 1992 White Paper was
approved by Parliament only in June 1993. Nevertheless, some preliminary comments may be offered.

A high level of generalisation may be expected and accepted at the
level of policy prescription. In order to be implemented effectively,
these prescriptions need to be operationalised. Responsibility for this
is vested in the aid administration and shared between the Ministry of
Foreign Affairs and the implementing agency (NORAD). To what
extent have the objectives, strategies and modalities been operationalised? To what extent has the policy been communicated to
Norway's main partners in development? How far and how clearly
have the consequences been spelled out of a failure to meet the expectations? To what extent are the policy and performance of the
recipients monitored, and what are the criteria, the framework,
routines and level of ambition of that exercise? To what extent has the
Norwegian aid administration prepared the staff to handle these new
issues and how greatly does it rely on external expertise and institutions? In addition, what are the rules and routines for follow-up?
These are basic questions to identify the kind of regime which is (unilaterally) established.

The answers to them may tell the real story. At this stage, it is possible only to indicate certain answers with reference to the immediate
past. The main conclusion is that little seems to have been done so
far, other than in a few exceptional cases.

The annual high-level policy dialogue with programme countries
has been identified as a major instrument for pursuing these objectives. To what extent and in what way has this instrument been used
effectively to pursue identified objectives?

During the 1980s, concern for human rights and democracy entered
the dialogue only in exceptional cases: those of Sri Lanka in 1984,
Bangladesh in 1986 and Kenya in 1988. In both of the latter cases, a

low profile was maintained.[29] The norms on which Norway's aid rests have been communicated in general terms and specific cases of grave violations have been raised occasionally. Since the mid-1980s, however, the message has been more direct (albeit discreet), in particular to programme countries that are most dependent on aid. Nevertheless, in no case has improved performance on these criteria been explicitly set as a condition for continued aid. It follows that the *specifics* of such a policy (if they exist at all) have not been communicated to the programme countries. However, even discreet pressure, without the stick, may yield results [*Mushi, this volume*].

Very few of the requirements necessary to pursue a bilateral conditionality policy have materialised. The office of the NORAD resident representative, now integrated in the embassies of programme countries, reports routinely on developments in the host countries as part of normal follow-up, and reports from the missions are taken into consideration when the budget is prepared. However, no country-specific strategies have been devised. No specific criteria have been drawn up to govern policy decisions (such as the check-list with specific indicators for the criteria involved and the *Länderkonzept*, established by Germany [*Waller, this volume*]), nor are there specific procedures for how to proceed in situations where the overall guidelines might apply. Moreover, there has been no staff-training on how to handle the new tasks. The administration has not prepared itself for the challenges involved at the bilateral level. The main reason for this may be that Norway has decided not to act on its own and – except in extreme situations – not to use the bilateral channel in order to exert pressure for policy reform, involving denial of aid.

However, some steps have been taken. Certain mechanisms have been developed for monitoring the human rights performance of the programme countries both within the aid administration and outside – although external institutions (Amnesty International and the UN Human Rights Commission) represent the main sources relied on.[30]

---

29. A low profile in bilateral negotiations involving human rights and democracy issues can be rooted in several considerations, not the least concern for a good co-operative atmosphere. The negotiations on the country programmes may not be the best suited forum for raising these issues, since the recipient side is not represented by people in charge of them. The negotiations may, however, be used for opening up for contact with those in charge (the Minister of Justice, PM or President), but then involving the political level also at the donor side (a visiting Minister or the Ambassador).
30. As noted by Andreassen *et al.* [*1985:10-12,32 ff*] there were no efforts at systematic research and documentation in any of the Nordic countries until the mid-1980s. Such efforts had, in contrast, been made by aid administrations in the US and the Netherlands (the ministries of foreign affairs), resulting in annual reports on the human rights situation in the main recipient countries; the US efforts, starting in the

Positions as special advisors on human rights have been established both in the Ministry of Foreign Affairs (MFA) and NORAD. In 1991, following the Kenyan experience, an intra-administration committee was established to attend to the human rights *problématique*. In addition, external monitoring has been stimulated: for almost ten years, the MFA has provided financial support for an annual report scrutinising the human rights performance of the governments of the programme countries.[31] In 1991, a Nordic intra-ministerial/agency study was commissioned to consider ways and means of implementing policy on human rights.

The dialogue involving the international agencies and main bilateral donors was identified as a useful instrument in promoting the objectives set, with reference to both conditionality and supportive measures. The Consultative Group serves as the primary instrument for aid co-ordination and also as the main forum for policy dialogue with the recipient governments. Occasionally, this forum has exerted pressure for policy reform [*Stokke, this volume*]. Norway has participated in meetings involving its programme countries, and when policy reforms have been set as conditions for continued aid. In these settings, the pressure is increased: for the individual donor, sharing the potential negative effects lessens them. By and large, Norway has been a free-rider in these settings; it has not been particularly active in driving initiatives.

The main modality of the 1992 White Paper – a development contract – in theory provides a way out of the dilemma. Some time has lapsed since the concept was first coined; however, it remains at a very high level of generalisation and no efforts have been made to

---

mid-1970s, have grown into an extensive annual survey (*Country Reports on Human Rights Practices for [year]*) of the human rights situation in all UN member countries (the focus is, however, limited to civil and political rights).

31. This effort was, however, initiated and driven from outside; two Norwegian research groups (the Chr. Michelsen Institute in Bergen and the Human Rights Project, which later developed into the Human Rights Institute, Oslo) took advantage of the commitment to human rights included in Report No. 36. The first volume appeared in 1985 [*Andreassen et al., 1985*], covering the Norwegian programme countries and also providing a summary of the 1984 White Paper with reference to human rights (with comments). The first issue appeared in Norwegian, but for later issues this was changed to English. The base was broadened, initially to include other Nordic countries, and it is now published jointly by human rights institutes in Austria, Denmark, the Netherlands, Norway and Sweden [*Skålnes and Egeland, eds., 1986; Andreassen and Eide, eds., 1988; Nowak and Swinehart, eds. 1989; Andreassen and Swinehart, eds., 1991; Andreassen and Swinehart, eds., 1993, and Baehr et al., eds., 1994*]. The first three volumes were supported financially by the Norwegian aid administration; the base has now broadened to include the aid administrations of the countries quoted with the exception of Austria (the Norwegian 1992 contribution amounted to about US$ 100.000 [*Report No. 9, 1993:98*]).

operationalise and adapt it to the bilateral negotiations involving the country programmes. As an idea, it aspired towards a broader application. The necessary process has not yet taken place to make the concept workable and to adapt it to serve such a function. This process should start at home. The lack of follow-up, therefore, indicates either a very low priority or a lack of confidence in the idea; the experiences emerging from the agreement between SADCC and the Nordic countries may have contributed to this.

The ground has not been particularly well prepared for so-called 'positive conditionality', involving additional support for good performance. The existing planning system which provides commitments on a long-term basis, does not easily allow for quick responses of this kind, whether in the context of conditionality or as political 'relief assistance' to fragile democracies where a change of regime has taken place. This form of support was conceived in the mid-1970s *vis-à-vis* a limited numbers of governments (*inter alia*, Portugal and Jamaica) [*Stokke, 1979*]; a similar idea was nurtured in the late 1980s with the proposal for a Nordic fund for development, democracy and independence [*Andreassen, 1987:12-13*]. In 1988, major Norwegian NGOs established the Norwegian Human Rights Fund with the aim of providing rapid and flexible support for organisations, groups and individuals falling outside traditional aid channels [*Egeland, 1988*]. The fund relies partly on private donations and receives generous public funding (about two-thirds); it is governed by the NGOs who launched it.

Such efforts fall outside the conditionality mechanism and may be subsumed under the umbrella of so-called positive measures. Since the late 1960s, provision has been made within the Ministry of Foreign Affairs for a budget item with funds from the ODA budget at its disposal in order to support victims of human rights violations – which was used from the 1970s to provide humanitarian aid to victims of the apartheid regime in South Africa and to support liberation movements in southern Africa. After the 1984 White Paper had brought human rights more firmly on to the aid agenda, the use of this particular post has been extended to include the promotion of democracy and human rights; however, its size is modest (US$ 2-8 million a year). These funds have been distributed to support a variety of activities, such as the publication of trade union papers and judicial assistance to victims of human rights violations; they are channelled, in particular, through NGOs.

In 1992, an 'aid for democracy' strategy [*MFA, 1992*] established this kind of support as a regular part of aid, oriented towards:

- national and regional efforts for peace and stabilisation,
- electoral processes and elected assemblies,
- judicial protection and the rule of law,
- economic planning and control,
- decentralisation and organisational pluralism, and
- the promotion of mass media and information.

Norwegian expertise in the various areas was drawn upon and a resource bank for democratic development was initiated. The Nordic Group on Human Rights and Development, established in 1990, serves a co-ordinating role in these efforts.

A varied mosaic of activities have received support which in turn has been drawn from a variety of budget items, within both the country and the regional programmes. In addition, a separate budget item was established in 1990 to provide flexible support for new fragile democracies [*Proposition No. 96*]; in 1992, this support amounted to about US$ 8 million, of which a large proportion went to Latin America (Chile, El Salvador) [*Report No. 9:1993:98-99*].

If priority is measured from the resources allocated, these objectives would hold a low priority: only a tiny proportion (1-2 per cent) of the ODA budget is allocated to 'positive measures'. Nevertheless, these budget items constitute only a minor component of the positive measures; although not framed in such terms, the ODA budget supports several activities and institutions as 'ordinary' aid which are associated directly or indirectly with the good government agenda, including competence and institution-building.

VI. SOME CONCLUDING OBSERVATIONS

The discussion has been based explicitly on a broad definition of the conditionality concept. It includes both coercive and supportive measures aimed at obtaining policy reform on the recipient side using aid as the instrument. A policy consists of many components, involving intentions and objectives, strategies, norms and guidelines as well as instruments. The result is what ultimately matters, deciding the extent of success or failure *vis-à-vis* the objectives set. In addressing Norway's conditionality policy, attention has been directed towards all these aspects; it has not been restricted to the technical features which constitute its core elements: namely, the denial of foreign aid if specified conditions were not met or (positive conditionality) offers of additional aid as a reward for good performance. Also aid targeted specifically towards policy reforms or to improve good government has been considered. In addressing the main question posed in the introuction, the main components will be discussed in turn.

The Objectives: Democracy, Human Rights and 'Good Governance'

The main elements of the 'good government' agenda have been included in the objectives set for Norwegian aid since the 1970s. Although omitted from the formal, overall objectives until 1984, promotion of *democracy* has been entrenched in the declared aid policy since the start; the fact that India was a working democracy made it a natural first choice as partner for bilateral development cooperation in the early 1950s. Promotion of human rights by the means of aid also remained unformalised until 1984; in 1976, however, Parliament made respect for *human rights* a condition of inclusion as a programme country for a recipient government. Competence-building in general, focusing on management in particular, combined with institution-building, were early features of the declared and implemented aid policy.

What then was the novelty of the 1990s? First, there is greater urgency in the stated policy which is expressed in direct language. Moreover, democracy and human rights have become objectives in their own right; they are no longer considered merely as preconditions for economic, social, cultural and political development. The stronger emphasis in declared policy becomes particularly pronounced when examined in a somewhat longer-term perspective, and is evident in a comparison between objectives and prescriptions for implementation as set out in the first government White Paper which addressed the foreign policy aspects of human rights, Report No. 93 [*1977:13-15*] and those of the 1992 White Paper. In the first, there was recognition of the close link between the attainment of economic and social rights and opportunities to pursue political and civil rights. However, it emphasised that the industrialised countries should be careful not to make aid transfers dependent on political factors. In 1992 the political framework conditions had attained first priority: economic and social development depended on an enabling political environment.

To what extent came this new priority as an adaptation to the international 'wind of change' of the late 1980s? The strong influence of international environments, particularly the World Bank, transpires in the way the policy is phrased in the 1992 White Paper; both content and language are similar. This is underlined by a gradual weakening of the non-interference principle, particularly in relation to human rights issues; first generation conditionality policy was instrumental in this regard.

Nevertheless, the content of the White Paper policy is rooted in a domestic tradition. In that tradition, however, emphasis was placed not so much on democracy and *civil* human rights as on economic and *social* human rights. The latter have not been reduced in importance; poverty orientation remains an imperative for Norway in its stated aid policy.

Strategy and Instrumentality

All strategies have to be adapted to the specific circumstances prevailing; these framework conditions may themselves reflect the choice of strategy at an earlier stage. Since the early 1970s, the established system of aid administration has been of particular importance for Norwegian policy-makers. Bilateral aid relations have been established with a small number of principal recipient countries for a very long time on the basis of a revolving 4-year country programme which advances only after an annual process of consultations and negotiations. The system differs from programme- or project-based co-operation where the short-term horizon leads to a more *ad hoc* operation. Relations become more interwoven and interdependence tends to develop over the years.

This setting may explain the strategy chosen in the declared policy. The objectives set are to be pursued in a bilateral dialogue with the recipient government, particularly in the annual dialogue concerning the future direction of aid. In this context, issues known to be utterly controversial and which may have a negative influence on the smooth co-operative climate are apt to be avoided or addressed in general terms. This may also explain why the emphasis in the 1992 White Paper is on international dialogue, involving international fora; and why supportive rather than coercive measures are brought to the fore in the stated policy. The latter may also result from the norms on which the traditional policy stance was based: adherence to the principle of non-interference in the policy of recipient countries.

However, coercive elements are also contained in the declared policy. The criteria for the selection of new programme countries for bilateral aid – related to social justice and human rights – do not apply in this context since they did not imply a withdrawal of aid; they were intended to govern new relationships. In the 1990s, however, coercive conditionality is explicit, particularly as prescribed by NORAD: a failure to deliver results on the part of the aid recipient might lead to the aid relationship being broken off. However, it should be noted that this referred to contractual agreements in general, not necessarily involving the good government agenda. When first devised, the modality of a development contract was intended as an alternative approach to first generation conditionality; the good government agenda might have be totally absent. However, its design allows for it to apply to these objectives as well. In the 1992 White Paper the 'safety clause' of previous white papers is toned down, which signals a less flexible response.

The norms established in the 1984 White Paper – particularly those on the human rights agenda, where emphasis is placed on the civil rights but which includes social rights – were designed in the same vein, underlining supportive aspects. Moreover, there was a greater focus on the direction of human rights performance than on the degree of violations, provided these were not excessive. However, coercive aspects were not totally absent: if the violations of human rights were grave and consistent, with no intervention from the government, aid might be redistributed or even terminated. Again, the policy was designed before second generation political conditionality took off. However, the international emphasis on this agenda in the 1990s may have reinforced the concern for human rights.

Follow-up and Effects

In the 1970s and 1980s, follow-up on declared policy in terms of objectives as well as strategy and instrumentality had a very low-key profile. The criteria relating to social justice and human rights for the selection of programme countries were invoked only occasionally *vis-à-vis* countries which were already included, and then on the basis of grave violations of *civil* human rights. Reference to the recipient government's human rights record has, in a few cases, been given as the justification for freezing aid to the established nominal level. It is even more seldom that the government's political rights record has been brought on to the agenda in the annual dialogue on continued aid, other than in general statements which put on record the emphasis given to these aspects.

The main exceptions are the cases of Sri Lanka and Kenya. In Sri Lanka, human rights issues were raised in the dialogue and led to a redistribution directed towards humanitarian aid and assistance for the victims of violations of these rights.

In the Kenyan case, Norwegian concern about human rights violations was brought up at a late stage (autumn 1988). The termination of state-to-stat aid two years later was unintended. However, minor withdrawals of aid during this period indicated that the 'aid weapon' might be used. Low-key references to human rights violations in the annual dialogue from a minor donor did not impress the Kenyan government.

*

The main emphasis of the Norwegian policy, particularly as implemented, has been on 'positive measures'. Although keeping a high profile in its stated policy, attuned to the new drive of second generation conditionality, its intellectual and practical contributions in implementing a conditionality policy, in bilateral and multilateral settings, have been quite modest. Within the domestic setting, cherished norms relating to aid were conflicting. The international orthodoxy of second generation conditionality strengthened some of these conflicting values, particularly those related to democracy and human rights, especially the civil and political rights; however, the social justice rhetoric was not toned down. By the same token, it weakened other traditional values, particularly those related to the sovereignty of the recipient governments. However, this change was to a large extent self-generated and in progress already in the early 1980s, as manifest in the 1984 White Paper. Torn between competing values, Norway has been a somewhat hesitant free-rider in the conditionality drive, particularly with regard to the first generation but also to the second generation aid conditionality.

REFERENCES

Andreassen, Bård-Anders, Jan Egeland, Asbjørn Eide, Bernt Hagtvet, Tor Skålnes, Hugo Stokke and Bjørn Stormorken, 1985, *Menneskerettighetene i Norges hovedsamarbeidsland 1985* (Human Rights in the Programme Countries for Norwegian Aid 1985), Bergen and Oslo: Christian Michelsen Institute and The Norwegian Human Rights Project.
Andreassen, Bård-Anders, 1987, 'Ingen utvikling uten menneskerettigheter!' (No Development without Human Rights!), *Mennesker og Rettigheter*, Vol. 5, No. 1, Oslo: Institute of Human Rights.
Andreassen, Bård-Anders and Asbjørn Eide, eds., 1988, *Human Rights in Developing Countries 1987/88*, Copenhagen: Akademisk Forlag.
Andreassen, Bård-Anders and Theresa Swinehart, eds., 1991, *Human Rights in Developing Countries 1991*, Oslo: Scandinavian University Press.
Andreassen, Bård-Anders and Theresa Swinehart, eds., 1993, *Human Rights in Developing Countries Yearbook 1993*, Copenhagen, Lund, Oslo, Åbo/Turku: Nordic Human Rights Publications.
Baehr, Peter, Hilde Hey, Jacqueline Smith and Theresa Swinehart, eds., 1994, *Human Rights in Developing Countries Yearbook 1994*, Deventer: Kluwer Law and Taxation Publishers.
Edgren, Gus, 1984, 'Conditionality in Aid', in Stokke, ed., 1984, Volume 2.
Egeland, Jan, 1988, 'The Norwegian Fund for Human Rights – Supporting Third World Activities', *Mennesker og Rettigheter*, Vol. 6, No. 4, Oslo: Institute of Human Rights.
Griffin, Keith, 1991, 'Foreign Aid after the Cold War', *Development and Change*, 1991:4, London: Sage Publications.

Kaul, Inge, 1993, 'A New Approach to Aid', New York: UNDP (draft).

Kjekshus, Helge, 1992, 'Aid Conditionalities: Some Norwegian Perspectives', paper presented at a conference on 'The New Political Conditionalities of Aid' organised 23-24 April 1992 in Vienna by EADI (mimeo).

Lancaster, Carol, 1993, 'Governance and Development: The Views from Washington', *IDS Bulletin*, Vol. 24, No. 1, Brighton: Institute of Development Studies, Sussex.

Love, Alexander R., 1992, 'Remarks by Alexander R. Love, Chairman, Development Assistance Committee, Organisation for Economic Co-operation and Development, to the Norwegian Institute of International Affairs', Seminar 15 September 1992 (mimeo).

Lunde, Magne, 1991, Norsk bistand og menneskerettigheter (Norwegian Aid and Human Rights), hovedfagsoppgave (cand. polit. thesis), Oslo: University of Oslo, Institute of Political Science, 16 December 1991 (mimeo).

MFR, 1992, Strateginotat om demokratistøtte i bistandsarbeidet (A strategy for democracy support in development co-operation), Oslo: Ministry of Foreign Affairs (mimeo).

Mushi, Samuel S., 1994, 'Determinants and Limitations of Aid Conditionality: Some Examples from the Nordic-Tanzanian Co-operation', this volume.

NORAD, 1990, *Strategies for Development Cooperation – NORAD in the Nineties*, Oslo: Norwegian Agency for International Development.

Nowak, Manfred and Theresa Swinehart, eds., 1989, *Human Rights in Developing Countries 1989*, Kehl: N.P.Engel.

OECD, 1992, DAC and OECD Public Policy Statements on Participatory Development/Good Governance, Paris: DAC (OCDE/GD(92)67).

OECD, 1993, DAC Orientations on Participatory Development and Good Governance, Paris: OECD (OCDE/GD(93)191).

Ofstad, Arve, Arne Tostensen and Tom Vraalsen, 1991, 'Towards a "Development Contract" ', paper presented at a meeting of the North-South Roundtable, Ottawa, June 1991.

Proposition No. 96, 1990 (St.prp. nr. 96 (1989-90)), Om midler til tiltak til støtte for demokrati, utvikling og nasjonal selvstendighet (On financial support of measures in support of democracy, development and national self-determination), Oslo: Ministry of Foreign Affairs.

Proposition No. 1, 1990 (St.prp. nr. 1 (1990-91)) for the budget of 1990, Oslo: Ministry of Foreign Affairs.

Proposition No. 17, 1990 (St.prp. nr. 17 (1990-91)), Om endringar av statsbudsjettet for 1990 under kapittel administrerte av Utanriksdepartementet (On changes in the budget for 1990 under chapters administered by the Ministry of Foreign Affairs), Oslo: Ministry of Foreign Affairs.

Recommendation No. 192, 1976 (Innst. S. nr. 192 (1975-76)), Innstilling fra den forsterkede utenriks- og konstitusjonskomité om Norges økonomiske samkvem med utviklingslandene (Recommendation by Parliament's Extended Committee on Foreign Affairs and Constitutional Matters on Norway's economic relations with the developing countries), Oslo.

Recommendation No. 186, 1987 (Innst. S. nr. 186 (1986-87)), Innstilling fra utenriks- og konstitusjonskomiteen om Norges hjelp til utviklingslandene (Recommendations by Parliament's Standing Committee on Foreign Affairs and Constitutional Matters on Norway's aid to the developing countries), Oslo.

Recommendation No. 195, 1993 (Innst. S. nr. 195 (1992-93)), Innstilling fra utenriks- og konstitusjonskomiteen om utviklingstrekk i Nord-Sør-forholdet og Norges samarbeid med utviklingslandene (Recommendations by Parliament's Standing Committee on Foreign Affairs and Constitutional Matters on trends in the North-South relations and Norway's co-operation with the developing countries), Oslo.

Report No. 29, 1972 (St.meld. nr. 29 (1971-72)), Om enkelte hovedspørsmål vedrørende Norges samarbeid med utviklingslandene (On some major issues related to

Norway's co-operation with developing countries), Oslo: Ministry of Foreign Affairs.

Report No. 94, 1975 (St.meld. nr. 94 (1974-75)), Norges økonomiske samkvem med utviklingslandene (Norway's economic relations with developing countries), Oslo: Ministry of Foreign Affairs.

Report No. 93, 1977, (St.meld. nr. 93 (1976-77)), Norge og det internasjonale menneskerettighetsvern (Norway and the international protection of human rights), Oslo: Ministry of Foreign Affairs.

Report No. 36, 1984, (St.meld. nr. 36 (1984-85)), Om enkelte hovedspørsmål i norsk utviklingshjelp (On some major issues in Norwegian development assistance), Oslo: Ministry of Development Co-operation.

Report No. 34, 1987, (St.meld. nr. 34 (1986-87)), Om enkelte hovedspørsmål i norsk utviklingshjelp. Tilleggsmelding til St.meld. nr. 36 (1984-85) (On some main issues in Norwegian development assistance. Supplementary report to Report No. 36, 1984), Oslo: Ministry of Development Co-operation.

Report No. 51, 1992, (St.meld. nr. 51 (1991-92)), Om utviklingstrekk i Nord-Sør forholdet og Norges samarbeid med utviklingslandene (On trends in North-South relations and Norway's co-operation with the developing countries), Oslo: Ministry of Foreign Affairs.

Report No. 9, 1993 (St.meld. nr. 9 (1993-94)), Om Norges samarbeid med utviklingslandene i 1992 (On Norway's co-operation with the developing countries in 1992), Oslo: Ministry of Foreign Affairs.

Skålnes, Tor and Jan Egeland, eds., 1986, *Human Rights in Developing Countries 1986*, Oslo: Norwegian Universities Press.

Stokke, Hugo, 1985, 'Norsk uenighet og u-hjelp og overgrep', *Mennesker og Rettigheter*, Vol. 3, No. 2, Oslo: The Human Rights Project.

Stokke, Olav, 1979, *Norge og den tredje verden* (Norway and the Third World), Oslo: Universitetsforlaget.

Stokke, Olav, 1984, 'Norwegian Aid: Policy and Performance', in Stokke, ed., 1984, Volume 1.

Stokke, Olav, ed., 1984, *European Development Assistance*, Volume 1, *Policies and Performance*, Volume 2, *Third World Perspectives on Policies and Performance*, EADI Book Series No. 4, Tilburg: EADI.

Stokke, Olav, 1988, 'Norsk bistandspolitikk: kontinuitet og endring' (Norwegian Aid Policy: Continuity and Change), *Norsk Utenrikspolitisk Årbok 1987* (Norwegian Foreign Policy Yearbook 1987), Oslo: Norwegian Institute of International Affairs.

Stokke, Olav, 1989a, 'The Determinants of Aid Policies: General Introduction', in Stokke, ed., 1989.

Stokke, Olav, 1989b, 'The Determinants of Norwegian Aid Policy', in Stokke, ed., 1989.

Stokke, Olav, ed., 1989, *Western Middle Powers and Global Poverty. The Determinants of the Aid Policies of Canada, Denmark, the Netherlands, Norway and Sweden*, Uppsala: The Scandinavian Institute of African Studies.

Stokke, Olav, 1991, 'Norsk bistandspolitikk ved inngangen til 1990-tallet' (Norwegian aid policy on the doorsteps to the 1990s), *Norsk Utenrikspolitisk Årbok 1990* (Norwegian Foreign Policy Yearbook 1990), Oslo: NUPI.

Stokke, Olav, 1992a, 'Policies, Performance, Trends and Challenges in Aid Evaluation', in Stokke, ed., *Evaluating Development Assistance: Policies and Performance*, London: Frank Cass, EADI Book Series 12.

Stokke, Olav, 1992b, 'Nord-Sør-meldingen: Nye signaler?' (The North-South White Paper: New Signals?), in Stokke, ed., *Norsk Nord-Sør-politikk: Lever den opp til sitt rykte?* (Norwegian North-South Policy: Up to its Reputation?), Oslo: NUPI.

Stokke, Olav, 1992c, 'Mål, strategi og prinsipper for norsk bistand: Old bottles?' (Objectives, strategies and guidelines for Norwegian aid: Old bottles?), in Stokke, ed., *Norsk Nord-Sør-politikk: Lever den opp til sitt rykte?* (Norwegian North-South

Policy: Up to its Reputation?), Oslo: NUPI.

Stokke, Olav, 1994, 'Aid and Conditionality: Core issues and State of the Art', this volume.

Stoltenberg, Thorvald, 1989, 'Towards a World Development Strategy', in Louis Emmerij, ed., *One World or Several?*, Paris: OECD.

Sæter, Odd Jostein, 1984, 'Menneskerettighetenes plass i den nye prinsippmeldingen' (Human Rights in the new White Paper), *Mennesker og Rettigheter*, Vol. 2, No. 2, Oslo: The Norwegian Human Rights Project.

Sørbø, Gunnar M., Grete Brochmann, Reidar Dale, Mick Moore, Erik Whist, 1987, *Sri Lanka. Country Study and Norwegian Aid Review*, Bergen: University of Bergen, Centre for Development Studies.

Sørensen, Georg, 1993, 'Democracy, Authoritarianism and State Strength', *The European Journal of Development Research*, Vol. 5, No. 1, London: Frank Cass.

Waller, Peter P., 1994, 'Aid and Conditionality: The Case of Germany', this volume.

Wamwere, Koigi wa, 1989, *Kenya - selvstyre uten frihet* (Kenya: independence without freedom), Oslo: Pax.

World Bank, 1989, *Sub-Saharan Africa: From Crisis to Sustainable Growth*, Washington, DC: World Bank.

World Bank, 1992, *Governance and Development*, Washington, DC: World Bank.

6

Conditionality in Swiss
Development Assistance

JACQUES FORSTER

I. INTRODUCTION

Conditionality is as old as aid itself. What has varied over the years is both the prominence of conditionality as an explicit issue in development assistance and the various dimensions of the issue which have been highlighted at different stages of aid history. In the 1980s, conditionality was mostly discussed in the context of structural adjustment programmes propounded by the Bretton Woods institutions. Since the end of the Cold War, a 'new political conditionality' emphasising human rights has been added to the already vast paraphernalia of development assistance.

Our assumption is that conditionality is the donor's means of ensuring – or appearing to ensure – the implementation of the objectives pursued by its development co-operation policy. If the donor's and the recipient's agenda coincide, conditionality will not be regarded by the latter as a constraint but merely as a means of fulfilling efficiently and effectively a common purpose. The relationship between the United States and western European countries in the context of the Marshall Plan was by and large of that kind. If, on the other hand, the agendas differ, the conditions are regarded as concessions to be made as a *quid pro quo*, that is in exchange for development assistance. In fact conditionality is present whenever transactions involving transfers of resources occur outside market mechanisms.[1] In the domestic polity, subsidies are examples of such transactions. What then makes conditionality a particularly sensitive issue in development assistance? The following factors may provide an answer to this question:

---

1. This does not imply that conditionality is absent from all market-based transactions.

(a) the actors involved are sovereign states;
(b) they do not always share the same ideological and/or cultural values;
(c) the common purpose is defined in very broad terms and does not exclude conflicts of interests;
(d) the bargaining power of the partners is unequal;
(e) the time frame of the partners for the achievement of common objectives may not be the same;
(f) the donors may pursue other objectives than their declared developmental objectives.

Obviously, the nature of the aid relationship – and of the conditionality attached to it – varies according to different 'donor-recipient combinations'. As far as bilateral donors are concerned, broad categories can be defined, taking into account the size of the country, its historical links with developing countries, its role in international relations, and the magnitude of its aid programme. As far as the recipient is concerned, the size of the country, the relative importance of aid in the resources devoted to development, the authority of its government, and the competence of its administration are the main factors which affect its relationship – or bargaining power – with donors.

The purpose of this chapter is to examine the nature of this relationship in the case of Switzerland with particular reference to the recent developments on the 'new political conditionality'. Such an analysis, by clarifying the rationale of the donor's objectives and policies, may contribute towards enhancing transparency, an essential ingredient to improve the by nature 'awkward' relationship between donors and recipients.[2]

Conditionality in aid can be applied at different levels. Gus Edgren [1984] identifies five levels: (i) general political compatibility, (ii) policy level, (iii) project/programme level, (iv) financial conditions, (v) administrative conditions. The scope for application of political conditionality decreases as one moves from level (i) to level (v) and becomes very limited indeed beyond the project/programme level. This chapter will therefore concentrate on issues relative to the first two levels.

The first level determines the choice of recipient countries, either to initiate development co-operation or to terminate it. The criteria for assessment are to be found amongst the following: the recipient country's level of development; its present or potential importance as an

---

2. An insightful analysis of the donor-recipient relationship, with reference to its awkwardness, is provided by John White [1974: 200].

economic partner; the recipient government's general development policy; its foreign policy, in particular participation in military alliances; the nature of the political system, and general attitude towards human rights. The second level links the transfer of resources to specific measures in various areas (domestic economic and social policy, international economic relations, governance and human rights).

The objective of this chapter is to examine Switzerland's policy and – whenever possible – its practice of conditionality in development assistance. *Section II* briefly examines the distinctive features of Swiss development assistance policy as compared to that of other European middle powers. Conditionality being a means to achieve objectives, *Section III* describes what exactly the Swiss authorities mean when they state that their objective is to promote development and respect for human rights. As the promotion of 'good governance' has recently become the new universal catchword to define the donors' general political objectives in development co-operation, we shall also describe the content given by Swiss officials to this concept. *Section IV* analyses the policy on conditionality, whilst *Section V* attempts to illustrate the implementation of this policy at the two levels defined above. A sub-section is devoted to Swiss policy in the context of the Bretton Woods institutions.

II. DISTINCTIVE FEATURES OF SWISS DEVELOPMENT ASSISTANCE

The distinctive features of Switzerland's development co-operation policy can be identified by comparison with other DAC members. Considering its economic size and its strong integration in the world economy, Switzerland belongs to a group of six European countries (including Austria, Denmark, Finland, Norway and Sweden) which present the following features: small population, middle-sized economy, absence or quasi-absence of a colonial past. It is thus both relevant and useful to characterise its policy towards developing countries with the help of the analytical framework used in a recent comparative study of the aid policies of 'Western middle powers' edited by Olav Stokke [*1989*].[3]

Switzerland's development co-operation differs from that of most of the other above-mentioned five countries on two important and prominent points:

---

3. In this study the Western middle powers examined are Canada, Denmark, the Netherlands, Norway and Sweden.

- a consistently and significantly lower level of official development assistance (ODA). All these countries except Switzerland
  and Austria had, in 1991, an ODA/GNP ratio higher than the 0.7
  per cent target. However, Finland is a special case in this context;
  at the beginning of the 1980s, it had the same level of ODA as
  Switzerland and Austria, but reached 0.76 per cent in 1991 – in
  1992, however, it was sharply reduced to 0.50 per cent.
- a relatively weak degree of participation in multilateral development co-operation; the share of ODA channelled through multilateral agencies is much smaller for Switzerland and Austria than
  for the other four countries (respectively 22 per cent and 24 per
  cent whilst the other countries' share ranges from 30 to 39 per
  cent. Switzerland's lower commitment to multilateral ODA is an
  indicator of a more deeply-rooted reluctance towards participation in multilateral co-operation, signalled by non-membership of
  the United Nations Organisation, a very late entry into the
  Bretton Woods institutions (1992) and the refusal in December
  1992 of the Swiss people to join the European Economic Space.
  However, the official statistics quoted above do not reflect the
  actual Swiss contribution to multilateral agencies since an important share of this is disbursed as 'multi-bilateral' aid, that is, earmarked contributions to specific projects and programmes. Prior
  to Switzerland's full participation in the Bretton Woods institutions, its contributions to IDA were exclusively of the 'multi-bi'
  type.

On other aspects, such as geographical concentration and choice of recipients, Switzerland is closer to the group of Nordic countries than it
is to Austria. The list of main recipients of development assistance,
defined in Stokke's study as those who have received two per cent or
more of total ODA, which totals six countries in the case of Switzerland, includes three (Tanzania, Mozambique and India) which are also
on the list of main recipients of assistance from Sweden, Norway and
Denmark.

The commercialisation of aid is not as high for Switzerland as it is
for most of the other five countries. Taking as an indicator the percentage of totally untied ODA, the figures range from 17.3 per cent in
Finland to 53.1 per cent in Sweden. Switzerland, with 51.9 per cent,
ranks second in the reference group.[4]

A global characterisation of Switzerland's development co-

---

4. The statistical data quoted in paragraphs 8-10 comes from the OECD 1992 Development Co-operation report.

operation policy can be attempted using Stokke's typology of the basic values underpinning the policies of Western industrialised countries [*Stokke, 1989: 10-15*]. Switzerland's policy towards developing countries is close to that inspired by 'liberal internationalism' which 'combines the core component of humane internationalism with a strong commitment to an open, multilateral trading system ... Liberal internationalism is motivated by a humanitarian tradition in combination with an enlightened self-interest emerging from the increased North-South interdependence and the new opportunities opened up by the integration of the Third World into the Western market economy' [*Stokke, 1989: 13*].

The basic difference from the Scandinavian countries initially stemmed from the positive attitude of the latter towards reforms of the international political and economic system to the benefit of developing countries, an area in which Switzerland always proved to be amongst the most conservative industrialised countries. However, in the 1980s the Scandinavians by and large moved towards liberal internationalist attitudes [*Stokke, 1989: 298-299*], whereas Switzerland's increased experience in various North-South issues – notably, structural adjustment programmes – may have caused the policy-makers to rely less blindly on market mechanisms to reduce international imbalances.

Switzerland may thus be on its way to become less of a 'Sonderfall' (special case) in the concert of European middle powers, at least as far as development co-operation goes. The last very distinctive feature may well be the low level of its ODA compared to that of other European middle powers. In the perspective of Switzerland's relations with the European Community, this is one of the areas in which it should make an effort to improve its 'Euro-compatibility'.

III. DEVELOPMENT, GOOD GOVERNANCE AND HUMAN RIGHTS:
A SWISS PERSPECTIVE

Conditionality is, for the donor, a means to ensure that transfers of ODA resources contribute to the achievement of its objectives. If this premise is accepted, it is then necessary to know what the donor is trying to achieve through development assistance. In the context of this chapter, we have chosen to present the official Swiss perspective on three basic objectives of international – and Swiss – development assistance: the promotion of development, good governance and human rights.

The Concept of Development

The concept of development which underlies Swiss development co-operation embodies the following elements:

- development should enable a society to preserve its identity;
- all individuals should be offered – within their own community's endeavours – the means to live freely and in dignity;
- all individuals should, moreover, be in a position to meet, through their work and initiative, their basic needs and those of their dependents;
- the government's development policy should aim at improving the distribution of resources and at a fair distribution of the benefits of development so as to eliminate progressively social injustice [*DDA, 1991: 38*].

Looking more closely at the political dimensions of this concept of development, one very consistently and frequently comes across the idea, in formal policy statements, that the participation of individuals is a key element of the development process that the Swiss Development Co-operation (SDC)[5] wishes to promote in less developed countries (LDCs). The Swiss law on international development co-operation (article 6, 1, a) explicitly mentions participation in economic, social and cultural development as one of the goals to be pursued by technical co-operation.

A recent document circulated by the Swiss delegation at a DAC meeting states that 'genuine and sustainable development depends considerably on the definition and limitation of the areas of public responsibility, and on the space provided for the population to participate in the development process' [*SDC, 1992:2*]. Participation thus becomes a more important criterion by which to evaluate the development policy of a recipient country than formal criteria relating to the political system which may be too 'Eurocentric'. Participation and poverty alleviation are closely linked as the poor are generally deprived of political power. Poverty is related to lack of political strength 'in struggles to gain access to water, land, credit, governmental support services' [*DDA, 1991: 29*]. In line with this concept of development, empowerment of the underprivileged sections of the population is a prerequisite for social and economic progress. There is

---

5. SDC (DDA in French) is the agency within the Ministry of Foreign Affairs responsible for development co-operation. It shares this responsibility with the Federal Agency for External Economic Affairs (OFAEE in French) which is part of the Ministry of Economic Affairs.

little doubt that this perspective, the respect for human rights, is a key feature of any development policy and hence a key element in the relationship between aid donors and recipients. 'When people, even those who are least fortunate are offered an opportunity of fulfilling their potential ... the self-confidence of the individuals concerned and the freedom of action available to them, play a predominant role' [*Federal Council, 1977: 18*]. Furthermore, people's participation is also a key ingredient in programmes promoting environmentally sustainable development.

The Concept of Good Governance

In a paper presented in 1991 at the World Bank Annual Conference on Development Economics, two senior World Bank officials defined governance as 'the use of political authority and exercise of control over a society and the management of its resources for social and economic development' [*Serageldin & Landell-Mills, 1991: 2*]. Good governance 'depends on the extent to which a government is: perceived and accepted by the general citizenry to be *legitimate; committed* to improving general public welfare and *responsive* to the needs of its citizenry; *competent* in assuring law and order and in delivering public services; able to create an *enabling policy environment* for productive activities; and *equitable* in its conduct, favoring no special interests or groups' [*ibid.: 12*].

The Swiss concept of good governance as it was presented to DAC [*SDC, 1992: 2*] is very close to that definition as it stresses the need for accountability, transparency, and respect for human rights. However, three particular aspects are worth mentioning as they illustrate Switzerland's particular interests when it comes to analysing a recipient's policy in the perspective of good governance:

– As mentioned previously, *participation* is one of the basic tenets of the Swiss concept of development. One particular concern of SDC is to try to reconcile, though appropriate macro-economic policy, market-oriented economic development with the enhancement of poorer sections of society and of women.
– Policies to *alleviate poverty*. Does government policy encourage labour-intensive growth? Does it facilitate access of all sections of the population to productive resources such as land, water and credit as well as to basic social services?
– Issues related to *military expenditure* should not be neglected: not only those which directly concern LDCs (level of expenditure in relation to the security situation and to GNP; expenditure on

education and health; the role of the military in the society) but also those in which industrialised countries have a responsibility (arms trade).

Switzerland's International Human Rights Policy

In the wake of the growing concern for human rights expressed in the 1970s by Western countries, the Swiss government published in 1982 a report on its human rights policy in which it stressed that Swiss foreign policy should be more active than hitherto in that area.[6] The main reasons for this new emphasis were at that time (a) that the defence of human rights is implied by the principle of international solidarity which – together with neutrality – is one of the two pillars of Swiss foreign policy; (b) that respect for human rights contributes significantly to maintaining peace and security throughout the world. The defence of human rights thus contributes to Switzerland's external security.

In the same report, the government sets out a number of guiding principles to ensure that the implementation of this policy will not do more harm than good to the victims of human rights violations and/or to Swiss interests. In the first place, this policy should enjoy a high degree of credibility; this can be ensured

– if Switzerland itself has a faultless record on human rights;
– if the policy is universally applied – that is, regardless of the region or the political regime;
– if it is based on internationally accepted criteria – as incorporated in international law and reliable sources of information;
– if it aims at being effective, that is, bringing about an improvement in the situation of victims of human rights violations. The concern about effectiveness induces the government to intervene more readily in individual cases of human rights violations rather than at the general level of a country's human rights situation and to opt for discreet pressures through diplomatic channels rather than for public statements.

The country's neutrality has long been mentioned as a reason – for some as an excuse – for Switzerland's former passivity in this area. It is accepted today in government circles that 'neutrality cannot be equated with indifference'.[7] Nevertheless – at least in the context of

6. This section of the chapter relies on two articles: Kälin [1988] and Krafft and Vigny [1992].
7. Pierre Aubert, former Swiss foreign minister in Madrid, September 1983, quoted by Kälin [1988: 194].

the Cold War – Swiss authorities felt that it was crucial, when criticising a particular state, to avoid taking sides in relation to any East-West controversies and being identified with either of the two blocs. When it came to Communist states, what was criticised was repression rather than the socio-political systems as such [*Kälin, 1988: 194*].

An important feature of Swiss human rights policy is the strict separation that is maintained between this policy and other dimensions of foreign policy, particularly concerning international economic relations. 'The Federal Council (the government) has explained its refusal to use the human rights situation as a criterion in the definition of its economic relations policy towards other states on the grounds that the latter had to be conducted according to the principle of universality' [*Kälin, 1988: 204*]. In its 1982 report, the Federal Council explains that the universal extension of trade relations is necessary in order to maintain jobs in Switzerland in view of the increasingly tough international competition for market shares. Both this reason and the unwillingness of the government to interfere with private enterprise in economic activities explains why Switzerland has in the past consistently refused to join international boycotts, the case where this attitude drew most international and national attention being that of South Africa (cf. Section V). However, over the years, Switzerland was unable, in a number of instances, to disregard totally sanctions which had been decided on by the international community. In 1966, for example, it had to restrict its trade with Rhodesia to the level reached prior to the imposition of UN sanctions, in order not to assist Rhodesia in evading the sanctions [*Kälin, 1988: 206*].

Obviously, conflicts may arise over the implementation of two fundamental principles: the universality of the human rights policy and that of the country's international economic relations. These conflicts are generally resolved in favour of the latter, the only admitted exception being the ban of exports of military equipment to areas where human rights are grossly violated. The priority given in practice to one of the principles over the other is challenged by the political left and by NGOs.[8]

---

8. In June 1993, the Federal Council decided that Switzerland would associate itself with the economic sanctions concerning Haiti decided on by the UN Security Council; obviously Swiss economic interests in Haiti are not such as to be given priority over the defence of human rights.

IV. THE SWISS POLICY APPROACH TO CONDITIONALITY

Traditionally, the basic objective of Swiss development co-operation has been to contribute to the implementation by developing countries of policies which ensure that the poorer sections of the population share in the benefits of social and economic progress. In recent years, new dimensions have been added to this objective in the wake of international political and policy changes. Switzerland – along with other multilateral and bilateral donors – began to move away from exclusively project-oriented development assistance towards an approach which has also concerned global macro-economic and macro-social issues (structural adjustment, good governance, democracy through the promotion of political participation, and respect for human rights).

The concept of development adopted by the Swiss government, its interpretation of 'good governance', the values upon which its human rights policy rests are, by and large, the same as those of other European middle powers. The distinctive feature of Switzerland's policy probably lies in the *means* used to induce – where and when necessary – the recipient countries to put these concepts into practice.

Swiss development co-operation policy is part of the country's foreign policy; in the field of human rights it follows the policy briefly presented in Section III of this chapter. Basically, Switzerland is reluctant to use development co-operation as a means of pressure on the government of a recipient country. In other words it is reluctant to make use of conditionality. This policy has two separate sources which, although of a very different nature and origin, happen to lead to the same policy conclusions.

The *first source* is Switzerland's traditional reserve, in its foreign relations, about making declarations or taking action on political issues concerning another country. This is also valid when it comes to human rights (cf. Section III). Let us quote two policy-makers:[9]

> In principle, Switzerland strictly separates its external policy from its international policy on human rights. In other words, Switzerland does not consider respect for human rights as a criterion for its international economic relations, except when it comes to exporting military equipment. This attitude does not

---

9. Ambassador Mathias-Charles Krafft is Head of the Department for Public International Law in the Swiss Ministry of Foreign Affairs. Jean-Daniel Vigny heads the human rights section in the same department. This quotation is translated into English by the author of the chapter.

prevent it from intervening in order to safeguard these rights by approaching States with which we have economic relations or a development co-operation programme. In this respect experience shows that, on the contrary, our interventions are all the more likely to be effective if these relations are significant. Generally speaking, we doubt that the economic isolation of a country by another country can be conducive to the improvement of the human rights situation. Indeed social and economic development is as essential to the peace and security of a country as respect for the civic and political rights of its citizens ...

In this context, the perspective of our development co-operation is a positive one, by which respect for all human rights is recognised as the fundamental factor of genuine development. Our assistance itself must therefore be designed to contribute to the promotion of these rights. Respect for human rights is, in the long run, a necessary condition for successful development ... Taking into account the specific situation and needs of a given country, one must therefore combine 'positive' development co-operation measures aimed at the promotion of human rights ... with – if necessary, 'negative' actions, i.e. approaching the concerned governments to intervene in case of serious and repeated violations of human rights. In such instances, relations in the area of development co-operation should be maintained – except in extreme situations. It may, however, be necessary to adjust aspects of the co-operation, for instance by setting up programmes bringing direct benefits to the population, whenever possible through non-official channels, or by granting humanitarian assistance [*Krafft and Vigny, 1992: 232*].

Another often quoted reason for this reserved attitude is the size and power of the country: 'We are not sufficiently powerful, either economically or politically, to set conditions for our development assistance', declared the Head of the Human Rights section in the Ministry of Foreign Affairs just before the opening of the UN Conference on Human Rights in Vienna.[10]

The *second source* is Switzerland's development co-operation policy which for reasons related to humanitarian considerations, and in keeping with its concept of development, prefers positive measures to sanctions and dialogue to conditionality. What is the rationale for this attitude?

---

10. Jean-Daniel Vigny in an interview to the *Nouveau Quotidien*, 14 June 1993.

The link between human rights and development. Although human rights violations occur in societies which are experiencing various levels of economic development, some of the root causes of human rights violations can often be linked to situations which are specific to developing countries where structural deficiencies, particularly in the organisation of the state and its judiciary, prevent the application of the rule of law. Moreover, it can be warranted, for humanitarian reasons – specifically in conditions where gross human rights violations occur – to assist the most vulnerable sections of the population in their endeavour to satisfy their basic needs (health, food production). The gist of this line of thought is: 'As long as through aid, people in distress can be assisted, development co-operation projects must be pursued for humanitarian reasons' [*Kälin, 1988: 203*, quoting the 1982 government paper on human rights].

An important policy paper entitled 'Image directrice de la DDA' [*DDA, 1991*] elaborates on the attitude development co-operation agencies should have on human rights issues:

> According to the principle of non-interference in domestic affairs, international development co-operation has always been very discreet on domestic political issues ... One can't establish a simplistic link between successful development and economic liberalism. One must however take into account that the political regime, respect of human rights, as well as the respect of a minimum of economic freedom and of private initiative are prerequisites for genuine development.

One could consider a much more resolute commitment on the part of donor countries in that respect:

– in policy dialogue ... donors could insist on equity, human rights as well as on the priority to be given social expenditure (reduction of military expenditure);
– in day-to-day business, it is possible to support more efficiently local institutions which defend the political and economic rights of the population;
– finally, one could consider being more selective in the choice of recipient countries. When minimal criteria at the political level are not satisfied, one could forego giving assistance, except as humanitarian aid, and letting it be known why such measures are taken [*DDA, 1991: 34*].

Development co-operation and humanitarian assistance are instruments of Swiss human rights policy:

> We utilise them for instance to promote the development of a diversified society by supporting associations and groups defending the social and economic interests of underprivileged sections of the population. Supporting education and training can be considered to contribute to the development of a society concerned with human rights ... However, we do not want to make our aid dependent on respect for human rights. By doing so we may act against the interests of sectors of the population who are, as it is, victims of the non-respect for fundamental freedoms. In each case we examine concretely whether the human rights situation allows the general objectives of our co-operation to be achieved. If these conditions are not fulfilled, we abandon the planned programme [*Conseil fédéral, 1990: 42-43*].

Within SDC, a certain reluctance to apply conditionality also stems from the perception that conditionality as applied by Western donors is often Eurocentric or Americano-centric in its approach and does not sufficiently take into account the specific characteristics of a particular society. The view is that it sometimes also overlooks the fact that political change is a long-term process which must be implemented by endogenous social actors. Conditionality sometimes also conveys patronising attitudes, cynicism, opportunism or can reflect the hidden agenda of a particular donor country or agency. The policy implication of this attitude is to give preference, whenever possible, to a long-term approach leading to the building-up of confidence through bilateral dialogue with the recipient country, the support of endogenous processes of democratisation, and the identification of social actors likely to promote – and capable of promoting – changes in desired direction.[11]

V. THE SWISS APPROACH TO CONDITIONALITY IN PRACTICE

How is the policy we have described above implemented? The chapter does not attempt to give a detailed analysis according to recipient country or to make an assessment of Switzerland's practice of conditionality, but merely to illustrate this policy by examples. We shall

---

11. This approach is presented in a 1992 informal SDC paper.

deal with three issues: (i) the choice of recipients; (ii) the bilateral approach of the positive measures and (iii) the approach to conditionality in the framework of the Bretton Woods institutions.

Switzerland's Choice of Recipient Countries

A donor's decision to initiate or terminate a development co-operation programme with a particular country is based on an assessment of the 'general political compatibility' [*Edgren, 1984: 160*] between the two countries. In the case of Switzerland, the policy and practice of selecting recipients has gone through several phases.

Being a neutral country without colonial ties, Switzerland was at the outset basically open to co-operating with any developing country, development co-operation being yet another way of demonstrating the universality of the country's external relations. The choice of the first recipients was made in a very pragmatic way through the connections which the first actors on the Swiss development scene (missionaries, representatives of NGOs, civil servants, scholars) had established with some developing countries through different channels. For Switzerland at that time there was, as it were, an almost total absence of political incompatibility. In the 1960s, projects were initiated in developing countries encompassing a wide range of GNP per capita and of political regimes. However, as a small donor cannot be expected to grant ODA to every single developing country, certain countries were implicitly avoided as recipients for political reasons.

In the 1970s, two constraints influenced the geographical distribution of Swiss ODA:

(a) The law on international development co-operation, passed by Parliament in 1976, requiring that priority be given to under-privileged countries, regions and communities. This law, passed in the wake of the first oil shock, henceforth considerably reduced the scope for middle-income countries to receive Swiss development assistance. Ecuador (an oil-exporting country) thus ceased being one of the three main recipients of Swiss assistance in Latin America.

(b) The necessity of concentrating flows of financial and human resources on a limited number of recipients, in order to increase both the efficiency and the effectiveness of a relatively small aid programme.

A list of 19 countries and a region (the Sahel) emerged as the main recipients of Switzerland's bilateral technical and financial aid.[12] In 1990 these countries received 57.5 per cent of total bilateral technical and financial aid. This list has remained fairly stable over the years. In Africa, nine of the ten countries on the 1990 list had been on the list in 1980 (Cameroun was replaced by Benin). In Asia, no change in the list occurred between 1980 and 1990. In Latin America, the main emphasis in the programme for Central America shifted from Honduras to Nicaragua in 1990, and Bolivia was temporarily removed from the list as a consequence of Garcia Meza's brutal putsch in 1980. Ecuador was dropped from the list shortly after the first oil shock in 1973, to be reintroduced in the late 1980s.

In the late 1970s, with the beginning of Swiss development assistance to Nicaragua, we witness the first decision to select a new recipient country for reasons explicitly related to its development policy. Somoza's fall and the coming to power of a government seemingly committed to social and economic development was seen as an opportunity to initiate development co-operation with one of the poorer countries of the Western hemisphere. This choice did not go unnoticed by other governments, in particular that of the United States who, in 1986, claimed that Swiss official assistance to Nicaragua was biased in favour of Sandinista sympathisers. Other such 'political' choices were made in the 1980s in terms of the selection of new recipient countries or the significant stepping-up of aid to a traditional recipient.

In the latest (1990) Federal Council 'Message to Parliament concerning the continuation of its technical assistance and financial aid programme', comments are made with reference to two potential recipients who, for political reasons, are presently not receiving aid from Switzerland:

–   Myanmar, after the military junta failed to respect the results of the 1990 elections: 'If the population were to be granted opportunities for economic development as well as political and social rights, we would be willing to support this country's reconstruction' [*Conseil fédéral, 1990: 62-63*].

–   Haiti, after the coup against President Aristide: 'We see hardly

---

12. *Africa*: Benin, Burkina Faso, Chad, Kenya, Madagascar, Mali, Mozambique, Niger, Rwanda, Tanzania; *Latin America*: Bolivia, Honduras, Nicaragua, Peru; *Asia*: Bangladesh, India, Indonesia, Nepal, Pakistan.

This list, valid for 1990, is that established by SDC and is not binding on the OFAEE, the other official development co-operation agency. Moreover, NGO programmes receiving ODA support and humanitarian assistance do not necessarily give priority to the same recipient countries.

any possibilities at present for co-operating with this State. We shall, however, try to find opportunities for supporting educational programmes benefiting the least privileged sections of the population' [*Conseil fédéral, 1990: 73-74*].

What are the outcomes of the process through which Switzerland has progressively selected the recipients of its development assistance?

(a) Orientation towards low-income countries. An analysis of the main 20 recipients of Swiss bilateral development assistance at the beginning of the 1990s reveals that 15 of these have a per capita GNP of below USD 350. The country with the highest per capita GNP is Peru (USD 1010 in 1989) and the five recipients with per capita GNP of above USD 400 between them received (in 1988) 15.1 per cent of total Swiss bilateral ODA. One can therefore safely state that the priority is clearly given to low-income countries.

(b) Low commercialisation of aid. The choice of recipient countries does not appear to be influenced by commercial interests. A comparison between the list of the 15 main recipients of Swiss development assistance and the list of the country's 15 principal trading partners amongst developing countries shows that only one country – India – is present on both lists. This orientation is also corroborated by the relatively low percentage of tied aid.

(c) A human rights orientation corresponding to the DAC average. It is difficult – and controversial – to attempt to measure human rights violations, yet, as Peter Waller [*1992: 30*] has rightly pointed out, it is indispensable to have indicators to implement a human rights oriented development co-operation policy. In an attempt to evaluate the human rights record of Switzerland's main recipients we have taken as a base Charles Humana's human rights indicator which measures countries according to whether their performance is better or worse than the world average [*Waller, 1992: 32*]. For the years 1984-85 (on which Humana based his index) it appears that of Switzerland's 15 most important recipients, ten are below average and five above. The record of all DAC donor countries taken globally is exactly the same. We can tentatively conclude from this rough analysis that Switzerland's choice of recipients correspond to that of many other donors as far as human rights orientation is concerned. According to SDC officials, Switzerland tends to adopt a dynamic approach to the issue of human rights whereby the potential for improvement in a particular country

may be more important than the level of performance actually attained.

(d) Relative weight of military expenditure. We have seen that Switzerland attaches a certain importance to the significance of developing countries' military expenditure. To evaluate to what extent this concern is reflected in the list of recipient countries, we have calculated the relative weight of this expenditure for the main recipient countries. Two indicators were selected: ratio of military expenditure to GNP and ratio of military expenditure to health and education expenditure. As far as the first ratio is concerned, it appears that five of the 15 main recipients (Mozambique, Tanzania, Nicaragua, China and Pakistan) demonstrate a higher ratio than the average performance of all developing countries. The second ratio is above this average for only two recipient countries (Nicaragua and Pakistan), but it is noteworthy that the ratio has increased between 1977 and 1990 for nine of the main recipients, as it has done among LDCs in general. The record of DAC countries taken all together is seven out of 15 on the first indicator, one on the second. Five amongst the DAC main recipients demonstrate an increase in that ratio between 1977 and 1990.[13] There again, Switzerland's main recipients do not seem to have a profile which differs significantly from that of the main recipients of the Western aid community considered as a whole.

The conclusion that can be drawn is that Switzerland's choice of recipient countries has moved from an era of great pragmatism to one where, increasingly, 'general political compatibility' is taken into account in selecting new development co-operation partners. This trend has, however, had a limited influence on existing recipient countries as there are only very few examples of a total cessation of an aid programme for reasons of lack of political compatibility.[14] However, partial or progressive withdrawals, as well as the freezing of development funds, have occurred. The next sub-section will deal with political conditionality in recipient countries.

Positive Approach in Practice

How is the policy described in the preceding section put into practice? We have seen that respect for human rights has played neither a larger

---

13. The data on the recipient countries comes from the 1992 DAC report; the data on military expenditure from the UNDP Human Development reports 1993 and 1990.
14. The only example we have come across is the interruption of aid to Vietnam following the invasion of Cambodia in 1979 and the interruption of aid to Afghanistan following the Soviet invasion at the end of the same year.

nor a smaller role in the selection of recipients of Swiss assistance than it has for other DAC countries. A number of major – and traditional – recipients, have experienced severe domestic problems leading to a deterioration of the human rights situation: Bolivia (Garcia Meza's putsch in 1980), Nepal (attempts in the 1980s by the monarchy to thwart the democratic process) and Rwanda (ethnic and political tensions culminating in a civil war in 1992/93). The Swiss attitude to these has varied from case to case.

In that of *Bolivia* it led to the interruption of those projects which could no longer be pursued under the new dictatorship because their goals of encouraging participatory development ran counter to the new government's policy. Other projects, however, were not discontinued.

The case of *Nepal* is a good example of the use of a combination of pressure and positive measures. Switzerland let it be known to the Nepalese authorities that its co-operation would have to be reviewed if the democratic process was suppressed. On the other hand, SDC provided support to the Nepal Law Society, an association of independent jurists which played a significant role in the transition to constitutional monarchy.

Rwanda is the most recent example. Confronted with severe human rights violations in the most ancient of its recipient countries in Africa, the Swiss authorities 'speak frankly with our partners, with government ministers, but behind closed doors, not in the presence of journalists. Exposure to the media does not always produce the expected changes. It sometimes leads to tougher positions'.[15] Switzerland takes advantage of its influence to encourage negotiations. Threats to withdraw its assistance remain implicit. Amongst positive steps, Switzerland commissioned local lawyers to look into cases of arbitrary arrests.

The case of *South Africa* is certainly one of the most significant illustrations of this policy. After the South African government's decision to declare a state of emergency in July 1985 most Western countries adopted economic sanctions against the country. Switzerland was probably the only country to declare that, although it condemned apartheid, it would not apply sanctions. The reasons put forward were (a) the principle according to which Switzerland's economic relations are universal and cannot be made dependent on human right issues; (b) the Swiss government's doubts about the capacity of such measures to transform a political regime and its feeling that dialogue with the South African government is preferable to sanctions.

---

15. Ambassador Staehelin, Director of the Swiss Development Co-operation in an interview with the *Nouveau Quotidien*, 6 April 1993.

In 1981, SDC has started to support South African NGOs opposing apartheid. In 1986, the Federal Council decided to take positive action on South Africa by transforming this support into a more significant and prominent programme. This programme encourages actions in favour of human rights, civic education and dialogue between the various communities. It also supports training programmes, including scholarships, for professionals (such as lawyers and small entrepreneurs) from communities oppressed by the political system. In 1992, a new programme was initiated to facilitate the reintegration in South Africa of persons returning from exile. One of the institutions supported by SDC is the Legal Resources Centre, an institution employing about 100 lawyers over the whole country and offering legal advice and protection to victims of apartheid.[16] In quantitative terms, this programme started off with an annual disbursement of some 2 million Swiss francs which eventually increased to 7 million francs. In 1990, Switzerland was the sixth largest bilateral source of ODA for South African NGOs.

Other examples of positive steps in the area of human rights and democratisation include the support of democratic elections through financial assistance and the sending of observers to Paraguay, Nicaragua, Benin, Madagascar and Namibia and support for institutions in Latin America which help peasants achieve more secure land rights. In Central America, support was provided to human rights NGOs. As far as military expenditure is concerned, Switzerland was amongst the first donors to contribute (10 million francs) to Mozambique to support the demobilisation and reintegration of both government and RENAMO troops. The programme provided technical assistance and financial support to the demobilised soldiers to help them to engage in self-supporting economic activities.

Conditionality in Relation to the Bretton Woods Institutions

Switzerland was in an unusual situation up until 1992 in being the only OECD member not to be a member of the Bretton Woods institutions. This did not mean that it disagreed with their goals and policies, on the contrary, Switzerland has always been and still is one of the staunchest supporters of the liberal world economic order pursued by these institutions, and it has acted within their framework in respect of the macro-economic policy of recipient countries.

Non-membership did not prevent Switzerland from co-operating closely with the World Bank in selected recipient countries by

---

16. A programme of legal assistance was also initiated by the Swiss Development Cooperation in the territories occupied by Israel.

participating in the relevant consultative groups and by co-financing IDA loans or granting purely bilateral aid (for example in the form of balance-of-payments support) within structural adjustment programmes. Swiss bilateral aid is, in principle, granted only to countries whose economic policy programme as outlined in the Policy Framework Paper (PFP) has been approved by the IMF and/or the World Bank [*Frieden, 1990: 234*]. These procedures indicate that Switzerland shares by and large the World Bank's policy and practice when it comes to structural adjustment programmes, that is to say that it accepts conditionality as applied by these institutions. As a senior Swiss official has put it: 'Since large transfers of funds to a developing country were involved, and since money is fungible, it was evident – for everybody – that some conditions, increasing the chances of success of the entire operation, had to be fulfilled by the borrowing country' [*Wilhelm, 1992: 6*]. There have been, however, exceptions to this rule, as demonstrated in the case of Rwanda: between 1988 and 1992, when this country was in disagreement with the World Bank over structural adjustment issues, Switzerland maintained its support for the government's programme; but then Rwanda is a country SDC knows particularly well.

In May 1991, when it formally made the proposal that Switzerland should join the Bretton Woods institutions, the Federal Council reviewed the IMF's and the Bank's policies, including conditionality [*Conseil fédéral, 1991: 37-40 and 92-93*]. The government mentions the more usual criticisms directed at the Bretton Woods institutions, including the short-term perspective of structural programmes, and lack of concern for the impact of these programmes on the poor. The conclusions of this review are:

(i)   a global endorsement of the IMF's policy. The government paper notes that most of the issues raised by critics of the IMF have been or are being addressed by the institution itself;
(ii) that much of the criticism directed at the IMF should in fact be directed at the international community and particularly at the industrialised countries;
(iii) that, as a member of these institutions, Switzerland would promote within the World Bank group a policy based on Switzerland's principles and goals in development co-operation, encouraging a long-term perspective, the promotion of the poorer sections of the population, respect for human rights, the promotion of women, and a greater emphasis on environmental issues [*Message du 15 mai 1991: 93*].

It is obviously too early to make an assessment of Switzerland's participation in the World Bank and the IMF as a full member of these institutions from the point of view of the implementation of this policy.
However, in its participation in World Bank structural adjustment
programmes through the co-financing of components of these programmes, a special emphasis was placed on measures designed to
mitigate the social consequences of adjustment. The presentation of a
few examples of co-operation with the World Bank mentioned in the
1992 Annual Report of SAC demonstrates differences of approach between the two institutions which are frequently related to the nature
and the extent of people's participation in development programmes.
In those instances, it seems that it is not the Bank's conditionality *per
se* which raises questions with Swiss development officials but the
substance of the Bank's policy.

NGOs and Conditionality: the Swiss Aid Agencies Coalition

Swiss NGOs[17] have long been engaged in attempts to link Switzerland's development co-operation policy with the promotion of human
rights. When the Federal Council presented its 1982 report on human
rights (see Section III above), the Swiss Aid Agencies Coalition expected the government to examine to what extent all schemes which
related to the promotion of Switzerland's economic relations with
developing countries could be used as instruments of its human rights
policy. This attitude was consistent with the enduring concern of the
Coalition that each component of Switzerland's relations with developing countries should contribute to the promotion of development in
these countries – or, at least, not go against it.

On the specific issue of whether ODA should be made conditional
on respect for human rights in recipient countries, the Coalition takes
the view that the most vulnerable social groups are generally the ones
which are most severely affected by the interruption of aid programmes. If human rights violations warrant a reaction on the part on
the donor, ODA should no longer be granted through government
channels but through local NGOs. For example, as the Swiss government decided not to grant ODA to Myanmar (see above), Swissaid, an
NGO, supported local opposition NGOs.

It is difficult to asses the impact of Swiss NGOs on government
policy in this particular area, but it can safely be stated that they made

---

17. Since the world of Swiss NGOs is a very multifarious one, we restrict ourselves
in this short section to the policy followed by the Swiss Aid Agencies Coalition,
which includes the main development-oriented NGOs and which is the most influential NGO development lobby in the country.

a considerable contribution to the growing awareness of international human rights issues, in particular in countries such as Turkey and South Africa, and of the necessity for Switzerland to bring more coherence into its policy towards developing countries.

VI. CONCLUSIONS

Conclusions can be drawn from this chapter as far as the declared policy is concerned. However, it is not possible at this stage to come to conclusions about policy implementation as we were not able to conduct in-depth studies in a number of recipient countries.

The traditional reluctance of the Swiss government to join in international sanctions designed to promote human rights, on the grounds that such measures conflict with the universality of its international economic relations, coincides with its reserved approach to the use of conditionality in the context of bilateral development co-operation.

Switzerland's position on international sanctions can be explained by a number of factors: the country's traditional policy of neutrality; the wish to prevent 'politics' from interfering with international economic relations; and scepticism as to the ability of sanctions to change a state's policy.

In the field of development co-operation, developmental considerations lead to a similarly reserved attitude towards conditionality – at least within the scope of bilateral co-operation. First of all there is the belief that change comes from within and that pressure from external actors has limited impact. Preference is therefore given to supporting agents of change within the country. Secondly, there is the fear that withdrawal of development assistance – for instance for non-compliance with human rights related conditionality – will primarily affect the most vulnerable sections of the population. Thirdly, there is a realistic assessment that the country does not have the power to set conditions for its development assistance.

Over the years Switzerland's traditional 'apolitical' approach to international relations has undergone changes. The government's declared policy that sanctions were not an instrument of the country's human rights policy was not upheld in a number of cases [*Kälin, 1988: 206*]. The selection of recipient countries has moved away from the 'universal/pragmatic' approach of the early years towards one of seeking to identify countries in which participative development is genuinely encouraged. However, the list of recipients tends to remain stable and this policy is not followed by all government development agencies.

The choice of South Africa as a new recipient in 1986 arose from a combination of two different policies. Switzerland had had to face harsh criticism of its policy on sanctions not only internationally but also on the domestic scene. The announcement of 'positive measures' was not only an illustration of Switzerland's approach towards inducing political change but also a signal that the country was doing something to combat apartheid.

An evolution towards more politically minded co-operation and the introduction of more conditionality in the bilateral relations with recipient countries are, however, perceptible. In June 1993, the Federal Council issued a draft bill on co-operation with states from eastern Europe and the former USSR. This draft explicitly states that the objective of the co-operation is to promote and reinforce in these countries respect for human rights, democratic and stable political institutions and stable economies based on the market. It is moreover clearly stated that co-operation will depend on the will of concerned governments to undertake reforms which correspond to these objectives.

REFERENCES

A. Official documents

Conseil fédéral, 1977, *Message concernant la continuation de la coopération technique et de l'aide financière en faveur des pays en développement* du 23 novembre 1977.

Conseil fédéral, 1990, *Message concernant la continuation de la coopération technique et de l'aide financière en faveur des pays en développement* du 21 février 1990.

Conseil fédéral, 1991, *Message concernant l'adhésion de la Suisse aux institutions de Bretton Woods* du 15 mai 1991, Berne.

DDA/OFAEE, 1993, Rapport annuel 1992, Coopération au développement de la Confédération suisse, Berne.

DDA, 1991, *Image directrice de la DDA*, Cashiers de la DDA, numéro 1, Berne.

DFAE, 1993, Avant-projet d'arrêté fédéral concernant la coopération avec les Etats d'Europe de l'Est, Berne.

Loi fédérale sur la coopération au développement et l'aide humanitaire internationales du 19 mars 1976 (RS 974.0).

SDC, 1992, *Swiss Development Co-operation and Good Governance, State of Discussion* (mimeographed document circulated for information at the DAC Senior Level Meeting, Paris 16-17 June 1992).

B. Books and articles

Edgren, Gus, 1984, 'Conditionality in Aid', in Olav Stokke (ed.), *European Development Assistance*, Vol. 2 (Third World Perspectives on Policies and Performance), Tilburg: EADI Book Series 4.

Frieden, Jürg, 1990, 'Les balbutiements de l'aide-programme macro-économique,

Quelques considérations tirées de l'experience récente de la Suisse', in *Annuaire Suisse-Tiers Monde*, numero 9, 1990, Genève: IUED.

Kälin, Walter, 1988, 'Die Menschenrechtspolitik der Schweiz', in *Schweizerisches Jahrbuch für Politische Wissenschaft*, Vol. 28, Berne: Haupt.

Krafft, Mathias-Charles et Jean-Daniel Vigny, 1992, 'La politique suisse à l'égard des droits de l'homme', in *Noveau manuel de la politique extérieure suisse*, Berne: Haupt.

OCDE, 1992, *Coopération pour le développement, Rapport 1992*, Paris: OCDE.

Serageldin, Ismaïl and Pierre Landell-Mills, 1991, *Governance and the External Factor*, Annual Conference on Development Economics, 25-26 April.

Stokke, Olav (ed.), 1989, *Western Middle Powers and Global Poverty. The Determinants of the Aid Policies of Canada, Denmark, the Netherlands, Norway and Sweden*, Uppsala: The Scandinavian Institute of African Studies in co-operation with the Norwegian Institute of International Affairs.

Waller, Peter, 1992, 'After East-West Detente, Towards a Human Rights Orientation in North-South Development Co-operation', *Development* 1992-1, Journal of SID.

Weck-Hanneman, Hannelore, 1987, 'Politisch-ökonomische Bestimmungsgründe der Vergabe von Entwicklungshilfe: Eine empirische Untersuchung für die Schweiz', in *Revue suisse d'économie politique et de statistique*, numéro 4, décembre 1987.

White, John, 1974, *The Politics of Foreign Aid*, London: The Bodley Head.

Wilhelm, Rolf, 1992, ' "New Political Conditionality" as seen from the Swiss experience in Development Co-operation', paper presented at the Seminar on the Political Conditionality in Development Assistance, Vienna: University of Economics and Business Administration, April, 1992.

7

Determinants and Limitations of Aid Conditionality: Some Examples from Nordic-Tanzanian Co-operation

SAMUEL S. MUSHI

Political conditionality has become fashionable in the wake of the democratic revolutions in Eastern and Central Europe. In African countries, too, there are increasing pressures for democracy and the observance of human rights [*Kumado and Busia, 1991; Andreassen et al., 1991:ix*]. Part of this pressure has built up internally over three decades, but in the past few years the main push has come from external forces, especially Africa's major Western donors.

Before the disintegration of the Eastern bloc, Western aid was used partly as a foreign policy instrument in order to contain communist expansion. Often conditionality took philanthropic, economic or technical forms, thereby concealing political motives. In the 1960s, during the *détente* between the two superpowers, 'gunboat diplomacy' was replaced by 'cheque-book diplomacy' (aid). However, 'gunboat diplomacy' (of one superpower) is now back in, and political conditionality has become an open agenda.

Many Western donors and international organisations have recently delivered open statements making political reforms in Africa a firm condition for aid. For example, between 1989 and 1990 clear directives were given by Douglas Hurd (then British Foreign Secretary), Herman Cohen (then US Assistant Secretary for African Affairs), François Mitterrand (President of France), and Barber Conable (World Bank President).[1]

---

1. For statements by Douglas Hurd and François Mitterrand, see *The New Internationalist*, No. 221, September 1990, p. 19; and for that of Herman Cohen, see *The African Reporter*, September-October 1989, p.9. Barber Conable envisaged a political scenario that encouraged private entrepreneurs, see Kumado and Busia [*1991:12*].

Within Tanzania, donor agents have recently made use of the mushrooming private newspapers[2] in order to express their views on a variety of political issues – such as established laws, proposed laws, treatment of newly registered political parties, human rights issues – whilst avoiding the accusation of interfering in the internal affairs of the host country. For example, by 'seeking' to be interviewed by these newspapers, US and EEC representatives and ambassadors in Dar es Salaam were able to express negative views on a proposed bill which seemed to curtail the autonomy of the press. The EEC ambassadors expressed 'great concern' and said they would continue to discuss the matter in their regular meetings.[3] Such direct and open intervention is new in Tanzania: in 1964 the country broke off aid relations with West Germany over the Hallstein doctrine of conditionality.[4]

Where does the Nordic region stand on this? The purpose of this chapter is to explore NordicTanzanian aid relations in the context of the changing forms of conditionality. We are interested in the determinants and limitations of conditionality in general and political conditionality in particular. The chapter is guided by many questions that are being asked in Africa, with special emphasis on two of these. Who are the target and/or actual beneficiaries of aid conditionality – the donors or the recipients? Can conditionality be made 'reciprocal' or must it always remain a one-sided imposition?

In Section I we shall trace the origins of *Nordiphilia* within Tanzania and *Tanzaphilia* within the Nordic region, and how these cordial relations have affected conditionality. Section II examines the factors behind the practice, policy and philosophy of aid as it changed from being basically recipient-oriented (1960s-70s) to being largely donor-oriented (1970s-80s). Various instruments for achieving donor-centred interests (economic conditionality) are reviewed. Section III focuses on examples of Nordic political conditionality in Tanzania during the 1980s and 1990s, and contrasts the Nordic style with that of the major Western powers. Finally, in Section IV, we discuss the limits of conditionality in theory and practice.

In Figure 1 we have attempted to give a summary of the major orientational changes in Nordic aid policies, practices and conditiona-

---

2. Some 20 private newspapers now exist, but none has (by July 1993) been publishing on a daily basis: most are weekly or fortnightly.
3. *The Express*, 29 July-4 August 1993, Issue No. 076, p. 3. The bill was expected to come before Parliament in October 1993 despite opposition by private journalists who may have actively solicited the views of the ambassadors and donor agents to strengthen their position. It has not been tabled till now (i.e. end of March 1994).
4. For an analysis of the Hallstein doctrine of conditionality, see Mushi and K. Mathews (eds.) [*1982*].

lities from the mid-1950s to the early 1990s. The chapter is, in a sense, an elaboration of the contents of the 20 'boxes' included in the figure. However, it must be emphasised that the figure cannot be taken as an 'accurate', detailed picture of each country, but as an indication of a dominant pattern in the Nordic region as a whole during each period.

FIGURE 1
NORDIC AID: MAJOR ORIENTATIONAL CHANGES, 1950s-1990s

Phase	Dominant aid philosophy	Public opinion on aid in donor country	Main objective or focus of aid	Bilateral/ multilateral division of ODA	Dominant conditionality: explicit or implicit
Mid-1950s to late-1960s	Humanitarian, philanthropic, altruistic aid	Population generally supportive of a humanitarian mission	Economic growth: fighting poverty to improve – international peace – international security – national image abroad	Greater multilateral than bilateral aid; predominantly untied aid	Virtually no explicit conditionality
Late-1960s to mid-1970s	Philanthropy plus 5% to donor business community (enlightened selfinterest)	Supportive public opinion (Finland an exception in the 1960s)	Growth with equity: meeting basic needs	Generally multilateral-bilateral balance: some tying introduced	Social justice as implicit conditionality
Mid-1970s to mid-1980s	Officially altruism but self-interest growing	Generally supportive	Back to growth and economic liberalisation	Bilateral tied aid gaining ground; some tied multilateral aid	Economic policy reform: liberalisation and privatisation; aid tying is intensified, but some aid is converted into grants
Mid-1980s to the 1990s	Co-operation for development and mutual benefit	Generally supportive	Economic and political liberalisation	Increasing bilateral tied aid	Political reform: democracy and human rights

227

I. PHILANTHROPY, NORDIPHILIA AND TANZAPHILIA, 1960s-70s

Until the 1970s Tanzania was as Nordiphilic as the Nordic countries were Tanzaphilic. Treasury officials in Tanzania often refer to the four Nordic countries aiding Tanzania (Sweden, Norway, Denmark and Finland) as having a 'progressive profile'. This they attribute to the following factors:[5]

- the Nordic countries did not suspend bilateral aid to Tanzania when the latter refused to comply with the IMF conditionalities between 1979 and 1986;[6]
- Throughout the 1970s, each Nordic country gave to Tanzania a higher proportion of its ODA than to any other country in the aid programme: on average, 13 per cent of Swedish bilateral ODA (1975-81), 15 per cent of Norwegian (1970-81), 17 per cent of Danish (1975-81) and 34 per cent of Finnish bilateral ODA (1970-81);[7]
- The Nordic countries supported the liberation struggles in central and southern Africa to which Tanzania was passionately committed;
- they had not colonised Africa and therefore did not have an 'imperialist' stigma;
- they provided comparatively soft aid terms, with more grants than loans (in principle and initially untied, but later progressively tied);
- Sweden and Norway were the first OECD countries to reach the 0.7 per cent ODA target and even set their own target of 1 per cent and above;
- they targeted aid to the real poor, 'seeking solidarity with the world poor', as SIDA puts it [*SIDA and URT, 1987; Södersten, 1987*];
- they supported the declaration on the New International Economic Order (NIEO), and voted with Third World countries in various other UN resolutions [*Bergesen et al., 1982*]; and
- they supported progressive (welfare state) policies at home and abroad.

---

5.   Interview in the Treasury during May-June 1993, and relevant documents produced by donors and by the Tanzanian government.
6.   Available data show that Swedish assistance was rising when that of other capitalist countries was falling during this period.
7.   Data gathered from Stokke (ed.), [*1984. Vol. 1, chapters on Sweden, Norway, Denmark and Finland*].

In the 1960s and early 1970s Tanzania's rosy picture of the Nordic region was matched by the Nordic countries' similarly rosy picture of Tanzania. Nyerere's first state visit (just before Tanganyika's full independence in 1961) was to a Nordic country, Sweden. There a *Karibu* (welcome) association was formed by some Swedish experts, diplomats and former missionaries, to express feelings of solidarity with Tanzania and to lobby for support.[8] Nyerere's ideology of *ujamaa* had much in common with Nordic social democracy and welfarism, and he was quick to cultivate personal friendships with like-minded leaders such as the influential Olof Palme of Sweden and Urho Kekkonen of Finland. Impressed by Nyerere's vision of Tanzania's future, the Nordic countries jointly built the Kibaha Educational Centre in the l960s and continued to co-operate with Tanzania, particularly in the social services field.

Nordic countries' aid objectives, up until the mid-1970s, left little room for direct or short-term economic and political conditionalities. As small and medium powers caught between two roaring giants, Nordic countries were concerned above all to ensure peace and security at the international level, particularly through the United Nations [*Stokke, 1989; Kärre, 1989*]. Aid was seen as 'a means of cutting off potential sources of conflict between rich and poor countries' [*Kiljunen, 1984:151*]. Thus emphasis was single-mindedly on economic growth, as major theorists of the time had also advised [*Rostow, 1963, 1971*]. This objective is consistent with the fact that until the mid-1970s the larger part of Nordic ODA was distributed multilaterally (through UN agencies, the World Bank, regional banks, etc.) rather than bilaterally.

The officially declared principles guiding Nordic aid were generally altruistic and philanthropic. We shall illustrate this by a few examples. Both Norway and Sweden formulated their aid principles in 1962, and each was supposed to be 'disinterestedly' recipient-oriented. For Norway, a policy of 1962 declared that aid 'must be provided on a general humanitarian basis and should not be based on economic, political or religious particularistic interests' [*Stokke, 1984:319*]. Sweden's aid philosophy (spelt out in Government Bill 1962:100) went beyond the conventional emphasis on growth to include social justice (the fair distribution of resources), economic and political independence, human rights and democracy. However,

---

8. For example, Sweden and Finland were among only four developed capitalist countries to vote in the UN for economic rights and state responsibility, the other two being New Zealand and Australia. The resolution stipulated the right of developing countries to participate in the management of world economic affairs.

these were not made conditionalities for recipients, but remained guiding principles for the donor [*Kärre and Svensson, 1989; Ljunggren, 1986; Frühling, 1986*]. According to Jellinek *et al.* [*1984:367*], describing the period before the mid-1970s, 'SIDA's activities were characterised by a permissive attitude towards its programme countries, which were given relatively extensive freedom of action'. In fact democracy and human rights were not linked to Swedish aid until two decades later.

Denmark was to be guided by three DAC-recommended principles: '(i) Extension of development assistance without imposing political conditions on the recipient countries; (ii) Compliance with the wishes and priorities of the recipient countries, as established in their development plans; and (iii) Concentration of assistance on the poorest developing countries with special emphasis on the needs of the poorer strata of the population, in accordance with the basic needs strategy' [*Svendsen, 1984:136*].

The philosophy behind Finnish aid was rooted in the internationalist concerns of the UN Second Development Decade. The Finnish President, Urho Kekkonen, reflected this in his 1970 UN speech: 'The strategy for the new United Nations Development Decade is an important expression of the emerging philosophy of international responsibility which recognizes that the concepts of social justice must have a universal application.'[9] Consequently a Finnish Programme for International Development Co-operation adopted in 1974 emphasised 'the joint responsibility of all countries for the international development' and that the well-being of the international system depended on the well-being of its parts: 'All the nations share the advantages of international development... The government regards the principles of the international development as the starting point for its development cooperation policy.'[10]

Towards the end of the 1960s it was clear that the strategy for growth had widened the gap between the rich and the poor within individual developing countries and between rich and poor nations [*Pearson, 1969*]. Even the World Bank – the chief architect of the growth strategy – criticised it for ignoring the equity side of development [*McNamara, 1980*]. Tanzania was ahead of the UN Second Development Decade by three years. The Arusha Declaration (1967) and subsequent policies of the ruling party, Tanganyika African

---

9. The Ministry of Foreign Affairs, Helsinki, 1971. Statements and Documents on Foreign Policy, 1970, quoted in Kiljunen [*1984:155-6*]
10. Government of Finland, 1974, Programme and Principles for International Development Co-operation, 10 August 1974, quoted in Kiljunen [*1984:156-7*].

National Union (TANU), had laid down a people-based strategy emphasising growth with distributive justice. This policy further endeared Tanzania to the Nordic countries which supported the UN basic needs strategy. Thus they became leading supporters of the ambitious rural-oriented TANU social services programmes until the end of the 1970s. A leadership code introduced in 1967 gave confidence to the donors that their money would be used for development oriented towards people. The introduction in the 1970s of country programming, with a fouryear revolving planning period (three for Finland) and tentative figures for the period reviewable annually was expected to make aid more recipient-oriented.

Thus, apart from a sort of 'social conditionality' implied in the Nordic aid philosophies, the Tanzanian authorities were virtually unrestricted during this period. For example, the donors seem to have accepted – or at least condoned – the monopolistic position of the state in the development effort, the hegemonic position of the ruling party (TANU and, after 1977, Chama Cha Mapinduzi, CCM) *vis-à-vis* civic organisations, the primacy of central over local institutions, and so on. Neither the recipient nor the donors had 'discovered' the developmental and democratic significance of 'civil society' which currently receives so much attention. The Nordic countries were concerned more with economic rights (following the UN basic needs philosophy) than with civil and political rights. While in economic terms there was no contradiction with Tanzania's *ujamaa* philosophy, concern for the broader rights required the donor to repudiate the monopoly of power. No such repudiation was heard during the 1970s.

One outcome of Tanzaphilia and Nordiphilia was to mitigate criticism on both sides. This was particularly true during the Nyerere years, but has continued to underlie Nordic-Tanzanian relations.

II. THE RISE OF DONOR SELF-INTEREST AND ECONOMIC CONDITIONALITY: 1970s-1980s

If during the 1960s and early 1970s aid conditionality was hidden and insignificant, it became explicit and controversial after the economic shocks of the mid-1970s, and it took an economic form. Our hypothesis is that both the modality and conditionality of aid are determined by factors operating in three different arenas: the recipient country, the donor country and on an international level. Even where – as in the Nordic case – the rhetoric of official aid philosophy has remained the same, in practice it is distorted by factors located in these three arenas, and therefore the outcome is usually a compromise. During the 1970s and 1980s all the factors favoured economic reform which was then imposed as a condition for aid.

Significant factors within Tanzania were those relating to the performance of the economy and the state of the civil society. After the mid-1970s the Tanzanian economy deteriorated rapidly for a combination of reasons: these include the sharp rise in oil prices, the Tanzania-Uganda war, the break-up of the East African Community, floods in some parts of the country and droughts in others, the fall in (agricultural) commodity prices on the world market, and the rise of bureaucratic corruption and consequent fall in management standards. All this affected the state of civil society: a prosperous merchant class had arisen with a parallel underground economy,[11] feeding parasitically on the statemanaged economy and ready to unite with external forces to challenge the monopolistic position of the state. Civic organisations formerly under state control also began to search for autonomy and thousands of informal people's organisations (POs) appeared in both rural and urban areas as a way of ensuring survival under harsh economic conditions.

The war[12] against economic sabotage declared by the government on the merchant class in March 1983 was evidence of the government's awareness of the rise of alternative centres of power and their sense of vulnerability to internal and external manoeuvres. Thus the country's economic and socio-political situation provided fertile ground for conditionality. Nyerere's six-year resistance to the IMF conditionalities (1979-85) was sustained more by his personal charisma and fighting spirit than by the status of the economy, and eventually he had to give in.[13]

At the international level, the most important factor relating to conditionality was the rise of neo-conservatism which led to the election of ultra-conservative leaders in influential countries between 1975 and 1985. Outstanding examples were Ronald Reagan in the US, Margaret Thatcher in the UK and, within the Nordic region, the defeat

---

11. For a good analysis of the rise of the parallel economy, see Maliyomkono and Bagachwa [*1990*].

12. From the mid-1970s, the size of the unofficial, parallel economy grew rapidly, and was feeding on state economic corporations. By the early 1980s a large group of prosperous traders constituted a class of *nouveaux riches*. The activities of this merchant class were declared 'economic sabotage' by the government and campaigns against them started in March 1983, leading to the arrest of many and the confiscation of their property.

13. Before leaving the Presidency in 1985, Nyerere had accepted the proposal to privatise unproductive state farms (e.g. sisal estates) and had approved trade liberalisation measures in 1984.

of Social Democratic parties (as in Sweden 1976-82). Reaganism and Thatcherism provided the Western bloc with a powerful ideology seeking to 'roll back the frontiers of communism' and to create a new world with a liberal economy and polity [*Krieger, 1986*]. The Bretton Woods institutions (the IMF and the World Bank) took this ideology very literally in prescribing structural adjustment programmes for Tanzania and the rest of Africa, everywhere making economic liberalisation (and later political liberalisation) a pre-condition for aid. The other donors – Nordic countries included – could not remain unaffected by the ideology of the world pace-setters.

Domestic pressures within the Nordic countries vigorously challenged the altruistic assumptions of ODA and demanded a more donor-oriented aid policy. Soon aid became an important aspect of domestic politics and donor governments responded with a number of donor-centred packages ingeniously built into the ODA structure. This resulted in the commercialisation of ODA through various mechanisms, such as the following:

(1) the creation of new institutions or the streamlining of old ones;
(2) the tying of aid to ensure a higher return flow to the donor country;
(3) changing the forms or modalities of aid;
(4) making changes in the sectoral distribution of aid and in the principle of geographical concentration.

We shall examine these changes in donor policies and how they affected Tanzania in relation to economic conditionality, or diminished economic benefit.

Programmes which combined aid with commerce were created in all Nordic countries during the 1970s and 1980s so as to achieve the balance between recipient and donor orientation of aid which was demanded domestically [*Rudebeck, 1979; Lembke, 1986; Edgren, 1986; Beckman, 1978*]. A good example of this trend is Sweden's 'enlarged co-operation' programmes which were introduced in 1976/ 77 and by the early 1980s accounted for about five per cent of ODA. Unlike the previous 'development assistance' form of aid which focused on poor countries and poor sections of the population, these programmes focused on middle- and upper-income countries and sections – that is, areas of 'effective demand'. The aim was to consolidate long-term economic and other relations with the recipient countries. A recommendation by a government committee stated: 'When the aid budget is financing enlarged co-operation, it performs a dual function: it strengthens economic and social development in the recipient country and stimulates the development of Sweden's relationship with this country' [*Jellinek et al., 1984:387*].[14] The programmes were administered by the Swedish Commission for Technical Co-operation (BITS) established in 1979 under the Ministry of Foreign Affairs.

Other Swedish examples include SWEDFUND and Concessionary Credit. SWEDFUND was established in 1979 to promote joint industrial ventures between Swedish companies and partners in recipient (and other developing) countries. It would provide information and support pre-investment studies by interested Swedish companies. Concessionary Credit, introduced in 1981, was primarily a commercially motivated facility to support Swedish enterprises against stiff international competition in the developing countries, including recipient ones. The credits were to be subsidised up to 15-25 per cent, with much of the funding coming from the ODA budget. The credit funds, which had to be approved by BITS, were administered by the Swedish Export Credits Guarantee Board which acted as a guarantor to Swedish companies exporting to low-risk countries.

Norway also moved towards commercialising aid relations [*Havnevik et al., 1988*]. Government Report No. 35 of 1980/81 stressed that what was needed in the 1980s was broader co-operation which would stimulate Norwegian private industry to participate in the economies of recipient (and other Third World) countries through expanded trade and joint ventures. Although the philosophy of the Report – that effective demand rather than poverty should determine the type of aid – was rebuffed by the Norwegian Parliament, the new orientation and practice continued [*Stokke, 1984:345-48*]. NORDFUND, similar to Sweden's SWEDFUND, had been created in 1979. This provided credit, on favourable terms, for Norwegian firms which engaged in industrial enterprises in demand-effective Third World countries (countries in demand of the goods and services in question and with an ability to pay). Despite an initial intention to the contrary, part of the funding for this facility came from ODA [*Stokke, 1984:334-35*].

Integration of aid and business was even easier in Denmark because DANIDA had a board which was composed of representatives from major interest groups – including members from industry, agriculture, trade unions, youth groups and voluntary organisations. This met at least once a month during the 1970s to study and com-

---

14. Jellinek *et al.* [*1984:387*] quoting a recommendation by the Standing Committee of the Parliament on Foreign Affairs, document 1978/79:20, p. 81.

ment on aid projects and related activities. A similarly composed 75-member Council of International Development met twice a year to debate, among other things, DANIDA board reports and related aid issues. Pressure from these and other institutions led to the appointment of a Committee in 1981 to review the country's aid policy and practices. As in Sweden and Norway, the Committee recommended wider co-operation to include trade, technology and investments. During this time, close to 50 per cent of Danish bilateral aid was tied [*Svendsen, 1984:130-32*].

Although Finland was a latecomer in the aid business, it was probably the first in the Nordic region to describe aid in terms of self-interest. In 1967 a Finnish Foreign Minister used the term 'enlightened self-interest' (rather than altruism) to describe aid, and later a Finnish State Commission for Development Aid recommended the use of the term 'development co-operation' instead of 'development aid' to emphasise the expected mutuality of benefits [*Kiljunen, 1984:154*]. Specific devices to ensure the interests of the donor were developed in the course of the 1970s and 1980s: these included FINNFUND (on the same model as NORDFUND and SWEDFUND) in 1979, mixed credits in 1980, and an export guarantees system in 1981. As in the other Nordic countries, these commercially-oriented devices were financed partly from the regular aid budget, and as one analyst puts it: 'In the course of the 1970s, commercial interests gradually eroded the official development (aid) philosophy, as the commercial relations with the developing countries advanced' [*Kiljunen, 1984:159*].

Tying of aid to procurement from the donor country increased with the creation of new devices and growing pressure from potential suppliers. The four Nordic countries differed only in degree: all moved from virtually untied aid during the 1960s, to moderately tied aid after the mid-1970s and substantially tied aid during the 1980s.[15] Tying was even extended to the multilateral portion of ODA. For example, projects co-financed with the World Bank or regional banks usually engage Nordic firms for tasks such as feasibility studies, project preparation, construction, evaluation, provision of capital equipment, technical assistance, and consultancy. As Nordic exports to Tanzania increased during the 1980s and 1990s the emphasis on import and commodity aid led to examples of double and even triple tying of aid.[16]

---

15. For details see the chapters on Finland, Sweden, Norway and Denmark in Stokke (ed.) [*1984*].
16. Single tying is specifying the purpose of the aid; double tying is specifying the

Changes in modalities of aid after mid-1970s were at two levels. The first was in the ratio of bilateral and multilateral aid: in the mid-1960s, for Norway, Sweden and Denmark the ratio was about 40:60 and for Finland 20:80; by the mid-1980s all changed to about 60:40. Clearly, part of the reason for the reversal is that it is easier to tie aid which is bilateral rather than multilateral. However, this did not affect the position of Tanzania as a recipient of Nordic aid. The second level of change relates to the distribution of bilateral ODA. In this regard, all the Nordic donors were flexible enough to entertain Tanzania's requests for a combination that would meet its critical economic needs. For example, Nordic aid to Tanzania during 1986-92 reveals the following order of priorities: commodities/import support, project aid, technical assistance, and programme aid.[17]

The order accords well with Tanzania's own economic situation: this includes inadequate foreign exchange reserves for much needed agricultural and industrial imports, unbalanced budgets, and declining management capacity due to bureaucratic corruption. It so happens that the new modalities also accord with the export and consultancy needs of the Nordic business community.

Sectoral distribution of aid has been affected by the current focus on effective demand (rather than poverty) by the donors and their companies. This had led to the abandonment of the earlier principle of geographical concentration of aid on a few selected programme countries. Tanzania has been affected by these changes. The Nordic enthusiasm for rural-based projects for basic services seems to have declined, judging by the number of 'white elephant' projects which donors have abandoned [*Therkildsen, 1988*], and the virtual absence of foodproduction aid to the subsistence sector. Such projects have a relatively low return flow, and recent debates on the future of state welfarism in the Nordic region may help to explain this decline. However, the spread of Nordic aid to non-programme countries (in accordance with the 'enlarged co-operation' idea) has not led to a loss of the privileged position enjoyed by Tanzania during the 1960s and 1970s [*DAC, 1989, Jerve; 1991:71-78*].

III. MANIFESTATIONS OF POLITICAL CONDITIONALITY 1980s-1990s

Current political conditionality linked to human rights and democracy should be understood in its historical and theoretical context and its

---

purpose and linking it with sources in the donor country; triple tying is determining purpose, donor country and specific firms in the donor country.
17. Interviews in the Treasury, June 1993. Actual figures were not available.

background of self-interest. Previous theories related aid to democracy only indirectly in a theoretical chain linking aid with growth (growth theories), growth with general socio-economic prosperity (trickle-down theories), and economic prosperity with democracy (theories on economic prerequisites for democracy):

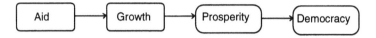

This formulation evolved from the history of democracy in the West, and human rights (coming at the end of the chain) were conceived as an integral part of the democratisation process.

The UN Second Development Decade modified this formulation in two ways. First, the basic needs, poverty-oriented strategy combined growth and general prosperity in the philosophy of 'growth with equity' [*Streeten, 1980*]. Second, the issue of human rights came to the surface as a distinct area of concern, and included a longer list of rights than those conventionally associated with liberal democracy: civil, political, economic, social and cultural rights [*Steward, 1989*]. Aid would stimulate equitable development among various groups in society and such development would promote democracy and respect for human rights:

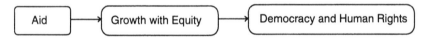

In this formulation democracy has a diminished domain, focusing mainly on political pluralism, since many civil and political rights were seen in the context of human rights. Because intervention to promote human rights is internationally more acceptable than intervention to export democracy, the expanded scope of the human rights sphere may have given donors some leverage for imposing political conditionality [*Donnelly, 1989*]. However, in practice, Western donors have rarely been willing to make aid conditional on improved performance in human rights [*Tomasevski, 1989; Brecher, 1990; Falk, 1981; Mathews and Pratt, 1988*]. In Africa, for example, regimes which violate human rights have survived and thrived, sustained by Western aid, including military support to crush internal opposition. This apparent contradiction can be understood only in terms of donor self-interest.[18]

---

18. Western countries' continued support of Moi's regime in Kenya until the 1992

The imposition of the IMF-IBRD structural adjustment programmes (SAPs) and economic recovery programmes (ERPs) on African countries – including Tanzania – throughout the 1980s reinstated the policy of growth at the expense of equity. The programmes also sought to break the monopolistic role of the state in the economy and to remove tariff barriers. Since aid was conditioned on policy reforms, it contained political conditionality, and as the World Bank admitted in 1985, 'More of our lending has become policy-based.'[19] However, the conditionality was not based on concern for human rights or democracy in the recipient countries but rather with the Reaganist-Thatcherist ideology of the 'free market'. In Tanzania and elsewhere in Africa the adoption of liberal economic policies after the mid-1980s led to the diminution of socioeconomic 'human rights' in the poorer sections of the population (such as the right to health, education, and an adequate living). Apart from indicating that development is as political as it is technical, this raised questions of whether some aspects of democracy and human rights could be traded. For example, should socio-economic rights be given priority over civil and political rights or vice versa? [*Howard, 1983*]

Some theorists (including Gorbachev on *perestroika* and *glasnost*) now emphasise the need for human and democratic rights to go in tandem with economic growth [*Howard, 1983; Donnelly, 1989*]; and some even argue that democracy is the parent of growth rather than the other way round [*Michanek, 1985*]. Such thinking has become current amongst donors as reflected in a 1989 statement of the Development Assistance Committee (DAC) aid ministers: 'There is a vital connection, now more widely appreciated, between open, democratic and accountable political systems, individual rights and the effective and equitable operation of economic systems' [*DAC, 1989*]. This perception ignores the historical development of democracy and human rights in the West and requires that aid be targeted simultaneously to economic development, human rights and democratic development [*Michanek, 1985; Steward, 1989; Donnelly, 1989*]:

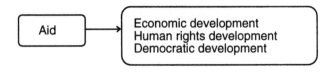

---

elections and Mobutu's regime in Zaire, despite their poor human rights record, illustrates this contradiction.
19. An interview published in the *Far Eastern Economic Review*, October 1985.

This simultaneous approach allows the selective use or combination of two forms of conditionality: explicit and implicit.

Explicit conditionality refers to the donor's attempt to encourage the recipient to observe human rights and the rules of democracy by threatening to take punitive action such as withholding or reducing development aid. Two drawbacks make this an unpopular choice. First, it may seriously affect the economic and social rights of the very people the action seeks to protect. Second, such action may jeopardise the donor's own economic and other interests in the recipient country.

Implicit conditionality refers to active support for human rights activities and for building democratic institutions, channelled either through the state or targeted groups such as women's groups, human rights activists, civic associations, and opposition parties. In this approach the 'violating' regime gets the message indirectly even where development aid continues; and even if the regime fails to respond to such signals, the donor's targeted assistance makes opposition groups better prepared for the struggle. In the current atmosphere between donors and recipients this option may lead to accusations of 'political interference' in the recipient country. Nordic political conditionality in Tanzania has been based largely on this implicit approach, and so far skilful use has preserved cordial relations.

Although some Nordic countries had mentioned that concern for democracy and human rights was among the principles and objectives of development assistance (for example, Sweden in 1962), they did not make them definite conditions for aid before mid-1980s. According to a Swedish government statement to Parliament in 1988: 'A main task in Swedish foreign policy is to safeguard human rights. All the political parties of Parliament stand united in that endeavour and Parliament and Government are supported by a united Swedish people.'[20] This commitment was re-emphasised by the Foreign Minister in 1989 before the UN Commission on Human Rights: 'Promotion of the respect for human rights is an increasingly important consideration in the Swedish programme of development co-operation, both in our continuing dialogue with major recipient countries and in the direction given to our assistance.'[21] Sweden illustrates two types of assistance built into ODA to support human rights and the transition to democracy.

---

20. Statement by the Swedish Assistant Minister of Foreign Affairs to Parliament on 7 December 1988, in commemoration of the UN Declaration on Human Rights, quoted in Duner [*1991:25*].
21. Quoted by Duner [*1991:19*].

The first is 'humanitarian aid' which is aimed at specific targets: it includes support for trade union education, for refugees and political prisoners and liberation efforts (as in South Africa). This received an allocation of SEK 500 million in the 1990/91 fiscal year. The second is 'Support for Democracy and Human Rights' (established in the late 1980s by Parliament). This offers more general assistance to various activities relating to human rights and the democratisation process (including sending observers to supervise elections). This received an allocation of SEK 50 million during the fiscal year 1990/91.[22]

This amount, a small percentage of the total aid budget, is also used to finance expensive international teams and organisations (including UN human-rights activities, supervision of elections, support for the International Court of Justice (ICJ), and regional organisations). This indicates that support for human rights and democracy does not constitute a priority area for Sweden. The same conclusion can be drawn throughout the Nordic area which consists of 'like-minded' countries as far as aid policies are concerned. However, funds are still sufficient to exert political influence in poor countries like Tanzania. Their Nordic donors employ the following four forms:

(1) The dialogue method or 'quiet diplomacy';
(2) The use of the multilateral voice;
(3) Support for political parties, human-rights groups, and civic organisations; and
(4) Support for specific measures for economic and political reform.

The dialogue method works through formal and informal consultations between donor and recipient officials and institutions both in devising policy and implementing it. Either side may initiate dialogue, but usually the aid agencies have retained the upper hand. It is interesting to note, for example, the role of dialogue as defined in the Swedish Development Co-operation Bill of 1987/88:

> It is an important task of the dialogue with the recipient countries for the two parties to formulate precise project goals... The short-term goals must be realistic. *In the long-term, Sweden should aim higher, which imply demands for changes in the policies of the recipient country.* (Our emphasis. Quotation from Kärre and Svensson [*1989:61*]).

The 'demands for changes in the policies of the recipient country'

---

22. Ibid., pp. 22-23.

constitute political conditionality, imposed through the dialogue method to prevent the recipient feeling the weight of the imposition. This subtle approach has generally succeeded in Tanzania. Described by Bertil Duner [*1991:23*] as 'quiet diplomacy', it avoids sensationalism when it comes to public media, dwelling only on technicalities for public consumption. This makes it difficult for the public to know the real state of relations at any given point. Writing about Sweden, Duner [*1991:23-24*] states:

> Since it is a quiet diplomacy, its implementation and effects are not well known and details that are officially disclosed are difficult to verify by independent sources. However, it is asserted in the Ministry of Foreign Affairs that questions of human rights are regularly addressed in the dialogues. Moreover, since human rights are a Swedish assistance goal rather than a criterion for sorting out misbehaving countries, such discussions aim at co-operative efforts, not at Sweden's enforcement of changes by means of threats and punishments.

The use of the multilateral voice is another method of imposing political conditionality favoured by Nordic donors.[23] The Nordic countries contribute substantially to multilateral aid organisations such as the World Bank, IDA, EEC, regional banks such as the ADB and, particularly, the UN system. This allows them influence in country programming or setting conditionalities. Usually the Nordic region co-operates closely on aid policy, co-ordinating their views through one spokesperson. The bilateral portion of ODA can be used therefore for more 'positive' purposes, or in accordance with a code defined multilaterally, without the individual donors appearing to pressurise the recipient.

The Nordic countries can also exert influence through their membership of the Paris Club.[24] It has now become customary for the Minister of Finance to fly to Paris for a meeting with creditor nations each year after presenting the government budget estimates. Criticism of Tanzania's performance in the July 1993 meeting was particularly direct and severe, contrasting sharply with the quiet diplomacy of individual Nordic countries. To quote one report:

---

23. This is not to suggest that the Nordic countries are always active in these institutions when it comes to setting conditionalities for Tanzania. Given their long and extensive aid relationship with Tanzania, they can also exert a moderating influence.
24. Club members who are Tanzania's creditors are Denmark, Finland, Norway, Sweden, Austria, Belgium, Canada, Germany, Ireland, Italy, Japan, Netherlands, Spain, Switzerland, Britain, USA.

Tanzania's creditors, the Paris Club, have said they are disappointed over Tanzania's pace of economic reforms, threatening to divert funds to other needy Third World countries if improvement is not seen... The Club has charged that the reforms have not been rapid enough to put the country on the path to sustainable economic growth.

The creditors have noted with concern that there was an obvious gap between the announced intentions to embark on reforms and actual implementation, particularly with regard to changes in the fiscal policy, the parastatal and social sectors... The creditors have warned that unless Tanzania showed improved economic performance, it stood to lose out to other developing countries which are competing for the rapidly diminishing financial assistance.[25]

The response by the Tanzanian Minister of Finance was, in contrast, desperately submissive: 'The government will intensify the pace of implementation and will strive to minimize slippages as much as is humanly possible,' and 'we recognize that we cannot afford to lose access to international support which our development partners are extending to us at a time when there is an increasing competition for international resources.'[26] Economic weakness in the recipient arena also makes for a weak rebuttal.

The positive approach (or implicit conditionality) has been used by all the Nordic countries to support various groups and activities relating to human rights and the democratisation process in Tanzania.

For example, they played an important role during the early years of agitation for multiparty rule. The critical period was 1989/90-1991/92 when opposition groups emerged with full determination to bring about political change, and the ruling party was impelled into action that eventually led to the formal adoption of the multi-party system in July 1992. Most of the 'party system' seminars and workshops organised during this period by both opposition groups and the ruling party itself had a contribution from one or other of the four Nordic countries aiding Tanzania [*Mushi, 1992*].

Since the support was open and extended to opposition and ruling party alike, the donors were not accused of taking sides or 'political interference'. However, it is virtually impossible to obtain precise information on the magnitude and the variety of assistance sought from, and given or rejected by the donors. In one extreme case, it is

---

25. *The Express*, Dar es Salaam, 15-21 July 1993.
26. Ibid.

understood that some groups consulted donors on the constitutions and political programmes of their future parties long before a multi-party system was accepted.[27]

At the same time, the Nordic countries gave financial support (directly and through multilateral institutions) to various processes, commissions and institutions engaged in economic and political reform. Examples include: (1) the process leading to the adoption of an investment code and the establishment of the Investment Promotion Centre; (2) the commission on financial and banking institutions; (3) the commission on the system and administration of tax; (4) the commission on privatisation of state corporations; (5) the Shelukindo Commission on the Union; (6) the Nyalali Commission on the party system. Support included financing trips abroad (including to the Nordic region) to learn from the experiences of other countries.

IV. THE CONTRADICTIONS AND LIMITS OF CONDITIONALITY

Conditionality does not act on a *tabula rasa*; its efficacy is limited by factors in the three arenas which give rise to it: the recipient, the donor and the international arenas. This chapter is concerned with only two limiting factors, namely (1) the political boundaries of economic conditionality (or reform), and (2) the economic boundaries of political conditionality (especially in relation to democracy and human rights).

Political boundaries of economic conditionality refer to the point where the aid-receiving regime feels that continued implementation of economic reform entails more political costs and risks than non-implementation. The liberalised political situation in Tanzania already provides evidence that conditionality to promote democracy can contradict or constrain conditionality favouring economic reform. In contrast to the Paris Club's view that reform was too slow, leading political figures[28] and a growing number of Members of Parliament (now 'free' to talk) have criticised the government for moving too rapidly and without proper planning under pressure from the donors. The handling of the parastatal reforms, external investments, and particularly the social sectors under the Economic Recovery Programme (ERP) have been targets of MPs' criticism. Members of the public (using the growing private press) have also expressed concern about the direction of change. Thus conditionality promoting democracy is itself placing brakes on conditionality encouraging economic reform.

---

27. Interviews with party leaders and donor officials in Dar es Salaam, May 1993.
28. Particularly Mwalimu Nyerere, the former President.

The peasants see a real contradiction between their situation and the declared benefits of the donor-driven reforms. For example, the IMF-sponsored ERPs of the 1986-92 period may have contributed to a rise in agricultural output, but low commodity prices mean that real earnings are even less than those of a decade ago. Thus the government has only reluctantly and hesitantly implemented ERP conditions such as cost-sharing in health and education. In July 1993, the government found it necessary to suspend a scheme of cost-sharing in the health field due to widespread complaints in the popular press and among Members of Parliament. Similarly, a scheme of cost-sharing in higher education introduced two years ago is still in abeyance. While such schemes could have been implemented bureaucratically under the one-party system, under pluralism they are subject to a political process.

Economic boundaries of political conditionality refer to: (1) the point where the donor feels that continued insistence on political conditionality (for example widening democracy) jeopardises its economic interests, and (2) the extent to which the economy of the recipient country can sustain the political reforms on which aid is made conditional. For the donor, the main limiting factor is the extent to which aid relations have consolidated its own interests in the economy of the recipient country. Our hypothesis is that the more donor-oriented the aid practice becomes, the less the likelihood that political conditionality relating to democracy and human rights will be applied vigorously. Thus conditionality is imposed only as a way of seeking influence and maximising national interests. Human rights and democracy are asserted rhetorically and when convenient by donors as long as it remains in fashion to do so.

The Nordic-Tanzanian case, however, is not a good test of this hypothesis. Consolidation of donor interests in the recipient economy entails links in aid, trade and investment. In this case, only aid links have been fully developed. Trade links are still limited to areas directly related to aid, and very little investment has been made by Nordic companies in Tanzania. This is despite the various facilities (and inducements) created by each Nordic country in the 1980s and a liberal investment code and promotion effort in Tanzania since 1990. Sweden provides an example: of the 20 companies which had established themselves in Tanzania by 1992, only one (Saab-Scania) was purely commercial. The rest offered professional consultancy services to Swedish-aided projects.

The extent to which the economy of the recipient country can sustain the political reforms on which aid is made conditional requires particular attention for donors. For example, it is still uncertain whether democracy and human rights can be sustained in conjunction with widespread poverty. The point is not whether donors should or should not encourage recipients to be democratic or to observe human rights, but that they should bear in mind economic imperatives, and provide substantial assistance. With regard to African aid, it seems ironic that real development assistance should be declining at a time when the crusade for democracy and human rights is at its peak. In comparison with the democratising Eastern Europe, Africa has been getting a raw deal. As Kumado and Busia have documented [1991:15]:

> The aid package to the ACP group from the EC countries concluded under the Lomé IV agreement amounted to USD 10 per capita, while a similar package is being prepared for Poland and Hungary of which per capita amounts to USD 60. The US is pouring USD 2 billion to a few East European countries, but yet gave Namibia USD 500,000 in 1990 on occasion of the latter's independence.

In judging recipients by economic performance account must be taken of constraints originating from the international system. Prices of commodities are a good example of factors over which many recipient countries have no control. The following figures for Africa as a whole tell the story[29]:

- Real non-oil commodity prices fell by about 40 per cent between 1973 and 1990;
- From the early 1980s world market prices for coffee, tea and cocoa fell by 11 per cent (with the cocoa price falling by over 60 per cent between 1979 and 1990);
- It is estimated that the fall of commodity prices alone cost Africa USD 19 billion in 1990;
- Despite an annual 2.5 per cent increase in exports, Africa's global earnings fell by 16 per cent between 1986 and 1990 in nominal terms, from USD 65.2 billion during 1981-1985 to USD 54.8 billion during 1986-90; the fall in real terms was drastic considering the rising prices of imports;
- The fall in commodity prices was coupled with the debilitating effects of the rising African debt. This rose from about USD 7

---

29. Most of the figures have been drawn from Salim [1993].

billion in 1965 to USD 28 billion in 1974, USD 152 billion in 1984, USD 203 billion in 1986, to USD 290 billion in 1992. It continues to rise;
– Whereas the debt in 1986 represented 54 per cent of Africa's GDP, it had risen to 110 per cent by 1992, making a mockery of any notion of recovery (through aid) in Africa;
– Service on the debt in 1992 alone was estimated to have cost poor, aid-receiving Africa about USD 27 billion or 32 per cent of the continent's total exports.

Needless to say, such a reverse flow of resources perverts Africa's efforts to mobilise domestic savings for investment, leading to poor economic performance and further conditionality by donors. The current situation can be described in a circular fashion as follows:

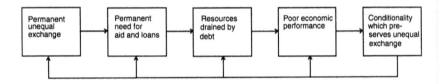

Permanent unequal exchange in the international system leads to the permanent need for aid and loans for poor countries. Borrowing leads to the debt burden which drains resources and leads to weak economic performance. Performance-based conditionalities do not question the unequal exchange in the international system: rather they seek to preserve it, and the cycle continues.

These problems may appear irrelevant to Nordic-Tanzanian aid relations since they reflect the unfavourable global environment faced by Tanzania and other sub-Saharan African (SSA) countries. But the truth is that donors (Nordic and non-Nordic alike) have tended to play down this global dimension in judging economic performance in recipient countries (including Tanzania). During the 1970s, the Nordic countries supported Third World demands for reform leading to the establishment of a New International Economic Order (NIEO), but now the focus is solely on economic (and political) reforms for the recipient.

As to the specific Nordic-Tanzanian relations, there are paradoxes to be explained. The flow of aid has remained remarkably stable long after the conditions promoting Tanzaphilia (such as Nyerere's leadership and *ujamaa* ideology) ceased to apply, and despite the absence of significant Nordic investment. Several factors help to preserve Tanzania's privileged position: (1) the historical cordial relations which, though partially eroded, still provide a comparative advantage; (2) the long-term aid policy maintained by the Nordic countries; (3) the large amount of previous investment (the theory of sunken costs), and the presence of a huge Nordic aid establishment in Dar es Salaam; and (4) the presence of a strong Tanzanian lobby (with experience in Tanzania) within aid administrations in the Nordic capitals.

REFERENCES

Andreassen, Bård-Anders and Theresa Swinehart (eds.), 1991, *Human Rights in Developing Countries: 1990 Yearbook*, Strasbourg: N.P. Engel Publisher.

Beckman, B., 1978, *Aid and Foreign Investment: The Swedish Case*, Uppsala: AKUT 7.

Bergesen, Helge Ole *et al.* (eds.), 1982, *The Recalcitrant Rich: A Comparative Analysis of the Northern Responses to the Demands for a New International Economic Order*, London: Frances Pinter Publishers.

Brecher, Irving (ed.), 1990, *Human Rights, Development and Foreign Policy: Canadian Perspectives*, Halifax: Institute for Research on Public Policy.

DAC (Development Assistance Committee), 1989, *Development Co-operation in the 1990s*, Policy statement by DAC Aid Ministers and Heads of Aid Agencies, Paris: OECD, December 1989.

Donnelly, Jack, 1989, 'Repression and Development: The Political Contingency of Human Rights Trade-Offs', in David P. Forsythe (ed.), *Human Rights and Development*, London: Macmillan.

Duner, Bertil, 1991, 'Swedish Development Policy and Human Rights', in Andreassen, Bård-Anders and Theresa Swinehart (eds.), *Human Rights in Developing Countries: 1990 Yearbook*, Strasbourg: N.P. Engel Publisher.

Edgren, G., 1986, 'Changing Terms. Procedure and Relationships in Swedish Development Assistance', in Pierre Frühling (ed.), *Swedish Development Aid in Perspective*, Stockholm: Almqvist & Wiksell International.

Falk, Richard, 1981, *Human Rights and State Sovereignty*, New York: Holmes and Meier.

Frühling, Pierre (ed.), 1986, *Swedish Development Aid in Perspective*, Stockholm: Almquist and Wiksell.

Havnevik, Kjell J., Finn Kjærby, Ruth Meena, Rune Skarstein, Ulla Vuorela, 1988, *Tanzania: Country Study and Norwegian Aid Review*, Centre for Development Studies, University of Bergen.

Howard, Rhoda, 1983, 'The Full-Belly Thesis: Should Economic Rights Take Priority Over Civil and Political Rights? Evidence from Sub-Saharan Africa', *Human Rights Quarterly*, Vol. 5, No. 4.

Jellinek, Sergio, Karl-Anders Larsson and Christina Storey, 1984, 'Swedish Aid: Policy and Performance', in Olav Stokke (ed.), *European Development Assistance*, Vol. 1, *Policies and Performance*, Tilburg: EADI Book Series.

Jerve, Alf Morten, 1991, 'The Tanzania-Nordic Relationship at a Turning Point?', in Jeannette Hartman (ed.), *Re-thinking the Arusha Declaration*, Copenhagen: Centre for Development Research.

Kärre, Bo, and Bengt Svensson, 1989, 'The Determinants of Swedish Aid Policy', in Olav Stokke (ed.), *Western Middle Powers and Global Poverty*, Uppsala: The Scandinavian Institute of African Studies.

AID AND POLITICAL CONDITIONALITY

Kiljunen, Kimmo, 1984, 'Finnish Development Co-operation: Policy and Performance', in Olav Stokke (ed.), *European Development Assistance*, Vol. 1, *Policies and Performance*, Tilburg: EADI Book Series.

Krieger, J., 1986, *Reagan, Thatcher and the Politics of Decline*, Cambridge: Polity Press.

Kumado, Kofi and Nena K.A. Busia, Jr., 1991,'The Impact of Developments in Eastern Europe on the Democratisation Process in Africa: An Exploratory Analysis', in Andreassen, Bård-Anders and Theresa Swinehart (eds.), 1991, *Human Rights in Developing Countries: 1990 Yearbook*, Strasbourg: N.P. Engel Publisher.

Lembke, H.H., 1986, *Sweden's Development Co-operation Policy*, Berlin: German Development Institute.

Ljunggren, Börje, 1986, 'Swedish Goals and Priorities', in Frühling, Pierre (ed.), *Swedish Development Aid in Perspective*, Stockholm: Almquist and Wiksell.

Maliyomkono, T.L. and M.S.D. Bagachwa, 1990, *The Second Economy in Tanzania*, London: James Curry.

Mathews, R.O. and C. Pratt (eds.), 1988, *Human Rights in Canadian Foreign Policy*, Kingston and Montreal: McGill-Queen's University Press.

McNamara, R.S., 1980, *World Development Report*, Washington D.C.: The World Bank.

Michanek, Ernst, 1985, 'Democracy as a Force for Development and the Role of Swedish Assistance', *Development Dialogue*, 1981:1.

Mushi, S.S. and K. Mathews (eds.), 1982, *Foreign Policy of Tanzania, 1961-1981*, Dar es Salaam: Tanzania Publishing House.

Mushi, S.S., 1992, 'Development of Democratic Institutions and Democratic Culture in Tanzania: Background to Political Pluralism', PDRC Occasional Paper No. 1.

Pearson, B.L., 1969, *Partners in Development*, Report of the Commission on International Development, London: Pall Mall Press.

Rostow, W.W. (ed.), 1963, *The Economics of Take-off into Sustainable Growth*, London: Macmillan.

Rostow, W.W., 1971, *The Stages of Economic Growth*, Cambridge University Press.

Rudebeck, L., 1979, *Third World Policies of the Nordic Countries*, Uppsala: AKUT 9.

Salim, A., 1993, 'Africa Loses its Strategic Position', *The Express*, Dar es Salaam, 12-18 August.

SIDA and the United Republic of Tanzania, 1987, *Annual Joint Review of the Swedish Support to Education and Vocational Training, 1986*, Dar es Salaam.

SIDA, 1993, *Redefining the Role of the State and the Market in the Development Process*, Skara: Västergotlands Tryckeri.

Steward, Frances, 1989, 'Basic Needs, Human Rights and the Rights to Development', *Human Rights Quarterly*, Vol. 11, No. 3.

Stokke, Olav, 1984, 'Norwegian Aid: Policy and Performance' in Olav Stokke (ed.), 1984, *European Development Assistance*, Vol. 1, *Policies and Performance*, Tilburg: EADI Book Series.

Stokke, Olav, 1989 (ed.), *Western Middle Powers and Global Poverty*, Uppsala: Scandinavian Institute of African Studies.

Streeten, Paul, 1980, 'Basic Needs and Human Rights', *World Development*, Vol. 8.

Svendsen, Knud Erik, 1984, 'Danish Aid: Consolidation and Adjustment in the 1980s', in Olav Stokke (ed.), *European Development Assistance*, Vol. 1, *Policies and Performance*, Tilburg: EADI Book Series.

Södersten, Bo, 1987, 'Towards a Realistic Internationalism', unpublished Mss, University of Toronto.

TANU, 1967, *The Arusha Declaration and TANU's Policy of Socialism and Self-Reliance*, Dar es Salaam: Government Printer.

Therkildsen, O., 1988, *Watering White Elephants? Lessons from Donor Funded Planning and Implementation of Rural Water Supplies in Tanzania*, Uppsala: Scandinavian Institute of African Studies.

Tomasevski, Katarina, 1989, *Foreign Aid and Human Rights*, New York: St. Martin's Press.

Wilkens, A., 1990, *Development Aid in the 1990s – Swedish Experience and Perspectives*, Stockholm: SIDA.

Wood, R.E., 1980, 'Foreign Aid and the Capitalist State in Underdeveloped Society', *Politics and Society*, Vol. 10, No. 2.

Wood, R.E., 1986, *From Marshall Plan to Development Crisis: Foreign Aid and Development Choices in the Third World Economy*, Berkeley University Press.

World Bank, 1989a, 'Sustainable Growth with Equity, Long Term Perspective for the Sub-Saharan African Machinery', Washington, DC.

World Bank, 1989b, *World Development Report 1989*, New York: Oxford University Press.

World Bank, 1989c, *From Crisis to Sustainable Growth*, Washington, DC.

8

Aid Conditionalities and Development Imperatives of Bangladesh

MOSHARAFF HOSSAIN

I. INTRODUCTION

Aid conditionalities refer to the terms specified by a donor in order to govern aid flows to a recipient country. Instances of unconditional aid are almost non-existent. Both the form and content of these conditions have changed over the last decades. The international community now broadly agrees on the need for consistent conditions which determine the nature and composition of aid and the development goals of recipient countries. Bangladesh has received aid from many different donors for over three decades. This chapter analyses the extent to which donor conditionalities can be regarded as consistent with the development goals of Bangladesh.

Large-scale economic assistance from one country to another began after World War II. Despite its relatively long history, the justification for the flows of aid, particularly from OECD countries to the poverty-stricken Third World, remains somewhat undefined. Many critics are of the opinion that aid is provided both to safeguard and bolster the economic and business interests of the donor community. This argument appears untenable in view of the fact that nearly 49 per cent of the huge amounts of foreign aid received by Bangladesh since Liberation has been in the form of grants and the remainder through concessionary loans. The provision of billions of dollars to LDCs (least developed countries) such as Bangladesh, in the form of grants or loans on highly concessionary terms, does not indicate good business sense for the tax payers of the donor country even when conscious efforts to promote business are included in aid policies. The promotion of business interests is therefore not the most important determinant, though it undeniably plays a role in formulating some of the conditionalities.

It is equally difficult to subscribe to the view that aid is provided in order to accelerate the economic and social development of recipient countries. Aid flows to Bangladesh began in the early 1960s. It is clear that genuine development requires both an increase in income level and a decrease in the incidence of poverty and hunger. Available information shows that since then, there has been a steady decline in employment opportunities and average calorie intake, particularly in the rural areas. More than four-fifths of the population reside in rural areas, and the economic conditions of the great majority of the rural people have deteriorated. Aid flows have not, therefore, succeeded in initiating a process of sustained economic development in Bangladesh.

This makes the term 'development aid' a misnomer, which ought to be a major cause for concern among the OECD countries and the multilateral development agencies who provide nearly 90 per cent of total aid to Bangladesh – particularly in view of their declared intention to reduce poverty.

In 1975, Robert McNamara, then President of the World Bank, stated categorically in his *Assault on World Poverty: Problems of Rural Development, Education and Health* that 'poverty which blights the lives of ... millions of people is unacceptable'. In 1993 Lewis T. Preston, the current President of the World Bank, reiterated that 'poverty reduction is the prime objective of the Bank' (*Getting Results – The World Bank's Agenda for Improving Development Effectiveness*). The World Bank is both a major donor and also responsible for co-ordinating aid flows to Bangladesh. According to the Bank's own data the per capita income of Bangladesh in the late 1980s (at 1980 constant US dollar prices) was similar to that in the late 1960s. It is clear that during the last few decades income distribution has become more uneven. Why large-scale aid flows to Bangladesh failed to bring about significant development is an inescapable question not only for the government and people of Bangladesh, the donors and the scholars, but also for others in Asia and Africa who are experiencing a similar plight. Is the amount of aid insufficient? Alternatively, have aid funds been improperly utilised? Plainly, in the case of Bangladesh, the problem is due to the latter. Utilisation of aid funds is determined by their conditions: the examination of the types of conditions imposed and whether they should be restructured is central to the discussion of foreign aid.

For OECD countries to give aid, parliamentary approval is necessary, and the quantity and structure of aid are matters of increasing concern for MPs of these countries. However, the logical basis for

the allocation of aid funds between various claimants and the rationale for aid conditionalities have rarely been the subject of serious
debate in the donor countries. These issues appear to be regarded as
matters of detail and considered unsuitable for serious discussion by
parliamentarians: they are consigned to the officials responsible for
administering the aid programmes. This means there is little compulsion on donor governments to examine carefully the needs and effectiveness of aid conditionalities. A recipient government such as that
of Bangladesh cannot question the merits of donor choices concerning
aid policies: an aid-dependent country has to abide by the wishes of
the donors. A lack of eagerness to examine the critical issues in
administering aid, evident in both donor and recipient countries, may
be regarded as the principal reason for increasing dissatisfaction with
aid in most parts of the world.

It is true that humanitarian considerations have acted as powerful
inducements for OECD countries to give aid. Humanitarian sentiments are usually stirred when people see the suffering that disasters
inflict on fellow human beings, whether inside or outside their national borders. Many people give regular donations to charitable foundations, including OXFAM, Save the Children Fund, Christian Aid and
Concern, to support both disaster relief and programmes to develop
education, health and various income-generating activities. The
resources provided to local NGOs by these international NGOs and
the official donors have a positive economic and social impact in
countries such as Bangladesh. However, most development assistance
given to Bangladesh by OECD countries and international development agencies, such as the World Bank, Asian Development Bank and
UNDP, is made available to the government, to finance its own programmes.

From the perspective of LDCs, it is impossible to regard Christian
or other moral values as the principal motivations for aid: the level of
aid flows does not correlate closely with that of the impoverishment
in the Third World. Moreover, the major donors have failed to insist
on the adoption of specific programmes and policies aimed at a veri-
fiable reduction of poverty. What appears as an important justification
is the enlightened self-interest of the donors, arising from the perception that increasing social conflicts, even in far-off lands, do not
always remain confined within national boundaries. Conflicts in poor
countries eventually threaten the interests of the developed countries.
Post-colonial societies tend to have exacerbated social tensions for
reasons which include:

- rising expectations on the part of rapidly growing populations;
- a widening gap between needs and available resources;
- ever-increasing social divisions resulting from unequal access to resources;
- the growth of fundamentalist and extremist ideologies in poverty-stricken countries;
- problems created by the arbitrary nature of national boundaries drawn up during colonial rule; and
- the attempts of the major powers to build up client states during the Cold War period, which had a pernicious effect on the character of government.

In Bangladesh, aid flows have failed to lessen social conflicts: this makes it necessary, even from the point of view of enlightened self-interest, for donors to examine seriously the impact of aid conditionalities.

II. NATURE OF AID CONDITIONALITY

Analysis of the impact is not easy because the conditionalities are rarely set out clearly and separately. They are usually included in the small print of aid agreements entered into between donor and the recipient, which are not generally made available to the public. The avoidance of transparency in aid conditionalities is difficult to understand: aid agreements are binding not only on the government currently in power, but on all its successors for their duration, transcending even state structures. The people of Bangladesh were horrified to find that the aid agreements ratified by Pakistan before Liberation were still binding after the establishment of their new state. The only justification was the Pakistani claim (with which most of the donors concurred) that a proportion of the aid provided to pre-1971 Pakistan had been used to undertake development activities in the territory comprising Bangladesh, committing the Bangladeshi government to take over responsibility for the obligations of the aid agreements. There was little choice but to accede to donor pressure in this case. However, if conditionality imposes obligations on the people of a recipient country, its citizens have a right to know what commitments their government is making on their behalf. This is particularly important in Bangladesh where democratic institutions are not yet flourishing. An autocratic government which accepts aid without paying attention to the terms and conditionalities attached by the donors may prefer to keep its people in the dark while the rulers are able to reap private or sectarian gains from its continuance. A donor government, however, cannot be a party to such an arrangement, if it wishes the people of the recipient country to be bound by aid terms. The process of democratisation in recipient countries requires transparency in the conditions laid down by aid donors.

Any attempt to determine the rationale of aid conditionalities imposed on Bangladesh is bound to be somewhat speculative since conditions are not widely publicised. However, we may assume that they aim, on the one hand, at securing the perceived interests of the donors and, on the other, at efficient utilisation of aid funds. Analysis of the conditions imposed until the early 1980s shows that they were designed for a number of different purposes:

(a) to specify the activities which would be financed under particular aid programmes, thus ensuring that there were no leakages or wastage of aid funds;

(b) to identify the sources from where aid-financed goods and services should be obtained and the modalities to be observed by the Bangladeshi government. This conditionality could either promote the donor's own interest, if any, in supplying the aid-financed goods and services or that of preferred market economies and LDC sources. Bilateral aid often stipulates country of origin for procurement. Presumably the system of open competitive bidding, where specified, was meant to discourage recipients from using aid funds to buy costly, or even not so costly, domestically-produced goods and services[1];

(c) to specify the administrative and accounting procedures which the recipient government was expected to comply with. The expatriate consultancy services to be used and the facilities which the expatriates involved in administering the aid programmes would enjoy, were also listed;

(d) to specify the kinds and amounts of contributions which the recipient government itself would have to make for implementing selected aid projects and programmes;

(e) to outline the rates of interest, grace period and repayment obligations in cases where aid was provided as loans on concessionary terms;

---

1. Some of the most glaring examples of donor conditionalities leading to non-utilisation of capacities built up with aid funds during the 1960s and 1970s are the enterprises of the Bangladesh Engineering and Shipbuilding Corporation. For example, conditions relating to the procurements of the Rural Electrification Board resulted in imports of many equipments from abroad which could be supplied easily by the General Electric Manufacturing Company of Bangladesh.

(f) to ensure prompt response to the demands of the management-intensive aid programmes by recipient governments despite their low aid-absorptive capacity and shortage of personnel capable of responding satisfactorily to all the concerns or queries of the donors;

(g) to ensure that the performance criteria determined by the donors were duly observed by the aid recipients.

Even on the assumption, hard to justify in many cases, that the aid programmes were formulated within the broad framework of the development plans and programmes of Bangladesh, the conditions appear to imply a belief on the part of donors that, without supervision, recipient governments would either 'waste' or misappropriate aid funds. Aid conditions were framed, on the one hand, to prevent misuse and, on the other, to educate recipients about donor concerns and exert pressure on them to observe set procedures for the smooth disbursement of funds and procurement from sources preferred by the donors. However, the conditions mainly related to resolving the micro-management problems of individual projects and programmes rather than eliminating the real causes of arrested development in recipient countries. Thus, such conditions were unsatisfactory both to donors and recipients in terms of the overall aim of external aid flows: to hasten the process of sustainable development.

The failure of aid was most obvious in its change from being an operation over a comparatively limited period to a process which threatened to become never-ending. The academics and planners of aid in donor countries in the 1950s and the early 1960s, believed that no more than 10 to 15 years of aid flow would be required to set in motion a process of self-sustained development in an LDC. The inability of most LDCs, including Bangladesh, to become self-reliant after several decades naturally raised doubts about the effectiveness of aid and conditionalities. It appears that this was the context for a shift in donor perceptions about the factors necessary to achieve development, leading to changes in their aid conditionalities [*Woodward, 1992*]. In addition to the multifarious micro-management conditionalities already in force, the donors began to insist on improved macro-economic performance with a more rigorous implementation of market-oriented policies by recipient countries such as Bangladesh. The donor-designed macro-economic reform packages came to be known as structural adjustment programmes.

The International Monetary Fund began to express concern about the rapidly rising prices in Bangladesh following the first oil shock

and a disastrous flood in the early 1970s. While accepting that inflation and imbalances in the external payments position were likely to
be due to severe exogenous shocks, the IMF considered that the
government's failure to enforce monetary stability or to fix the currency at a realistic external value had accentuated price instability in
the country. They envisaged no rigidities in the system of production
likely to hinder the effort to maintain economic stability and ensure
economic growth. IMF experts appeared to believe that exogenous
shocks could be absorbed by the Bangladesh economy and that
exports and imports would adjust to changes in world market
conditions, provided the government took certain measures: it should

– refrain from undertaking deficit budgeting;
– control unwarranted increases in money supply and bank credit;
– set the external value of the currency on the basis of a realistic
  assessment of its purchasing power; and
– offer a positive rate of interest to counteract incentives for a
  'flight from money'.

In order to qualify for IMF loans, Bangladesh agreed to these conditions and received the support necessary to tide it over the 'temporary
difficulties'.

However, when these measures failed to resolve the economic
problems of the country, the World Bank, acting as the co-ordinator
of the donor community, insisted on the adoption of a structural
adjustment programme (SAP) in order to improve macro-economic
management. The most important aspects of the SAP in the case of
Bangladesh were

– privatisation;
– total withdrawal of subsidies;
– limiting bank credit to public sector enterprises whilst enabling
  rapid increases in borrowing for the private sector;
– increased efforts to mobilise more resources by reforming the tax
  system;
– emphasis on the implementation of development projects
  financed by donors rather than undertaking projects in the hope
  of implementing them with government support;
– liberalisation of trade through measures such as the abolition of
  tariff protection.

These programmes were initiated in the early 1980s. They were extended and streamlined a few years later, when the government launched a medium-term programme at the behest of the IMF under the Structural Adjustment Facility (SAF), and again during 1990-93 under the scheme of Enhanced Structural Adjustment Facility (ESAF) of the IMF [*Gotur, 1991, 1992*].

The programmes appear to have been designed to accelerate the growth process in the country. According to the donors, including the Bank, the nationalisation policy of the early 1970s was a strong disincentive to domestic private investment, for which privatisation was the necessary remedy. The implicit belief appeared to be that the private sector, operating on the profit motive, was most likely to ensure the optimum allocation of investible resources in the country, while subsidies and trade restrictions led to distortions in the allocative pattern. It was necessary for the government to abolish them to achieve rapid development in the economy. The government's tendency to undertake development projects to be financed with its own resources was tantamount to misuse of funds: there were delays in implementing donor-aided projects due to the government's failure to mobilise sufficient resources to meet local costs. Moreover, most projects of high priority were financed already by donors. The capacity of private investors to accelerate investments in productive activities was held back by limitations in credit facilities. Restrictions on government borrowing for the operation of commercially non-viable public enterprises would enable producers in agriculture, industry and tradeable services to expand their operations. It was on the basis of these assumptions that aid conditionalities were designed. The suggested reforms were expected to generate necessary growth impulses within the economy.

Fundamental to donor perceptions of the necessary policy environment for development was an anti-statist logic [*World Bank,1991*].[2]

---

2. Until the mid-1980s the World Bank provided strong support to military-authoritarian regimes around the world under the impression that they were sufficiently strong to implement reforms for integrating their economies into the world market. The Bank seemed to believe that the non-democratic regimes were in a better position than democratic ones to overcome domestic pressures and resistance in order to adopt and implement reforms [*Lal, 1983, 1987*].

The inability of the reform programmes to produce the desired results in most non-democratic regimes and the collapse of the Soviet block at the end of the 1980s led to changes in the Bank's position on the role of the state. Emphasis on democratisation, privatisation, decentralisation and decision-making at the grassroots level, combined with channelling aid funds through the NGOs and other civil bodies, inevitably leads to sidetracking if not delegitimising the functions of the state. Does such a scenario leave enough opportunities and compulsions for the multifarious, disparate and disunited participants on the recipient side to rally round a common cuase? What impact will these developments have on bodies such as employers' and labour

This makes sense, given the declining efficiency of the state sector in the administration of development programmes, its strong propensity to give higher priority to private accumulation than to the need to maximise the rate of growth and the linkages with rent-seeking vested interests in the country. However, the existing social and economic structures in the country and the absence of effective democratic institutions raise another pertinent issue: the possibility that the ruling class in Bangladesh may continue its private accumulation activities in the absence of sustained development, with or without SAP. The issues of supply elasticity of capable entrepreneurs in Bangladesh and conditions for the creation of a congenial climate for private investment can not be separated from the arguments put forward in support of the SAP, if aid flows and conditionalities are to produce the desired results. It appears that these aspects were not given due importance in the formulation of aid policies, presumably because the donor community has not yet reached a decision on the extent of its involvement in the search for workable solutions to the development problems of the country.

III. BANGLADESH'S DEVELOPMENT EXPERIENCE

Before examining the extent to which aid flows and conditionalities were conducive to rapid growth in its economy, it is necessary to outline briefly the development experience of Bangladesh, focusing particularly on the period since the early 1970s, after Liberation. Total development aid during the whole of the 1960s amounted to less than US$ 1 billion. The average annual rate of growth of GDP before 1971 was just over four per cent. With the population increasing at more than 2.5 per cent a year, the rise in per capita income was very low. Nearly 95 per cent of the population was rural. With the great majority of people engaged in farming, the rapid growth in population led to a steep decline in the average size of holdings, leading in turn to increasing landlessness and a higher growth rate in labour supply than was possible to absorb in gainful activities. The result was increasing impoverishment, particularly in the rural areas. The failure of the Government of Pakistan to resolve these problems accentuated popular resentment and indirectly helped to create the independent state of Bangladesh.

The foreign assistance increased dramatically after Liberation. Aid

---

unions? [*Beckman, 1992*]. The Bank's lack of concern about these issues is somewhat surprising.

funds helped Bangladesh to complete the reconstruction and rehabili-
tation of its war-ravaged economy by 1975. GDP regained its pre-war
level by the mid-1970s. However, the increase in population between
1969-70 and 1975-76 had resulted in a decline in per capita income of
about one-sixth compared to the level of the late 1960s. This level, it
has already been noted, was not regained until the late 1980s, which is
surprising in view of the fact that Bangladesh received annual
external assistance amounting to nearly eight per cent of GDP between January 1975 and June 1993. Despite these increases in aid, the
annual growth in GDP was little over 3.5 per cent. The annual flow of
aid per capita was rarely more than US$ 18, which is much lower than
the average for developing market economies other than India. Still,
compared to the pre-Liberation period, aid to Bangladesh rose steeply
while the rate of growth in GDP actually declined.

There are various reasons for the unsatisfactory performance of the
Bangladesh economy. Most important is the drastic decline in domestic savings after Liberation which have continued to remain at a very
low level. The structure of production has been changed in a manner
which is detrimental to the rapid alleviation of poverty. The proportion of the tradeable goods sector in GDP has declined over the last
two decades.

An important aspect of the productive system is the sectoral
distribution of employment. The great majority of the labour force in
Bangladesh (more than 35 million strong) are either self-employed or
work as unpaid family help. There are roughly 21 million households
in the country: up to 14 million (with more than 20 million workers)
are engaged in farming, of which nearly 11 million cultivate small or
marginal amounts of land. Between two and three million households
are engaged in traditional cottage industries. Modern manufacturing
employs fewer than two million labourers, including the 'low value
added' export-processing sector such as the garments industry.
Another one million people are employed in government or parastatals. The remaining 10 million work either as landless agricultural
labourers, fishermen, traders, or in the various service sectors.

The figures demonstrate that more than four-fifths of the work
force are engaged in unorganised traditional activities, despite three
decades of planned development.[3] Huge aid inflow and large-scale
government development activities, in particular improvements to the
economic and social infrastructure, have not had a significant impact

---

3.   The UNCTAD Report on the Least Developed Countries, 1991, shows that the
proportion of the manufacturing sector in GDP declined from ten per cent in 1980 to
seven per cent in 1989.

in terms of increased productivity and levels of consumption of the masses. As a result, the incidence of poverty grows in parallel with rising unemployment and underemployment. In addition, the deepening economic crisis due to limitations in the labour market is leading to the development of a 'frontier situation' in the country. A decline in social order and levels of efficiency in public services has stimulated 'transaction charges', 'mediation fees' and 'involuntary donations', resulting in an uncongenial climate for investment.

Despite government adoption of structural adjustment programmes in the early 1980s, with the consequent privatisation of public sector enterprises, the withdrawal of input subsidies and rapid expansion in credit to the private sector, private investment activity has not increased. Available data show that its rate of just over five per cent of GDP in the mid-1970s went up to just over nine per cent in 1980-81; however, since then there has been a steady decline and it is now no more than 5.6 per cent.

The most powerful disincentives to private investment activity in a country such as Bangladesh include uncertainty and the high risks on irreversible investment. This applies to all the least developed countries. The low proportion of modern enterprises means that establishing a new productive venture involves undertaking lumpy investment which cannot be easily disposed of, if found unprofitable. An established company in a developed market economy can substitute new production for unprofitable units without having to incur large additional expenditures on, for example, construction and power supply. The ratio of irreversible investment to expected value of output is far higher in a country without old indigenous business concerns or a significant industrial base compared to industrialised countries or even newly industrialised countries (NICs). The emerging class of entrepreneurs in countries such as Bangladesh lacks sufficient expertise and experience in modern management techniques, making the elements of uncertainty and risks of investment far higher than would be the case in developed market economies or the NICs. Investment both in industry and in agriculture is consequently deterred.

The majority of the peasant producers in the country own and cultivate very small holdings, of which just under 50 per cent are less than one acre (0.4 hectares) in size. The average size was approximately 3.5 acres in 1960, which has been reduced to less than 1.7 acres over the last three decades. Roughly five per cent of the farming households own comparatively large holdings of more than 7.5 acres, although often made up from many small, scattered plots. Small cultivated holdings mostly produce crops required for consumption by the family members of the cultivators. Even when production is insufficient to meet the domestic needs, smallholders are often obliged to sell a portion of their yield in order to meet cash costs of seeds, fertilisers, irrigation, water and pesticides. Cash costs also include the expenses of hiring labour. Even though all poor peasant households have surplus labour due to the lack of alternative gainful employment opportunities during agriculturally slack seasons, hired labour is required to prepare lands for cultivation and for planting and harvesting crops during peak seasons. The majority of marginal peasants are also obliged to hire power tillers or ploughs with draught animals because they own neither bullocks nor ploughs. Average cash costs of cultivation thus work out at a high figure. Available estimates show that the cash outlay necessary to produce high-yielding varieties (HYV) accounts for nearly 45 per cent of their total value.

Most of the peasantry rent land from large landholders in order to make the maximum use of labour time in addition to agricultural tools and equipment such as ploughs. After meeting cash costs and the landowner's share of the produce, these sharecroppers are left with only a small portion of their output. In most cases, the peasants then need to borrow in order to stay in production. In view of the uncertainties surrounding agricultural activities, which include droughts, floods and pest attacks, there is an understandingly low incentive to borrow in order to maximise the level of output. Landless labourers have limited opportunities to earn a living: this acts as a powerful inducement on poor peasants to avoid innovative activities which might lead to loss of their lands. Thus, 'fierce resistance to landlessness', survival and 'safety first' are the principal determinants of peasant behaviour in Bangladesh.

Given the geographical characteristics of the country, government programmes to develop the infrastructure, many of which are donor funded, have not resulted in eradicating the risks attendant on fluctuations in agricultural output levels and in the prices of farm products in Bangladesh. Thus whether it is technically feasible to increase yields or the potential gains of crop diversification are matters of far less significance to the peasant producers than the overriding need to meet the consumption requirements of the ever-increasing family [*Hossain, 1994b*].

IV. AID CONDITIONALITIES AND POLICY IMPLICATIONS

It is imperative for a government to widen the gap between the prices of output and input if it is to mitigate the effects of decline in the size

of holdings. Aid conditionalities leading to the withdrawal of subsidies have prevented the government from adopting this course. The
conditions are based on the mistaken belief that productivity depends
on yield alone. Within the agriculture sector, they have been determined by market demand, supply conditions and the desire to avoid
perceived distortions in resource allocation rather than by the level of
calorie intake of the poverty-stricken masses. Those designing aid
conditions for Bangladesh appear to endorse astronomic government
expenditure on physical infrastructure to eliminate the threats posed
by recurrent droughts, floods, and pest attacks. Likewise, they coun-
tenance high levels of spending on building and maintaining all-
weather farm-to-market roads and undertaking rural electrification
programmes, to generate external economies to the agricultural producers and, at the same time, incurring transfer expenditures for those
who are unable to find jobs. However, there is surprisingly little encouragement for the far lower expenditure required to reduce the cost
of modern inputs, eliminating the international asymmetry and reducing risks; nor for increasing the provision of domiciliary services to
the poor, illiterate, marginalised and exploited peasantry: the donors
do not support these measures because they violate the doctrines on
which aid conditionalities are based.

There is a sense in which the deepening economic crisis in Bangladesh and many LDCs poses a more serious challenge to the donor
community than to policy-makers in the countries receiving aid.
According to Alan Fowler [1992]: 'When a state depends on external
aid rather than national economy for its existence, it effectively
becomes a local government in the global political order.' Donors
must fully recognise that 'sovereignty is a meaningless concept in a
situation where primary governmental functions, i.e. security, economic management, the selection and implementation of public policies, cannot be minimally guaranteed or undertaken unless externally
negotiated and financed'. While discussing the problems caused by
Bangladesh's dependence on aid, Van Arkadie and de Wilde
remarked that 'aid put the country on the map and kept it afloat in the
difficult first years of independence'. The situation has worsened
since then.

V. THE DONORS, THE GOVERNMENT AND THE PEOPLE

In the late 1970s and early 1980s, the government was able to finance
at least a quarter of development expenditure from its own resources.

By the late 1980s, aid flows exceeded the government's entire budget for development. Decades of aid dependence have resulted in a gradual transformation of the state structure into a semi-autonomous local government with increasing pressure from the donors to reshape policies to conform with aid conditionalities. The compulsion on the government, and even its capacity, to design and implement development programmes on the basis of the objective conditions obtaining in the country has inevitably eroded to a great extent. Informed opinion in the country doubts whether the government, acting on its own, can achieve its development goals. There is probably still less expectation that donor officials will become more responsive to the pleas of enlightened sections of indigenous Bangladeshis to restructure aid policies. There is inadequate recognition among donors that their interests will not be served by aid flows that continue either for an indefinite period or until an inevitable ending when their domestic public opinion begins to believe that aid objectives are inherently unattainable. In order to foresee an end to aid flows, with Bangladesh securely on the path to sustainable development, aid policies have to be restructured, substituting the basis of neo-classical tenets which are not universally applicable with a focus primarily on the objective conditions obtaining in Bangladesh. Aid conditionalities and programmes need to be redesigned to ensure that the contributions and commitment of the Bangladeshi people are sufficient for developing their country. This is certainly an attainable goal.

A relevant quotation in this context comes from the head of the Swedish delegation at the Bangladesh Aid group meeting held in Paris, 27-28 April 1993: 'Bangladesh has, no doubt, taken important steps towards a more coherent development policy. Still, further measures are necessary, and, more importantly, so is a much more firm commitment to poverty alleviation through rapid and sustainable labour-intensive growth. We know from other countries that such a commitment is of crucial importance. What is needed is a clear *development agenda*, defined through a process of national dialogue, on the basis of which a national consensus can be built, a consensus that includes the government, the opposition, NGOs, intellectuals etc. Such an agenda could also form the basis for a longer term *contract* between Bangladesh and the donor community.'

This may be the first time that a representative of a donor country has publicly acknowledged three important factors: the absence of a firm commitment in Bangladesh to attain development goals; the need to draw up a development agenda on the basis of a national consensus; and the importance of using this agenda as a basis for reaching a long-term agreement between the donor community and Bangladesh. It should be noted that in the course of the same statement some of the merits of the structural adjustment programmes were also highlighted. However, by emphasising the need for Bangladeshi initiative in their own development, the Swedish spokesman had legitimately cast doubts upon the donors' ability to formulate programmes capable of inspiring enthusiasm in the people of the country and making them more willing to implement them.

It is somewhat surprising that throughout the long period of aid administration, there has been no attempt by donor officials to take into account the impact of their demands for a prompt and dutiful government response on the morale, initiative and responsibility of the government functionaries involved. In Bangladesh, there has been a dramatic reduction in pay in real terms of all grades of employees since independence. Senior government officials have no reason to feel excited when less senior officials of aid agencies expect them to fix the prices of public utilities according to donor criteria, bring about a sharp reduction in 'systems loss' in electricity distribution, get rid of employees when the size of the payroll appears too large to the expatriate experts, appoint expatriate consultants when qualified Bangladeshis are obliged to remain idle or seek their fortunes in foreign countries, import development inputs even when these are available in the country, or when representatives of the companies from the donor countries mutter veiled threats about 'uncooperative attitudes' without any clear understanding of the social and political realities within the country. The Swedish plea for assumption of responsibility by Bangladesh for its own development could certainly produce a desirable impact in terms of changing the attitude of the donor community about the need for a 'strong government presence in development planning and execution'.

However, withdrawal of agricultural input subsidies, which never exceeded one per cent of GDP, at the donors' insistence failed to stop the steep decline in public savings. Donor conditionalities could not check the unfettered rise in public consumption. The decline in public savings resulted in reduced aid absorption ability.

Since independence, the amount of aid pledged annually to Bangladesh invariably has fallen significantly short of commitments, due to government failure to identify areas suitable for external financing. Moreover, donors frequently express preference for sectors and projects without regard to their compatibility with government programmes. Consequently, many areas of high priority do not secure adequate financing and the pledged amounts cannot be translated into firm commitments. There are still further consequences: the lack of public savings impedes government allocation of funds to meet the local costs of projects financed by aid. This creates an inevitable gap between annual commitments and disbursements of aid. During the last two decades more than a quarter of the amounts pledged by the various donors could not be disbursed.

The absence of public savings also tends to prevent the country from undertaking the detailed surveys and research necessary to identify potentially profitable areas for investment and to determine an effective sequencing of projects. This leads to widespread dependence on donor financing and expatriate consultancy. In many areas, including rural development, transport and communication, education, health and family planning, considerable indigenous expertise is available. Despite this, expatriate consultancy services are widely used due to lack of government resources, accentuated by conditions specifying such use laid down by both bilateral and multilateral aid agencies. Frustration inevitably follows, with underutilised local capacity and indifference to the work of expensive expatriate consultants. More seriously, the lack of involvement by local experts and officials in the design of development programmes and projects leads to both the inadequate transfer of technology and the adoption of inappropriate implementation procedures due to expatriate ignorance of the local conditions; it also undermines any serious local commitment to implement these expatriate-designed and donor-financed development projects and programmes, thus increasing dependence on 'experts' of doubtful competence. The problems which arise in attempts at the efficient implementation of development programmes based on borrowed, and frequently inappropriate, ideas and technology are well known. The chief difficulty is the donors' tendency to ignore them.

The government of Bangladesh alone has the capacity to finance programmes for the rapid development of skills consistent with the increase in demand, and for the provision of funds sufficient for the research and development necessary to initiate the process of assimilating borrowed technology. In addition, only government can ensure that local expertise is fully utilised, and that the package presented for donor finance is made up of high priority, fungible and properly-designed projects, consistent with the available resources, and that those responsible for implementation are involved in the process of design. This would help

–   eliminate the gap between pledges and disbursements;

– avoid unnecessary delays in completing project work, due to a lack of available funds;
– ensure adoption of high priority projects for development financing; and
– ensure that no important projects are left out because of lack of donor interest.
– It would also help the government to enter into a serious dialogue with the donors on the wisdom and feasibility of recommendations apparently of doubtful merit, and
– would increase the confidence of donors in the usefulness of aid programmes, once convinced of the government's commitment to take a responsible and executive role in the development process.

In the light of all this, it is difficult to understand the donors' inability or lack of success in persuading the government to raise the level of public savings, despite this being a prominent feature of conditionality, particularly of the World Bank and the IMF. Successful pressure would have reduced their burden and would avert the threat of donor fatigue arising from unsatisfactory performance on the part of recipient countries.

The current pattern of aid administration involves protracted negotiation between officials of donor and recipient countries in order to secure approval for the disbursement of funds. Time-consuming monitoring of performance records according to criteria set by donor officials is required, in addition to a careful scrutiny of the extent to which the government is observing the various conditions. As a result, the decision-making process is rendered more cumbersome. Increasing conditionalities have intensified pressures on management of aid-financed development activities from the point of view both of the recipients and the donors. This is not conducive to increasing the operational efficiency of implementation agencies in the country.

It is possible that globalisation of the market, reduction of trade restrictions and increasing currency convertibility around the world will reduce the stringency of micro-management conditionalities imposed by the donors. However, macro-economic management conditionalities will continue to impede rapid development of the Bangladeshi economy. The success of structural adjustment programmes can be judged only by their impact on levels of savings, investment, employment and output. The experience of the last decade demonstrates that adjustment efforts in Bangladesh have not produced the desired results.

The SAP in Bangladesh is restricted by being based on assumptions which are not strictly tenable in the prevailing conditions.[4] For market forces to function efficiently, the government needs to take note of certain essential economic and social factors and to adopt corrective action. These factors include:

- the absence of a developed capital market;
- the inability of the interest rate to act as an effective instrument to discriminate between good and bad borrowers;
- the absence of a close correlation between public investment in building up infrastructure and private investment in production;
- the lack of a linear relationship between investment and output due to structural rigidities in many sectors;
- inelasticity in the supply of competent entrepreneurs to compensate for the absence of an established indigenous business class;
- informational asymmetry;
- a restricted domestic market due to low level of productivity in both agriculture and industry;
- inability on the part of the government to ensure rapid increase in required external economies because of the severe shortage of resources for investment;
- the tendency for domestic savings to remain very low because of pressures for currency devaluation due to external imbalances, and the propensity to resort to capital flight to avoid taxes and involuntary donations;
- the impact of the very low level of retained earnings since the opportunity cost of investing funds is lower than the price of borrowed funds;
- market imperfections due to monopolistic competition;
- gross income inequalities;
- the relationship between the climate for private investment and the degree of social and political stability;
- the limited external market for goods produced by vast masses of unskilled labourers; and
- the negative impact caused by the risks of lumpy irreversible investment.

---

4. This is true both for Bangladesh and for most other Third World countries that were compelled to adopt structural adjustment programmes. Chahond [*1991*] has rightly stated that 'IMF crisis management leads regularly to economic overkill for the debtor economies: the GNP declines, the volume of import has to be cut and investment falls. The principal victims of failed adjustment policies are the members of the lower social strata'.

It is essential to recognise that these constraints to the growth of market forces cannot be eliminated by simply liberalising trade, expanding credit facilities to the private sector and reducing government intervention in the economic sphere. Rapid increases in bank credit to private borrowers, far from raising the level of private investment in Bangladesh, has led inevitably to massive debt default.[5]

Both the policy makers and the donors have to recognise the 'social dysfunctions of the market': the inability of market forces to ensure absorption of surplus labour caused by changing market conditions which threatens to create an underclass of impoverished masses with an inevitable subsequent adverse impact on development. This reality is as fundamental to the existing socio-political conditions of the country as the government's incapacity to design and implement workable development projects and programmes. The situation requires a combination of market and 'strong government presence in planning and execution'. Market forces can become stronger only if appropriate policies are adopted by the government. This cannot be achieved by weakening the desire and capabilities of the government machinery to perform their assigned role. Thus aid conditionalities have to be redesigned so that government is induced to prepare a national development agenda with no external input; and it should be accepted that efforts to strengthen market forces and achieve trade liberalisation must be consistent with the need to enhance growth in productivity and expand the domestic market. The level of skill and capacity to assimilate borrowed technology needs to rise sufficiently to enable Bangladesh to compete in the world market with the NICs in selling skilled-labour-intensive products. Until then, encouraging efficiency for domestic producers should be given higher priority than the urge to hasten globalisation of the market.[6]

---

5. Historic specificity and the socio-economic peculiarity of the objective conditions in each country under review need to be recognised and addressed seriously. The structural adjustment programme, instead, formulates a general set of conditions based on pure neo-classical logic that very rarely conforms to the actual operations of any economy. Moreover, adjustment becomes necessary not simply because of the incompetence of the people of the country concerned, despite the attempts of the IMF and the World Bank to make the debtor countries subscribe to that view: it is the result of uncertainties and fluctuations in the global market where their role is minimal. See, for example, Woodward [1992].

6. The UNICEF study *Adjustment with a Human Face* [*Cornia et al., 1987*] also prescribes moderation of aid conditionalities with a wider role for the government particularly through a restructuring of public expenditure towards an increase in social programmes and investments for the poor. This is not simply for their maintenance, but more for their empowerment. The adoption is also encouraged of *meso* policies that influence the allocational and distributional impact of macro variables within the frame of adjustment. In the case of Bangladesh this should be the central focus rather than a package of balancing provisions in the preparation of conditionalities for aid.

Conditionalities are as significant as the magnitude of aid flow in an LDC such as Bangladesh for the process of developing the economy. The design of aid policies should take into account the following facts:

- The inadequate contribution and commitment of the government impedes an accelerated process of development.
- Regular misappropriation and misdirection of aid funds result from donor officials being motivated by objectives other than maximising the efficiency of aid utilisation for development in recipient countries.
- The absence of flourishing democratic institutions, respect for human rights and lack of education combine to inhibit public information about the purpose of aid and expressions of popular concern about its misuse.
- Donor officials are apt to exert pressure on the recipient government to create a context in which policies are formulated without adequate analysis of objective local economic and social conditions. Insufficient attention is paid to the need for consistency between the proposed policy environment and the development goals and needs of the recipient country.
- Disbursement imperatives often outweigh the need to take decisions solely on economic logic.

Low productivity and a somewhat low rate of growth in the output of tradeable goods exacerbate the economic crisis. The country's dependence on aid is increasing rather than declining. The weak power base of the civil-military bureaucrats and business interests, whose regime ended recently, made them highly susceptible to donor pressure. However, despite the necessity to do so, donor officials failed to persuade the government to design development programmes aimed at achieving economic and social objectives while gradually increasing the country's own financial contribution. This may have been due to fears that excessive pressure to neglect private and sectarian gains might tempt the military rulers to take advantage of the Cold War to seek undesirable patrons. Despite the welcome change in this area, aid objectives will remain unattainable unless the donor community's new-found commitment to democracy and human rights – of which economic security is an integral element – is combined with a readiness to redesign the pattern of aid flow and the conditionalities. The aims should be to increase self-determination and strengthen the commitment towards self-financing of development.

Aid conditionalities are essential for democratic institutions to take root in countries such as Bangladesh. There are ample opportunities for collusion between the ruling classes in recipient countries and business corporations in the developed market economies: the lengthy process of eliminating market imperfections calls for unqualified support from aid donors. There is a strong urge to respond to narrow self-interest rather than enlightened self-interest. If aid ceases to be the preserve primarily of the officials and business interests of donor and recipient countries and becomes a subject of serious and informed discussion everywhere, it is still possible that the phenomenon of aid dependence and the endemic poverty of billions in Third World countries will become a thing of the past.

REFERENCES

Altvater, E., K. Hübner, J. Lowentsen and R. Rojas, eds., 1991, *The Poverty of Nations: A Guide to the Debt Crisis from Argentina to Zaire*, London: Zed Books Ltd.

Asaduzzaman, M., 1989, ' "Feeding Our Future Towns" An Overview of Urbanization and Associated Food Policy Issues', in *Food Strategies in Bangladesh: Medium and Long Term Perspectives*, Dhaka: University Press Limited.

Bangladesh Bureau of Statistics, 1988, *Agricultural Census Report, 1983-84*, Dhaka: Government of Bangladesh.

Bangladesh Institute of Development Studies, 1992, 'A Profile of Poverty in Bangladesh', Dhaka (mimeo).

Beckman, Björn, 1992, 'Empowerment or Repression? The World Bank and the Politics of African Adjustment' in Gibbon *et al.*, eds., *Authoritarianism , Democracy and Adjustment*, Uppsala: The Scandinavian Institute of African Studies.

Chahond, Tatjana, 1991, 'The Changing Roles of the IMF and the World Bank' in Altvater *et al.*, eds., *The Poverty of Nations: A Guide to the Debt Crisis from Argentina to Zaire*, London: Zed Books Ltd.

Cornia, G.A., R. Jolly and F. Stewart, 1987, *Adjustment with a Human Face*, Oxford: Clarendon Press.

Fowler, Alan, 1992, 'Distant Obligations: Speculations on NGO Funding and the Global Market', *Review of African Political Economy*, Nov.

Gibbon, P., Y. Bangura and A. Ofstad, eds., 1992, *Authoritarianism, Democracy and Adjustment*, Uppsala: The Scandinavian Institute of African Studies.

Gotur, P., 1991, 'Bangladesh: Economic Reform Measures and the Poor', *IMF Working Paper* WP/91/39.

Gotur, P., 1992, 'Bangladesh: Tackling the Problem of Poverty, Assessing the Impacts of Economic Reforms on the Poor', *Finance and Development*, June.

Hossain, Mosharaff, 1984, 'A Note on Aid Conditionality' in Olav Stokke, ed., *European Development Assistance*, Vol.II, Tilburg: EADI Book Series.

Hossain, Mosharaff, 1993a, 'A Sustainable Medium Term Development Strategy for Bangladesh' in Salahuddin Ahmed, ed., *Sustainable Medium Term Development for Bangladesh*, Dhaka: Centre for Economic, Social and Environmental Research.

Hossain, Mosharaff, 1993b, 'The Real Issues in Development Strategy' in Salahuddin Ahmed, ed., *Sustainable Medium Term Development for Bangladesh*, Dhaka: Centre for Economic, Social and Environmental Research.
Hossain, Mosharaff, 1994a, 'Bangladesh Economy, a Statistical Outline' (forthcoming), Dhaka: Centre for Economic, Social and Environmental Research.
Hossain, Mosharaff, 1994b, 'Structural Changes in Bangladesh Economy, 1972-1992' (mimeo).
Killick, Tony, 1992, 'Continuity and Change in IMF Programme Design 1982-92', *ODI Working Paper* 69, London: ODI.
Killick, Tony, 1993, 'Issues in the Design of IMF Programmes', *ODI Working Paper* 71, London: ODI.
Lal, D., 1983, *The Poverty of Development Economics*, London: London Institute of Economic Affairs, Hobert Paperbook, 16.
Lal, D., 1987, 'The Political Economy of Economic Liberalisation', *World Bank Economic Review*, Vol. 1, No. 2.
McNamara, Robert, 1975, *Assault on World Poverty: Problems of Rural Development, Education and Health*, Washington, D.C.: World Bank.
Preston, Lewis T., 1993, *Getting Results – The World Bank's Agenda for Improving Development Effectiveness*, Washington, D.C.: World Bank.
Singer, H.W. and S. Sharma, eds., 1989, *Economic Development and World Debt*, London: Macmillan.
Sobhan, R., 1982, *The Crisis of External Dependence*, Dhaka: University Press Limited.
UNCTAD, 1992, *The Least Developed Countries 1991 Report*, New York.
Woodward, D., 1992, *Debt, Adjustment and Poverty in Developing Countries*, Vols. I and II, London: Pinter Publications and Save the Children.
World Bank, 1989, *Sub-Saharan Africa: From Crisis to Sustainable Growth*, Washington, D.C.: World Bank.
World Bank, 1991, *World Development Report 1991*, Washington, D.C.: World Bank.
World Bank, 1993, *World Development Report 1993*, Washington, D.C.: World Bank.

9

Conditionality, Structural Adjustment and Development: The Case of Egypt

GOUDA ABDEL-KHALEK AND KARIMA KORAYEM

I. INTRODUCTION

The government of Egypt has been implementing stabilisation and structural adjustment measures since the mid-1980s[1], often without formal agreement with the IMF or the World Bank. A stand-by arrangement concluded with the IMF in May 1987 collapsed soon afterwards. Despite some interruption, the implementation of stabilisation measures continued. It was only in 1991 that Egypt reached formal agreements with the two Bretton Woods institutions: a stand-by arrangement (SBA) with the Fund in May, and a structural adjustment loan (SAL) with the Bank in November. The set of measures supported by the SBA and the SAL together form the backbone of Egypt's so-called economic reform and structural adjustment programme (ERSAP).

The SBA and the SAL agreements contain a multitude of conditions, embedded in a curious web of front-loading, policy understandings and performance criteria. Cross-conditionality is also a basic feature in both, and hence the ERSAP package. The main concern in

Note of acknowledgements. A preliminary version was discussed in the Workshop on Aid and Conditionality, EADI Working Group on Aid Policy and Performance, Berlin, 13-15 September 1993. The authors would like to thank the participants at the Workshop, especially Rashid Faruqee and Olav Stokke, for helpful comments and suggestions.

1. In fact, Egypt's experience with stabilisation is much longer. The first Stand-by Arrangement (SBA) dates back to 1962. But relations with the Bretton Woods institutions were strained for the rest of the 1960s and until the mid-1970s because of disagreement on fundamental policy issues as Egypt moved towards a centralised public-enterprise economy. The move towards Open-Door Economic Policy in the early 1970s paved the way for an SBA in 1976, which collapsed under the political pressure of mass riots in January 1977. An Extended Fund Facility was concluded in 1978, followed by an SBA in 1987. But none of these policies was fully implemented. For details see Abdel-Khalek [*1987*] and Korayem [*1987*].

this chapter[2] is to address the following question: what are the likely effects of conditionality (and cross-conditionality) on prospects for sustainable and equitable development in Egypt? Two dimensions of the impact of ERSAP will be focused upon: the potential for economic growth and structural change conducive to development, and the effects the programme may have on poverty and equity.

The first phase of ERSAP ended in September 1992. Even before ERSAP, Egypt was following many of the same policies under previous agreements with the IMF [*Korayem, 1987: 67-73*]. Although all such agreements were discontinued at some stage for political, social or economic reasons, ERSAP may be considered as just one link in a chain of policies continued since the 1980s. Hence a preliminary assessment of ERSAP is feasible even at this early stage of its implementation.

A caveat is in order at the outset. This exercise is undertaken against the background of fundamental differences in the field of conditionality: an increasingly important aspect of international economic relations (in particular relations between the Bretton Woods institutions and indebted developing countries). Uncertainty in definition has led to sharp divisions in views in this area, examined in Section III.

The chapter is organised as follows: Section II outlines the main elements of ERSAP. Section III deals with the question of conditionality, drawing both on the literature and on Egypt's experience. Section IV is devoted to examining the impact on growth, and sections V and VI deal with the effects on poverty and equity. Section VII concludes the chapter.

II. ELEMENTS OF ERSAP

ERSAP was concluded against the backdrop of a serious deterioration in Egypt's economic conditions.[3] The annual growth of GDP came close to the population growth in the late 1980s-early 1990s; in fact GNP growth was negative in 1990/91 (see Table 3). Interest payments as a proportion of exports of goods and services exceeded 20 per cent, and the country was in arrears on its external debt. The fiscal deficit reached 18 per cent of GDP in 1989/90 (see Table 1).

---

2. This chapter draws on previous work by the two co-authors [*Abdel-Khalek, 1987, 1993; Korayem, 1987, 1994*].
3. One of the main reasons was the deterioration in the country's terms of trade. The index of the terms of trade dropped from 100 in 1987 to 76 in 1990. See World Bank [*1992b, Table E6*].

The objective of ERSAP[4] is thus to restore economic growth and creditworthiness, and to improve living standards in a sustained fashion. It focuses on three policy areas: stabilisation, structural adjustment and social policies. The main components are the following: macro-economic reforms; public enterprise reform; domestic price liberalisation; foreign trade liberalisation; private sector reform; and the Social Fund for Development (SFD).

Macro-economic Reform

Macro-economic reform aims to achieve sustainable economic growth consistent with the country's ability *to service foreign debt*. This is the stabilisation foundation for ERSAP. It encompasses fiscal policy, interest rate and monetary policy and the exchange rate regime.

Fiscal adjustment lies at the heart of the stabilisation package, and involves cutting the fiscal deficit, including that financed by banks. As shown in Table 1, the target is to bring down the ratio of the overall budget deficit to GDP from an estimated high of 22 per cent for 1990/91 to a mere 1.5 per cent by 1995/96. It stipulates a slight reduction in the ratio of public expenditure to GDP[5], and a substantial increase in the share of public revenue (from about 25 per cent to about 40 per cent of GDP). However, central government non-tax revenue will provide most of the targeted adjustment with revenue raised through price increases, particularly energy prices. The increase in tax revenue relies mainly on indirect taxation (such as a comprehensive sales tax or escalation of stamp tax).

The large shift in the structure of total expenditure over the period of the programme is extremely important in terms of both equity and efficiency. Table 1 shows that the fiscal component of the programme involves almost trippling the ratio of interest payments to total government expenditure and almost halving the ratio of capital expenditure. In fact, interest payments doubled in just one year – between 1989/90 and 1990/91 – corresponding to the liberalisation of domestic interest rates and the issuance of treasury bills (TBs) and selling them to the public. The steep rise in interest payments is expected to have a negative social impact; it tilts the distribution of income in favour of the rentier or clipping class[6] at the expense of wage and profit earners.

---

4. Information in this section is drawn from IMF [*1991*], World Bank [*1991a*] and Central Bank of Egypt [*1991/92*].
5. Abstracting from the exceptionally high ratio in 1990/91, for the reasons explained in the note to Table 1.
6. 'Clipping class' was the term used by Keynes to describe people who lived off income from government debt after the Second World War. According to data of the Central Bank of Egypt, the stock of treasury bills outstanding at the end of June 1992

Expenditure measures include cutting food and agricultural-input subsidies and a reduction in public investment. The latter is obviously the more significant for growth. Public sector investment outlays were to be reduced by five percentage points in real terms between 1989/90 and 1992/93. It is assumed that such government withdrawal will lead to a major increase in private investment. The package also stipulates strong wage restraint, actually amounting to a squeeze on labour.

With regard to *monetary policy*, ERSAP removes all interest rate ceilings, imposes specific domestic credit ceilings that favour the private sector, eliminates any direct credit line between the Central Bank of Egypt (CBE) and the government, and develops a market for TBs. Interest rates were liberalised and the first TB auction held in January 1991.

ERSAP policy on the *exchange rate* includes devaluation, simplifying the system and ensuring a competitive rate. Anticipating the formal agreement with the IMF in May 1991, a dual exchange rate system consisting of a primary and a secondary market came into effect on 27 February 1991.[7] This replaced the multiple exchange rate system, involving partial unification and a maxi devaluation of the Egyptian pound of some 20-25 per cent in 1991 [*Abdel-Khalek, 1994: Table 10*]. The control mechanism for the entire system is the rate in the secondary market, which is determined freely; the rate in the primary market is set within five per cent below the former.[8]

All payments and transfers for international transactions, both current and capital, may be effected without restriction. Egypt has thus moved to full capital mobility for the first time in more than 40 years. On 8 October 1991, the free foreign exchange market was established, involving the unification of the exchange rate and a dirty float.[9]

Public Enterprise Reform

Structural adjustment measures which relate to public enterprise reform address issues of autonomy and restructuring. Autonomy is affected by a new Public Investment Law that gives freedom to public enterprises (PEs) and the establishment of a new regulatory

---

exceeded £E 17 billion. More than 80 per cent of the treasury bills stock is held by the banking sector, about 6 per cent each by private business and insurance companies, and about 4 per cent by the household sector.
7. This is an interesting example of front-loading of conditionality.
8. For details of the transactions in the two markets see: CBE [*1991*].
9. According to the new system, the Egyptian pound is pegged to the US dollar. The CBE intervenes in the foreign-exchange market to stabilise the £E/US dollar rate. Exchange rates of the pound *vis-à-vis* other currencies seem to be derived from the exchange rate of the US dollar with these currencies, given the pegged £E/US $ rate.

environment common to both public and private sectors. Restructuring involves the reorganisation of PEs as affiliate companies under the umbrella of holding companies; and privatization, including asset sales, divestiture and contracts with private management teams.

Domestic Price Liberalisation

Measures include a programme to withdraw control of ex-factory prices of *industrial sector* products. Policy on *energy prices* includes the gradual raising of domestic petroleum product prices to eventual parity with world prices by June 1995. Electricity prices will also be adjusted upwards, aiming for equality with the long-run marginal cost also by June 1995. In the *agricultural sector*, measures include raising cotton prices to bring them closer to world prices, lifting the price control of pesticides, fertiliser and animal feed, and allowing the private sector to distribute such inputs.

Foreign Trade Liberalisation

The main measures include: (i) reducing the list of commodities protected by import bans to no more than 30 per cent of industrial domestic output; (ii) changing the tariff structure to a maximum tariff rate of 80 per cent and a minimum of 10 per cent; (iii) gradual elimination of non-tariff barriers (NTBs), such as export and import bans and suspensions (see Table 2 for details); and (iv) eliminating the discretionary allocation of foreign exchange by the banking system.

Private Sector Reform

The most important measures are: (i) automatic approval of all private investment projects, domestic or foreign, except those on a negative list to be officially published; (ii) lifting price controls on the private sector, with the exception of a limited number of strategic items; (iii) entitling private-sector companies to distribute products handled by public-sector monopolies (for example cement and fertilisers).

The Social Fund for Development (SFD)

This is the palliative for the bitter medicine of ERSAP. It is a temporary measure to provide short-term relief to groups negatively affected by these adjustment measures. Financial resources equivalent to US$ 500-600 million are to be made available for SFD by the Egyptian government, UNDP, IDA, and other bilateral and multilateral donors.

III. CONDITIONALITY: THEORY AND PRACTICE

Theory of Conditionality

A theory of conditionality should address the following questions. *What* is conditionality? *Why* conditionality? And *how* does conditionality manifest itself in practice?

Conditionality may be defined as a side condition in a contractual agreement, stipulated to ensure the execution of the agreement [*Mosley et al., 1991: 65*]. The subject has attracted increasing attention in recent years. This may be attributed to two simultaneous and interrelated developments: the eruption of the debt crisis, and the introduction of World Bank policy-based lending more than a decade ago. This is known as first generation, *economic* conditionality. The collapse of the bi-polar world system, and the disintegration of the *dirigiste* regimes in eastern and central Europe and the former Soviet Union have led to the emergence of second-generation, *political* conditionality.

Inevitably, the line between economic and political conditionality is often blurred. The World Bank, though concentrating on economic conditionality, has recently stressed good 'governance'. The thrust of economic conditionality is liberalisation, through the promotion of contract-based free exchange, involving some measures which may be in conflict with the spirit of political conditionality. For example, a wage freeze imposed by fiat, would run counter to wage bargains struck through contract-based negotiations.

There is no unanimous view in the literature regarding the motivation or justification (the 'why') of economic conditionality, especially that associated with the flow of official aid. Division of opinion is particularly sharp regarding the conditionality of the Bretton Woods institutions.[10] One may distinguish three main positions. The *first* is that of the two Bretton Woods institutions, subscribed to by some academics [*Stern, 1983*]. It justifies conditionality on the grounds of maximising the chances of repayment, the equivalent of collateral in normal commercial-bank lending. The *second* is the opposite: neither IMF nor World Bank conditionality can all be justified simply on the grounds of maximising the chances of repayment [*Dell, 1982; Spraos, 1986*]. The *third* is that while IMF stand-by conditionality is

---

10. It should be noted that IMF conditionality was *formally* incorporated only in the 1969 amendment of the Fund's Articles of Agreement. For almost 25 years, Fund conditionality was implicit and rather non-uniform. World Bank conditionality became relevant only with respect to policy-based lending since the beginning of the 1980s.

justifiable on these grounds, World Bank policy-based lending is not [*Mosley et al., 1991: Ch. 3*].[11]

It should be observed that the Bank and the Fund are increasingly resorting to cross-conditionality: the decision of one institution to provide resources to a member country is made contingent on the other institution approving certain measures taken by the country in question. As a result, it may be incorrect to analyse the conditionality of each *separately*. We maintain therefore that the second position is more plausible. For *both Bretton Woods institutions*, conditionality is much more than simply a substitute for collateral. It is a means of influencing the economic and social policy of debtor member countries. The study of Egypt's experience supports this position.

Finally, we deal with the question of 'how': how does conditionality manifest itself in practice? No reading, however careful, of the various documents exchanged between the Fund, the Bank and the member country will be sufficient to spell out the various conditionality 'clauses'. In fact the term is rarely mentioned explicitly in official documents, which in turn may reveal only the tip of the iceberg. In many cases the country is required to take specific measures in advance, anticipating the formal agreement. This is known as front-loading of conditionality. In this context the two basic documents which the member country 'submits' to the Fund and the Bank (the Letter of Intent and the Letter of Development Policy, respectively) may be the main source of information on conditionality. But in themselves they are insufficient.[12]

Conditionality: The Case of Egypt

Against this background, we discuss the specifics of conditionality as it affected Egypt under ERSAP. For the sake of clarity, first IMF and then World Bank conditionality is examined although the two have become so closely linked that they should be considered together.

---

11. Mosley *et al.* argue, following Killick [*1984*], that IMF conditions are unambiguous and easy to monitor. As such, they are simply put and enforced to maximise the likelihood of repayment. World Bank conditionality involved in policy-based lending (or SAL operations since the early 1980s) is different in three important respects: purpose, nature and enforceability. The *purpose* of World Bank SAL conditions is to remove what the Bank perceives as fundamental policy-based impediments to economic efficiency. By their very *nature*, some SAL conditions are either unquantifiable or institutional, and thus leave much scope for honest disagreement about compliance. The Bank concedes cases where policy-based funds were eventually released to member countries with some conditions unenforced [*Mosley et al., 1991: Ch. 3*].

12. Another important source of information on conditionality is the Memorandum of Understanding, agreed upon by the IMF and the government of the member country.

IMF conditionality. IMF conditionality is based on the stand-by arrangement which was concluded after prolonged negotiations. Part of it is front-loaded, specifying prior actions; most is expressed in terms of performance criteria.

The objective of IMF conditionality is to create a decentralised economy that is market-based and outward-oriented. It aims to restore non-inflationary growth and creditworthiness. The IMF paradigm is strongly liberal in the economic sense and this is manifested by the emphasis on the market and outward orientation.

IMF conditionality encompasses fiscal and monetary measures, pricing policy and foreign trade and payments. The main fiscal measure was the imposition of a General Sales Tax as a means of curbing aggregate demand. This was front-loaded to clear the way for the SBA. Pricing measures involve raising domestic energy prices gradually to the level of world equivalents. However, most IMF conditions relate to performance. The satisfaction of specific performance criteria is a precondition for tranche release. These criteria are:

1. Credit ceilings, both overall and public-sector specific.
2. Minimum target levels for the net international reserves of the Central Bank of Egypt.
3. Elimination of arrears on external debt, through rescheduling, debt forgiveness or cash payments.
4. Ceilings on the increase in public external debt.
5. Exchange-rate unification (*cum* devaluation).
6. Trade and payments liberalisation.

It is important to note that the 1991 SBA to Egypt was explicit in committing the Egyptian government to the necessary adjustment required to achieve the fiscal target, *regardless of any unfavourable external shocks.*

> *In particular, if there are adverse developments in world interest rates, imported food prices, oil export prices, restructuring costs, and foreign grant and loan disbursements, or if the major macroeconomic targets (e.g., the exchange rate, domestic interest rate, or the path of inflation) deviate from the assumptions underlying the fiscal estimates in a manner that adversely affect the government's finances, compensating fiscal measures will be implemented to keep fiscal policy on track [IMF, 1991:21; emphasis added].*

This illustrates quite clearly the draconian nature of IMF conditions. Such conditions are hard to defend on technical, let alone moral, grounds. Their effect is to force the deficit country alone to carry the burden of adjustment in an increasingly disorderly international economic environment.[13]

World Bank conditionality. The November 1991 SAL conditions also fell into the two categories of up-front and second-tranche. Front-loading involved actions taken prior to presenting the SAL to the Board of Executive Directors for approval[14], as well as specific loan-signing conditions, that is on or before signing the loan. Of these, the most important are: actual promulgation of the Public Investment Law; the acceptance of a formula to gradually adjust cotton prices to reach an equivalent international price; extending the liberalised investment and production licensing and registration system of Law 159 to enterprises organised under Laws 43 and 230 (foreign investment codes).

Second-tranche conditions include the following:

(1) Macro-economic framework: achieving *satisfactory* progress with an external financing programme (either debt relief or an equivalent support); reducing budget deficits for fiscal years 1992 and 1993, and pursuing consistent monetary and exchange rate policies.[15]
(2) Public enterprise reform: legal and institutional reforms and privatisation; progress, *acceptable to the Bank*, in implementing the 1991/92 privatisation programme; and adoption of a further privatisation programme, again meeting Bank criteria, for 1992/93.
(3) Price liberalisation in industry, energy and agriculture: implementation of the agreed Action Plan to free the prices of Group IV products; raising domestic energy prices towards eventual parity with world prices/long-run marginal cost, according to the

---

13. It would have been more appropriate for Egypt to obtain Fund resources under the Compensatory and Contingency Financing Facility (CCFF) instead of the SBA. We shall not go into the technical details about eligibility here; our intention is to highlight the point in the text.
14. These include: (i) reducing the coverage of import bans from 35 per cent to 23 per cent of total tradable goods output in agriculture and manufacturing; (ii) narrowing the minimum-maximum tariff margin from 0.7 per cent-120 per cent to 5.0 per cent-100 per cent (with some exceptions); (iii) submitting a schedule for reducing tariff preferences; and (iv) abolishing foreign-exchange allocations to public-sector enterprises.
15. Progress is to be evaluated according to indicators attached to the Letter of Development Policy.

agreed formula and phasing; raising cotton procurement prices towards eventual parity with international prices, eliminating subsidies on fertilisers and pesticides by the fiscal year 1993.

(4) Trade liberalisation: reduction of production coverage of import bans to 10.6 per cent of tradable goods output. Further reduction of export bans.

(5) Private sector development: a commitment to allow public sector cement and fertiliser companies to sell 40 per cent of their output to private distributors by 1 July 1992.

Furthermore, there is a requirement of *satisfactory* implementation of other elements in the government's economic reform programme, as stated in the Letter of Development Policy.

Some observations conclude this part on World Bank-IMF conditionality. *First*, continued Bank support and second-tranche release require monitoring on the basis of variables, both of performance (outcome) and policy nature. But the policy variables are simply means to achieve the various policy targets and should be judged accordingly, not as ends in themselves. *Second*, continued IMF support of the Egyptian government's structural adjustment programme is necessary to ensure its continuity and potential financing [*World Bank, 1991:42*]. *Third*, there is a tightly-knit web of cross-conditionality: the IMF requires an indication from the World Bank that its conditions are met regarding privatisation and price decontrol; in turn, the Bank insists on expressed satisfaction by the IMF that its conditions regarding interest and exchange rates are met. This point is crucial: it reveals a type of generalised cross-conditionality which has become prevalent in recent years. Egypt is no exception in this respect. Informal cross-conditionality between the two Bretton Woods institutions, as well as the similarity in policy recommendations for the countries seeking their support, has become quite common in recent years [*Sarkar, 1991*].

IV. IMPACT ON GROWTH

Developments in four areas indicate the impact of ERSAP on output: savings, investments, GDP growth rate, and income per capita. Gross domestic investment, which averaged 22.5 per cent of GDP over the period 1987/88-1990/91 was accompanied by a low rate of gross domestic saving, averaging 6.4 per cent of GDP (Table 3). This indicates an average savings-investment gap of 16.1 percent of GDP. The second indicator, also discouraging, is the negative rate of growth of gross domestic investment (GDI). Real gross domestic investment decreased from £E (Egyptian Pound) 11368 million in 1987/88, to £E 10378 million in 1990/91 (Table 3). This reflects the decrease in government investment over the previous few years in order to reduce the budget deficit; public investment represents about three quarters of GDI (Table 3).

The third indicator of the poor performance of the Egyptian economy in correlation with the investment development is the low and declining growth rate of GDP over the period 1987/88-1990/91. GDP at constant prices grew from £E 47 billion in 1987/88 to £E 50.8 billion in 1990/91, with a real annual growth rate falling from 3.9 per cent in 1987/88 to 2.3 per cent in 1990/91 (Table 3). The GDP growth rate fell further to 1.5 per cent in 1991/92 [*World Bank, 1992a: Vol. III, Table AIII.6*].

The fourth indicator is the development in income per capita. This increased from £E 996 in 1987/88 to £E 1606 in 1990/91 (Table 3). But in real terms, income per capita has declined slightly over the period, falling from £E 840 in 1987/88 to £E 835 in 1990/91. This indicates an average annual growth rate of -0.3 percent (Table 3).

In assessing the impact of the implementation of ERSAP on savings, investment, output, and per capita income, the following points should be considered: First, ERSAP pricing policies and exchange reform increase the cost of living, which will raise private consumption expenditure. Since private consumption represents the largest share in total consumption (88.9 per cent of the total in 1990/91 (Table 3)) this behaviour will have a significant impact in raising total consumption and decreasing gross domestic savings. However, the large increase in interest rates for deposits is expected to encourage domestic savings. The final impact on domestic savings will depend on the net outcome of these two opposing effects of ERSAP measures.

Second, ERSAP is expected to have a detrimental effect on investment, at least in the short run, for two reasons: one is the application of a strongly contractionary monetary policy, which has reduced the growth rate of domestic credit to 1.5 per cent in 1991/92 compared to an average annual growth rate of 21 per cent over the period 1987/88-1990/91 [*Korayem, 1993: Table 6*]. The second reason is the tight fiscal policy which resulted in reducing government expenditure on investment by 28.2 per cent in 1991/92, compared to 1990/91 (calculated from Korayem [*1993: Table 5*]). This reduction significantly affects total investment, since public (or government) investment represents more than three-quarters of total gross domestic investment in Egypt (Table 3). However, public-sector reform in ERSAP aims to compensate for the fall in the government investment by an increase in private investment through privatisation and by the introduction of appropriate laws and regulations to encourage private participation in economic activities.

Public enterprise reform will take a relatively long period to be implemented, and for the results to be felt.[16] Meanwhile, exchange rate reform and changes in investment laws favouring the private sector may encourage capital inflows, partly directed towards investment. However, the devaluation of the Egyptian pound and high differentials between domestic and international interest rates make profit easy to realise by portfolio shifts from foreign-currency to Egyptian-pound deposits; this makes investment in projects a less attractive alternative for private capital.

The impact of ERSAP on GDP will depend on its net effect on investment as described above. If it succeeds in increasing private investment to exceed the decline in public investment, GDP growth rate will increase. However, the effect of ERSAP implementation in 1991/92 is not encouraging: the growth rate fell to 1.5 per cent [*World Bank, 1992a: Vol. III, Table AIII.6*] from an average annual growth rate of 2.9 per cent during 1987/88-1990/91 (Table 3). It should be noted that, according to ERSAP, government revenues from the sale of public enterprises are not to be re-invested, but instead allocated to cover current government expenditure. For the government, this amounts to the liquidisation of its assets in order to cover its consumption expenditure. For the society, the impact of privatisation on investment will be simply to substitute private for public capital without any net addition to total investment. This policy is quite consistent with the Fund's objective of creating a market-based economy with a minimum government role in economic activity. This goal will not be achieved if the revenue from privatisation is re-invested in new public projects. An alternative worth considering would be to use the revenue to re-structure loss-making public enterprises and to upgrade strategic enterprises that are planned to remain in public ownership.

ERSAP's impact on real income per capita depends on its effects on the cost of living, and on GDP growth rate, given that the population growth rate in Egypt was 2.8 per cent in the 1980s [*CAPMAS, 1992*]. This means that the real GDP growth rate has to exceed 2.8 per cent annually, which does not seem to be a feasible target, in the short term at least.

---

16. Chile, for example, started privatisation in the mid-1970s and was still carrying it out throughout the 1980s.

V. IMPACT ON THE POOR

Egypt may not be among the poorest countries in the world, but poverty is relatively widespread. Moreover, its incidence has been rising since the early 1980s. Nationally, the percentage of households below the poverty line rose from 30 per cent to 33.8 per cent between 1981/ 82 and 1984 [*Korayem, 1987: Table 1-2*], and then to 45.8 per cent in 1990/91 [*Korayem, 1994*]. The average household's standard of living appears to have deteriorated slightly between 1981/82 and 1990/91 in both rural and urban areas [*El-Leithy and Kheir-El-Din, 1992*].

The impact of ERSAP on the population in general, and on the poor in particular, will be felt in three areas: cost of living, income, and social services provided by the government.

Cost of Living

Devaluation, increases in the price of energy, transportation and commodities from public enterprises; the elimination of subsidies, raising indirect taxes and widening their base: these are major ERSAP measures that will raise the cost of living for the population as a whole. But the effects will be felt most severely by the poor. Subsidies are given to essential consumer goods and services, such as basic foods and transportation services. The reduction in subsidy will hurt the poor most, since a large portion of their budget (up to 48 per cent for those in the lowest expenditure brackets) is spent on subsidised food; 60 per cent of the urban population in Egypt spent between one-fifth and a half of their total budget on subsidised food items, according to the 1974/75 Household Budget Survey [*Korayem, 1980: Table 8*]. In addition, devaluation of the Egyptian pound increases the price of imported commodities, including basics such as wheat and flour, whilst raising the prices of imported capital and intermediate goods, which in turn raise the cost of production for locally produced goods. This further contributes to the general price rise and hence the cost of living of the population, including the poor.

Income

By raising prices ERSAP also reduces real incomes. The working poor, usually illiterate or poorly educated, already earn low incomes, making them vulnerable to any increase in prices. Moreover, the application of tight monetary and fiscal policies and the reduction in government investments reduce prospects for job creation. Since the poor tend to be the least educated and lacking in influential social connections, their chances of getting a job diminish as the labour market contracts.

Social Services

ERSAP has an effect on social services provided by the government, either free or at a low subsidised price to the consumer. In spite of the increase in real investment in education and health in 1991/92 compared to the previous year, the level has not yet reached that already achieved in the late 1980s [*Korayem, 1993: Table 9*]. The increase in the number of students and population has led to a decline in real investment per student and per capita in education and health. Consequently, an improvement in the quality of education provided is unlikely, despite the introduction of a small fee paid by students at all levels of education. Similarly, there is increasing pressure on the supply of health services of reasonable quality and low subsidised cost. Yet again, the implementation of ERSAP has negative effects on the poor. This has already been acknowledged by both the Fund and the Bank [*World Bank, 1991b*]. Consequently, some compensatory measures are necessary to minimise hardship for the poor. The creation of the SFD is intended to serve this purpose. It is questionable, however, whether the SFD, with its limited resources, can realise such an objective.

VI. IMPACT ON EQUITY

No official data on income distribution are available for Egypt before 1990/91. Before that date, estimates based on Household Expenditure Surveys are available for 1974/75 and 1981/82 [*Korayem, 1987: Table 1-1*]. According to these, there is a significant improvement in the pattern of income distribution in 1981/82 compared to 1974/75, then a considerable deterioration takes place in 1990/91 compared to 1981/82, evident in the fall in the Gini index [*Korayem, 1994*].

The impact of ERSAP on income distribution may be assessed using two mechanisms. The first studies the effect on personal income distribution of policies on taxes, subsidies, and wealth; and the second looks at the impact on wages and prices.

Personal Income Distribution

No change in direct taxes (such as income tax or profit tax) has taken place so far. A global income tax is expected, but not enough is known about it to make a preliminary assessment about whether its effect will be relatively progressive or regressive compared to the prevailing tax system. Indirect taxes are by their very nature regressive. Levying new indirect taxes on commodities and services (such as the sales tax), widening the base of the prevailing ones, and raising their rates are measures which have been implemented as part of ERSAP. Inevitably, their impact has been most severe on the incomes of the population in lower income brackets. This is because the low income earners have a higher marginal propensity to consume, and accordingly allocate a larger share of their incomes to buy goods which form the base for indirect taxes.

Wealth effects (of foreign currency deposits) resulting from devaluation has a negative impact on equity [*Abdel-Khalek, 1987*]. Devaluation increases the wealth of owners of foreign currency deposits, and augments their incomes by raising the return to those deposits in Egyptian pounds. The effect is redistribution of income in favour of the owners of foreign currency deposits.

Wages and Salaries

According to the 1990/91 Expenditure and Income Survey, wages represent 49.1 per cent of urban households' income and 26.4 per cent of rural households' income [*CAPMAS, 1993*]. ERSAP requires the government to reduce expenditure on wages by 15 per cent in real terms. So its impact on the incomes of government employees is detrimental. However, the effect on distribution among the employees depends on whether the government decreases wages evenly across the ranks, or if it reduces them unevenly, favouring the low-ranking employees as it has done previously. The reduction in real government wages between 1973 and 1987 was borne mainly by high-ranking employees [*World Bank, 1991b*].

In the private sector too, the increase in prices as a result of the ERSAP measures threatens to reduce real wages. However, the resulting decline in the standard of living for employees in the private sector would be less than for those in the public sector if the pattern of wage distribution were to show a greater prevalence of high wages in the private compared to that in the public sector. But this does not seem to be the case. The distribution pattern of wages in both public and private sector establishments is similar. For example, according to wage data in 1990, 26.5 per cent of employees in the public sector received a monthly income of more than £E 300; while in private sector establishments of ten workers and more, those receiving the same level of income represented 26.0 per cent of the total number (calculated from: World Bank [*1992: Vol. III, Table AX.6*]). Another view, based on the assessment of the 1987 IMF stand-by arrangement, is that the impact on the private sector's wages is not immediately apparent [*Abdel-Khalek, 1987*]. According to this view, the devaluation of the Egyptian pound encourages emigration to Arab countries, raising nominal wages in the domestic market. The final outcome depends on the growth rate of inflation, in relation to that of nominal wages [*Abdel-Khalek, 1987*]. However, with relatively scarce job opportunities in the Gulf countries, and a high unemployment rate in the domestic market, the decrease in real wages in the private sector seems to be more likely, at least in the short term.

The impact of ERSAP on non-wage earners should also be considered. The measures eliminate the input subsidy in agriculture as well as the procurement prices for main crops, other than for cotton and sugar cane. This will probably raise the nominal incomes received by small farmers because they are the main producers of traditional crops, previously subject to compulsory delivery at controlled procurement prices. The input subsidy received by those farmers was less than the amount of income lost by selling their products to the government at low procurement prices [*Korayem, 1982*]. However, although their nominal incomes are expected to increase, the impact on their real incomes, which is more significant, is not unequivocal. This is because small farmers are also consumers of subsidised commodities. Cutting, or eliminating, subsidies on those commodities, will raise their cost of living and reduce their real incomes. The final outcome for small farmers will depend on the rate of increase in their nominal incomes compared to the increase in their cost of living.

Non-wage earners in the private business sector will be affected both negatively and positively: disadvantages are the high interest rates, the tightening of domestic credit, and probably trade liberalisation, at least in the short term, while they will gain by the freeing of prices, the promotion of competition between private and public sectors in production and by the devaluation of the Egyptian pound. The final impact of ERSAP's implementation on this group will be dictated by the financial position of the individual enterprise, especially with respect to the proportion of borrowed capital.[17] The higher this proportion, the more likely are the negative factors to outweigh positive ones, and the enterprise will be a net looser, and may even declare bankruptcy. The reduction in aggregate demand due to the tight policy measures applied by ERSAP will be another negative factor that will hurt the business sector (both public and private). The fall in purchasing power and the accumulation of inventories seem to be concomitant with the implementation of ERSAP, in the short term at least.

---

17. The impact of ERSAP on such a socio-economic group as consumers is not considered, because of their relatively low marginal propensity to consume, and also because their gain as producers normally outweighs the increase in their cost of living.

VII. BRETTON WOODS CONDITIONALITY AND ALTERNATIVE MEASURES

In assessing economic reform programmes there are various alternative approaches: the internal approach, the before-after approach, and the counter-factual approach. The internal approach examines the extent of achievement of the programme targets. The second compares the performance of the economy before and after the programme. The third compares what happens under the programme with what would have happened if the programme were not implemented. The before-after approach is most common, and it is the one used in this study.[18] On the basis of the foregoing analysis, the implications of the Egyptian case study for the more general analysis of conditionality are underlined, and the main effects of ERSAP on growth, poverty and equity are summarised. Finally, the question of an alternative to Bretton Woods conditionality is briefly addressed at the end.

(1) ERSAP is a good example of first-generation *economic* conditionality. It reflects quite clearly a type of generalised Bretton Woods conditionality. Except in its emphasis on privatisation, it does not reflect strongly the second-generation *political* conditionality that stipulates changes in the system of government and the management of public affairs.[19] However, many aspects of economic conditionality embodied in ERSAP have strong implications for the role of the state, and may thus be tantamount to political conditionality.

(2) ERSAP conditionality is in many ways excessive: for example, the fiscal target should be achieved irrespective of the magnitude and nature of external shocks. But it is interesting to note that the conditions met with far less resistance than expected. This applies to aspects such as trade and price liberalisation as well as the reduction of the fiscal deficit. Privatisation may be the only part of ERSAP which is generating strong political opposition. Concern about the

---

18. In justifying this approach, two familiar criticisms should be addressed. The *first* is that it may be premature to judge the results of ERSAP since the programme has been through one phase only, with another still to follow. The *second* is that it may be difficult to separate the effects due to ERSAP from effects due to other factors. The first criticism is addressed in the Introduction. The second calls for careful attention in attributing results to the programme.
19. In the Egyptian context, privatisation may be the only example of political conditionality. It entails fundamental changes in the economic system as defined by the Constitution, which stresses that Egypt's politico-economic system is democratic socialism and assigns a principal role to the public ownership of the means of production.

detrimental effects of privatisation was expressed by political parties, the trade union movement and representatives from the public sector and some intellectuals. The privatisation programme, therefore, is behind schedule and this has led to delay in the second-tranche release.

(3) ERSAP is expected to have a detrimental effect on output and employment in the short term, mainly due to its contractionary fiscal and monetary measures. Public enterprise reform will enhance the negative impact on employment. The impact in the medium term will depend amongst other things on the success of structural adjustment measures in enhancing productivity and output, creating additional employment, and encouraging the private sector to compensate for the reduction in public investment.

(4) For the poor ERSAP is harmful in the short term, mainly because of its effect in raising prices and reducing employment opportunities. The medium-term impact will depend on how successfully the programme can stabilise prices, increase total investment and raise output. The capacity of the Social Fund for Development (SFD) to minimise hardships resulting from ERSAP measures should not be exaggerated. SFD resources are limited, and those living in ultra poverty are not among its beneficiaries.

(5) In terms of income distribution, the conclusion must be that ERSAP has a negative impact on wage earners. For non-wage earners the conclusion is equivocal and depends on several factors pulling in opposite directions. The effect on farmers, for example, depends on whether the gains from lifting the control of crop prices outweighs losses resulting from the elimination of subsidies on agricultural inputs and basic consumer goods. For non-wage earners in the business sector, the net effect will depend on the gains from decontrolling prices and export promotion outweighing losses resulting from the raising of interest rates, lowering of credit ceilings and liberalisation of foreign trade.

These conclusions concerning the effects of ERSAP should not be construed as a defence of the policies the programme sought to replace. Such policies were deficient in a number of important ways, and the resulting situation was untenable. Rather, the conclusions are based on the nature of ERSAP and the Bretton Woods conditionality involved. This leads to a consideration of an alternative to Bretton Woods conditionality.

Egypt, as a developing economy, suffers from institutional under-development and structural inflexibility. The most important restric-tions are the fundamental nature of the food deficit, the prevalence of public ownership, significant idle capacity in manufacturing, and dollarisation [*Abdel-Khalek, 1994*]. Given these inflexible factors, ERSAP's plan to transform the Egyptian economy within three to five years to an open market economy, with prices and incomes determin-ed freely by demand and supply conditions, would be difficult to achieve without inflicting a high social cost. The structuralist approach is probably more suitable than the neo-classical approach underlying ERSAP; a heterodox package may therefore be a better alternative.

In contrast to ERSAP, the alternative package should have the fol-lowing features:

(1) a more balanced mix of measures to augment supply and reduce demand. Emphasis should be placed on increasing the supply of food;
(2) a better balance between market forces and price mechanism on the one hand and planning and direct control on the other [*Banuri, ed., 1991*];
(3) more measures to promote better economic management; and
(4) different sequencing of measures implemented, starting with reform of the real economy.

In conclusion, we believe that some government intervention by means of investment, production and price controls on certain goods and services is necessary for a smooth transition to a market-oriented economy. Government investment is required to combat unemploy-ment until GDP growth is sustained, aggregate demand expands, and the private sector is capable of contributing to society's economic well-being. Moreover, it is necessary to freeze the prices of selected basic commodities and services until inflation is brought under con-trol and the deterioration in real income is contained.

TABLE 1
FISCAL VARIABLES UNDER ERSAP
(PER CENT OF GDP)

	Fiscal Year						
	89/90	90/91	91/92	92/93	93/94	94/95	95/96
Total Revenue	25.37	29.56	36.89	36.69	38.27	39.29	39.96
o/w							
Central Government							
Tax Revenue	14.91	18.48	23.77	23.12	23.65	23.91	23.95
Central Government							
nontax	4.93	7.63	9.59	10.51	11.55	12.32	12.98
Total Expenditure	43.81	51.47	47.12	45.15	44.65	43.45	42.08
Current Expenditure	28.05	32.40	33.80	35.92	35.48	34.75	33.86
o/w Interest	4.60	9.33	11.29	13.20	13.08	12.93	12.54
Capital Expenditure	15.76	19.06	13.32	10.22	9.17	8.70	8.22
Fiscal Deficit	18.44	21.91	10.24	6.58	5.42	3.33	1.52
o/w							
Bank Finance	9.68	1.81	0.87	0.00	0.00	0.00	0.00

Notes and Sources: Capital Expenditure includes public entreprise investment and structural-reform-related expenditure. For 1990/91, it includes £E 6.1 billion (= 6% of GDP) as government transfer to the four public-sector banks to close their foreign-currency exposure. This was mainly financed from Gulf-crisis related extraordinary foreign financing.
Source: World Bank [*1991a:13*]

TABLE 2
DOMESTIC PRODUCTION COVERAGE OF NTBS
(AS PER CENT OF DOMESTIC OUTPUT)

	Public Sector		Private Sector		Overall	
	(1)	(2)	(1)	(2)	(1)	(2)
Exports						
Export Bans	9.5	4.2	1.9	1.1	4.9	2.3
Other NTBs	15.2	4.5	1.5	0.0	7.0	1.9
All Export NTBs	24.8	8.8	3.3	1.1	11.9	4.2
Imports						
Import Bans	49.2	41.2	29.3	10.3	37.2	22.7
Agriculture	n.a.	n.a.	n.a.	n.a.	35.9	9.8
Manfacturing & Mining	n.a.	n.a.	n.a.	n.a.	37.8	28.5
All Import NTBs	76.4	47.5	36.3	10.9	52.5	25.6

Notes and Source: (1) March 1990
(2) June 1991
World Bank [*1991a, Tables 4 and 5*]

TABLE 3
SELECTED ECONOMIC INDICATORS
£E MILLIONS

	1987/88	1988/89	1989/90	1990/91
	At Current Prices			
1. GDP Deflator (1986/87=100)	116.0	135.4	158.9	194.3
2. Urban Consumer Price Index (CPI)				
(1986/87=100)	118.6	138.4	167.7	192.4
3. Gross Domestic Product (GDP)	54553	65577	78907	98664
4. Consumption (C)	50102	61812	75120	91713
4.a Private Consumption (PC)	42729	53623	65888	81488
PC/C	85.3	86.8	87.7	88.9
4.b Gov. Consumption (GC)	7373	8189	9232	10225
GC/C	14.7	13.2	12.3	11.1
5. Gross Domestic Investment (GDI)	13187	15269	17276	20164
GDI/GDP	24.2	23.3	21.9	20.4
5.a Change in Stocks	150	240	360	420
5.b Fixed Capital Formation	13037	15029	16916	19744
Private Investment (PRI)	2015	3549	2665	4677
PRI/GDI	15.5	23.6	15.8	23.7
Public Investment (PBI)	11022	11480	14251	15067
PBI/GDI	84.5	76.4	84.2	76.3
6. Gross National Product (GNP)	52603	63934	77280	91410
7. Gross Domestic Saving (GDS)	4451	3765	3787	6951
GDS/GDP	8.2	5.7	4.8	7.0
8. Population Estimates				
(in thousands)	52827	54188	55571	56910
9. Income Per Capita (£E)[1]				
(= 5 ÷ 7)	996	1180	1391	1606
10. Average Nominal Deposit Rate[2]	11.0	12.0	12.0	16.0
11. Average Nominal Lending Rate[2]	15.0	16.0	17.0	18.0
12. Private Dollarization[3]	53.7	56.5	57.9	62.0
13. Interest Payments/EXPGSR[4]	8.4	20.9	22.2	20.9
14. DOD/GDP[5]	155.0	127.9	144.3	119.1
	At Constant Prices[6]			
	1987/88	1988/89	1989/90	1990/91
GDP	47028	48432	49658	50779
GDP growth rate (%)	3.9	3.0	2.5	2.3
C	42245	44662	44794	47668
GDI	11368	11277	10872	10378
GNP	45347	47219	48634	47046
GNP growth rate (%)	2.9	4.1	3.0	-3.3
Income per capita (£E)	840	853	829	835

Notes:

1. Assuming gross national income = GNP, i.e. without adjusting for the terms of trade factor. The terms of trade adjustment for Egypt were negative in 1987/88 and 1988/89, which are the latest data available [*World Bank, 1991d*].
2. On deposit and loans with maturity of one year or less.
3. Defined as the ratio of private sector's foreign currency deposits to private sector's total deposits.
4. Interest payments are calculated on actual basis from 1988/89; prior to 1988/89, data on cash basis. EXPGRS is exports of goods and services including workers' remittances.
5. DOD is debt outstanding and disbursed.
6. Deflated by GDP deflator, except for income per capita which is deflated by CPI.

Sources: Central Bank of Egypt [*1991/92*], World Bank [*1992a, Vol.III*], and CAPMAS [*1992*].

REFERENCES

Abdel-Khalek, Gouda, 1987, *Stabilization and Adjustment Policies and Programmes: Country Study 9, Egypt*, Helsinki: World Institute for Development Economic Research.

Abdel-Khalek, Gouda, 1994,'Egypt's ERSAP: The Orthodox Recipe and the Alternative', in Gouda Abdel-Khalek and Hanaa Kheir-El-Din (eds.), *Economic Reform and Its Distributive Impact*, Cairo: Al-Mostaqbal Al-Arabi.

Banuri, Tariq (ed.), 1991, *Economic Liberalization: No Panacea; The Experience of Latin America and Asia*, Oxford: Clarendon.

Central Agency for Public Mobilization and Statistics (CAPMAS), 1992, *The Annual Statistical Yearbook*, Cairo: June (in Arabic).

Central Agency for Public Mobilization and Statistics (CAPMAS), 1993, *Research in Income, Expenditure and Consumption in the Arab Republic of Egypt, 1990/91*; 3 volumes (composed of 5 parts), December (in Arabic).

Central Bank of Egypt, 1991 & 1992, *Report on Monetary and Credit Conditions 1990/91 & 1991/92* (in Arabic).

Central Bank of Egypt, *Annual Report, 1991/92*, Cairo (in Arabic).

Dell, Sidney, 1982,'Stabilisation: The Political Economy of Overkill', *World Development*, Vol. 10 (8).

El-Leithy, Heba and Hanaa Kheir-El-Din, 1992,'Assessment of Poverty in Egypt Using Household Data', a paper presented in the Conference of Economic Reform and Its Distributive Impact, Faculty of Economics and Political Science, Cairo University, 21-23 November.

IMF, 1991, *Memorandum on Economic Policy of the Egyptian Government*, 19 April, Washington, DC: International Monetary Fund.

Killick, Tony, 1984, *The Quest for Economic Stabilisation: The IMF and the Third World*, New York: St. Martin's.

Korayem, Karima, 1980, *The Impact of the Elimination of Food Subsidies on the Cost of Living of Egypt's Urban Population*, the International Labour Office, World Employment Programme Research, Working Paper 91, August.

Korayem, Karima, 1982,'The Agricultural Output Pricing Policy and the Implicit Taxation of Agricultural Income', in Gouda Abdel-Khalek & Robert Tignor (eds.), *The Political Economy of Income Distribution in Egypt*, New York: Holmes & Meier Publishers Inc.

Korayem, Karima, 1987,'The Impact of Economic Adjustment Policies on the Vulnerable Families and Children in Egypt', a Report prepared for the Third World Forum (Middle East Office) and UNICEF (Egypt).

Korayem, Karima, 1993,'Structural Adjustment and Reform Policies in Egypt: Economic and Social Implications'. United Nations, the Economic and Social Commission for Western Asia (ESCWA), October.

Korayem, Karima, 1994, *Poverty and Income Distribution in Egypt*, Cairo: The Third World Forum.

Mosley, Paul, Jane Harrington and John Toye (eds.), 1991, *Aid and Power: The World Bank and Policy-based Lending*, Vol. 1, New York: Routledge.

Sarkar, Prabirjit, 1991,'IMF/World Bank Stabilisation Programmes: A Critical Assessment', *Economic and Political Weekly*, October.

Spraos, John, 1986,'IMF Conditionality: Ineffectual, Inefficient, Mistargeted', *Essays in International Finance*, Princeton University Press, No. 166, December.

Stern, Ernest, 1983,'World Bank Financing of Structural Adjustment', in John Williamson (ed.), *IMF Conditionality*, Washington, DC: Institute for International Economics.

World Bank, 1991a, *Report and Recommendation of the President of the International Bank for Reconstruction and Development to the Executive Directors on a Proposed Structural Adjustment Loan in an Amount Equivalent to US $ 300 Million to the Arab Republic of Egypt*, June.

World Bank, 1991b, *Egypt: Alleviating Poverty During Structural Adjustment*, Washington, DC.

World Bank, 1991c, *World Tables*; 1990-91 Edition.

World Bank, 1992a, *Egypt: Financial Policy for Adjustment and Growth*, Vols. I & III, Appendices and Annexes, October 30.

World Bank, 1992b, *Global Economic Prospects and the Developing Countries*. Washington, DC, April.

10

Conditionality and Compliance: The Sustainability of Adjustment in Turkey

OLIVER MORRISSEY

I. INTRODUCTION

The experience of Turkey with economic policy reform (structural adjustment) in the 1980s is worthy of study for at least two reasons. Turkey was one of the first countries to receive a World Bank structural adjustment loan (SAL), the only country to receive a full programme of five SALs, and it received almost one-third of all SAL funds allocated between 1980 and 1986. Furthermore, the Turkish experience has been analysed extensively. It has been hailed as a success by the World Bank (hereafter referred to as the Bank) and many commentators [*Baysan and Blitzer, 1991; Krueger and Turan, 1993; van Wijnbergen et al., 1992*], although others have been more ambivalent [*Boratav, 1987; Önis and Webb, 1993; Kirkpatrick and Önis, 1991*]. This chapter examines the Turkish case, and compares it to other adjusting countries, by concentrating on three issues: conditionality, compliance and sequence. It will be helpful to clarify some terminology at the outset.

Conditionality refers to the specific economic policy reforms that were integral to the SALs negotiated between the Bank and the Turkish government. Each SAL programme supported by the Bank comprises a list of economic reforms to be undertaken by the recipient, such as removal of quantitative restrictions (QRs) on imports, reduction of tariffs, reform of public enterprises and cuts in public spending. These reforms are conditions because the funds associated

Note of acknowledgements. I am grateful to all of the participants at the Berlin workshop on 'Aid and Conditionality' on 13-15 September 1993; the conversation over the three days had a strong influence on the manner in which this chapter has been revised. I am especially grateful to a number of people for specific comments: Olav Stokke, Gouda Abdel-Khalek, Karima Korayem and Samuel Mushi. None are implicated in the final product.

with the loan, or some part thereof, will not be released unless the reforms are undertaken. *Compliance* refers to the extent to which these reforms are implemented. While in practice it is difficult to grade the degree of compliance, attempts are made to do so and, from the recipient's perspective, the critical issue is whether compliance is sufficient to satisfy the Bank (so that funds are released on time). Turkey did not dissatisfy the Bank, and the nature of its conditionality and compliance are discussed in Section II. *Sequencing* refers to the order in which economic reforms are attempted, taken here to include the speed of reform, and is also addressed in Section II.

A wide range of methods for evaluating adjustment episodes, or economic reform in general, have been proposed and used. We make no attempt to summarise the alternatives, even briefly [for a discussion see *Greenaway and Morrissey, 1993; Krueger, 1992; Mosley et al., 1991a*]. However, it is important to comment on what we mean by claiming that a series of reforms were a 'success' as this can be contentious. There are likely to be winners and losers from any reform (Pareto optimal reforms do not seem to be observed in practice) and the former are likely to consider the reform a success while the latter would disagree. However, there is broad agreement that if the reformers (the Bank and government) specify the targets or objectives of the reform, then the extent to which these targets are reached is an indicator of how successful the reforms have been. In this sense reforms can be successful (in attaining their objectives) without necessarily being desirable or optimal to outside observers, or to groups affected by them (the losers). It is in this narrow sense that the term 'success' is used as an operational concept rather than a value judgment. Section III considers if Turkish adjustment has been successful by examining indicators of economic performance, while Section IV addresses political economy issues. Section V offers a conclusion and some lessons for other adjusting countries.

Turkey in 1980 exhibited many of the economic problems which signalled the need for structural adjustment. Persistent budget deficits fuelled inflation: interest rates were below inflation so credit rationing became prevalent. The proliferation of controlled prices, import licences, foreign exchange and credit controls gave rise to distortions, reflected in high effective protection, rent-seeking and rationing. Public enterprises accounted for large shares of investment, output and employment, with favourable access to scarce resources such as rationed credit, but were relatively inefficient with low productivity [*Baysan and Blitzer, 1991*]. The low return on public investment contributed to debt-servicing problems and undermined the effectiveness of aid inflows. Furthermore, Turkey had an overvalued exchange rate, which reduced the domestic cost of debt-servicing but discriminated against exports and reduced the foreign exchange earnings which could be used to meet debt interest payments.

Inappropriate policies generated a wide variety of distortions throughout the economy. Consequently, growth required wide-ranging economic reform. By the end of the 1970s, the Turkish lira (TL) was again overvalued and the country had an unsustainable current account deficit. In January 1980 the government announced major reforms: a devaluation of almost 50 per cent and a commitment to maintain the real exchange rate, supported by an IMF stand-by agreement. There followed a programme of five SALs worth some $1.5 billion over 1980-84. This chapter offers a comparative evaluation of that adjustment programme. Section II looks at the conditionality of Turkey's adjustment programme and the degree of compliance, drawing a comparison with other adjusting countries, and highlights the central importance of sequencing. Section III reviews the economic performance of Turkey in the 1980s, revealing why some commentators have hailed its adjustment as a success. Section IV evaluates the political economy factors, and Section V concludes.

II. TURKEY'S STRUCTURAL ADJUSTMENT PROGRAMME

The conditionality underpinning SALs evolves in a process of negotiation between the Bank and the recipient government, although the two parties do not have equal bargaining power. Recommendations are made for reforms and disbursement of SAL funds is conditional upon the acceptance of these reform proposals. The process can be thought of as a stick and carrot mechanism. The carrot comes most obviously through quickly disbursed finance on concessional terms. The stick takes the form of a threat by the Bank not to offer further finance if the recipient reneges (slips) on the conditions. The extent of slippage can be difficult to define and it would appear that the Bank places greater emphasis on compliance with some conditions than with others. A recipient's scope for slippage will, therefore, depend on the nature of the conditions attached to the loan and its relative bargaining power with the Bank.

Table 1 provides details of the conditionality content of Turkey's SALs in comparison with other classes of adjusting countries. For example, 45 per cent of the conditions attached to Turkish SALs (all five taken together) involved trade policy reforms, such as the elimination of QRs and tariff reductions. This is not surprising given that the principal objective of adjustment was to remove anti-export bias and reduce protection. The emphasis on trade was much higher for Turkey than for all SALs taken together (where 28 per cent of conditions related to trade policy reform). The prominence of trade, in general, is attributable to the beliefs that outward-orientation facilitates more rapid economic growth and liberal trade policies minimise price distortions and encourage a more efficient allocation of resources. Furthermore, protectionist trade policies, particularly those grounded in direct controls, encourage rent seeking. Finally, many of the instruments of trade policy are readily identifiable and compliance with particular conditions is relatively easily monitored. Techniques of policy analysis are fairly well-developed for trade issues, such as incidence and effective protection, which facilitates the design, negotiation and implementation of policy. In the latter respect, the first Turkish SAL included the condition that a detailed study of protection be undertaken.

TABLE 1
CONDITIONALITY CONTENT OF SALS
VARIOUS POLICY AREAS AS A PERCENTAGE OF ALL CONDITIONS

Item	SSA (13)	HIC (22)	All (51)	Turkey (5)
Exchange rate	4	2	2	2
Trade policy	25	32	28	45
Tax/Public spending	20	20	21	39
Public enterprises	19	17	16	12
Financial sector	4	13	11	18
Industry/Energy policy	8	5	9	6
Agricultural policy	17	10	11	0
Total	100	100	100	100

Notes: Table 1 provides an indication of the relative importance of particular policy areas among the conditions required as part of the adjustment package. Conditions in each area are implicitly given the same weight (each is counted as one). Numbers in parentheses are total numbers of loans; 'All' refers to all SAL recipients over the period 1980 to 1987 inclusive; 'SSA' is sub-Saharan Africa; 'HIC' is Highly Indebted Countries.
Source: World Bank [1988], Table 4.2; figures for Turkey are estimated by the author and derived from the list of conditions provided in Kirkpatrick and Önis [1991], Table 11.2.

Liberalisation of import policy may in itself encourage export, as complete liberalisation will, *ceteris paribus*, result in neutrality in the structure of relative prices (between imports and exports). In SAL programmes, complete liberalisation is not typical, either because reforms are gradually phased in or because a certain level of protection is conceded. Thus, positive export policy is frequently recommended, as it was in the first two Turkish SALs. Export promotion is assisted by exchange rate devaluation, which increases the (domestic currency) price of exports relative to imports. As the costs and risks associated with exporting tend to be greater than those of competing in the home market, an overvalued exchange rate disadvantages the export sector in particular (which appears to have been the case in Turkey).

The area which has been least subject to conditionality is exchange rate policy, which accounted for only two per cent of all conditions attached, and Turkey is no exception. This reflects the fact that the exchange rate is traditionally in the sphere of influence of the IMF. Recipients of SALs are usually recipients of stabilisation loans from the IMF in which the exchange rate is a major target of conditionality. This clearly applies to Turkey where an IMF stabilisation programme preceeded the first SAL (Table 3). In looking at the percentage composition of conditions, as in Table 1, it is important to understand that the same weight is given to each condition listed in the SAL agreement. Thus, a condition such as 'devalue by 50 per cent' is treated on a par with a condition such as 'undertake a comprehensive study of protection' although the importance of each is obviously very different. Table I therefore offers little more than an indication of the number of economic reforms in particular policy areas.

Other major policy areas for all SALs are the public sector, agricultural policy, and financial sector reform. It is curious that agriculture did not feature directly in any of the conditions attached to Turkish SALs. The public sector, especially expenditure reduction, did feature prominently for Turkey. Many of the conditions imposed on Turkey in this area related to public investment, which was to be reduced in scale and redirected towards infrastructure, away from public enterprises. Interestingly, Önis and Özmucur [*1991:31*] observe the trend in public investment after 1980 as being away from manufacturing and towards infrastructure, which they criticise as a 'tendency towards disequilibrium' (in terms of future debt-servicing). However, the trend is consistent with implementation of SAL conditions, infrastructure is an appropriate area for public investment and may not crowd-out private investment. Another significant area for Turkish conditions was reform of the public enterprises which dominated heavy industry but were relatively inefficient. The conditions were intended to reduce the prices, wages and favourable access to credit of public enterprises and to increase their efficiency. The financial sector featured more prominently for Turkey than for SALs in general, largely because Turkey is relatively developed; most of these conditions related to the provision of credit and establishing a stock exchange, and featured in the fifth SAL.

The range of policy instruments affected by SAL programmes makes their negotiation and agreement difficult for two main reasons. First, there are problems of policy interdependence. For example, tariff reductions may reduce government tax revenue whilst another condition requires the government to reduce its budget deficit; the two may be inconsistent making it difficult for the government to implement all of the conditions. Turkish conditions were relatively well integrated. For example, the reforms of public enterprises would also reduce public expenditure and the budget deficit while facilitating private sector expansion. Second, the greater the number of policy areas involved in a particular reform package, the greater the number of government agencies involved in the negotiation of the package. As the number of interested parties increases, the potential trade-offs between agencies increases. This also is unlikely to have been a critical problem for Turkey as it was rarely the case that any one SAL related to a large number of conditions, and Turkey had a relatively skilled and capable bureaucracy. In conclusion, Turkey's conditions were more focused on trade and better integrated than for most SALs.

Compliance with Conditionality

In assessing the effects of SALs an important distinction can be made between the 'success' of the Bank in obtaining compliance with proposed conditions, and the effects of the reforms that were implemented. Countries that did not comply with the conditions imposed would not be expected to achieve the expected gains (for general evidence on this see Mosley *et al.* [*1991a:212-4*]). In fact, if slippage undermines credibility, countries with high slippage could be worse-off after the reforms than before [*Rodrik, 1989*]. Assessing compliance appears to be a relatively simple exercise: we look at the stated conditions and assess the degree to which they were implemented. Any such assessment would necessarily be qualitative in judging when a condition was 'fully implemented', and when 'substantial progress' had been made. The World Bank [*1988*] assessment for all SALs is summarised in Table 2 with a comparable exercise for Turkey (our difficulty in assigning percentages for Turkey calls into question the process of assigning values, although the relative magnitudes are remarkably similar). For the 40 countries in the World Bank sample, 68 per cent of all conditions were assessed as fully implemented. In our judgment, Turkey made somewhat less progress largely because of dubious compliance with conditions on import liberalisation and public enterprise reform.

This approach avoids (and may even disguise, through the use of apparently objective numbers) the fact that not only is slippage difficult to measure, but it is also difficult to interpret. Simple figures for percentage slippage are unable to distinguish cases where recipients did not implement conditions they had never, even at the negotiating stage, intended to implement from cases where slippage occured because recipients were unable to implement the conditions (either because the terms were too ambiguous or too ambitious). For Turkey, the trade policy conditions in the third SAL were vague ('further progress to be made on import liberalisation'). There were further

TABLE 2
COMPLIANCE WITH CONDITIONALITY, 1980-87
PERCENTAGE OF SAL CONDITIONS IMPLEMENTED DURING THE LOAN PERIOD

Item	All SALs[1]		Turkey[2]	
	(1)	(2)	(1)	(2)
Exchange rate	70	90	80	100
Trade policy reform	55	84	40	80
Reduce QRs	63	93	40	50
Reduce Import tariffs	62	77	50	60
Export incentives	61	82	60	80
Tax/public expenditures	64	78	40	80
Public enterprises	61	87	50	60
Financial sector	71	86	60	90
All conditions	68	84	50	70

Notes and *sources*:
1. data on all SALs from World Bank [*1988*], Table 4.3; percentages refer to the share of conditions in each policy area that were deemed: (1) 'fully implemented' and (2) fully plus 'substantial progress'. Original source gives figures to one decimal place but this would appear to be spurious accuracy (all values should be interpreted as relative; see discussion in the text).
2. estimates for Turkey derived from Kirkpatrick and Önis [*1991*], Table 11.2; percentages are judgements (as are the figures for all SALs).

cases where conditions were met but their effects undermined by subsequent policies, such as in Turkey where the 'ambiguous' moves towards import liberalisation were partially offset by increased use of the import levy scheme from 1984. The evidence in Table 2 indicates that, overall, most conditions were met. It does not, however, indicate whether the conditions were sustained, nor if they actually involved significant reforms.

The evidence in Table 2 reveals differences in implementation by policy instrument. For instance, the percentage of import liberalisation conditions fully implemented was relatively low, but for exchange rates the percentage was relatively high. This may have something to do with the nature of the reforms involved: if those for exchange rates involve clearly stated devaluations but those for trade policy require reductions in effective tariffs, one can see how the greater complexity of the latter could increase the difficulty of compliance. Another possibility is that greater political interests may be at stake with import liberalisation than with, for example, export promotion. This would also explain Turkey's failure to reform public enterprises. A further issue is sequencing. It may be appropriate to implement some conditions before others so that compliance increases over time (see below).

It may be the least important conditions which are adhered to, and the most important which are resisted. There is a distinct possibility that this applies to Turkey. Two important areas of conditions were complied with to a high degree, namely exchange rates and export promotion. While there was initial compliance with the demands to reduce the budget deficit, public investment grew after the restoration of parliamentary democracy in 1983 and significant reductions did not occur until the late 1980s. In two important areas compliance was not convincing: while quota lists and tariffs were reduced, many imports remained subject to restrictions; while the staffing levels of public enterprises and access to credit were reduced, legislative reforms were delayed (and the second tranche of SAL II was delayed in response) and internal reforms to increase productivity were never implemented [*Kirkpatrick and Önis, 1991*].

Sequencing and Timing

Having taken a decision to liberalise, should the programme be implemented rapidly or gradually? There are two general arguments for rapid reform: it gives strong signals to economic agents who will respond quickly and it does not provide the political opposition with time to mobilise. If factors are perfectly mobile and there are no distortions, economic theory favours rapid liberalisation: under the 'big bang' approach adjustment would be smooth. Michaely *et al.* [*1991*] argue that the evidence favours abrupt liberalisations, although their evidence is open to different interpretations. However, the reality of adjustment under SALs is that there *are* distortions and factors are *not* perfectly mobile, hence the presumption that rapid adjustment will be smooth and relatively costless cannot be made.

A number of arguments to favour gradual reform. First, adjustment costs, notably unemployment, are likely to be higher if reform is rapid [*Thomas and Nash, 1991*]; even without distortions adjustment might be painful if some factors are sector specific. Second, gradualism can be defended on grounds of income distribution: by slowing the rate at which rents to factors in the unfavoured (post-reform) sector are reduced, those factors have more time to move into alternative uses [*Falvey and Kim, 1992*]. This argument has a political dimension as opposition may be less vociferous if adjustment costs are mitigated. Third, there is a credibility argument for gradualism. If a government does not have a reputation for credible reform, then introducing a series of gradual reforms to which it demonstrates commitment can allow that government to build up a reputation for credibility. Turkey had many failed, unsustained attempts at stabilisation and reform in the 1960s and 1970s. Reforms in the 1980s were initiated by a new government and implemented through five SALs over six years: this gradual approach helped the government to establish credibility.

Closely related to the speed of reform is the issue of sequencing: in what order should reforms be attempted? There is fairly broad agreement on some principles of sequencing [*Greenaway and Morrissey, 1993*]. Macroeconomic stabilisation, in particular devaluation to a realistic (and maintained) exchange rate and control of the fiscal deficit, should be the first element of reform. Import liberalisation can then take place. This will normally comprise a conversion of QRs to tariffs, which contributes to tax revenues, and a staged reduction of tariffs. The provision of export incentives is optional. Liberalisation of the domestic financial market can commence once trade liberalisation is well underway. The last stage should be relaxation of capital controls. The sequencing of Turkish adjustment is summarised in Table 3 and can be related to these general principles.

We have noted already that the Turkish reforms (conditions) were reasonably well integrated and concentrated in a few policy areas. This is even more true when one examines the individual SALs: stabilisation and export promotion featured heavily in the early loans, then reducing public investment and reforming public enterprises attracted

303

emphasis, and finally financial sector reforms were conditions of the fifth SAL (import liberalisation also reappeared in SAL V because earlier conditions had not been implemented). Once the political (a government committed to and capable of reform) and economic (stabilisation) foundations have been laid a country should find it easier to liberalise imports. Turkey followed a rather different sequence. SAL I emphasised a variety of export promotion measures and control of the budget deficit via restricting public investment. The latter is suitably sequenced as reducing the deficit is an initial macro-economic target. The former makes sense for credibility reasons: as potential exporters have always experienced relative discrimination, offering real incentives will encourage the shift of resources to exporting sectors.

TABLE 3
SEQUENCING IN TURKISH ADJUSTMENT PROGRAMME

	Loan ($m)	Major Policy Conditions	Compliance
IMF (June 1980)	SDR1.25b	Devaluation	**full**
SAL I (25.3.80)	250.0	**5 conditions** Export promotion	**moderate** good
SAL II (15.5.81)	300.0	**17 conditions** Exchange rate Export promotion Reduce quota list Budget deficit Public enterprises	**good** full good moderate good poor
SAL III (16.7.82)	304.5	**8 conditions** Public investment Public enterprises	**good** good good
SAL IV (23.5.83)	300.8	**5 conditions** Reduce QRs Public investment	**poor** moderate poor
SAL V (14.6.84)	376.0	**12 conditions** QRs and tariffs Public investment Financial sector	**good** moderate moderate good

Notes: Dates in parentheses relate to when the loan programme was agreed. Evaluation of degree of implementation is subjective: 'full' implies quantifiable condition fully implemented (e.g. devalue by 20 per cent); 'good' implies conditions were largely implemented and policy stance changed (e.g. export promotion); 'moderate' implies partial implementation with no major change in policy (e.g. import liberalisation); 'poor' implies weak conditions largely ignored and no effective change in policy (e.g. reform of public enterprises).

The full range of trade policy conditions were introduced in SAL II. Again, exchange rate and budget deficit conditions were designed to sustain macroeconomic stability, and further export promotion to encourage adjustment. However, implementation on reducing the quota list (effectively transforming QRs to tariffs) was slow and ambiguous, as was progress on public enterprise reform. It was not until 1984 that significant progress was made in reducing the share of restricted commodities in total imports, but even then almost half of all imports by value were 'subject to permission' and it was 1988 before this share fell below ten per cent [*Togan, 1992*]. It is not inconceivable that the whole programme could have come unstuck were it not for the fairly quick export response to the devaluations and promotion measures. This is a lesson for other reformers: early export incentives not only encourage adjustment but can compensate for slow import liberalisation. The export incentives were put in place in SALs I and II but little import liberalisation occurred until SALs III and IV. Detailed analysis of the import regime in Turkey reveals that nominal and effective protection rates, on average, rose between 1983 and 1984 and were not reduced significantly until 1989 and 1990 [*Togan, 1992*].

Good overall compliance on SALs II and III ensured that SAL IV was forthcoming. By then the Bank was heavily committed and sufficient momentum had been generated so that, despite poor performance on IV, SAL V was released. This is, perhaps, a lesson to recipients on how to sequence implementation so as to avoid the threat of a tranche or loan being suspended. By SAL IV there is evidence that parts of the programme were coming unstuck and Turkey may not have been the success so frequently portrayed. We have argued already that little significant import liberalisation actually occured. It is clear also that public enterprise reform was limited: although we evaluate compliance as good under SAL III, the reforms in question were to hold budgetary transfers to public enterprises below an agreed level, which was implemented, and 'progress required on legal reforms' which is rather vague. The good overall performance on SAL V is attributable to reforms in the financial and energy sectors. Having evaluated the inputs to reform, outputs may now be examined.

III. PERFORMANCE UNDER ADJUSTMENT PROGRAMMES

Evaluating the effects of a reform programme is a difficult exercise. First, there is no way of accounting for the counterfactual, events that would have occured without reform, nor are there reliable means of accommodating the effects of exogenous shocks. Consequently, evaluation is frequently by reference to the achievement of targets. Second, many of the SAL reforms are supply-side, directed at altering relative incentives in the medium to long run. It may therefore take some time for the reforms to have an impact on economic activity. Third, other lending programmes could interact with a SAL, notably IMF stabilisation loans; how does one disentangle the effects of the two programmes? Fourth, in any cross-section study different countries start from different positions, they face different conditionality, the sequencing of programmes may be different, and so on. Finally, as already discussed, the conditions of a given SAL may not have been fully adhered to. Notwithstanding these difficulties, there have been several attempts to evaluate the impact of SALs [*World Bank, 1988 and 1990; Mosley et al., 1991a and 1991b*].

To assess SALs one must first select the relevant targets, then choose the methodology to evaluate the success of the SAL in achieving these. Medium-term growth, the sustainability of the balance of payments and export growth are seen as key objectives. These are obvious indicators. There are two standard methods: 'before and after', and 'with-without' SALs. The former traces the path of, for example, export growth before the SAL and compares it with post-SAL performance, the difference being attributed to the impact of the lending programme. There are two major shortcomings with this. First, it presupposes sustainability of preexisting policies, as the implied counterfactual, whereas most recipents are facing a crisis brought on by unsustainable policies. The other problem is that it is difficult to control for exogenous shocks such as commodity price changes. 'Withwithout' compares the performance of SAL countries (the 'with' group) against that of non-SAL countries. Differences are then attributed to the impact of adjustment lending. The principal problem here is in the choice of control and the impact of other factors. This, however, is the approach used by the World Bank [*1988, 1990*] and Mosley et al. [*1991a*]. One can note that, in effect, this approach compares the 'with' and 'without' groups both 'before' (when they are expected to be similar) and 'after' (when they are expected to differ).

This section considers both approachs to evaluating Turkish adjustment. We begin by examining the trends in a range of macroeconomic indicators over the 1980s, identifying four important sub-periods: 1978-80 is the 'pre-crisis' period which establishes the initial state of the economy; 1981-83 covers the initial adjustment period when the country was ruled by a military dictatorship, hence is termed

'SAL-MD', and essentially refers to SALs I-III; 1984-87 covers SALs IV-V when there was a parliamentary democray, 'SAL-Dem', and is the final adjustment period; and 1988-90 is the 'Post-SAL' period when the sustainability of reforms can be considered. This approach allows us to consider the extent to which targets were achieved. The second approach is 'with-without' and Turkey's performance is compared with that of Greece, a satisfactory if not ideal pairing.

Macroeconomic Indicators of Turkey's Performance

Table 4 provides some summary data on the Turkish economy, distinguishing the four periods mentioned. The pre-crisis years witnessed negative growth, high inflation and large budget and current account deficits. The result was political and economic instability, with the

TABLE 4
COMPARATIVE DATA FOR SUB-PERIODS

VARIABLE	Pre-Crisis 1978-80	SAL-MD 1981-83	SAL-Dem 1984-87	Post-SAL 1988-90
Broad indicators: [a]				
Real GDP growth	-0.5	4.4	6.6	2.3*
Current account % GDP	-3.5	-3.0	-2.1	0.4
Govt revenue % GDP	22.7	21.5*	17.3	18.0
Budget deficit % GDP	-4.0	-2.5*	-6.0	-4.7
Inflation (CPI)	71.3	33.0	41.8	69.7
Export growth	3.0	46.3	14.5	11.7
Various indicators as % GNP: [b]				
Exports	7.3	14.3	19.3	24.9
Imports	13.7	15.1	20.4	26.3
Public consumption	9.2	10.1	9.2	9.0
Public investment	16.4	15.9	14.4	10.8
Debt	28.4	37.7	52.4	52.7
Labour market data:				
Unemployment rate [b]	8.6	7.1	7.7	8.1
Real manuf. wages [a]	133.0	120.7	100.5	95.5*
Exchange rates: [c]				
Nominal TL/$US	46.6	168.1	613.5	2024.9
PPP TL/$US	29.1	43.5	52.0	47.1

Notes and *sources:* Figures are simple annual averages based on non-overlapping sub-periods: 1978-80 (3 years); 1981-83 (3 years); 1984-87 (4 years) and 1988-90 (3 years). For full data and definitions see Appendix Table A1.
a. from Önis and Webb [*1993: Table 1*]; * indicates data for one year missing.
b. derived from data in the Appendix of Uygur [*1992*].
c. from Krueger and Turan [*1993: 342*].

country in crisis by early 1980. Turgut Özal, who had worked at the World Bank, was appointed to head the economic team of Suleyman Demirel's government in November 1979, remaining in this position after the military takeover of September 1980, and resigning in June 1982 following the 'Banker's Crisis' (Turkey's largest securities house collapsed [*Önis and Webb, 1993:5*]). A new constitution in November 1982 heralded elections in November 1983 which were won by Özal's ANAP (Motherland Party). The 'second wave' of economic reforms date from the start of 1984, and took place under a democratic government. The sustainability of reforms can be considered from the final period; ANAP lost the general election of 1991, although Özal had made himself President in 1989.

The most important reforms took place in 1981-83, and perhaps the most significant impact was on trade policy (which accounted for almost half of all conditions). 'Trade policy reform can be divided into three inter-related yet distinct components: real devaluation and commitment to a more flexible exchange rate policy; export promotion measures; and the liberalisation of imports' [*Önis and Webb, 1993:44*]. In the SAL-MD period there was little effective import liberalisation. A variety of export incentives were introduced, a number of which were direct subsidies: the effective export subsidy averaged 22 per cent over 1980-83, the most important elements being export credits and tax rebates (including a rebate of VAT even before its introduction), but was much higher for industrial exports [*Önis and Webb, 1993:49*]. This created a new lobby of exporters in favour of the reforms, while at the same time little had been done to alienate the import and import-competing lobbies. Imports grew slightly but exports grew rapidly, averaging an annual growth of 46 per cent over three years, which helped reduce the current account deficit. We can note that the export growth was concentrated in 1981 and 1982; it then slowed down dramatically and the current account deficit began to rise (Appendix Table A1).[1]

In January 1980 the Turkish Lira (TL) was devalued by 33 per cent and most multiple exchange rates were eliminated. It is clear from Table 4 that the SAL-MD period witnessed a dramatic devaluation, even in purchasing power parity terms. Although the figures suggest a reduction in the budget deficit, this was probably achieved for 1981

1. Note that the current account deficit, here measured as a share of GDP, need not equal the trade deficit. Furthermore, while an indication of the trade deficit can be derived from the figures in Table 4 for export and import shares, these are measured as percentages of GNP. Finally, in reading Table 4 remember that the figures are simple period averages.

only and missing data exagerates the period performance: while public investment was reduced, public consumption spending rose (see Appendix Table A1). Adjustment appears to have been immediately successful in so far as it elicited export growth, devaluation, economic growth and some reining in of the current deficit. It was less effective in controlling the fiscal deficit and was associated with an increasing debt burden. Labour bore the brunt of adjustment costs. The military government outlawed trade unions and weakened the position of labour: real wages fell and continued to fall throughout the decade (Table 4). The policy of the military government was to achieve cheap labour but not unemployment, so employers were required to agree not to make workers redundant [*Önis and Webb, 1993:28*]; unemployment did remain fairly stable throughout the decade.

The second wave of reforms, in the SAL-Dem period, included exchange rate liberalisation and devaluation (Table 4), with some import liberalisation, especially the removal of QRs but also tariff reduction. While 'the level and dispersion of nominal and effective rates of protection was reduced [this was] partly offset by taxes and surcharges' [*Önis and Webb, 1993:57*]. Liberalisation was greatest for intermediate goods; tariffs on capital goods were reduced, but such goods remained listed; QRs were removed from most consumer goods but tariffs were increased. Although export subsidies were cut in 1984, this was not sustained. As already observed, compliance with SAL IV was poor, although after 1984 there were reductions in public investment, further import liberalisation and financial sector reforms (Table 3).

Export growth was sustained over 1984-87 at a moderate annual rate of 14 per cent. This outstripped import growth and the current deficit was reduced. Public spending fell overall, albeit only slightly, but the budget deficit widened and inflation rose to an annual average rate of over 40 per cent. The burden of adjustment continued to fall on labour: real wages fell significantly while unemployment rose. Other than export growth and real GDP growth, the success of the early adjustment period was fading as the 1980s progressed.

There has been some dispute over how real the export growth was: many cite widespread incidence of over-invoicing as an (accepted) means of rent-seeking, although the econometric evidence supports significant real export growth responding to the real exchange rate [*Önis and Webb, 1993:78*]. The reorientation of incentives led to a rapid growth in exports which made a major contribution to growth. The sustained export growth defied the sceptics: exports were not simply out of excess capacity, therefore vulnerable to rises in domestic demand; they were not overly reliant on Middle East markets; nor on over-invoicing [*Krueger and Turan, 1993:372*].

The 1987 elections represented the completion of 'the process of re-establishing electoral democracy' but major economic reforms remained to be completed in the Post-SAL period: import liberalisation, reducing fiscal deficits and controlling inflation. The most substantial tariff reductions were in 1987-90. Average tariff rates fell from 30 per cent in 1987 to 11 per cent by the end of 1989: over the same period, average tariffs on the highly taxed consumer goods fell from 45 per cent to 17 per cent; on agriculture, which had relatively low protection, it halved to 11 per cent [*Önis and Webb, 1993:67; Togan, 1992*]. Many of the benefits were offset by the imposition of levies, which were highest on consumer and agricultural goods and accounted for about one quarter of the nominal protection on such goods. Many characteristics of an importsubstituting economy remained in place. The situation was further complicated by the prevalence of exemptions: over two-thirds of imports in 1988 were exempt from all import taxes [*Önis and Webb, 1993:70*].

Turkey moved towards a neutral trade stance not through effective import liberalisation but by subsidising exporters to compensate for the preferences shown to importers. This may make political sense (see Section IV) but it imposes economic costs: distortions are increased rather than reduced and a burden is placed on the budget. In the Post-SAL period this burden was borne by public investment, which was reduced fairly significantly. Exports continued to grow, the current account was in surplus in 1988 and 1989, and economic growth remained positive.

Comparative Evaluation of Turkey's Performance

Before commenting on the results, summarised in Table 5, an observation is in order, regarding the method of comparing adjusting countries (with SAL) and non-adjusting countries (non-SAL). In the Bank studies the data were pooled: all SAL countries were treated as one discrete sub-sample, all non-SAL countries as a separate sub-sample. Mosley *et al.* [*1991a*] regard this as flawed because the countries in each subsample may be unrepresentative. They match SAL and non-SAL countries on a pairwise basis using information on, *inter alia*, economic structure, income per capita, and growth of GDP. This is defended as allowing for the non-randomness of the two sample groups and the degrees of slippage. Despite this difference, one is struck by the similarity of outcomes (Table 5, top panel). Overall, both studies appear to suggest that adjustment lending might encourage real export growth and might contribute to improvements in the current account of the balance of payments. On the other hand, they imply that the impact on real GDP growth is neutral, whilst the effect on investment is negative.

Turkey's performance was relatively good on all criteria, notably in a significant increase in exports which contributed to more rapid economic growth. Exports nearly trebled in real terms between 1980 and 1985 and such growth was 'promoted by explicit incentives to manufacturers to compensate them for reduced domestic demand' [*Baysan and Blitzer, 1991:281*]. Table 5 also includes a limited comparison of Turkey and Greece. The rapid economic and export growth compares very favourably with Greece and can be attributed substantially to high compliance with export promotion, noting that Greece's current account balance deteriorated over the period. It is also worth noting that Turkey performed far better than Greece in maintaining investment: over 1980-85, gross domestic investment rose an average annual 3.6 per cent in Turkey whereas it fell an average annual 4.6 per cent in Greece [*World Development Report 1987: 141*]. Import growth in Turkey remained substantial during 1980-85, especially for iron and steel, machinery and transport equipment [*Baysan and Blitzer, 1991:280*]. However, Turkey reduced the current account deficit throughout the late 1980s and actually attained a surplus by 1989 whereas Greece still faced a substantial deficit. Unlike adjusting

TABLE 5
COMPARISON OF RESULTS ON EFFECTIVENESS OF SALS
PERCENTAGE OF SAL COUNTRIES WHICH OUTPERFORMED NON-SAL COUNTRIES

Study	Growth of real GDP	Investment % GDP		Growth real exports	Current account % of GDP	
World Bank [*1988*]	53	37		57	70	
Mosley *et al.* [*1991 a*]	50	36		65	79	
Performance:[a]	ave. annual	gross domestic		ave. annual	net balance	
	1980-89	1979	1989	1980-89	1979	1989
Turkey	5.1%	21	22	11.4%	-1.3	1.3
Greece	1.6%	30	18	4.1%	-4.8	-6.4

Notes and *sources:* From Greenaway and Morrissey [*1993*], Table II, except:
a. Greece was paired with Turkey in Mosley *et al.* [*1991a*]; data reported here are from World Development Report [*1981, 1987 and 1991*]. The columns are as for the top panel, respectively: GDP growth, investment, export growth and balance of payments. Current account balance is after official transfers.

countries in general, Turkish gross domestic investment actually increased following the SALs whereas it declined in Greece.[2]

Sustainability of Turkish Adjustment

It appears that adjustment lending is associated with investment slumps. As investment is related directly to growth this does not augur well for the future. The World Bank [*1990*] argues that since an integral aim of adjustment lending is to curtail inefficient private and public sector investment, some reduction was to be expected. This is not a convincing explanation, if only because proponents of adjustment lending would also argue that reduction of the public sector should have 'crowded in' private sector investment. A convincing explanation for the failure of private investment to increase relates to the role of credibility [*Rodrik, 1989*]. In the early stages of a SAL, the private sector has doubts about its sustainability and holds off from making investments until it is clear whether or not the change in regime is permanent. In view of the unstable policy environment in many developing countries, this is an appealing explanation and is certainly consistent with the facts. The essential point is that investment responses take time, both to occur and to impact on the economy. Optimists may argue that the positive investment response will occur once the reforms are seen to be permanent. Similarly, optimists may argue that any impact on growth rates will also take time to materialise but should follow from export growth and the improved structure of the economy.

The evidence for Turkey in the Post-SAL period offers limited encouragement to the optimists: although the rate of economic growth was not sustained and inflation and unemployment rose, export growth was maintained and the current account deficit was virtually eliminated while the fiscal deficit was reduced (Table 4). Public investment, however, had been reduced substantially and the debt burden remained high. In fact, Turkey's debt burden rose considerably from 28 per cent of GNP in 1980 to over 50 per cent from 1986. While the initial rapid export growth reduced the debt to export ratio from 284 per cent in 1980 to 175 per cent in 1982, it had climbed back to 260 per cent by 1986, largely due to the impact of successive real devaluations on the value of debt [*van Wijnbergen et al., 1992:58*]. Managing this debt will impose a major burden on fiscal

2. Some have observed that Turkish interest in joining the European Community may have had an effect on its economic policy stance from the mid-1980s. This is possible, especially in respect of import liberalisation and reducing export subsidies, but we can note that membership of the Community has not obviously helped Greece to adjust its economy.

policy in the 1990s. On a more positive note, private sector investment seems to be responding: it fell from about ten per cent of GNP in 1980 to nine per cent in 1983, recovered to ten per cent in 1986 and rose to almost 14 per cent by 1990 [derived from *Uygur, 1992:56*]. As the period since 1989 has been one of global recession, it is fair to conclude that Turkey has made substantial progress in placing its economy on a more solid footing. In this sense, adjustment in Turkey has been a success. This success has been bought with a distributional cost: labour and agriculture bore the brunt of adjustment, and these groups are unlikely to see the period as successful.

IV. THE POLITICAL ECONOMY OF REFORM IN TURKEY

The principal objective of trade liberalisation is to encourage the growth of real exports. A realistic exchange rate is a first step as it increases the relative returns to exporters. Reducing protection, and so removing many price distortions, will encourage exports as it reduces the input costs facing exporters and discourages resources from going into import-competing industries. For reform to succeed, however, it is important that exporting becomes attractive so that resources are released by import-competing sectors and are absorbed by exporting industries. Export promotion measures assist this transition. But, if agents are to respond, they must believe the reforms are permanent. The government's committment to the reforms and its ability to signal commitment will depend on political stability and the state of the macroeconomy.

This scenario applied to Turkey in 1980. The Ecevit administration of 1978-79 sought agreement with the IMF but viewed this 'as a short-run expediency to deal with the immediate balance of payments crisis' [*Kirkpatrick and Önis, 1991:11*]. This would not have instilled credibility. However, Turgut Özal, who had been at the World Bank, was responsible for economic policy in the Demirel government that resumed power in 1979, was supported by technocrats and was appointed deputy Prime Minister in charge of economic policy when the military assumed power in September 1980. He became the elected Prime Minister in 1983. His commitment to economic reform did serve to instill credibility and, no less important, was an important factor ensuring external (IMF and World Bank) commitment to Turkish reform.

The Turkish state ruled on an extensive patron-client network, rent-seeking was widespread, and business success was due as much to government intervention as entrepreneurial efforts. Özal undertook a number of institutional reforms intended to enhance the potential for policy co-ordination, dispense with political patronage and weaken the powerbase of those opposed to the economic reforms. The chief measure was to establish a new post of Minister of State for Economic Affairs in 1983: economic policy was determined by a team headed by Özal and his new minister, with other ministers and technocrats [*Önis and Webb, 1993*]. The power of the Central Bank was enhanced and from 1983 it was dominated by Western-trained economists who shared Bank/IMF views on economic policy, stabilisation and adjustment. Overall, the technocrats in the Turkish government during the adjustment period, especially after 1983, were willing and able to promote the types of reforms favoured by the the Bank and Fund.

From the Bank's perspective, given that it wanted to promote adjustment, Turkey was an attractive proposition in 1980. Although the government was military, it had retained the economic policymaking team which was known to and in agreement with the Bank, and a stabilisation agreement had been reached with the Fund. In the context of the need to implement reforms, there were benefits from a military government, notably the ease with which the voice of losers could be suppressed. Economists would recognise that reforms entail losers, but could suggest mechanisms whereby the gainers compensate losers. This principle does not seem to have guided Bank adjustment programmes: they appeared to adopt the view either that rapid adjustment would be costless or that short-term losers would benefit from long-term growth (the 'trickle-down' view). Such beliefs are, at the very least, optimistic. It should be clear from our preceeding discussion that the gainers in Turkey were exporters (who received direct benefits) and importers or import-competing sectors which lost few of their preferences; public enterprises, which were not obliged to institute any effective reforms, were largely sheltered from the effects of adjustment; labour, facing a consistent decline in real wages, and the agricultural sector, through a large reduction in the scale and scope of support prices, were the losers. It is not surprising that a military government could impose reforms with such distributional effects; what is somewhat surprising, and perhaps admirable, is the ability of Özal to lead a political party (ANAP) to democratic victory only one year after leaving the military administration.

Much of ANAP's appeal lay in how it distanced itself from the military (an achievement by Özal in one year), the popularity of Özal himself, the party's perceived ability to institute successful economic reforms and to distribute favours to supporters, notably through allocation of bank credits, extra budgetary funds and export subsidies [*Önis and Webb, 1993:17-19*]. The period 1984-87 was characterised by effective exchange rate and trade reforms: a number of major devaluations were undertaken, and the real exchange rate was maintained at a fairly stable level; export promotion measures appeared to be successful; import liberalisation took place, but in a rather half-hearted manner. Thus, even under the parliamentary democracy phase of adjustment the benefits all accrued to business while labour and agriculture remained the losers. It is not obvious why the losers accepted their position once democracy was restored. One possibility is that remittances from emigrant workers fulfilled the functions of a social security system. Certainly they were significant: 1985 remittances were estimated as worth $1714m compared to a current account deficit of $1030m [*World Development Report 1987: 230*]. By 1988 these distributional pressures emerged as a political issue and the persistent high inflation and macroeconomic instability was proving insoluble, undermining the political support for ANAP and the effectiveness of trade reforms. It is perhaps unsurprising that ANAP lost the next election (in 1991).

Önis and Webb [*1993*] and Krueger and Turan [*1993*] provide comprehensive reviews of the political economy of Turkish adjustment. They are in broad agreement on the factors contributing to the ability to implement (some) successful reforms (although the latter writers see more successes than the former): a Western-trained leadership committed to reform; political liberalisation, but with power concentrated in the executive and a weak opposition; streamlined economic policy-making concentrated in a small elite, supported by institutional reform; and military rule in a crucial period. Another factor, not emphasised by these commentators, is the importance of external financial support: although Turkey ceased to be a major aid recipient in the 1980s it received considerable capital inflows, especially during the adjustment period when the SAL revenues were received. The first SAL was equivalent to over a quarter of net aid to Turkey in 1980 and subsequent SALs accounted for about 15 per cent of capital inflows to Turkey in each of the four subsequent years. The real value of capital inflows remained around five per cent of GNP over 1980-86, but the composition altered significantly and became far less concessional [*Morrissey, 1993*]. The funds that arrived to support adjustment were part, at least, of the cause of what has the potential now to be a debt crisis.

There is also evidence that the benefits of bilateral aid to Turkey were questionable. The manner in which aid can support capital imports would have reinforced some of the imbalances in Turkey, as the aid tended to be concentrated on capital-intensive infrastructure investment and import support, thus favouring non-tradeables and imports rather than export sectors. There is clear evidence, at least for the late 1960s and early 1970s, that agricultural sectors in Turkey (potentially strong exporters) faced negative protection while import-competing sectors were heavily protected [*Baysan and Blitzer, 1991:309-11*]. Aid policies would have done little to improve the relative position of agriculture while at the same time providing an avenue for donor exporters to circumvent protection against imports [*Morrissey, 1993*]. On the other hand, the availability of aid may have made it easier (and cheaper in the short run) for Turkey to restore public sector investment in infrastructure. There is a potential cost if the investments generate insufficient returns to meet future debt-servicing but this can be offset, and more than offset if the adjustment programme is successful, by the contribution of infrastruture to industrial development. On balance, aid and adjustment may have interwoven beneficially for Turkey, but the aid has created a debt burden.

A number of the factors identified for Turkey have also been observed as contributing to 'successful' adjustment in other countries. It appears that 'new' governments have an advantage [*Mosley et al., 1991a; Papageorgiou et al., 1991*]. They are not tarnished with the failures of previous governments and are more likely to be able to instil credibility. Strong new governments, such as military dictatorships, are better able to withstand opposition to reforms: from bureacrats and public employees who are losing influence, if not their jobs; from those who had earned rents in protected activities; and from other losers from reform. This was made easier for the Özal government by the military clampdown on trade unions from 1980. External and internal commitment, a strong technocracy and weakened unions all rendered it easier for Turkey to implement a successful reform package. Even then, however, the strength of vested interests in public enterprises and import-competing sectors offers an explanation as to why adjustment was very slow in those areas.

V. LESSONS FROM TURKEY'S EXPERIENCE

Adjustment in Turkey in the 1980s can be described as a success in a number of senses. The principal targets were achieved: high rates of real export and GDP growth and elimination of the current account deficit. More generally, the structure of incentives in the Turkish economy was improved and anti-export bias largely eliminated, albeit more by subsidising exports than through import liberalisation. While many distortions persist, and inflation and the debt burden threaten the sustainability of reforms, the Turkish economy is now more flexible and dynamic than it was in 1980. Finally, there is a political success to the extent that democracy was restored during the adjustment period. However, it is clear that the success is limited: effective import liberalisation had only been achieved by 1989 while public enterprises remain in need of reform; patronage has imposed a high budgetary cost and is an inefficient use of scarce resources. In distributional terms, adjustment has been a failure as labour and agriculture are relatively, if not absolutely, worse-off now than they were in 1980.

We have indicated already that favourable initial conditions were in place: the creation of political commitment and laying support for reform through political stability (Özal represented continuity even if regimes changed). The principal macroeconomic condition of a realistic exchange rate was also in place (although the IMF agreement in Table 3 is dated after SAL I the devaluation preceded its implementation). The government was also in a position to resist the losers, namely labour and agriculture. It is also important that the lending agencies offered support and that they may have felt that they 'knew who they were dealing with' and viewed the government as committed to the reforms. A remarkably auspicious beginning to an adjustment programme.

Strong support from the Bank can obviously come via conditional finance with regular and efficient monitoring to minimise slippage. This was done fairly carefully: the Bank would have expected Özal to be reliable, but had invested so much in Turkey that they needed to ensure its success. This may be one reason why the Bank appeared to adopt a policy of condoning 'selective compliance' and accepted poor implementation of many conditions (or defined the conditions in a vague way which allowed flexibility). Sufficient adjustment took place to meet the principal targets. Failure to implement effective import liberalisation and public sector reform was not punished seriously by the Bank, perhaps because it recognised the political advantages of not creating an influential body of losers. The general failure to control the fiscal deficit also seems to have been accepted by the Bank; to some extent, Turkey may have been permitted to maintain public spending to support the restoration of democracy. The evidence does, however, suggest that public spending was used to support the patron state and dispense favours. This served Turkey's shortterm political interests but was not consistent with the ideology underlying adjustment programmes.

In conclusion, Turkey's apparent success is attributable to early export promotion measures but not to strong compliance with the conditions laid down by the World Bank. Turkey benefited from what we term 'selective compliance' as it was able to create a lobby in favour of reform (exporters) before alienating the potential losers from import liberalisation. Public sector reforms were rather limited and the basic nature of the Turkish patron state remained unchanged. The principal losers were silenced almost before adjustment began. Perhaps the single most important lesson to emerge from this study is that the Bank did not interfere, nor did it enforce those conditions likely to interfere, with Turkish politics: SALs were granted under a military dictatorship and a parliamentary democracy, both of which were allowed to continue their patronage system of government. The conditions in Turkish SALs were oriented predominantly towards trade policy, and only the export promotion conditions among these were fully implemented during the adjustment period. Most other conditions related to the public sector but effective compliance was minimal. Few conditions related to industry and none to agriculture, nor did the Bank intimate any concern with the treatment of labour. The Bank did not ask very much of Turkey, and required even less.

There are a number of lessons for countries attempting adjustment. First, gradualism makes sense because it eases the process of adjustment, allows governments to alter some conditions and may allow a recipient to obtain subsequent loans without fully complying with conditions. The latter two points are not necessarily disadvantageous to the adjustment process. The Bank does not always impose the most appropriate conditions and a government should have some flexibility if circumstances change. The lesson for the Bank is that it too should exercise flexibility. It may be appropriate to endorse 'selective compliance' as a general principle. Second, and following these points, the Bank must learn to see its role as a facilitator rather than an enforcer, but here decisions on how rigorously to monitor slippage on different conditions will require political and economic judgements. In the 1990s, the Bank seems to be requiring political conditionality, and enforcing conditions with major political ramifications. Our study of Turkey suggests that this is the wrong approach; at the least, economic targets can be achieved without altering the political system. This is not intended to condone every political system, rather the intention is to re-emphasise the principle of sovereignty. Third, and perhaps foremost, initial political commitment (to the types of reforms favoured by the Bank and Fund) and capacity are essential to ensure adherence to any adjustment programme, and may even be essential to ensure that a programme can begin. This, with programme design, sequencing and monitoring, is essential for even narrowly defined success.

REFERENCES

Baysan, T. and C. Blitzer, 1991, 'Turkey', in Papageorgiou *et al., Volume 6: New Zealand, Spain and Turkey.*
Boratav, K., 1987, *Stabilization and Adjustment Policies and Programmes: Country Study 5, Turkey,* Helsinki: WIDER.
Falvey, R. and C. Kim, 1992, 'Timing and Sequencing Issues in Trade Liberalisation', *Economic Journal,* Vol. 102, No. 413.
Greenaway, D. and O. Morrissey, 1993, 'Structural Adjustment and Liberalisation in Developing Countries: What Lessons Have We Learned?', *Kyklos,* 46.
Kirkpatrick, C. and Z. Önis, 1991, 'Turkey' in Mosley *et al.*
Krueger, A., 1992, *Economic Policy Reform in Developing Countries,* Oxford: Blackwell.
Krueger, A. and I. Turan, 1993, 'The Politics and Economics of Turkish Policy Reforms in the 1980s', in R. Bates and A. Krueger (eds.), *Political and Economic Interactions in Economic Policy Reform,* Oxford: Blackwell.
Michaely, M., D. Papageorgiou and A. Choksi, 1991, *Liberalizing Foreign Trade: Lessons of Experience in the Developing World,* Volume 7 of Papageorgiou *et al.* Oxford: Blackwell.
Morrissey, O., 1993, 'Foreign Aid and Adjustment in Turkey', *CREDIT Research Paper 93/2,* University of Nottingham.
Mosley, P., J. Harrigan and J. Toye, 1991a, *Aid and Power: The World Bank and Policy-based Lending. Volume 1: Analysis and Policy Proposals,* London: Routledge.
Mosley, P., J. Harrigan and J. Toye, 1991b, *Aid and Power: The World Bank and Policy-based Lending. Volume 2: Case Studies,* London: Routledge.
Önis, Z. and S. Özmucur, 1991, 'Capital Flows and the External Financing of Turkey's Imports', *Technical Paper No. 36,* OECD Development Centre, Paris.
Önis, Z. and S. Webb, 1993, 'The Political Economy of Policy Reform in Turkey in the 1980s', *Bogaziçi Research papers ISS/EC 93-05,* Bogaziçi University.
Papageorgiou, D., M. Michaely and A. Choksi (eds.), 1991, *Liberalizing Foreign Trade,* Seven Volumes, Oxford: Blackwell.
Rodrik, D., 1989, 'Credibility of Trade Reform - a Policy Maker's Guide', *The World Economy,* 12:1, 1-16.
Thomas, V. and J. Nash, 1991, 'Reform of Trade Policy: Recent Evidence from Theory and Practice', *World Bank Research Observer,* 6:2, 219-240.
Togan, S., 1992, *Foreign Trade Regime and Liberalization of Foreign Trade in Turkey during the 1980s,* Ankara: Turkish Eximbank.
Uygur, E., 1992, 'Foreign Aid as a Means to Reduce Emigration: The Case of Turkey', *World Employment Programme Working Paper MIGWP 64,* Geneva: International Labour Office.
van Wijnbergen, S., *et al.,* 1992, *External Debt, Fiscal Policy and Sustainable Growth: A Case Study of Turkey's Recovery from the Debt Crisis,* Baltimore: Johns Hopkins University Press for the World Bank.
World Bank, 1988, *Report on Adjustment Lending,* Document R88-199, Country Economics Department, World Bank, Washington, DC.
World Bank, 1990, *Report on Adjustment Lending II: Policies for the Recovery of Growth,* Document R90-99, Washington, DC: World Bank.

APPENDIX TABLE A1
MACROECONOMIC INDICATORS, 1977-90

Year	GDP %Δ [1]	CPI [2]	X %GDP [3]	X %Δ [4]	CA %GDP [5]	CGR %GDP [6]	Deficit %GDP [7]	Real Wages [8]
1977	7.5	27.0	4.9	-18.0	-6.6	22.0	-5.0	133.0
1978	-2.9	45.0	5.7	14.0	-2.4	23.0	-3.0	138.0
1979	2.1	59.0	4.9	-9.0	-2.0	23.0	-5.0	142.0
1980	-0.8	110.0	6.6	4.0	-6.0	22.0	-4.0	119.0
1981	4.4	37.0	10.4	85.0	-3.4	23.0	-1.0	125.0
1982	5.0	31.0	14.9	40.0	-1.8	na	na	119.0
1983	3.7	31.0	15.7	14.0	-3.8	20.0	-4.0	118.0
1984	5.7	48.0	19.6	20.0	-2.8	15.0	-10.0	104.0
1985	5.1	45.0	20.9	12.0	-1.9	18.0	-7.0	100.0
1986	8.3	35.0	17.6	-1.0	-2.5	18.0	-3.0	96.0
1987	7.4	39.0	20.8	27.0	-1.2	18.0	-4.0	102.0
1988	3.6	75.0	24.6	20.0	2.3	17.0	-4.0	97.0
1989	1.0	70.0	22.5	5.0	1.2	18.0	-5.0	94.0
1990	na	64.0	na	10.0	-2.4	19.0	-5.0	na

	NER TL/$ [9]	PPP NER [10]	U & [11]	Debt %GNP [12]	GCons %GNP [13]	GInv %GNP [14]	X %GNP [15]	M %GNP [16]
1977	17.92	28.03	9.50	24.00	7.83	19.41	7.30	22.79
1978	24.04	26.92	9.60	28.50	8.66	16.05	7.82	14.77
1979	38.14	28.42	8.40	23.20	8.47	16.89	6.80	13.20
1980	77.78	32.05	7.90	33.40	10.57	16.32	7.20	13.21
1981	112.42	37.84	6.90	34.10	10.29	16.67	11.70	13.99
1982	163.66	44.51	6.90	38.20	10.03	16.28	14.83	14.25
1983	228.14	48.19	7.60	40.90	9.83	14.67	16.32	17.15
1984	370.87	53.38	7.50	44.80	9.45	13.20	18.42	19.10
1985	526.18	52.62	7.00	45.00	9.26	15.46	19.63	19.65
1986	676.53	50.70	7.80	58.00	9.13	15.38	17.95	20.44
1987	880.39	51.25	8.30	61.60	8.80	13.67	21.23	22.59
1988	1468.18	52.72	8.30	59.30	8.65	11.38	24.60	22.11
1989	2155.80	48.38	8.50	53.60	8.87	10.53	25.06	25.35
1990	2450.69	40.10	7.40	45.10	9.36	10.40	25.03	31.44

Sources:
[1]-[8]Önis and Webb [*1993: Table 1*].
[9]-[10] Krueger and Turan [*1993: 342*].
[11]-[16]Uygur [*1992*]; various Appendix Tables.

Notes to Table A1:
[1]   Real GDP annual percentage growth (original source IMF).
[2]   Annual average increase in consumer price index.
[3]   Exports of goods and services as a percentage of GDP.
[4]   Annual percentage growth rate of real exports.
[5]   Deficit on current account as percentage of GDP.
[6]   Central government revenue as a percentage of GDP.

[7] Difference between central government revenue and expenditure as a percentage of GDP.
[8] Real wage per worker in manufacturing sector, 1985 = 100 deflated by CPI.
[9] Annual average nominal exchange rate: selling rate for Turkish Lira (TL) against US dollars.
[10] Purchasing Power Parity nominal exchange rate TL/$US: ratio of US wholesale price index to Turkish wholesale price index, multiplied by official Turkish nominal exchange rate [9].
[11] Unemployed as a percentage of labour force (original source is the Household Labour Force Survey).
[12] Total foreign debt as a percentage of GNP (original source World Debt Tables).
[13] Public consumption as a percentage of GNP (in constant 1988 prices).
[14] Public investment as a percentage of GNP (in constant 1988 prices).
[15] Total exports as a percentage of GNP (in constant 1988 prices).
[16] Total imports as a percentage of GNP (in constant 1988 prices).

11

Aid Dialogue between Russia and the West: Climbing the Learning Curve

STANISLAV ZHUKOV

I. INTRODUCTION

Economic interaction between Russia and the international financial community is a comparatively new phenomenon, both as a concept and in practice. From the beginning it raised fundamental questions, which went beyond the issues normally seen as important when major creditor governments, international organisations and commercial banks start to seek a mode of relations with a new member. From the Russian perspective the most crucial question is the following: how do the established conditions, or 'rules of the game', correspond to the country's two strategic goals for the transition, those of moving from a Leninist central planning system to a market economy and of simultaneously creating an open democratic society? Clearly, too, that question has global implications.

This chapter concentrates on some important problems which have emerged in the course of dialogue between Russia and the West. The discussion is organised in five sections: dealing with the problems of mutual understanding, debt relief, the vicious circle of the standard stabilisation packages, the need for an ideological breakthrough, and recent changes in the agenda. As the International Monetary Fund and the World Bank seem currently to play a co-ordinating role in the West's economic interaction with Russia, the chapter mostly focuses on the ideology and activities of the Bretton Woods agencies as well as on negotiations with the Paris Club.

A number of factors add to the complexity and uncertainty surrounding the subject. These include: the rapidly changing international context of economic interaction between nations, caused first of all by the elimination of the bi-polar world system; profound shifts in the geo-economic and geo-politic configuration; mounting economic difficulties in the leading developed market economies; incomplete decentralisation within the Russian federation; and the absence of a clear understanding of whether the federal government can meet its foreign obligations in a satisfactory fashion.

In the case of Russia two sets of factors are particularly powerful in influencing economic co-operation and aid patterns, namely the asymmetry of interdependence of Russia and the West, and the growing diversity of interests within the Western community since the end of the cold war and collapse of the Soviet Union. Although in some respects the standard 'donor-debtor' dichotomy exists, broad security and economic considerations change the whole picture. As Russia poses the most dangerous potential threat to Western security (because of its nuclear and chemical weaponry, environmental degradation, and the danger of uncontrolled mass migration, etc.), its bargaining power is far above the average. Moreover, since Russia is undeniably more developed technically and militarily than any peripheral or semi-peripheral country it is currently trying to secure a place within the group of leading world nations. Not surprisingly, all crucial decisions concerning Western economic relations with Russia are taken by the Group of Seven (G7) nations.

The second set of factors is exemplified by the Japanese position, linking aid with the solving of the dispute on the 'Northern territories' and by the German position, where aid is tied to withdrawal of Soviet military troops.

The newness of these tendencies and a lack of documentation preclude at this point a detailed study of the problem from this particular angle. Thus, the study focuses on Russia's relations with the international financial institutions, representing the West in general.

II. THE PROBLEMS OF MUTUAL UNDERSTANDING

During 1992 and the first half of 1993 Russia's economic dialogue with the West was particularly concerned with two problems: Soviet debt repayment and the introduction of a stabilisation policy in line with the IMF/World Bank recommendations. Political conditionality, such as the necessity of observing human rights and developing an open democratic society, was taken into account but until now has played a secondary role. On the one hand it is apparent, that in the given socio-economic and political-administrative situation contemporary Russia's leadership does the best it can to put democratic principles into practice. On the other, Russia's case reveals clearly the secondary role of this type of aid conditionality in general. Unexpectedly, the Russian side was the one which tried to devote more attention to human rights and the consolidation of democracy. The Western side preferred to concentrate purely on economic interaction.

While the IMF was continuously insisting on a standard stabilisation package, leading Russian officials found that the international financial organisations with whom it conducted talks in 1992, tried to narrow the dialogue with Russia to purely technical matters, avoiding discussion of democracy consolidation [*Aven, 1993:14*]. The deputy Prime Minister, A. Shohin, who replaced the former Minister for Foreign Economic Relations, P. Aven, as a key figure in Russia's talks with Western creditors in 1993, was particularly straightforward. He stated that if the IMF continued its 'arithmetics' and refused to help Russia, this would give an opportunity to 'communists and patriots to prove the correctness of their slogan, that co-operation with the Fund leads the country into a deadlock' [*Edemsky, 1993:12*].

It would be a simplification to see the two clearly different approaches as tactical manoeuvres, typical of situations of bargaining. In my view, the difference in the approaches reflects a difference in perception of what, using international jargon, is defined as 'aid'. For the West, specifically the Bretton Woods agencies, aid is a natural two-way process, which economically benefits both sides of the deal – the donor and the recipient. Meanwhile, it seems, that until very recently the majority of post-Soviet politicians in Russia has seen aid as a one-way act by the 'giving side', made in the interests of the 'receiving side', which is not bound to any strict commitments.

This approach has foundations in both Soviet and pre-revolutionary Russian thinking, the egalitarian-utopian mentality being found in very different, often opposing ideologies. Some of the elite in Russia treat 'aid' as a kind of free payment in return for implementing unpopular reforms. The same redistributionist approach manifests itself in the claims of the opposition, that Western aid is not a real aid, but part of a well thought-out long-term policy, and motivated by self-interest – as if there could be any other motivation in a market economy!

Signs of a utopian egalitarian mentality in relation to foreign aid were evident in the refined intellectual constructions of the ex-Soviet high-ranking bureaucrats of the Gorbachevian epoch [*Kvittsinski, 1993:2*]. As egalitarism and redistributionism originate in the mass consciousness, they are widely supported at the bottom of the society.

Only since mid-1993 have there been indications of a more realistic approach from the Russian side, with 'aid' being more regularly treated as a normal market deal, a specific social contract, implying certain obligations for both participating sides [*Agafonov, 1993:3; Fedorov, 1993:2; Chernomyrdin, 1993:1,5*].

III. DEBT RELIEF

Immediately after the failed coup d'état in August 1991 the problem of Soviet and then of ex-Soviet debt repayment moved to centre stage in Russia's interactions with the West. In October 1991, at the first meeting of the G7 representatives and officials of the 12 ex-Soviet republics, a 'Memorandum on mutual understanding on the USSR and successor states' debt to foreign creditors' was agreed upon [*Government Newsletter, 1991:2*]. The memorandum signed by nine republics envisaged a principle of joint (and several) responsibility on Soviet foreign debt. For its part the G7 took responsibility for proposing measures which could help the republics meet their obligations to donor countries.

In November 1991, at the second meeting of G7 and post-Soviet states, only eight former republics confirmed the Memorandum. The total sum of Soviet debt was divided proportionally between the republics, taking into account their economic potential and the share of credit received. Russia's share comprised about 61 per cent of the total debt, the Ukraine's 16 per cent, Byelorussia's and Kazakhstan's about four per cent, and that of all the other republics less the two per cent each [*Kisiliov, 1992*].

Measures worked out by the G7 included:

– deferment of payment on main short- and medium-term official debt, accumulated before 1 January 1991, until the end of 1992, with intermediate confirmation in March 1992 in case the stabilisation programme prepared under the recommendation of the IMF was adopted;
– continuity in provision of short-term export credits and warranties;
– the possibility of depositing remaining Soviet gold in Western banks.

At first glance, given the revolutionary disruption of the Soviet Union and the chaotic state of relations between and within USSR successor states, it would appear that Western creditors succeeded in solving the problem of debt repayment in a rather satisfactory manner. But that would be a wrong conclusion. The principle of joint responsibility in debt repayment proved its inefficacy since none of the former Soviet republics except Russia 'channelled a cent' into foreign debt-servicing obligations [*Gromyshkin, 1993*].

The idea of separate repayments by each republic was opposed first by the Paris Club and then by Western creditors in general. Consequently, Russia proposed the so-called 'zero variant' agreement, under which it has assumed sole responsibility for repayment of the debt of the former Soviet Union. The 'zero variant' not only gave practical dimensions to agreements of principle, but also simplified the process of negotiation for all sides involved.

By proposing the 'zero variant' Russia aimed at strengthening its bargaining position in the forthcoming talks on debt restructuring. As can be seen from Table 1, repayments peak in 1992-1993. Having assumed full responsibility for the Soviet debt Russia naturally felt that the main donors could respond in similar manner and considerably ease the terms of debt repayment.

In fact these expectations were based on several economic and political assumptions. Even if both ex-Soviet and new Russian foreign obligations are included in the calculations the ratio of medium- and long-term debt repayments in 1992 to annual export slightly exceeded 2:1, which is considerably lower than that of Brazil, Bulgaria, Poland and other countries which have experienced the 'debt crisis' [*Government, 1992:56*]. Taking into account rich natural endowment and, more important, an artificially low rouble-to-dollar exchange rate, giving a strong incentive to national exporters, there exist firm grounds for concluding that the Russian debt situation is far from critical.

TABLE 1

STRUCTURE OF SOVIET FOREIGN INDEBTEDNESS (PAYMENTS DUE IN BN US$)

	1992	1993	1994	1995	1996	1997	1998	1999	2000	>2000	Total
Middle-term untied credit	1.9	2.5	3.0	4.2	2.8	1.8	1.3	0.9	0.6	1.2	20.2
Middle- and long-term tied credit	4.6	8.4	8.1	5.2	2.2	1.6	0.9	0.7	0.4	0.6	32.7
Commercial credit	2.1	2.2	1.0	0.8	0.2	0.1	0.1	-	-	-	6.3
Percentages	4.3	3.7	2.7	2.1	1.5	1.1	0.8	0.6	0.3	0.3	17.4
Other	6.6	0.6	0.6	1.2	0.7	0.1	0.1	-	-	-	9.9
Total	19.5	17.4	15.2	13.5	7.4	4.7	3.2	2.2	1.3	2.1	86.5

Source: Vneshekonombank, Ministry for Foreign Economic Exchanges, USSR

At the same time the democratic forces which came to power in Russia also expected that the leading world nations would not subordinate their policy to narrow economic considerations. Jacques Attali, ex-President of the European Bank for Co-operation and Development, echoed these expectations by stating that 'democracy should not repay the debts of dictatorship' [*Attali, 1993:14*]. The Russian side's expectations in relation to aid perspectives were strongly encouraged by some Western advisors to the Gaidar government [*Sachs, 1992*].

In April 1993, after intensive talks, the Paris Club agreed on Russia's debt deferral and restructuring. According to the agreement reached, Russia should repay only US $3.5 bn in 1993 instead of about US $17.5 bn. Repayment of the rest of the sum was deferred by ten years with a five-year grace period [*Kommersant-Daily, 1993, 7 April:11*]. The other positive outcome of the meeting was a decision to continue with talks about the rest of the debt.

IV. THE VICIOUS CIRCLE OF STANDARD STABILISATION PACKAGES

In Russia's case the IMF/World Bank tandem tried from the very beginning to follow the traditional approach to economic reform. Intensive discussions between Russia and the IMF, started in November 1991 after Gaidar's government came to power, resulted in February 1992 in a government memorandum on macro-economic policy in line with traditional stabilisation logic. In this the Russian government agreed to cut the budget deficit to less than five per cent of GDP and bring monthly inflation down to single digits. On the basis of the memorandum the IMF approved a request by the Russian Federation for a stand-by arrangement in the first credit tranche, authorising a drawing of up to the equivalent of about US $1.04 bn.

The stand-by arrangement was for five months' duration and constituted the first stage of collaboration with the IMF. If the proposed programme was successfully implemented, it could lay the basis for a second stage of financial support from the IMF, including a possible upper tranche stand-by agreement. Further tightening of monetary and fiscal policy, and bringing the overall 1993 inflation rate down to a low single digit, were seen as a prerequisite for this. As Russia's quota in the IMF reaches US $4 bn, the second stage could involve at least US $3 bn [*IMF Press Release, 1992*].

In the third stage Russia would be able to use a multibillion-dollar fund to stabilise the rouble. Apparently, demand constrained policy is seen as a key to reform and one of the main criteria for aid provision.

None of the goals proclaimed in the memorandum to the IMF has been achieved. Frequent economic concessions, made by Gaidar's government, to the growing opposition, and the general chaos of the ex-Soviet economic space, serve as the main explanations for the failure of the stabilisation efforts. But that is only one side of the real problem. The other is that the commitments made were unrealistic from the very beginning, given the existing institutional and structural features of the economy and society.

Also, judging by Polish and former German Democratic Republic (GDR) experiences, the enforcement of strict monetary and fiscal constraints, as well as rapid liberalisation, would lead to a huge drop in production, combined with massive unemployment – early a third of the economically active population. It is true that inflationary expansion, chosen as an alternative to shock therapy did not stop the decline in production either (see Table 2). But at least this was not followed by huge unemployment. For the combination of the two would, surely, provoke massive social unrest, gravely endangering the fate of weak proto-democratic institutions in Russia.

At the end of 1993 about 33 million people in Russia, more than a fifth of the total population, live below the official poverty line. Although registered unemployment figures as yet are low, hidden unemployment, especially among women, is rapidly spreading. According to the tentative estimates made by using the International Labour Organisation concept, there were 3.8 million unemployed in December 1993 [*Goskomstat, 1994:7*]. Vulnerable social groups whose numbers are growing and whose fatigue from the recurrent adjustment shocks is accumulating, enormously strengthen the basis for political opposition.

TABLE 2

MACRO-ECONOMIC DATA ON RUSSIAN ECONOMY IN 1992 AND PROJECTIONS FOR 1993 (IN %)

	1992	1993
GDP	-19	-12
Consumer inflation	1600	940
Industrial inflation	2400	1000
Budget deficit as % of GDP	25-28	10-15

Source: Goskomstat [*1994:7*]; Frenkel and Galitsky, [*1993:6-7*]; and own estimates.

The reluctance of the IMF/World Bank to pay more attention to the political dimensions of reform in Russia continued at least to the end of 1993. Even leaving aside the problem of democracy consolidation and the restoration of economic growth after the shock of the transition, the programme of financial austerity supported by the IMF could in principle be implemented only through dictatorship or a strong military government (such as Pinochet in Chile and the military in Turkey) or by a civil leadership resting on overall national consensus (as in Poland in 1990). None of these prerequisites exists in contemporary Russia and actions proposed do not provide adequate incentives to the main political and economic blocks. Moreover, a combination of vested interests entrenched in the society forces all key national actors, except a tiny group in the upper echelons of the government bureaucracy, furiously to oppose measures supported by an external coalition of major donors, financial organisations and commercial banks. Not surprisingly, powerful internal groups are becoming increasingly intolerant of the current mode of Russia's relations with the external agencies. What is worse, anti-Western attitudes are reaching the general public.

Nevertheless, after the inauguration of the second government, headed by Victor Chernomyrdin, history repeated itself. Once again the Russian government and the Central Bank signed the agreement on co-ordination on economic policy issues, envisaging the same goals as in spring 1992: bringing monthly inflation down to single digits and cutting the budget deficit [*Podlipsky and Slavyk, 1993:3*]. Needless to say, many independent observers predicted – not without grounds – that the current economic course would have the same fate as that of the Gaidar government. The economic results for 1993 clearly supported this pessimism (see Table 2).

It is fair to conclude that although the IMF and the World Bank made some important concessions to Russia, mostly on technical matters, their general approach in 1991-first half of 1993 resembled the largely discredited 'quick-fix' adjustment scenarios tried in the 1970s and early 1980s in many developing countries [*Nelson, 1989*].

V. THE NEED FOR AN IDEOLOGICAL BREAKTHROUGH

Two years' experience gained by Russia in dealing with the donor governments, international financial organisations and commercial banks on issues of economic interaction, as well as the lessons learnt by the Central European countries, made it clear that significant

329

amendments to the current approach were needed. Changes were required, not only in terms of the volume, and direction of aid and related technical issues, but in the whole ideology of interaction. The Western world should acknowledge that assistance to countries in transition is completely different from development aid and requires a more flexible, and probably very different, regime of conditionality. The inadequacy of the traditional Western stance on aid in relation to the former socialist countries in general and Russia in particular was also felt within the international financial community. Some ideas aiming at improving the current situation were combined and developed in a more or less comprehensive plan by the Bank of Austria and described in a special report entitled 'The Marshall Plan for Eastern Europe' [*Belov and Popov, 1993:3*].

The IMF and – to a lesser extent – the World Bank base their recommendations on the neoclassical mainstream, which advocates a diminishing state and its withdrawal from economic processes. Meanwhile even the short-term tasks of transition demand a strong and effective state. Historical evidence attests to the fact that in developed market economies and especially in the economies which have successfully caught up, economic growth required the building of an effective state bureaucracy, providing a collective rationale in the Weberian sense [*Weber, 1978,1981; Gershenkron, 1962*]. The general weakness of the state and the lack of modern bureaucracy in today's Russia are, probably, the most serious obstacles to pro-market democratic reform. Paradoxically, liberal institutions inclined towards an anti-state ideology face the task of helping to create a modern state in Russia.

This is especially true if one takes into account that unlike other post-socialist countries in transition and developing market economies, where private property, elements of the market and the foundations of civil society already existed before the beginning of reform, Russia started its transition adventure from a particularly unfavourable position. In the totalitarian Soviet society every element of market economy and democracy was for decades not only compressed and distorted, but completely absorbed by the party-state. When the party-state collapsed the USSR and – later – Russia found themselves in a situation of unstructured social chaos. Thus, contemporary Russia faces, not a typical problem of a weak inefficient state, but almost an absence of any state. Looking from this perspective, the institualisation of the market and of civil society, with the modern state being one of the most important pillars of both, should be given the highest priority. It seems that in Russia's case institutional criteria need to play a decisive role in assessing the progress of reform and, in turn, in determining aid conditionality.

Another paradox is that international institutions should devote a large part of their assistance to such an unusual task as the creation of a modern social system. In now-prosperous economies this was naturally a task for the state [*Polanyi, 1944*]. But as post-socialist experience in Russia shows, a tendency towards extreme versions of liberalism, the new political elite, who came to power with the wreckage of communism, is trying by all possible means to evade any social responsibility and is enthusiastically most exclusively concentrating on building an outdated version of capitalism. In a society with a deeply-rooted tradition of 'socialist justice' (embedded in the pre-revolutionary legacy too) the unprecedent pace of income reduction and wealth redistribution, and mounting political and social alienation, immediately resulted in intense polarisation and open violence. Thus, the international community should intelligently compensate for the shortsightedness of the ruling elite.

Besides helping with the creation of a modern state and the provision of a safety net external players should direct their efforts towards nurturing and encouraging the private sector. Given the fact that for decades all private initiative was stifled, a special system of support is needed to help the natural carrier of market relations to grow up and consolidate. Eventually, the national private sector should become the main recipient of aid, under a system of international scrutiny and monitoring. Otherwise more billions of dollars will be irrevocably lost, as happened with Soviet petrodollars in the 1970s and early 1980s. A shift of emphasis in assistance efforts from the state towards the private sector is in line with the IMF's ideological rhetoric. Nevertheless until recently national states were its strategic partners.

VI. RECENT CHANGES IN THE AGENDA

Currently the outline aid package to Russia widely discussed in international financial circles remains essentially the same as it was when the Soviet Union existed. On 15 April 1993 the G7 announced in Tokyo an aid package of US $28.4 bn. Taking into account the Paris Club deferral of about US $15 bn, the total sum of aid is US $43.3 bn, only a small part of it consisting of fresh funding.

The bulk of the package is supposed to be channelled through the IMF, World Bank, EBRD and bilateral credit lines (see Table 3).

TABLE 3
STRUCTURE OF TOKYO AID PACKAGE TO RUSSIA

Programme	Channel	Amount of aid	Terms
Initial stabilisation support	IMF	1st stage: US $1.5 bn	Clear commitment by Russian government to stabilisation
	IMF	2nd stage: US $1.5 bn	Progress in combatting inflation
	World Bank	US $1.1 bn	Tied export credits
Full stabilisation programme	IMF	US $4.1 bn reserve credits	Targeted to concrete projects of stabilisation
	G7	US $6 bn	Rouble stabilisation fund
Structural reforms and foreign trade liberalisation	World Bank	US $3.4	Loans to agricultural and energy sectors, privatisation, critical import
	EBRD	US $0.5 bn	Additional support to energy sector
	EBRD	US $0.3 bn	Fund for small and medium private business support
	G7	US $10 bn	Export credits and warranties

Source: WE [*1993:1*].

Despite three years of discussions and declarations the comprehensive package of aid remains an unattained dream. Many internationally recognised experts have had severe doubts about the vague decisions made in Tokyo ever being realised in practice. Thorough examination of the commitments and actual inflows into the Russian economy leads to the following conclusions. First, the volume of commitments is far below the amount of resources needed to ensure a socially bearable transition in line with standard IMF recommendations. Calculations for developing countries with populations exceeding one million, in a study undertaken by the World Institute for Development Economics Research (WIDER), showed that to facilitate a capacity growth of one per cent a net inflow of more than US $35 billion is required annually [*Taylor, 1991*]. At least comparable amounts of external financial resources are needed for Russia's transition. Second, in spite of growing commitments the level of actual disbursement is strikingly low. High-ranking Russian officials explained the gap by pointing out the poor co-ordination between decision-taking (G7, G24) and subordinate (the IMF, World Bank) levels [*Aven, 1993:14*]. Third, the composition of the aid package shows that complementary forms of aid (debt relief, rouble convertibility) and tied export credits – neither of which involves a transfer of cash resources to Russia – predominate. Fourth, a minor portion of aid, involving real transfer of money, concentrates in hard-currency generating sectors and also represents commercial loans, not grants.

A serious deficiency also arises because different purposes do not match each other. For instance, the devaluation of the rouble and the introduction of inner convertibility on current transactions – which constitute the core of IMF/ World Bank adjustment programmes – were supposed to compensate for the reduction in internal demand caused by monetary and fiscal restrictions. Nevertheless, Russian industries face enormous difficulties in gaining access to US and European markets, where tariff and non-tariff barriers remain in place [*Kommersant-Daily, 1993, 27 May:9; Business World, 1993, 28 May:4*]. Meanwhile, for Russia transition access to export markets is undoubtedly more important than financial and technical aid.

There exist certain indications that 1993 witnessed some changes in terms of approaches to aid to Russia. The G7 political decision in April 1993 to create the IMF Facility For Systemic Transformation for former Soviet republics signalled important new thinking. First, the leading world nations seem to acknowledge the unique character of transition from central planning to market economy, with no precedents in recent history. The historical experiment demands completely new approaches in aid and economic assistance. Second, the creation of the special common fund for post-Soviet states reflects the growing understanding that these heavily disrupted, but largely surviving economies should be treated, if not as united, at least as a strongly interlinked economic zone. Third, the G7 leaders in effect demanded that the Bretton Woods agencies work out a new operational approach to interaction with Russia. As some observers exaggeratedly hurried to conclude: 'financial considerations do not determine aid to Russia any more' [*Balls and Lloyd, 1993:1*].

Nevertheless, these shifts in thinking have yet to be transformed into practical steps. Given the incredibly fast and often contradictory developments since the end of the cold war, it is extremely difficult to speculate on even the nearest perspectives in this particular field. However, several important tendencies, related to interaction between Russia and the West on aid issues, can be discerned. First, at the inter-state level, aid in the form of financial transfers will lose its relative importance compared with technical assistance and flows of know-how and professional expertise. Mounting economic difficulties, in particular rising unemployment in major donor countries, make this shift unavoidable. Second, taking into consideration increasing debt obligations and the limited capacity to absorb large injections of financial resources effectively, Russia could also try to minimise external borrowing. Third, the problem of better disbursement of diminishing aid flows and its efficient allocation will be given special attention. Fourth, with the progressive opening-up of the Russian economy and the development of national market agents, non-state or private channels for economic interaction should develop. Fifth, the enormously changed geo-political and geo-economic structure of the contemporary world seems to increase the importance of political conditionality for inter-state aid. This in turn will lead either to the strengthening of the G7 co-ordinating role, or to increasing separatism in aid channelling among major international donors.

Fundamentally, the core problem does not reside in aid as such. Recently, broader and more important issues concerning economic interaction between Russia and the West have moved to the centre of the discussion. The relative stabilisation of the Russian post-Soviet state, the maturing of the political elite, and real problems encountered in the process of transition from central planning to market economy, have constituted a powerful demand for a change of focus in the ongoing dialogue. The old agenda is gradually being replaced by new considerations: Russia's problems in gaining recognition by the international community as a country with a market economy; the need for the removal of numerous legal and operational barriers and of discrimination blocking Russian integration into the world economy; and the need to activate Western support for post-Soviet states, thus easing Russia's burden as donor in relation to these [*Kalashnikova, 1993; Shokhin, 1993*].

Evidently, the further development of dialogue in these particular directions demands restructuring of aid mechanisms on both the conceptual and the practical level. It is also apparent that traditional agencies such as the IMF and the World Bank were created to fulfil very different tasks. Logically, the G7 has decided to open its special representation in Moscow by setting itself the goal of co-ordinating international aid efforts to Russia and of playing a role in setting the political problems that arise. There are good reasons to expect that, if the reform dynamic does not lose its momentum, we may witness the development of a new paradigm of political conditionality. Historical evidence and the current world situation prove that for many different reasons Europe should play a more active role in shaping out a new approach towards interaction with Russia.

REFERENCES

Agafonov, S., 1993, 'Gaidar in Japan', *Izvestia* (in Russian), 27 May, Moscow.
Attali, J., 1993, 'Democracy should not repay the debts of dictatorship', *Moscow News* (in Russian), 25 April, No. 17, Moscow.

Aven, P., 1993, 'The West should draw out conclusions', *Moscow News* (in Russian), 17 January, No. 3, Moscow.

Balls, E. and J. Lloyd, 1993, 'The West reconsiders approaches to aid to Russia', *The Financial News* (in Russian), 8-14 May, No. 28, Moscow.

Belov, I. and Y. Popov,1993, 'A Marshall Plan for Eastern Europe. Will the idea be realised?', *Russian News* (in Russian), 26 December, Moscow.

Business World (in Russian), Moscow.

Chernomyrdin, V., 1993, 'I'm not going to ask for anything in America', *Izvestia* (in Russian), 31 August, Moscow.

Edemsky, A., 1993, 'Russia expects IMF understanding', *Kommersant-Daily* (in Russian), 12 January, Moscow.

Fedorov, B., 1993, 'We will not ask for aid at Tokyo meeting', *Independent Gazette* (in Russian), 7 July, Moscow.

Frenkel, A. and B. Galitsky, 1993, 'Russia's economy in 1993', *Business World* (in Russian), 5 January, Moscow.

Gershenkron, A., 1962, *Economic Backwardness in Historical Perspective*, Cambridge, MA: Harvard University Press.

Goskomstat, 1994, 'On the Socio-Economic Situation in Russia in 1993', *Economy and Life. Your Partner* (in Russian), February, No. 6, Moscow.

Government of the Russian Federation, 1992, 'Program of deepening of economic reform', *Problems of Economy* (in Russian), August, No. 8, Moscow.

Government Newsletter (in Russian), 1991, November, No. 48, Moscow.

Gromyshkin, Y., 1993, 'Russia's foreign debt: how to repay it', *Russian News* (in Russian), 29 January, Moscow.

IMF Press Release, 1992, 5 August, Washington, DC.

Kalashnikova, N., 1993, 'Russia seeks equal partnership', *Kommersant-Daily* (in Russian), 8 June, Moscow.

Kisiliov, D., 1992, 'Russia wants to repay debts itself', *Economy and Life* (in Russian), October, No. 42, Moscow.

Kommersant-Daily (in Russian), 1993, Moscow.

Kvittsinski, Y., 1993, 'This elusive aid', *Modus Vivendi International* (in Russian), No. 10, July, Moscow.

Nelson, J.M. *et al.*, 1989, *Fragile Coalitions: Politics of Economic Adjustment*, New Brunswick (USA) and Oxford (UK):Transaction Books.

Podlipsky, N. and A. Slavyk, 1993, 'The Government and the Central Bank have reached agreement', *Kommersant-Daily*, 26 May, Moscow.

Polanyi, K., 1944, *The Great Transformation*, New York: Rinehart.

Sachs, J., 1992, 'An optimist's view', *Moscow News* (in Russian), 7 April, Moscow.

Shokhin, A., 1993, 'Russia intends to introduce new language in dealing with the G7', *Kommersant-Daily* (in Russian), 1 June, Moscow.

Statistical Committee for the Commonwealth of Independent States, 1993, 'CIS Economy in 1992', *Business World*, 2 March, Moscow.

Taylor, L., 1991, *Foreign Resource Flows and Developing Country Growth*, Helsinki: WIDER.

WE (in Russian), 1993, May, No. 9, Moscow.

Weber, M., 1978, 1981, *General Economic History*, New Brunswick, NJ: Transaction Books.

12

Conditionality and Programme Food Aid: From the Marshall Plan to Structural Adjustment

EDWARD CLAY

I. PROGRAMME FOOD AID: DEFINITIONS AND RESOURCE TRANSFERS

Programme food aid offers an interesting case for looking at the evolution of donor practice in linking official development assistance (ODA) to various forms of conditionality. This chapter is a preliminary exploration of the subject, focusing particularly on the bilateral assistance provided by the United States and the European Community (EC) as community action. It is based on a review of legislative and other documentation for the two major food aid donors, the United States and the EC. It draws also on previous research concerned with Bangladesh [*Clay, 1981*], a study of US programme food aid [*Clay and Singer, 1982*] and studies of the evolution of food aid donor policies [*Clay, 1985; Shaw and Clay, 1993*]. The documentation of practice raises questions about the consequences and effectiveness of donor action which are explored elsewhere [*Clay and Benson, 1993; Clay and Stokke, 1991*].

Programme Food Aid Defined

For policy and analytical purposes food aid (and aid more generally) is conventionally classified in terms of programme, project and emergency or disaster assistance. In practice, the different categories are not always distinct, but there are broad distinguishing characteristics:

- Project food aid is usually provided as one of the resources within a narrowly circumscribed conventional project framework: for example, the wages in kind in a normal food-for-work activity or the food to be supplied as a school meals programme;

336

- Relief aid provides rations for those affected by disasters, refugees and displaced people;
- Programme aid provides commodities which are sold or, according to more recent jargon, 'monetised' within the recipient economy.

The other important characteristics of programme aid are that commodities are provided to achieve national or sectoral food security and development objectives through one or more of the following outcomes:

- foreign exchange saving;
- generation of local currency revenue; and
- increase in the supply of commodities.

The provision of programme food aid is linked almost invariably (and so far no contrary examples have been identified) to some form of conditionality. This may concern the uses of the commodities, the counterpart funds generated from sales and the wider policy framework in which the aid is provided.

Conditionality is, however, an ambiguous concept and it is therefore useful to distinguish between the different forms of condition associated with programme food aid. Much recent analysis of conditionality has been particularly concerned with the 'policy based lending' of the World Bank and agreements between governments and the IMF. An interesting issue, therefore, is whether focusing on bilateral commodity aid modifies or extends the discussion on conditionality. Others have drawn attention already to the ambiguity in the use of concepts such as conditionality, policy dialogue and leverage [*Cassen, 1986*].

A review of food aid donor practice since the US Foreign Assistance Act of 1948, the legislative basis for the post-war European Recovery Programme or Marshall Plan, leads to the following useful distinctions in the discussion on conditionality.

Explicit and Implicit Conditionality

Donor legislation, regulatory frameworks typically indicate aspects of an agreement between donor and recipients and related recipient behaviour that involve *explicit* conditions, criteria and procedures for determining *compliance*. The second form of conditionality is the statement of aims and objectives where policy dialogue or participation by the donor (as in the Marshall Plan) is expected to help ensure the effective use of aid in a context of appropriate policies and the furthering of donor goals. The Marshall Plan documentation and much subsequent US policy analysis and legislation refer to 'self-help' measures expected on the part of 'participating' countries, that is, aid recipients [*USECA 1948, 1951*]. The 1948 Act also established an Economic Cooperation Administration (USECA) and envisaged US missions in participating countries that would liaise with governments on national recovery programmes. Implicit conditionality is the opaque zone of policy dialogue, consultation and leverage.

Aid Use and the Policy Environment

From the outset food aid conditionality has been concerned with:

– the uses of aid, what it should be used for and how;
– the policy conditions which the recipient or 'participating' country (Marshall Plan usage) should satisfy to be eligible and to continue in the donor's programme.

Some attempts have also been made to specify the provision of aid in terms of internationally and regionally agreed guidelines, such as the Resolutions of the World Food Conference 1974 and the CFA Guidelines and Criteria for Food Aid,[1] regional initiatives such as the Food Aid Charter for the Sahel [*CILSS, 1989*], and also, as discussed in more detail below, donor legislation.

Donor Goals

Recipient development and donor self-interest conditionality has characteristically attempted to embrace:

– a constructive environment for developmental policy in the recipient country;
– regional and global foreign policy concerns of the donor; which overlaps with
– the trade and domestic economic interests within the donor country.

The support for development can be construed as 'enlightened self-interest' or part of a 'humane-internationalist' policy [*Stokke, 1989*]. The other conditions reflect the explicit promotion or protection of donor country interests, even at the expense of developmental

1. Shaw and Clay [*1993, Ch. 1, Appendix 1*].

objectives. The attempt to load onto a single policy instrument – concessional exports or grants of food for sale in the recipient economy – has had, unsurprisingly, a complex and chequered history which has engendered much controversy. This is illustrated by the experience of the United States since 1948 and the European Community since 1967. The large scale of resource transfers involved, at least initially, also helps to explain these ambitious attempts at conditionality.

II. PROGRAMME FOOD AID AS A RESOURCE TRANSFER: 1948-1991

The controversies that have surrounded US programme food aid in particular indicate the economic and political significance of this type of resource transfer. The most celebrated controversies concern LBJ's 'short tether' policy towards India [*Lipton and Toye, 1990*], and Kissinger's use of 'food power' in support of the war effort in Vietnam and against Chile [*Wallerstein, 1980*] as well as its insensitive use in pressurising the newly independent Bangladesh [*Faaland, 1981; McHenry and Bird, 1977*]. Controversy arose again in the 1980s concerning the use of food aid in support of foreign policy objectives in Central America [*Garst and Barry, 1990*].

All this controversy raises the question of why programme food aid has been regarded as such a powerful instrument in aid diplomacy and whether the scale of resources involved justifies the attention that has focused on the 'food weapon'.

Programme food aid is potentially a resource of considerable significance to the governments and economies of the recipient countries. So-called supply imbalances or shortages of basic food staples have potentially severe economic and political implications for economies with severe foreign exchange constraints. Engel's Law makes issues regarding food policy more important in low and lower-middle income countries [*Timmer et al., 1983*]. In many of these countries the politics of food has implied, at least until structural adjustment programmes involved dismantling public food distribution and subsidy arrangements, that certain groups are likely to be favoured by assured and characteristically subsidised access to basic food stuffs. They are typically the military, police, civil servants, unionised urban workers, party cadre and hostel-based students. Outside these privileged groups short-term shortages and spiralling prices in parallel markets threaten severe distress and famine amongst the informal sector of peri-urban and rural populations. Where there is acute difficulty in assuring supplies – post-war Europe, India in 1966, many Asian and African countries in 1974 – the capacity to provide access to finance and to supply food rapidly on a large scale provided the donor with considerable, but temporary, influence.

Food aid has been linked closely to the management of exportable market surpluses and is typically provided only on an annual basis, even where there have been longer-term contractual relationships between donor and recipient governments. The short-term nature of programme food aid support therefore provides a regular context for dialogue on policy and examination of the economic and political situation in the recipient country. It also provides an instrument of leverage.[2]

Where there are problems of national food insecurity, that is, lack of assurance in aggregate supply and access to supplies on a national level, bulk food imports offer the instrument to fill a supply 'gap' and to sustain directly the 'entitlements' of the urban population and priority groups. Programme food aid provides immediate support to the balance of payments precisely because the alternative for most governments confronted with acute food insecurity is to acquire food through commercial imports. Food aid is potentially, therefore, a highly fungible transfer.

The sale of imported food directly to the private sector or through the operations of public distribution systems also provides budgetary support that perhaps cannot be directly calibrated in terms of the overall share of revenue generated. Again the dynamics of the economy and aid flows need to be taken into account when assessing the balance between aid and influence. For example, in a crisis such as that following the 1991/92 drought in southern Africa, the governments of affected countries were confronted with upward expenditure and the contraction of revenue. Substantial short-term flows of concessional or grant-financed imports enormously ease immediate pressures on the treasury. A quickly disbursing, highly fungible form of aid which can be used directly to cover politically sensitive supply imbalances is a powerful instrument.

Another important reason for the close attention to programme food aid is that it was a very important part of all ODA in the formative period 1948-1970. Historically, programme food aid was relatively most important as part of international aid flows in the immedi-

2. Prior to the Title III provisions of the 1977 Act, programme food aid was committed by an agreement to make an allocation within a single financial year. A typical multi-annual programme, for example under PL480 Title III or an EC multi-annual agreement, involves a donor commitment in principle to supply food aid over three years, but still provides for a process of annual review of the actual import requirements of the recipient country.

ate postwar era, and as a share of American aid until the early 1970s. In the initial three-month phase of the Marshall Plan up to mid 1948 bread grains alone represented US$200 million out of US$653 million of appropriations; food, feed and a small provision for fertiliser accounted for 49 per cent of all procurement [*USECA, 1948*]. The share of food declined steadily within the European Recovery Programme and its successor the Mutual Defence Assistance Programme (MDAP), but nevertheless it represented overall 27 per cent of US$12 billion appropriations up to 1951 [*USECA, 1951*]. Practices in aid administration and perceptions of the importance of food aid were created which have continued until the present day, when food aid is a significant resource to only a few low- and middle-income countries (Table 1).

Following the ending of the Marshall Plan and the Mutual Defence Assistance Programme, the United States continued large-scale food aid under the Agricultural Trade Development and Assistance Act of 1954, the so called Public Law (PL) 480. Grant aid was, however, largely replaced by soft loans repayable in the form of non-convertible currencies. Total annual volumes of shipments ranged between 16 million and 18 million tonnes of commodities annually at the height of the programme between 1961 and 1966. The value of soft credit sales from programme food aid ranged annually between US$1.6 and US$2.2 billion between 1957 and 1967. In the period between 1948 and 1970, the year in which regular Organisation for Economic Co-operation and Development (OECD) data on food aid transfers became available, food aid (largely programme aid from the US) appears to have declined from just under 50 per cent to 23 per cent of all aid transfers or official development assistance (ODA). This was in retrospect the real era of food power, but both US policy makers and many political economic analysts of Third World developments became interested in food power, perhaps excessively, only in the subsequent era of decline.

In the period between 1970 and 1989 food aid accounted for only ten per cent of ODA from all OECD Development Assistance Committee (DAC) countries, declining from 17 per cent in the period 1970-74 to eight per cent in the period 1985-89. The major reason for this decline was the reduction in US food aid operations from a peak level of $2.4 billion in 1963 to around $1.2 billion in current prices in 1970 and afterwards. In contrast, during the two decades since 1970 other (non-food) aid rose almost continuously in both current and real terms.

The other important feature of food aid in the period since 1970 is

the involvement of other donors, particularly the European Community and its member states, Japan and Canada (on an increased scale)
following the ratification of the Food Aid Convention in 1967. The
US share of total food aid volumes declined from over 90 per cent to

TABLE 1
RECIPIENT COUNTRY ANNUAL AVERAGE PER CAPITA FOOD AID RECEIPTS AND EC
COMMUNITY ACTION SHARE OF SHIPMENTS 1989-1991

Recipient Country[a]	Global Food Aid: Per Capita Receipts[b] ((kg/person)	EC Community Action[c] as a percentage of glo- bal food aid
Cape Verde	158.9	6.2%
Jamaica	104.9	-
Sao Tomé & Principe	97.1	17.0%
Jordan	84.2	2.3%
Guyana	57.0	3.5%
Dominica	53.0	-
Nicaragua	40.5	10.0%
Tunisia	40.0	11.9%
Mauritania	35.1	35.5%
El Salvador	35.0	0.3%
Grenada	32.2	-
Mozambique	31.6	20.3%
Bolivia	30.9	7.6%
Egypt	30.6	8.0%
Liberia	29.4	16.1%
Malawi	29.1	24.2%
Honduras	27.4	0.5%
Djibouti	24.3	26.7%
Guatemala	21.1	1.6%
Lesotho	20.1	29.6%
Haiti	18.7	9.9%
Maldives	18.5	-
Sri Lanka	16.8	8.1%
Peru	16.2	7.1%
Costa Rica	15.5	-
Ethiopia	15.0	33.9%
Gambia	14.7	0.8%
Lebanon	14.6	21.7%
Sudan	14.5	24.0%
Yemen, Republic of	13.0	6.2%
Somalia	12.7	37.2%
Eq. Guinea	12.3	6.3%
Morocco	11.6	5.4%
Bangladesh	11.2	13.9%

Source: WFP INTERFAIS Database
Notes: [a] Countries receiving over 10 kg per capita per annum on average over the period
1989-91.
[b] Three-year average per capita receipts of cereals aid.
[c] EC Community Action as organised by the Commission.

around 55 per cent after 1972-73 and in terms of aid expenditure to under 50 per cent. The European Community emerged as the second most important donor with Community and member state actions collectively accounting for more than 30 per cent of all food aid expenditure by 1991. However, food aid is disproportionately a Community undertaking, accounting for 24 per cent of Community Action aid between 1970-1989 – and 14 per cent in the five years 1985-1989. In contrast, food aid has changed little as a share of member states' bilateral ODA: 5.5 per cent over the two decades and five per cent in the period 1985-1989. Food aid to countries in Eastern Europe and the Soviet Union since 1989 is not reported as part of DAC aid, but these flows have substantially increased the EC share in global food aid flows.

Within these totals programme food aid initially represented as much as 90 per cent of food aid in the immediate postwar era. In the period since the mid 1970s programme aid has accounted for 55-65 per cent of total flows if measured in physical terms. But in terms of expenditure in the late 1980s, probably less than half of food aid ODA was programme aid because of the high unit costs of emergency and project aid.

The changing policy framework of programme food aid is closely related to two important developments: the continuing relative decline in food aid as a component of ODA and the emergence of the European Community as the second important source of assistance.[3]

III. CONDITIONALITY IN US FOOD AID 1948-1990

The different forms of conditionality are set out above: explicit and implicit; related to resource use or the policy environment; variously promoting developmental, foreign policy and internal economic effects in the donor country. These different aspects of conditionality are illustrated in the evolution of food aid as provided under the Marshall Plan and subsequent US programmes up to the most recent legislation in 1990.

The Marshall Plan

The Foreign Assistance Act of 1948 provided the legal framework for large-scale US-financed assistance to support economic recovery in Europe. This act also provided for the beginning of US economic

---

3. For a detailed analysis of the emergence of the European Community and Member State food aid, see Clay and Benson [*1993*].

assistance to developing countries, with bilateral aid to 'friendly' countries of the Pacific rim in Asia. An economic cooperation agreement with each participating country was the formal instrument through which aid could be organised. These agreements involved explicit conditions about the uses of aid and the policy environment. The agreement also provided a formal frame for implicit conditionality – a context within which the United States government could participate in planning measures for economic recovery. As all the agreements were formally similar, these may be illustrated by a single case: the agreement with Italy signed in June 1948 [*USECA, 1948*].

The Italian agreement included explicit conditions regarding the uses of assistance to further the overall recovery in Italy, and more broadly in Europe. These explicit conditions were reflected in *Article II: General Undertaking* requiring the Italian government to use the resources for the general purposes outlined in a schedule to be furnished in support of requirements for assistance. The agreement also provides for the establishment of a local currency counterpart fund account in which would be deposited the lira equivalent of the commodities and services provided by the United States (Article IV). The agreement involves a number of conditions regarding the policy environment in which assistance is to be provided and used. The Italian Economic Recovery Programme was to be part of the Joint Recovery Programme for Europe. The framework for the JRP was the Organisation for European Economic Co-operation (OEEC). A distinctive feature of the Marshall Plan was the explicit promotion of regional economic co-operation. The general undertaking included a commitment to stabilise the currency, establish or maintain a valid rate of exchange, and balance the governmental budget as soon as practicable (Article IIc). The agreement also committed the participating country to the liberalisation of regional and international trade (Article IId).

Conditionality and Donor Goals

As already noted, the Marshall Plan agreement specified in considerable detail conditions concerning uses of aid and the policy environment considered to be most conducive to rapid recovery, and enabling the US to terminate its assistance within the four-year limit of the plan.

Wider foreign policy concerns were implicit in the condition that recovery measures should be organised within the context of the OEEC's Joint Recovery Programme and that Italy was an eligible 'participating country' as a signatory to the report of the committee on

European Economic Co-operation, Paris, 22 September 1947 (Foreign Assistance Act 1948, Section 103A [1]).

The Italian agreement and other conditions written into some of the subsequent agreements with participating countries also reflected an explicit attempt to promote or protect the general economic interest of the United States and special sectional interests within the USA. The Marshall Plan guaranteed the US access to scarce and strategic materials for stockpile and other purposes through sale, exchange or barter (for example, US/Italy agreement, Article V). The agreement committed governments to settle or refer claims by nationals of either country to the International Court of Justice (Article X). More generally, the 1948 Foreign Assistance Act envisaged that Marshall Plan assistance would use, where available, commodities that were in surplus in the United States. However, the tying of aid was only partial, and the first report of the USECA [*1948*] indicated as initial sources of commodity appropriations: USA 57 per cent; Canada 21 per cent; Latin America six per cent; participating countries ten per cent; others six per cent.

Promoting Special Interest Groups

The US Constitution allows Congress to place severe constraint on federal expenditure. The administration is able to provide assistance only as mandated under congressional legislation. This division of powers has involved detailed and difficult negotiation of all foreign assistance legislation since 1948 and offers opportunities for the promotion of special interest groups through additional clauses in the legislation. An early example was the requirement under the Merchant Marine Act of 1936 that 50 per cent of goods be delivered in US-registered vessels under the Marshall Plan and the Mutual Assistance Programme. This practice of attaching what one US foreign service officer characterised as 'spigots' to general legislation has remained a characteristic feature of US foreign assistance. The introduction of many requirements into legislation and agreements is probably another reason for the preoccupation since the Marshall Plan with detailed and regular monitoring of 'required compliance' on the part of both the US administration and the participating or recipient countries.

Instruments of Influence

The Marshall Plan agreement envisaged a regular process of consultation between the two governments and information from the recipient covering:

- detailed information on projects, programmes and measures proposed or adopted to carry out provisions of the agreement;
- a full statement of operations under the agreement including uses of the funds, commodities and services to be received on a quarterly basis;
- information regarding its economy and any other relevant information not provided through the OEEC;
- information regarding (strategic) materials (US-Italy Agreement, 1948, Article vii: Consultation and Transmission of Information).

The need for monitoring national economic performance on a consistent basis was the reason why the USA supported the Cambridge National Accounting Project through the OEEC.

The special Mission for Economic Cooperation established in each participating country was, apart from the OEEC arrangement, the major instrument enabling the United States to 'participate' in planning the process of economic recovery through consultation. Agreements also provided for up to five per cent of counterpart funds to be placed at the disposal of the United States for financing the activities of these missions and supervising the implementation of programmes.

The formal arrangements provided the opportunity for dialogue on policy and leverage. The reality of bilateral aid as documented, for example by Price [1955] and as reflected in reported information, varied considerably. These differences are reflected in the agreed uses of counterpart funds.

Counterpart fund arrangements provided for five per cent of funds to be deposited for the use of the United States government in the recipient country. In the Italian case local currencies were also available for meeting what are now known as internal transport, storage and handling costs (ISTH) of NGO relief operations.[4] The agreement provided for the remaining balance to be used for :

- Projects and programmes for the development of productive capacity;
- implementation and development of strategic materials; and
- effective retirement of national debt.

A comparison of the implementation of counterpart fund arrangements for different participating countries indicates the varying extent

---

4.   In the US context non-profit-making voluntary organisations (PVOs) are to be regarded as one of the specific interest groups which seek, with considerable success, to influence foreign aid legislation [Ruttan, 1993].

to which the United States was involved in determining internal public expenditure. Norway and the United Kingdom attributed counterpart funds almost entirely to the retirement of public debt, in effect leaving them free from detailed discussions with the USA on the uses of part of public expenditure. Such action involved only formal, not substantive, conditionality.[5] At the opposite extreme was Greece, where counterpart funds were allocated to a wide range of directly productive and infrastructural activities, public building, housing and relief [*USECA, 1951, Table C3*]. Again the role of the ECA mission varied from that of a small liaison and monitoring group (Norway) to a team actively involved in planning economic reconstruction (Greece) or, as in East Asia, a mission with a virtual pro-consular authority.

Most of the institutional and formal regulatory elements which were characteristic of US foreign assistance were put in place in the Marshall Plan era. However, the purely bilateral arrangements in East Asia were more characteristic of continuing practice than the system in Western Europe, where the OEEC was the primary institution ensuring that the regional development co-operation objectives of the Marshall Plan were met. Only in the unique OEEC framework have countries receiving aid genuinely participated in decisions about the allocation of bilateral American aid.

The Mutual Defence Assistance Programme

The major change in conditionality introduced in this programme which began on 1 July 1950 was in the additional requirement placed upon participating countries to commit themselves to higher levels of military expenditure including hardware. In practical terms this required re-direction of public expenditure from investment in recovery to defence. Price [*1955*] reports from interviews with officials of participating governments that intensive persuasion or leverage was required to obtain the agreement of several OEEC member states.

PL480 - Food for Trade

With the ending of the Korean war, US food assistance took a radically different direction. New legislation in 1954 provided for large-scale food aid with the objectives of managing burgeoning US

---

5. The retirement of public debt, that is repayment of government bonds, was nominally financed with counterpart funds receipts. But since this action did not preclude the issue of new bonds, these countries with full US agreement managed the public debt as they chose.

surpluses and expanding commercial export markets, combined with the desire to help friendly nations develop and stop the spread of communism [*Baker, 1979; Wallerstein, 1980*]. Under PL480 the major food aid programme, Title I, involved the sale of commodities on soft credit terms for local currencies of beneficiary countries. This programme, which was part of the budget of the US Department of Agriculture, rapidly came to represent the major single element in US foreign assistance. As recently as 1970, aid under PL480 accounted for 38 per cent of gross US official development assistance (ODA).

As Title I was a credit rather than grant programme, conditionality focused particularly on areas concerned with US economic interests. Both the original legalisation and subsequent amendments reflected the coalition of interests in Congress necessary to extend or modify legislation. Actual legislation reflected proposals emanating from both the executive branch and from within Congress. US agricultural trade interests were protected by requirements prohibiting the re-export of commodities. In addition, the US and other agricultural exporters agreed on Rules on Surplus Disposal within the framework of the FAO Committee on Commodity Problems in 1954, which established procedures for vetting each food aid agreement with an importing country [*FAO, 1980*]. The Sub-Committee on Surplus Disposal established Usual Marketing Requirements based on the average level of commercial imports during the last three years. As part of the food aid agreement the importing country was required to maintain this level.

The position regarding local currency proceeds of sales was different. The US was now receiving payment in the frequently non-convertible currency of the recipient country. The legislation provided for a range of uses including the local costs of US government operations, the acquisition of buildings and of overseas material for the Library of Congress and measures to promote US agricultural exports. In practice the scope for use of the funds soon proved to be extremely limited other than those used as with Marshall Plan counterpart funds for agreed development and other co-operation activities. In an attempt to exploit these unspent funds the legislation was amended in 1959 to allow loans for business development to US-registered companies for operations in recipient countries. These were named after the congressman, Cooley, responsible for introducing the legislation. The problem was resolved eventually by a switch from credits repayable in foreign currencies to dollar credits. But as this in turn excluded many low-income countries, a grant form of programme aid was re-introduced in 1977 (see below).

Food for War

As the US Congress considered revisions to the food aid legislation in 1964, certain issues particularly focused their attention: what to do with the excess currencies held by the United States, how to help to satisfy the expectations of developing nations and how to adjust PL480 to fit US foreign policy towards South East Asia, Egypt and Eastern Europe. Two important changes in the legislation were to have far-reaching implications. First, the definition of 'common defense' in the legislation was amended to include measures taken for 'internal security' as legitimate purposes for grants of foreign currencies held by the United States. Second, the definition of 'friendly nation' determining eligibility to Title I was re-written to exclude any nation controlled by a communist government, or any nation which permitted its ships or aircraft to transport commodities to and from Cuba. Thus the programme was re-drafted in ways that made it possible for the administration to fund the war in Vietnam through the food aid programme [*Wallerstein, 1980*]. The definition of friendly country was subsequently used in attempting leverage over the Egyptian government and to exclude Chile under Allende. Bangladesh also fell foul of this requirement by exporting jute bags to Cuba in 1974 [*McHenry and Bird, 1977*]. Another important change dictated by US interest was the shift from soft currency and barter to long-term dollar loans. In the light of the difficulty in using foreign currencies, credit sales were combined into a new Title I in 1966 (Food for Peace Act, PL 89-808) calling for an orderly transition to sales for dollars from 1971.

Food for Development

Parallel to the US preoccupation with strategic and agricultural interests, a theme gaining ground in Congressional debates and administration circles was the need to make US food aid a more effective instrument for development. Initially much attention focused on developing the grants channelled through NGOs and subsequently multi-lateral agencies. The 1959 legislation known as the Food for Peace Act also extended the range of uses of local currencies for developmental purposes and widened the scope for grant food aid. The United States in particular was able to support the newly established World Food Programme (WFP) from the grant component of PL480 (Title II) from 1963 onwards.

A series of developments resulted in a radical restructuring of food aid, shifting the balance of objectives and the framework of conditions towards developmental objectives. This restructuring involved the elaboration of detailed conditionality concerning the uses and policy environment in the recipient country and restrictions on foreign aid 'abuses'.

In 1965/66 India suffered a severe food crisis and the US responded by authorising emergency assistance of 3.5 million tonnes in addition to 6.5 million tonnes already scheduled for shipment. The US again provided massive food aid in 1966/67 involving US$500 million and 6.6 million tonnes of grain. The Johnson administration then, in perhaps the most widely cited example of bilateral donor leverage, attempted to use its influence to push the Indian government towards changes in internal economic policy. This attempt to link continued food aid to economic policy conditions, the 'short-tether' policy, succeeded in providing additional political impetus to India's drive towards self-reliance in food. The concept of linking food aid to economic policy measures in the recipient country as a means of promoting development was inserted into the legislation. They were considered 'self-help' measures, and were reminiscent of the Marshall Plan's concern with aid for reconstruction. The so-called Mondale Self-Help Amendment permitted the use of loan repayments in foreign currency for mutually agreed development activities.

In the early 1970s domestic public opinion in the United States turned against the war in Vietnam. Rising prices and the disappearance of surpluses in this period also added impetus to further changes. There was a rapid fall in the volume of US food aid, because it was budgeted in financial terms and Congress would not agree to higher appropriations. The direct outcome was to shift the balance of objectives in the legislation sharply towards developmental and humanitarian concerns, but this change would have far wider implications.

The Foreign Assistance Act of 1973 precluded the use of foreign currency funds for common defence or internal security from mid-1974. In response to the international food crisis of 1973-74, the 1974 Act further required that not more than 30 per cent of concessional food aid could be allocated to countries other than those designated by the United Nations as those most seriously affected by food shortages, except in the case of humanitarian assistance. Further legislation in 1975 and 1977 reshaped American programme food aid in a form that subsequently influenced the newly emerging food aid programmes of other donors. The amended legislation attempted to restrain severely the use of food aid in support of US strategic and agricultural trade objectives, except where these were more consistent with development. The act required the allocation of at least 75 per cent of Title I sales to countries eligible to borrow from the World Bank's International Development Association (IDA), with the effect of reducing food aid to Indonesia and most of Latin America. The 1977 legislation also included conditionality concerning 'gross violations' of human rights. Finally the 1977 Act introduced a new Title III 'food for development' programme with detailed sectoral conditionality.

Food Aid to Reduce Food Aid Dependence

The objectives and conditionalities associated with food aid between 1948 and 1977 had emphasised general economic development in terms of uses, the policy environment in the recipient country, US foreign and agricultural interests. The 1977 legislation placed new emphasis on making food aid an instrument for reducing developing countries' dependence on food aid.[6] The Food for Development provision was intended to encourage countries to use proceeds from sales of Title I commodities to *increase food supplies*, provide access to these supplies for the poor and improve the general well-being of the really poor. The emphasis would also be on assistance to small farmers, share croppers and landless agricultural labourers. Countries undertaking additional self-help measures to boost production, improve storage, transport and distribution of food as well as reduce population growth would be eligible for debt 'forgiveness', or writing off of food aid credit obligations. This new Title III emphasised consultation and reviewing performance in the recipient country with incentives for compliance.

The sectoral focus in the 1977 legislation was important in implicitly recognising the greatly reduced role of food aid within American and global aid flows. The US Department of Agriculture increasingly used other credit sale arrangements outside the food aid legislation to support its trade promotion activities.

The sectoral emphasis of the legislation was further underscored by the so-called Bellmon requirement, an amendment again named after the proposing congressman. This required the USDA and the United States Agency for International Development (USAID) to show that food aid was not having a negative impact on agricultural production and prices in the recipient economy. The Bellmon Amendment in the 1977 Act, strengthened in 1979, is an important example of the attempt to place the burden of conditionality on the donor agency. This device became a characteristic feature of environmental protection practice in the 1980s. The implication is that it is the aid administration as well as the recipient that now have to work within a narrow, regulatory, monitored framework.

---

6.   The Development and Food Assistance Act of 1977, PL 95-88.

The Ever-shifting Balance

The subsequent legislation up to and including the 1990 Farm Bill reflects the changing balance of influences on US foreign assistance and foreign agricultural policy. These changes have implied little in terms of modified conditionality for recipient countries, but substantial changes in availabilities and terms. The more restrictive conditions of PL480 led USDA to find an additional more flexible vent for surpluses as food aid under Section 416 of the 1949 Agricultural Trade Act in 1985. The 1990 Farm Bill divided responsibility for food aid between the Department of Agriculture, which administers Title I (Concessional Sales) and the USAID, responsible for Title II (Donations) and Title III (Multi-annual Programme Aid).[7] In fiscal year 1992 approximately one third of PL480 resources were programmed under Title I, whilst half were donated under Title II and the remainder under Title III. The pressure of domestic interest groups has been sustained: for example, in 1985 cargo preference was increased from 50 per cent to 75 per cent of commodities to be shipped in US flag vessels.

The programme aid resources of Food for Peace which represent a decreasing share of agricultural imports in developing countries have been directed towards politically high priority countries including Egypt and Central America. Emergency aid, and in 1992 the whole range of resources, have been targeted on countries which have international priority such as southern Africa following the recent drought. Apart from politically important countries, policy increasingly appears to place whatever influence US programme food aid has in a country such as Bangladesh behind the agenda for economic reform promoted by the World Bank and the IMF.

IV. EUROPEAN COMMUNITY FOOD AID

Origins

Three important developments resulted in the European Community (EC) becoming a major food aid donor. With the establishment in 1963 of the World Food Programme (WFP), the first and only multilateral body concerned exclusively with food aid, the EC and also European Free Trade Association (EFTA) countries were drawn for the first time into the provision of food aid on a regular basis.

---

7. The Food, Agriculture, Conservation and Trade Act of 1990 (PL 101-624) [*Hanrahan, 1991*].

During the Kennedy Round GATT negotiations in 1966-67 another US initiative brought the EC and other rapidly growing OECD economies into further commitments to provide food aid on a regular basis. There was a desire to achieve a wide GATT agreement, encompassing industrial products, and the EC also wanted tacit acceptance of its relatively new Common Agricultural Policy (CAP). Consequently the EC, the EFTA states and Japan agreed to make formal commitments to provide minimum amounts annually of cereals food aid, or the cash equivalent, under a Food Aid Convention (FAC). This convention was formally part of an international grains agreement, itself part of the wider Kennedy Round process.

The third important factor in the growth of EC food aid programme arose directly from the management of the CAP. The success of the CAP in promoting agricultural growth within the Community was quickly reflected in the build-up of surpluses in the protected European market, especially of dairy products. In looking for ways to manage these surpluses, the Community agreed in 1969 to provide dairy products as food aid. Since the surpluses were a Community problem, the dairy products were provided from the outset as what came to be known as *Community Action* food aid. This was organised by the Commission and acquired either from stocks or purchased directly from the processor by national agencies through tenders on behalf of the Community.

The institutional solution adopted by the EC for cereals aid was to divide responsibility for the FAC minimum contribution between national actions of members states and Community actions organised as an additional, separate programme by the Commission. This was combined with the new dairy aid programme and financed as new titles of the Community budget by direct additional budgetary subventions from the member states. The Commission was also given the opportunity to find constructive ways to manage or dispose of surplus dairy products. These decisions reflected the way internal markets were managed: cereals were regulated by national interventional authorities, but dairy intervention was organised on a Community-wide basis.

The Search for a Policy Framework

The next challenge was for the Community institutions to formulate a policy framework for the Food Aid Programme, which had been acquired more by accident than by a deliberate act of policy. The small unit, later a division, within Directorate General (DG)VIII (Development) of the Commission initially looked for relatively simple ways of allocating and shipping the food aid for which it was responsible. A simple option was to provide substantial allocations of programme aid for balance of payments and budgetary support to developing country governments on a bilateral basis. The WFP was also able to absorb large quantities of dairy aid, particularly through the then new Indian national dairy development programme, Operation Flood.

Bilateral food aid agreements were initially relatively simple, especially as the Community was providing food aid on a large scale to countries outside the Lomé group, where the Commission was not strongly represented in the field. Agreements included provisions regarding the uses for development and on accounting for counterpart funds. In 1974 the Commission produced its first substantive paper on food aid policy which emphasised the use of food for development, particularly in countries suffering acute temporary shortages and a specified combination of a developmental criterion that would influence allocations (COM (300) final, 1974). The main elements of these country agreements reflected established practice of the United States and Canada, but were without clear procedures for monitoring and ensuring compliance. The programme acquired a reputation for inefficiency reflected in highly critical reports of the EC Court of Auditors and independent evaluations. The eventual response included the elaboration of the 'national food strategy' as the thematic basis for providing programme food aid.

National Food Strategies

In around 1979 proposals began to emanate from the World Food Council secretariat that least developed countries should prepare 'national food strategies'. These were strongly influenced by the US PL480 Title III Food for Development initiative. A food strategy was to be an organising framework for greater agricultural self-reliance and food security, incorporating food aid as a constructive element. Food aid under Title III was to be provided on a multi-annual basis in ways that did not disrupt local markets and funds generated from sales were to be used to support agricultural development. Developed countries were encouraged to co-operate bilaterally with individual developing countries to prepare food strategies.

In 1982 the new Commissioner for Development, Edgard Pisani, adopted the food strategy approach with enthusiasm as part of a re-organisation of food aid. Administratively, the previously separate Food Aid Division became part of an enlarged division for supporting agricultural development. Under the new policy bilateral programme food aid was to be linked as closely as possible to national food strategies and sectoral projects promoting agricultural production. This initiative was reflected in the 1982 food aid management regulation of the EC Council:

The granting of food aid shall, if necessary, be conditional on the implementation of annual or multi-annual development projects, priority being given to projects which promote production of food in the recipient countries. Where appropriate, the aid may contribute directly to the implementation of such projects. This complementary may be assured through the use of counterpart funds where the produces supplied by the Community's aid are intended for sale (O.J. No L352/1 14.12.82).

The Commission attempted from 1983 until the late 1980s to make such national food strategies the organising framework for programme food aid (COM (83) 141 final). There were linked constructive developments, such as that allowing the substitution of financial support for food aid where, despite a food aid commitment, food imports were temporarily unnecessary (OJ/L165/7, 19 July 1984). The issue of possible conditionality also emerged in EC-ACP Lomé III and Lomé IV negotiations. But in practice there were few multi-annual agreements with recipient countries based on nation food strategies.

Whether the Community could have organised its bilateral food aid effectively around those forms of agreement raises questions about the capacity of one donor contributing only a limited proportion of the food aid imports to enter into substantive bilateral arrangements with recipient governments (see Table 1). In the context of wider discussions on conditionality, it is notable therefore that first the US then the other major donor moved from general economic to sectoral conditionality.

The shift to sectoral conditionality appears to have had two important impulses. First, the world food crisis of the mid 1970s and growing controversy concerning food aid made it increasingly necessary to provide a policy framework in which food aid was envisaged as not damaging agricultural development but ultimately leading to its own disappearance. Second, by the 1980s it became clear that, with few exceptions, no donor provided a sufficient quantity of food aid to any recipient for it to be used as a serious basis for macro-economic conditionality. Table 1 illustrates this limitation on donor influence: those developing countries are listed where all food aid, including relief, exceeded 10 kg a year per person during 1989-91, representing approximately five per cent or more of minimum requirements of cereals and other basic staples for human consumption. The share of EC community action in that total suggests that there is then limited potential for influence on national policy through a policy dialogue based only on food aid. This latter consideration may also explain the most recent development, the increasing interest on the part of donors in linking food aid to structural adjustment programmes.

V. FOOD AID AND STRUCTURAL ADJUSTMENT

In the early 1980s, the attempts of the US and other individual donors to impose bilateral macro-economic and sectoral conditionality raised problems of coherence and consistency. Bilateral 'dialogue' or leverage became less likely to be successful than in the preceding era when the US was effectively the only food aid donor of significance. World Bank consultative groups and UNDP round tables were emerging as the context for joint donor-government dialogue on the macro-economic policy framework and total aid requirements.

H.W. Singer and the author argued that IMF stabilisation agreements provided a less unsatisfactory policy framework for macro-conditionality than a separate bilateral food aid agreement [Clay and Singer, 1982]. They cited examples such as an agreement between Canada and Jamaica sterilising funds generated from sales of food aid and so contributing in the context of an IMF stand-by agreement to a reduction in an unsustainable budgetary deficit.

The emergence of World Bank co-ordinated structural adjustment programmes in the early 1980s provided another widely available framework in which to supply food aid. Gradually, donors responded to this, the major aid policy initiative of the decade, by looking for ways to use food aid in support of structural adjustment.

This tendency is illustrated by food aid policy statements by the European Community emphasising the benefits of linking food aid to structural adjustment programmes. Examples of this gradual shift in policy towards providing aid within a multi-donor framework include the European Community Council resolution on food security policy in sub-Saharan Africa (23 Nov. 1988), a subsequent Council resolution on food aid (29 May 1990) and a Council resolution on the use of counterpart funds generated by various development assistance measures (27 May 1991). The Lomé IV convention in 1990 gives particular significance to the use of counterpart funds from the European Community import support programmes, including food aid, as a means of mitigating the social costs of structural adjustment.

VI. TENTATIVE CONCLUSIONS

This brief review of programme food aid has indicated how many characteristic elements in recent discussions on conditionality emerged with the major US food aid programmes first in Europe and in East Asia from 1948 and subsequently with PL480 from 1954. Programme food aid evolved from being almost the single most important form of aid through a checkered history of political misuse, with attempts at sectoral conditionality, into the mainstream of macro-development policy. By the early 1990s programme food aid was being assimilated increasingly into broader packages of commodity assistance to countries involved in structural adjustment.

Are there lessons of wider relevance? Since the Marshall Plan, the whole history of the donor seeking to influence the use of local currency and counterpart funds has raised repeatedly so-called 'problems of implementation' that still preoccupy policy analysts and aid agencies.[8] An interesting question is why policy-based aid continues to be preoccupied with counterpart funds. Is this in part because this form of aid requires some measurable performance criteria for purposes of accountability that can be monitored by public audit bodies in donor countries?

The way in which US food aid accrued more and more stipulations advancing special interests is a model which Europe should seek to avoid. The adoption of ever more detailed provisos as the result of human rights, environmental and development lobbying is ambiguous in its implications, even when seeking to prevent bad practice.

A more general lesson is the need for genuine realism amongst those whose 'realistic' development policy practice involves the attempt to load a complex mix of conditions on a single instrument.

REFERENCES

Baker, J.E., 1979, 'Food for peace, 1954-1978: major changes in legislation', Washington, DC: Congressional Research Service.
Carlyle, M. (ed.), 1952, *Documents on international affairs 1947-1948*, London: Oxford University Press.
Cassen, R. H. and Associates, 1986, *Does Aid Work?*, Oxford: Oxford University Press.
CILSS/Club du Sahel, 1989, *Food Aid Charter for the Countries of the Sahel*, Ouagadougou: Permanent Interstate Committee for Drought Control in the Sahel, December.

8. For a critical exploration of this issue of reiterative practices that leads to implementation problems, see Schaffer [*1984*].

Clay, E.J., 1981, 'Poverty, Food Insecurity and Public Policy in Bangladesh', *Bank Staff Working Paper* No. 473, Washington DC: World Bank.

Clay, E.J., 1985, *Review of Food Aid Policy Changes since 1978*, WFP Occasional Paper No. 1, Rome.

Clay, E.J. and C. Benson, 1993, 'Food Aid Programmes of the European Community and its Member States: A Comparative Statistical Analysis', *ODI Working Paper* 72, London: Overseas Development Institute.

Clay, E.J. and H.W. Singer, 1982, 'Food Aid and Development: The Impact and Effectiveness of Bilateral PL 480 Title I - Type Assistance'. *USAID Program Evaluation Discussion Paper* No. 15, Washington DC: US Agency for International Development.

Clay, E.J. and O. Stokke (eds.), 1991, *Food Aid Reconsidered: Assessing the Impact on Third World Countries*, London: Frank Cass.

European Communities Commission, 1974, 'Food Crisis and the Community's Responsibilities Towards Developing Countries. (Memorandum on Food Aid Policy of the European Economic Community.)' COM (74) 300 final, Brussels: March.

European Communities Commission, 1983, 'Food Aid for Development: Commission Communication to the Council.' COM (83) 141 final, Brussels: April.

European Communities Commission, 1984,'Council Regulation (EED) No. 1755/84 of 19 July 1984 on the Implementation in Relation to Food of Alternative Operations in Place of Food-Aid Deliveries', OJ/L165/7, Brussels: June.

European Communities Commission, 1990, 'The Lomé IV Convention', *The Courier* No.120, Brussels: March-April,

European Communities Council, 1983, 'Food Aid Policy - Council Resolution' (Press release), 10543e/83 (Presse 189), Brussels: 15 Nov.

European Communities Council, 1988, 'Council Resolution of 23 November 1988 on Food Security Policy in sub-Saharan Africa', Brussels: 15 Nov.

European Communities Council, 1991, 'Consolidated Text: Council Conclusions on Food Aid Policy', Brussels: 29 May.

Faaland, J. (ed.), 1981, *Aid and influence: the case of Bangladesh*, London: Macmillan.

FAO, 1980, *Principles of Surplus Disposal and Consultative Obligations of Member Countries*, Rome: Food and Agriculture Organisation of the UN.

Garst, R. and T. Barry, 1990, *Seeding the Crisis: US food aid and farm policy in Central America*, Lincoln and London: University of Nebraska Press.

Hanrahan, C.E., 1991, 'The 1990 Farm Bill: Food Aid Reauthorization Issues', Washington, DC: Congressional Research Service, Jan.

Lipton, M. and J. Toye, 1990, *Does aid work in India?*, London: Routledge.

McHenry, D.F. and K. Bird, 1977, 'Food Aid and Diplomacy', *Foreign Policy* No. 27. Summer.

Pinstrup-Andersen, P., 1991, 'Food Aid to Promote Economic Growth and Combat Poverty, Food Insecurity and Malnutrition in Developing Countries, and Suggestion for How to Increase the Effectiveness of Danish Aid to the World Food Programme', Report to DANIDA, Ithaca, NY: Cornell University, Sept.

Price, H.P., 1955, *The Marshall Plan and its meaning*, Ithaca: Cornell U.P.

Ruttan, V.W., 1993, *Why Food Aid?*, Baltimore: Johns Hopkins University Press.

Schaffer, B.B., 1984, 'Towards responsibility: public policy in concept and practice', in Clay, E.J. and B.B. Schaffer (eds.), *Room for Manoeuvre*, London: Heinemann.

Shaw, D.J. and E.J. Clay, 1993, *World Food Aid: experiences of recipients and donors*, London: James Currey.

Singer, H., J. Wood and A. Jennings, 1987, *Food Aid. The Challenge and the Opportunity*, Oxford: Clarendon Press.

Stokke, O. (ed), 1989, *Western Middle Powers and Global Poverty. The Determinants of the Aid Policies of Canada, Denmark, the Netherlands, Norway and Sweden*, Uppsala: Scandinavian Institute of African Studies.

Timmer, C.P., W.P. Falcon and S.R. Pearson, 1983, *Food Policy Analysis*, Baltimore:

Johns Hopkins University Press for the World Bank.

United States Government, Economic Cooperation Administration, 1948, *1st Report to Congress for quarter ended June 30, 1948*, Washington, DC.

United States Government, Economic Cooperation Administration, 1951, *Thirteenth Report to Congress for quarter ended June 30, 1951*, Washington, DC.

USAID, 1989, 'The Development Impact of US Program Food Assistance: Evidence from the A.I.D. Evaluation Literature', Washington, DC: United States Agency for International Development, Bureau of Food for Peace and Voluntary Assistance, August.

Wallerstein, M.B., 1980, *Food for war - food for peace*, Cambridge, MA: MIT Press.

13

Political Conditionality: Strategic Implications for NGOs

MARK ROBINSON

I. INTRODUCTION

The debate about political conditionality has largely taken place within official donor circles, and bilateral aid policy in this area has been the prerogative of aid agencies and foreign ministries in the donor countries. Little consultation has taken place with NGOs and human rights agencies in the formulation of bilateral policy on conditionality, even though such organisations have long pressed for stronger linkage between human rights performance and aid commitments. Moreover, in the few cases where political conditionality has been applied to particular countries an NGO perspective has not generally been taken into consideration.

Yet while NGOs have been marginalised in the policy debate over political conditionality, its application has significant implications for their operations in developing countries and relations with governments and donors. This has three main elements, each of which will be dealt with separately in this chapter. First, the suspension or termination of bilateral aid programmes to countries which are judged to have poor records on human rights or repressive political systems can have significant repercussions for NGO programmes. The poorest people, who are the principal clients of NGOs, can be adversely affected by political conditionality if aid is reduced or terminated, perhaps compounding the effect of austerity measures adopted at the instigation of donors as part of a structural adjustment programme. It can also provoke retaliation against NGOs and human rights agencies by recipient governments in the form of more restrictive legislation or by closing off funding channels. Second, NGOs are looked to as vehicles for channelling political aid to promote empowerment, civic education and democratic reform, by virtue of their prominent role in civil society and grassroots involvement. And third, NGOs and rights agencies can offer insights on how common standards and criteria might be devised and suggest alternative approaches.

In this chapter it is recognised that NGOs constitute a diverse assemblage of organisations. Beyond the obvious distinction between northern and southern NGOs, there are also major differences among the latter, which include development organisations offering services, those providing humanitarian aid, and advocacy groups and human rights agencies. In the North, NGOs and human rights agencies have largely functioned with very different remits; the former concerned with funding and supporting development work in the South, and the latter with monitoring abuses and lobbying governments to improve conditions and existing practices. These organisations have begun to come together over the issue of political conditionality in the recognition that their work is complementary and that they might be able to intervene more systematically in the conditionality debate by combining insights from development practice at the grassroots with more informed advocacy of universal standards of human rights derived from international law.[1] This found expression in the high degree of consensus exhibited among NGOs and human rights agencies present at the World Conference on Human Rights in Vienna in June 1993, when a common position was articulated on the desirability of linking aid to human rights and the indivisibility of rights. At the same time, it should be noted that NGOs are far from homogeneous in their world view, and that sharp differences exist between NGOs along ideological and strategic lines, even though it is not possible to explore these differences in any depth in this chapter.

II. THE POLITICAL IMPACT OF CONDITIONED AID

Since the adoption by most donors of the principle of political conditionality, aid has been reduced, suspended or terminated in several countries, either bilaterally or by donors acting in concert through aid consortia. While seeking to promote changes as varied as improved human rights, increased government accountability, and political

---

1. A workshop in the Netherlands sponsored by the International NGO Training and Research Centre (INTRAC) in June 1993 brought together these various groups, along with representatives of official aid agencies to discuss the donor policy agenda on governance, democracy and conditionality, its implications for NGOs and the potential role they might play in modifying and improving existing policies. In examining these issues, this chapter draws on the discussions that took place in the course of the workshop around the theme of political conditionality.

reform by legalising political parties and holding elections, these actions have had a mixed record of success. In Africa, where these policies have been applied with greatest vigour, there is some evidence to suggest that political conditionality has helped to foster a process of political liberalisation when instigated by pro-democracy forces in countries ruled by insecure and economically weakened authoritarian regimes, as the experience of Francophone West Africa would appear to indicate [*Robinson, 1993a*]. When donor pressure is applied through decisions to suspend aid at aid consortia meetings, as in the cases of Kenya and Malawi, this has been successful in prompting recalcitrant autocratic governments to seek a popular mandate for their continued right to rule, either by means of elections or by holding a referendum on multi-party democracy [*Robinson, 1993b*].

Yet there have also been instances where, despite the termination of aid by certain bilateral donors, little progress has been made. Belgium, the United States, and the EC have all suspended their aid programmes to Zaire but President Mobutu remains in power while the country slides deeper into economic and political chaos. Donor action in the case of the Sudan has similarly had little effect on the political complexion of the regime or led to any appreciable improvements in the country's human rights situation. Even in countries where elections have been held incumbent rulers have remained in power (for example Moi in Kenya and Rawlings in Ghana), either by controlling access to the media and by indulging in electoral malpractice, or as a result of splits in the opposition. In such cases donor conditions have been complied with but the election outcome has favoured the status quo in the guise of multi-party democracy. And in countries where elections have resulted in victory for the opposition, such as Zambia and Benin, very little democratisation has taken place beyond a purely formal process of transferring power from one group of elite political leaders to another, and there are signs that autocratic practices persist.

III. POLITICAL CONDITIONALITY AND THE POOR

While this is not the place to discuss the experience of individual countries from the point of view of the success or failure of political conditionality, donor decisions to suspend or terminate aid can have profound effects on NGOs and the people with whom they work, principally the poor. At one level, reduced aid can create or exacerbate economic hardship for the poor, by causing governments to cut public expenditure on health, education and other public services. Withdrawal of aid for political reasons can create financial difficulties for countries undergoing structural adjustment where donor-imposed economic conditions are already in force.

The case of Malawi is of relevance here. Following the collective donor decision to withhold development aid in May 1992 the Banda government imposed cuts in public expenditure in response to a deterioration in the country's financial situation which in turn created financial problems for church-run hospitals in receipt of state support. A crisis was averted by NGOs, which increased the level of external funding to the health-care sector to make up for the shortfall [*Archer, 1993:19*]. In other countries which face similar financial problems as a result of aid withdrawal or suspension, such as Haiti, Burma, the Sudan and Iraq, the poor have been less fortunate since NGOs cannot operate with impunity, either as a result of political repression or of sanctions imposed by Western donors, and protect them from cutbacks in expenditure on essential services.

NGOs would not wish to perform a cushioning role to compensate for the adverse economic effects of political conditionality since their own resources are finite and their programme priorities might become distorted as result. There may be a role, however, for southern NGOs to monitor the impact of conditionality-induced public expenditure cuts on the poor, and for northern NGOs to lobby their governments to adopt a more discriminatory approach to conditionality, in which poverty-focused projects are insulated from aid conditions, and for higher levels of support for safety-net measures to protect the poor from sharp reductions in public expenditure.

Donors claim that humanitarian aid is exempt from conditionality. In Malawi, while development aid worth £72 million was suspended pending improvements in civil and political rights, £170 million was provided in humanitarian aid. Although difficult to substantiate, this was, according to the Malawian government, far less than the amount necessary for it to feed and clothe thousands of Mozambican refugees camped inside its borders [*Robinson, 1993b:64*]. Another illustration of how political conditionality might indirectly affect humanitarian aid is the case of the Sudan in 1990-91, where it was alleged that the donor response to warnings of impending famine was both slow and inadequate because of poor diplomatic relations with the military Islamic government and the suspension of development aid by bilateral donors [*Bailey et al., 1990*]. For their part, the aid donors claim that the government contradicted evidence coming from local early warning systems and repeatedly denied that there was an impending food crisis in the north of the country, thereby causing unnecessary delays. These examples, whilst not providing conclusive evidence of political conditionality adversely affecting humanitarian aid programmes, underline the importance of ensuring that humanitarian aid is kept free from political considerations and that every effort is made to treat requests for humanitarian aid assistance from governments deprived of development aid in accordance with normal emergency procedures. Since they are heavily involved in bilateral relief operations, NGOs are well placed to monitor humanitarian aid responses and to ensure that such governments, and more particularly the affected population, are not unfairly penalised.

IV. REPERCUSSIONS ON NGO OPERATIONS: INDONESIA AND KENYA

While political conditionality has in some cases had an adverse impact on the poor, inducing a response from NGOs in the manner outlined above, NGOs' freedom to manoeuvre has been directly affected in terms of the political response that it has induced from recipient governments. Two illustrations from Indonesia and Kenya are of relevance here.

In November 1991 the Indonesian military massacred hundreds of civilians during a peaceful student-led protest in occupied East Timor. This provoked sharp criticism of the military's action by Western donors, with the Netherlands, Canada and Denmark indicating that they would suspend their aid programmes in response. Japan and the World Bank, which have the largest aid programmes, refrained from taking any decisive action. In the event, only the Dutch government suspended its aid programme pending the outcome of an independent review of the incident. This produced a retaliatory response from the Indonesian authorities, resulting in the decision in March 1992 to terminate Dutch aid and dissolve the aid consortium chaired by the Netherlands, for its alleged use of development assistance as a 'tool of intimidation' [van Tuijl, 1993:2]. Besides raising questions about the efficacy of political conditionality when applied unilaterally and demonstrating how trade and foreign policy considerations can conflict with ostensible commitments to upholding human rights and good government, the application of political conditionality over the East Timor incident had important repercussions for Dutch NGOs and their partners in Indonesia [Robinson, 1993b].

Dutch aid to Indonesia accounted for only 2 per cent of the total volume of development assistance to the country, but there was a significant programme of financial support for Indonesian NGOs through the co-financing programme and private grants from Dutch NGOs, amounting to some US$ 15 million. A month after the termination of the bilateral aid programme, Dutch NGO aid was also banned; all Indonesian NGOs, whether development agencies, foundations, professional and consumer associations, legal aid institutes or religious organisations, were prohibited from receiving funds from Dutch sources. The Indonesian authorities declared that participation by Indonesian NGOs in the International NGO Forum on Indonesia (INGI), a vehicle through which Dutch and Indonesian NGOs could engage in policy dialogue with the official aid donors, was declared irrelevant.

These actions followed steadily mounting pressure on NGOs in the country, that had been repeatedly warned to stay out of political affairs and encouraged to form a code of ethics to regulate their activities. In December 1991, a month after the East Timor massacre, the Indonesian government announced that it had launched an investigation to find out whether any NGO had utilised foreign funds for 'anti-government' human rights activities. In April 1992, NGOs in Bali were prohibited from receiving funds from foreign NGOs, allegedly to prevent them from becoming dependent on external funds, rather than for political reasons [*van Tuijl, 1993:3-4*].

Although the Indonesian government sought to defend its decision as a patriotic act, concern was expressed in the national press about the potential impact of the termination of Dutch NGO aid on the poor. International NGOs responded by writing to the World Bank and other members of the new aid consortium, expressing concern over the rupture of bilateral relations between the Netherlands and Indonesia, and appealed to the Indonesian government to lift the ban and to allow NGOs in the country to operate without restrictions.

To make up for the shortfall in funding created by the termination of financial support from Dutch NGOs, other international NGOs took their place as the principal funders and 'swapped' projects with Dutch NGOs, especially where they formed part of a donor coalition. Despite this initiative, a number of Indonesian NGOs experienced severe disruption as a result of the banning order, especially small local organisations implementing development projects in the more remote outer islands of the archipelago, which did not have ready access to alternative sources of funding. These arrangements, while providing financial continuity, remain vulnerable to further government legislation to restrict foreign funding, and NGOs are hampered in their work by the security services and bureaucratic strictures.

The Kenyan case also offers some insights about the difficulties and the opportunities that can be created for NGOs when donors suspend official aid and attempt to redirect it through NGO channels. While the donor decision to suspend further aid to Kenya in December 1991 created new opportunities for Kenyan NGOs, it came at a time when the Kenyan government was introducing more restrictive legislation to limit their room for manoeuvre and make it difficult for them to receive funds directly from foreign donors.

The need to establish greater control over NGOs had been mooted by President Moi in 1987 but it was not until late 1991 that an NGO Registration Act was finally approved by parliament, at a time when the aid donors were exerting pressure on the government to introduce fundamental economic and political reforms. One of the intentions behind the legislation was to discourage donors from redirecting aid from state-controlled projects to Kenyan NGOs, as a means of promoting reform and bypassing official channels. Denmark, for example, withheld one-fifth of its bilateral aid to Kenya in November 1990 as a gesture of solidarity with Norway, with whom Kenya had severed diplomatic ties following Norwegian criticism of the arrest of a political refugee [*ODI, 1992*]. With the suspension of US$ 8 million worth of bilateral aid, the Danish government announced that it would channel the funds through Kenyan NGOs and grassroots organisations. Similarly, other donors employed a dual strategy of diplomatic and aid pressure combined with higher levels of funding to NGOs, which increased the resources at their disposal, but also provoked the government into introducing legislation to restrict their activities.

One of the lessons from the Indonesian experience is that attempts to impose political conditions will not always be received passively by governments accused of human rights violations, especially if donors fail to act in concert because other interests are at stake. Both the Kenyan and the Indonesian examples suggest that efforts to channel increased funds through NGOs to compensate for reduced aid through official channels might be thwarted by restrictive legislation limiting foreign funding and the capacity of indigenous NGOs to engage in policy advocacy and human rights work. The next section examines the prospects for directing political aid through NGOs to promote democracy and good government which many donors favour while at the same time attaching political conditions to their aid programmes.

V. POLITICAL AID THROUGH NGOS

Although the process of political reform in developing countries has been uneven, it has created new opportunities for NGOs and increased their room for manoeuvre [*Edwards, 1993*]. Similarly the good governance agenda, with a focus on greater accountability, transparency and the rule of law, can potentially widen the scope for NGO involvement in public policy and enable them to operate in a less restrictive environment [*Robinson, 1993c*].

Official aid donors regard NGOs as having not only the potential to reach the very poorest through development interventions but also the capacity to enrich civil society by supporting a range of programmes aimed at empowering poor and disadvantaged groups in countries where they are deprived of basic freedoms. Donors have provided assistance, often through small mission funds, for human rights groups, legal aid centres, and projects which involve participatory planning, to advance the good government and human rights agenda.[2] Of course NGOs are not the only vehicle for political aid funds, some of which go directly to political parties (for example through the German political foundations and various US organisations) or for the training of jurists, lawyers and journalists [*Pinto-Duschinsky, 1991; OECD, 1992*].

This strategy is not new. In countries under military dictatorships NGOs acted as conduits for aid funds which contributed to the struggle for the restoration of civilian rule. Chile provides the best illustration of this, where donors provided substantial levels of funding for human rights projects, legal services and related activities for many years, with NGOs filling the void created by the absence of legalised political parties and open media [*Loveman, 1991*]. In 1989, foreign funding for Chilean NGOs engaged in pro-democracy activities amounted to an estimated US$ 50 million, although with the transition to democracy in 1990, the volume of external aid for NGOs has fallen dramatically.

Channelling political aid through NGOs was also the preferred option for many donors in South Africa during the apartheid period. For example, the British Overseas Development Administration funded NGOs and church-based organisations for much of the 1980s when it was not possible to channel funds through the government; in 1990/91 this amounted to £8 million. There are now moves underway to bring about a more co-ordinated donor funding strategy as the country progresses towards majority rule.

---

2. The Swedish International Development Agency (SIDA), for example, channels US$ 10 million annually to NGOs in support of these activities.

NGOs in Africa have responded to the democratic revival sweeping the continent by becoming involved in promotional activities designed to complement the work of pro-democracy movements but without aligning themselves with political parties. These include civic education campaigns and electoral monitoring. In Zimbabwe, Silveira House, one of the oldest NGOs in the country, has been designing and testing civic education programmes for some years. In addition to stimulating debate on the social and economic issues that surround development interventions, this includes providing education on the Constitution and the functioning of the modern state, highlighting rights and obligations and the meaning of citizenship, stimulating awareness of the channels that are available to people to influence policy decisions, strengthening grassroots leadership to maximise people's involvement in decision-making, informing people of the resources they have the right to expect from the state, and fostering critical awareness of the political, economic and social structures within which people live. This combines the empowerment approach long favoured by NGOs with a more concerted effort to educate people about their political rights and the functioning of a democratic system [Fowler, 1993].

With the transition to multi-party democracy taking place in many countries by means of free and competitive elections, some NGOs in Africa have become involved in election monitoring. Following President Moi's announcement in December 1991 that multi-party elections would be held the following year, the National Christian Council of Kenya (NCCK) and its Catholic counterpart established a separate body to organise election monitoring teams throughout the country. The NCCK also set out to educate the Kenyan public, and churchgoers in particular, about electoral procedures and the rights and obligations of citizens in a democratic political environment. It published reports and booklets on democracy issues and organised seminars across the country for church, community and political leaders to examine the issues raised by the transition to democracy [Archer, 1992:10].

Another level at which NGOs have been intervening in the democracy process is in promoting decentralisation, which several countries have been attempting in order to diffuse ethnic tensions and to strengthen local administration. NGOs have much to gain if the process of decentralisation is effective and offers channels for participating in local-level decision-making. NGOs in Mali have actively contributed to the decentralisation process in the country which is intended to promote greater regional autonomy. The Near East

Foundation (NEF) has gone about this in an innovatory way, by producing papers in local languages which carry educational articles on decentralisation and on the country's political system. It has assisted in the setting-up of a rural radio station in which a Malian human rights organisation contracted by NEF produces programmes comprising news stories, interviews and analyses to convey the essence of the decentralisation process to a largely illiterate population.[3] It has also organised a series of theatre shows in rural areas which address current topical concerns and are intended to stimulate debate among villagers [*Deme, 1993*].

These examples suggest that there is some potential for channelling political aid through NGOs for promoting political reform and more accountable government. But there are limits on the extent to which it might be feasible for donors to channel increased levels of resources through NGOs for this purpose. Civic education programmes and election monitoring are activities which are favoured by donors and northern NGOs alike, but relatively few NGOs in Africa currently possess the expertise and resources to run such programmes on a large scale. Donors should therefore take care to avoid overloading NGOs' capacities for absorbing increased levels of funding without compromising their efficiency or objectives. There is also the danger that the availability of external funding would stimulate the formation of new organisations which command little legitimacy within the wider community, and create conflicts between NGOs over the allocation of such funds, which could ultimately prove inimical to the goal of strengthening civil society. A related problem is that this type of assistance can muddy the distinction between NGOs and political parties, and distance NGOs from their developmental objectives.

Another constraint is that a number of developing country governments have imposed restrictions preventing NGOs from accepting funds for political purposes. In Egypt, for example, the government imposes strict limits on the activities which NGOs can legitimately engage in, and would be hostile to the prospect of aid being channelled through NGOs to promote human rights and greater pluralism. Some donors also place restrictions on the use to which co-financing can be put.[4] It would therefore be unrealistic for donors to

---

3. It is interesting to note in this context that local newspaper projects and radio programmes are recommended as worthy of donor support to assist in the strengthening of civil society in the 'project portfolio' put forward by Osborne [*1993*].
4. The British charity laws are probably unique in the limitations that they place on British NGOs to fund activities considered to be of an explicitly political nature unless these can be shown to complement development objectives. These laws conflict with the official policy of promoting good government and political reform through NGOs, and it remains unclear which activities would be considered acceptable.

expect NGOs to be able to absorb political funds on a vastly increased scale without being counter-productive. Mission funds and co-financing through northern NGOs are likely to be the preferred routes for such support since normal bilateral channels cannot be easily used for political aid if the recipient government objects and local NGOs lack power and influence.

VI. NGO PERSPECTIVES ON POLITICAL CONDITIONALITY

NGOs have adopted very different positions on political conditionality. Some NGOs object to the principle of using aid to promote political reform as an infringement on national sovereignty and accuse western donors of double standards. While accepting the premise of linking aid with good government and human rights, others disagree with the way that conditionality has been applied in practice, either because there has been a lack of co-ordination among donors, or because they are inconsistent in its application to different countries. This critique has sharpened of late as a result of closer collaboration between human rights agencies and development NGOs. Their response to the donor policy agenda takes two principal forms: advocating a more consistent application of universal principles derived from international law, and proposing alternative conceptions of conditionality.

Over the past two years most donors have devised a broad set of criteria on good governance, human rights and democratic development, which differ in emphasis rather than on substantive issues [*OECD, 1992*]. But despite agreement on the basic tenets, the application of political conditionality in practice demonstrates that donors have different motives governing decisions to reduce or terminate aid to particular countries, which include trade and investment considerations, foreign policy objectives, the geo-political and strategic importance of recipient countries, as well as the nature of their political system and human rights record. This has produced a range of responses from individual donors, several of whom have taken action on a bilateral basis, either in response to a single gross and well-publicised abuse of human rights, or because of a combination of factors over time.

Inconsistency in the application of conditionality and a lack of clarity and transparency in decisions to suspend or terminate aid has led many NGOs and rights agencies to question donor sincerity and to argue for a more consistent approach to political conditionality derived from the principles and standards contained in international human rights law. It is argued that the principles of universality, indivisibility and reciprocity provide an objective basis for donor policy on human rights as opposed to the selective and subjective approach that currently underpins donor thinking on human rights criteria. There are widely accepted legal conventions on human rights which are laid down by the UN but applied indiscriminately; NGOs and human rights agencies argue for the need to look at means of enforcing these standards consistently without discrimination [*Dias, 1993*].

Using human rights as the standard for applying aid conditionality has a number of advantages. Compared to democracy and government accountability it can be monitored relatively easily. Donors already possess considerable experience of incorporating human rights criteria into aid allocation decisions [*Hill, 1991; Tomasevski, 1989*]. But there are problems of enforcement and deciding on appropriate thresholds for punitive action. In other words, should donors employ aid conditionality when there is a single gross violation of human rights or should this only be contemplated when there are systematic infringements? It is proposed by northern NGOs that aid donors should listen to the views of indigenous NGOs and human rights agencies involved in monitoring the situation in their own countries that will be alert to the potentially disadvantageous impact of aid conditionality on the poor. At present this type of consultation does not generally take place and donors are making decisions based on diplomatic considerations and the views of their staff in overseas missions without recourse to widely accepted human rights standards and clear criteria for applying conditionality.

Besides arguing for universal human rights standards as the starting point for political conditionality, NGOs and human rights agencies have also attempted to bring economic, social and cultural rights into the donor policy agenda, with some success, as the outcome of the Vienna conference would appear to indicate. Where donors have sought to define a clearer link between aid and human rights this has tended to centre on civil and political rights to the exclusion of other rights which have legal recognition in the Universal Declaration of Human Rights, but more particularly in the International Covenant on Economic, Social and Cultural Rights. The Covenant details the rights and freedoms proclaimed in the Universal Declaration and the obligation of states to ensure their realisation but, recognising that the achievement of these rights is conditional on their level of development, it only requires states to achieve progressively the full

371

realisation of economic, social and cultural rights to the maximum of their available resources [*UN, 1988*].

NGOs and human rights agencies are intimately concerned with such socio-economic rights as the right to employment and the right to food and shelter, since these are fundamental to the living conditions and development prospects of the poor. Moreover, there is concern that the suspension or termination of aid by donors in response to a country's infringement of civil and political rights may inadvertently lead to a violation of people's social and economic rights if resources for development programmes and public services are reduced as a result.

Although NGOs and human rights agencies are keen to press for greater attention to socio-economic rights in aid-policy circles, there is recognition that the enforcement mechanisms are not binding and that many Third World states do not have the resources to enable them to achieve the realisation of these rights. Despite these difficulties, the concept of 'people's conditionality' has been put forward in some quarters, both to capture the socio-economic dimension of human rights at a policy level, but also as a means of incorporating aid conditions into development projects and programmes at the micro-level from the perspective of those adversely affected by such interventions. First proposed by NGOs attending TOES (The Other Economic Summit) in Houston in 1990, the notion of 'people's conditionality' applies to people displaced by development projects, deprived of their subsistence base, and disadvantaged by environmental degradation. The idea would be to introduce conditions at the planning stage with a view to protecting certain rights (for example, the right to an anti-discriminatory employment policy), or to ensure that people are not adversely affected during the course of project implementation and that their rights will be guaranteed if the project entails displacement and loss of assets [*Dias, 1993*].

While this concept extends current understanding of conditionality and its potential application at the micro-level, it is less clear how it would apply at the policy level. However, it does raise the question of how people who are affected by aid conditions can exert influence over donor policy, both from the point of view of NGOs drawing attention to the negative effects of conditioned aid on people's welfare, but also in granting legitimacy to donor actions; political conditionality will be all the more effective if it has the support of those affected by aid suspension or termination.

More acceptable to donors, and complementary to the notion of micro-level conditionality, is the proposal that aid provision should be linked to the level of government spending on social services and on projects and programmes for the benefit of the poor. In other words, governments which place the interests of the poor at the forefront of their national development strategy should be rewarded with increased aid and those which fail to do so should be penalised. This ties in with the consistent demand from many northern NGOs that aid should be poverty-focused and designed to benefit the poor in the first instance, and forms a natural extension to their lobbying activities in this area.

Finally, northern NGOs have their own conditions which they adhere to in making decisions about which projects to fund. It has been argued that the way these are drawn up and implemented could have lessons for official aid agencies [Archer, 1993:15-17]. Most northern NGOs have devised guidelines for applicants which detail the types of projects that they are prepared to fund. If these guidelines are not adhered to then the funding is terminated. However, NGOs would claim that their decisions are governed by the principles of reciprocity and transparency where obligations are binding on both funders and recipients, and established through open negotiation and the adoption of agreed procedures. In the official aid context, reciprocity would imply that official donors should not impose conditions which are not adhered to in their own countries, to avoid imposing double standards and making unrealistic demands. As Archer [1993:11] has argued, 'Donors should set standards of performance for themselves that are at least as rigorous as those they expect recipient governments to achieve'.

VII. A ROLE FOR NGOS?

Donors believe that southern NGOs can contribute to policy on political conditionality in several ways: as providers of information on the human rights situation in a particular country, channelling humanitarian aid where aid to the government has been cut off, and as implementors of projects which aim to contribute to good government and political reform [Dias, 1993:9].

NGOs and human rights agencies have endorsed various components of the new donor policy agenda with its emphasis on democratisation and improving government accountability, but have not been consulted very much during the formulation of policy on political conditionality. They also perceive themselves to have a broader role than the one ascribed to them by donors. Hence NGOs have sought to adopt a more up-front position rather than simply accommodating themselves to donor agendas, principally by having greater involvement in the formulation and implementation of donor policies on aid conditionality, and by helping to produce universal criteria to govern aid policy decisions on conditionality. This has three components.

First, NGOs and human rights agencies are keen to ensure that political conditionality is premised on universal standards of human rights as laid down in international conventions, and that these are applied objectively rather than on the basis of narrow political reasons. They have sought to lobby individual donors on policies towards particular countries and to be consulted on a regular basis, which does happen in some cases.[5]

Second, human rights agencies possess considerable expertise on the technical aspects of international human rights law and the instruments that might be employed in refining donor policy on conditionality, although this again requires a willingness on the part of donor agencies to bring them into the decision-making process.

Third, many NGOs and human rights agencies would like to have a more systematic monitoring role which is not simply restricted to documenting human rights abuses and sharing these with donors. In view of the potentially adverse impact that political conditionality can have on their clients' well-being and their own operations, NGOs would also wish to monitor the unintended consequences of suspending or terminating aid and advise donors on appropriate responses and policy modifications. Southern NGOs can act as a sounding-board for domestic interest groups and membership organisations and alert donors to their views on the desirability of withholding aid to promote political reform and improved respect for human rights. This would not only add legitimacy to donor actions but also inject greater caution if political conditionality was thought to be ill-advised or lacked internal support.

VIII. CONCLUSION

It should be apparent that NGOs and human rights agencies could have greater input into donor thinking about political conditionality

---

5. In Britain, for example, the Minister for Overseas Development convened several meetings with NGOs and human rights agencies to discuss how the government might develop a more coherent human rights agenda. This led to the formation of an unofficial grouping called the Human Rights and Development Forum which is seeking to carry forward the process of policy dialogue.

than is the case at present. The potential for them to do so rests on the willingness of individual donors to allow them to have a more systematic involvement in policy formulation and implementation, and in policy dialogue with aid recipients. This will require a combination of lobbying and advocacy efforts to ensure their voices are heard. But NGOs and human rights agencies will have to prove that they have a positive contribution to make. The challenge lies in combining NGOs' knowledge of grassroots reality in developing countries with the legal expertise and monitoring capacity of human rights agencies. Until recently there was little information-sharing or collaboration between these sets of organisations. But the new policy agenda has created the space for a more effective exchange of ideas and combination of talents than existed before, which brings with it the possibility for fruitful engagement.

REFERENCES

Archer, R., 1992, 'Democracy in Africa: Democracy and Development in Kenya and Zaire', unpublished mimeo, London: Christian Aid.

Archer, R., 1993, 'Conditionality: Aid, Penalties and Incentives', unpublished mimeo, London: Christian Aid.

Bailey, J., M. Buchanan-Smith and S. Maxwell, 1990, 'Famine in Sudan: The Proceedings of a One Day Symposium', *Discussion Paper 283*, Brighton: Institute of Development Studies.

Deme, Y.,1993, 'Les ONG et le Mouvement Démocratique en Afrique Occidentale', case study presented at the INTRAC Workshop 'Governance, Democracy and Conditionality: What Role for NGOs?', Amersfoort, June.

Dias, C.J., 1993, 'Governance, Democracy and Conditionality: NGO Positions and Roles', paper presented at the INTRAC Workshop 'Governance, Democracy and Conditionality: What Role for NGOs?', Amersfoort, June.

Edwards, M., 1993, 'International NGOs and Southern Governments in the "New World Order": Lessons of Experience at the Programme Level', paper presented at the INTRAC Workshop 'Governance, Democracy and Conditionality: What Role for NGOs?', Amersfoort, June.

Fowler, A., 1993, 'Non-Governmental Organisations as Agents of Development: An African Perspective', *Journal of International Development*, 5(3).

Hill, D., 1991, *Development Assistance and Human Rights: Principles, Criteria and Procedures*, London: Commonwealth Secretariat.

Loveman, B. 1991, 'NGOs and the Transition to Democracy in Chile', *Grassroots Development*, 15(2).

ODI, 1992, 'Aid and Political Reform', *Briefing Paper*, London: Overseas Development Institute.

OECD, 1992, *Review of the Survey of DAC Members' Policies and Practices in Participatory Development/Good Governance*, OECD: Paris.

Osborne, D., 1993, 'Action for Better Government: A Role for Donors', *IDS Bulletin*, 21(1).

Pinto-Duschinsky, M., 1991, 'Foreign Political Aid: the German Political Foundations and their US Counterparts', *International Affairs*, 67(1).

Robinson, M., 1993a, 'Aid, Democracy and Political Conditionality in sub-Saharan

Africa', *European Journal of Development Research*, 5(1).

Robinson, M., 1993b, 'Will Political Conditionality Work?', *IDS Bulletin*, 24(1).

Robinson, M., 1993c, 'Governance, Democracy and Conditionality: NGOs and the New Policy Agenda', paper presented at the INTRAC Workshop 'Governance, Democracy and Conditionality: What Role for NGOs?', Amersfoort, June.

Tomasevski, K., 1989, *Development Aid and Human Rights*, Pinter: London.

United Nations, 1988, *Human Rights: A Compilation of International Instruments*, UN: New York.

van Tuijl, P., 1993, 'Conditionality for Whom? Indonesia and the Dissolution of the IGGI: the NGO Experience', case study presented at the INTRAC Workshop 'Governance, Democracy and Conditionality: What Role for NGOs?', Amersfoort, June.

14

State Formation Processes under External Supervision: Reflections on 'Good Governance'

MARTIN DOORNBOS

I. INTRODUCTION

State formation as a phrase already covers a number of concepts, but it appears pertinent now to add a further one to the amalgam: state formation under supervision, or, more precisely, state formation as a process evolving under external supervision and direction. The idea that this concerns something novel may seem surprising at first. External involvement with the processes of state formation, particularly in the Third World, has been present for a long time, usually from the very inception of the decolonised states concerned and thus virtually by definition. However, categorisation as a distinct variant of state formation appears justified, given the extent to which various forms of external, that is, international preoccupation with the *internal* policy frameworks and the structuring of political processes in formally independent Third World countries have come to be concentrated and made concrete in recent years. These tendencies imply a crystallisation of an increasingly explicit tutelage relation *vis-à-vis* the countries concerned.

Discussion of these issues has developed largely around the recently rediscovered, though by no means unequivocal, concept of 'governance' and the adoption of political 'conditionalities' by the global organisations and the major donor governments. This chapter aims at a preliminary reconnaissance of the emerging field: it looks at the effect of recent modes of external intervention in Third World

Note of acknowledgement. The author would like to thank Mark Robinson for his useful comments on a previous draft. An earlier Dutch version of this paper appeared in *Antropologische Verkenningen*, Vol. 12, No. 4, 1993.

countries in relation to their structuring of policy processes and public administrative frameworks. Subsequent discussion considers the concept of 'good governance' in a wider perspective. As a background, there is a brief review of some current concepts of state formation.

II. CONCEPTS OF STATE FORMATION

Concepts of state formation have already comprised a wide range of meanings. In the first instance, state formation must refer to the processes through which the first ever state structures were shaped, and to the factors which appeared to have an impact on them. This area of interest has already produced a rich and still growing literature (including Claessen and Skalnik (eds.), [1976], and subsequent works by participants in related early state networks). The debate as to the original stimulus for the earliest processes of state formation continues, and has not only intrinsic historical but also contemporary relevance: what prompted or prompts the initial steps towards state formation, that is, towards the creation of a body politic with a distinctive identity; and what caused or causes some of these to develop staying power? Does the genesis lie with power-holders and power structures which create their own political domain, or does it originate rather with particular social and economic transformations which generate new modes of control and political structures? When considering recent state formation processes focused on and instigated by the European Community, for example, one encounters aspects and questions not fundamentally different from those raised in discussions on the origins of the earliest state forms. By the same token this is also true for various other contemporary and historical examples.

Contemporary examples, nonetheless, imply concepts of state formation which differ at least in one regard from those which refer to the earliest processes: once the idea of 'state' has emerged, its independent development is conceivable in some other locations, but otherwise its evolution is likely to be largely a matter of replication and elaboration of existing models or of posing alternatives to these [Doornbos, 1986]. Generally, therefore, state formation processes almost by definition will also entail processes of incorporation and/or dismantling of pre-existing state forms which are superseded by new dominant structures. European as well as African and Asian history, colonial and pre-colonial, contains numerous illustrations of such patterns. In some cases this implies the establishment of new structures representing a direct, 'revolutionary' rupture with preceding forms, whereas other instances retain a certain degree of institutional continuity. The latter might obtain wherever – at least *vis-à-vis* the outside world – a facade of inherited formal structures is presented, but also where existing, culturally rooted patterns of social relations manifest themselves within changed institutional contexts, thus partly determining the content and sub-culture of the new state.

'State formation' based on replication thus refers to the formative processes of national states within Europe and subsequently beyond, and to the establishment of post-colonial states in the Third World as territorial political entities. However, the term 'state formation' can refer more specifically to the creation, development and differentiation of state structures and institutions; to the crystallisation and articulation of the role of the state and to corresponding manifestations of state power. It indicates also processes of incorporation of various social and political groupings and organisational networks within the overall state structure. In the latter sense 'state formation' must refer, among other things, to the dynamic aspects in the (changing) relations between state and society [*Doornbos, 1990*]. Thus, in certain historical contexts the state emerges as a force overarching all other ranks and subdivisions, whereas in others one witnesses a loss or shedding of state functions and responsibilities. The latter may result from fiscal crises or efforts to delineate more sharply the role of the state apparatus, in line with current persuasion. As a multifarious and dynamic concept, state formation thus also comprises historical and contemporary instances of state *re*formation and *de*formation.

III. EXTERNAL INVOLVEMENTS

In general terms, state formation refers to the processes through which state structures are being generated and regenerated. The effect is the transformation or relative degeneration of institutions which at an earlier stage were dominant or functional. In principle this concerns autonomous processes, neither hindered nor aided by external factors, and protected under the principle of sovereignty. During the past few years, however, externally-led direction has become increasingly important in determining the manner of adjustment, orientation and organisation of political structures, notably with respect to Third World states and particularly within the African context. This is not to suggest that there are no previous examples of external political pressures demanding a particular policy position. The relations between the United States and Latin America over almost two centuries constitute a continuing chronicle illustrating this practice. Also, from the very beginnings of the phenomenon of development aid, it has been recognised that aid without strings attached is illusory. Aid-receiving countries have been expected to display loyal behaviour in the international arena: with respect to voting patterns within the UN system, the granting of military facilities, or by safeguarding a receptive climate for foreign trade and investment. Moreover, setting 'conditionalities' of appropriate economic management before new loan applications are discharged has been common for some time. With the impostition of the IMF and World Bank structural adjustment programmes, these kinds of conditions have become very detailed and severe. But the posing of demands on theoretically sovereign states regarding the manner in which they should organise their administrative structures, policy-implementation procedures, and indeed their political systems, evidently goes a step further and touches on 'delicate issues', to use the phrase employed by World Bank President Connable when introducing the new Bank policy in this area at the World Bank Annual Conference on Development Economics, 1991.

Political conditionalities, therefore, are by no means a novelty: but conditionalities to politics, particularly in regard to the manner of structuring the political and administrative framework, certainly are. Over the past five to ten years, but especially since 1989, the international donor community, led by the major international organisations, has begun to set increasingly specified conditions with respect to the formation of institutional structures of 'client' states. This is motivated, among other things, by the conviction that African states and their economies in particular have been suffering from 'overdeveloped' and inefficient state structures – a viewpoint, incidentally, previously advanced by critical researchers [Doornbos, 1990]. But it also reflects the belief that 'liberalising' the market requires 'liberalising' the state.

The complex mixture of externally-led initiatives towards restructuring government machinery and introducing political reform which is directed at Third World countries has meanwhile crystallised into a formidable package of policy prescriptions. Together they account for a significant impact on, and a new phase in, the state formation processes of the countries concerned, even if they are often less than effective or have distorting or contradictory effects. But processes thus put 'under supervision' bear a qualitative difference from most historical examples of state formation, partial exceptions being the process of decolonisation in a number of cases and the organisation of regimes previously converted to the Soviet model, adopting the latter's party and state structures. In this sense, therefore, it appears justified to consider this type of process as a novel variant of 'state formation', leaving aside any merits one might wish to attach to it.

The policy packages concerned generally rest on a twofold strategy. On the one hand there is a supply side with a notably varied assortment of what might be termed 'political development aid'. This includes a range of positive measures designed to increase the effectiveness and efficiency of selected government bodies, although usually in trimmed-down form: support for judiciaries and media, training programmes for legislators and key government officers, logistic assistance for elections, and so on. Concrete examples are legion, but in this connection the World Bank's African Capacity Building Initiative, itself a whole package of measures, may be mentioned specially [World Bank, 1990]. On the other hand the strategy increasingly rests on the imposition of punitive 'conditionalities' of political or institutional reform which must be fulfilled in order to continue to qualify for financial assistance or economic co-operation. Thus for various Western governments the adoption of a 'pluriform' political framework has become one key conditionality for continued development co-operation, especially since the end of the East-West rivalry and the attendant possibility of alternative sources of support for the countries concerned.

A donor perspective on these matters was formulated in a World Bank staff paper in the following terms:

> Since poor countries generally have fragile polities and weak systems of accountability, with few autonomous institutions and little countervailing power to that exercised by the government at the centre, external agencies are potentially key political players capable of exerting considerable influence in promoting good or bad governance. In raising the shortcomings of a country's governance, external agencies are calling into question its government's performance. Clearly, this goes further than a critique of a particular programme or project (generally regarded as a legitimate concern of a financing agency), to touch on the ability of a regime to govern effectively in the interest of its citizenry [Landell-Mills and Serageldin, 1991: 13].

In the light of this perspective, conditions are being posed by the major international organisations and the main donor governments which, if implemented, should together produce different, more flexible and open, and more efficient state organisations. Among other things, they encourage a reduction on administrative structures, the privatisation of government services and the use of non-governmental organisations in aid operations. Also advocated is the establishment of autonomous, 'non-bureaucratic' organisations with wide jurisdiction over particular policy areas; and the engagement in 'policy dialogue' with donor representatives about the way policy is given shape in particular sectors. The term 'co-governance', pointing explicitly to a sharing of authority over specific project or policy matters, epitomises some of the new thinking on these issues. There is increasingly detailed specification of external instruments of evaluation and of instructions with respect to the formulation and elaboration of national budget chapters and policy priorities. Wide-ranging and substantial decentralisation of government functions is encouraged, paralleled in several countries by the promotion of donor interests to concentrate their aid efforts in particular 'adopted' districts or regions. There is a general promotion of measures to make government bodies more accessible, while also ensuring their effective accountability; and finally, multi-party systems are introduced in order to promote effective mechanisms of political accountability and control.

The emphasis placed by donors on the adoption of this package of measures, in full or in part, is motivated by various factors. These include: dissatisfaction with the role of governments in Third World countries generally; concern about the lack of institutional capacity for absorption of donor-initiated development programmes; the wish to induce the growth of recipient government structures to assist the implementation of complex development programmes; the desire to enhance general efficiency and effectiveness in the public sector; the determination – strongly increased since the termination of East-West rivalry – to reduce the influence of political factors, often considered arbitrary and in the last instance held responsible for failing government interventions, modifying their effect particularly in the area of public policy; and, more generally, interest in the initiation of political reforms which might break the continued hegemonic control by particular political strata or coalitions.

Within this general package of instruments and conditionalities for political reform, the demands with respect to the adoption of multi-party systems and democratisation have attracted particularly widespread attention. It is beyond the scope of this chapter to deal with the complex relation between political conditionalities and democratisation. It should be noted, though, that a positive correlation between these has not as yet been demonstrated [*Healey and Robinson, 1992; Sørensen, 1993*], and that there are very substantial differences with respect to the expectations and objectives between external actors and a whole range of different democratisation movements [*Rudebeck, 1992*]. The external interest generally appears to offer little or no support for democratisation movements 'from below' and in principle keeps itself focused on one particular, that is, liberal model, with the single assumption and criterion that a multi-party system holds the key to democratisation. Promotion of this model may be viewed as a way of complementing the structural adjustment programmes, in which the 'rolling back' of the state and the creation of open markets are central objectives. The ideological element is thus added to the economic vision of a liberal capitalist society. With a reduced role of the state the actual role of political parties may be expected to be a limited one, however; while at the same time there is likely to be considerable scope for external influence and direction over various branches of the state machinery.

IV. 'GOOD GOVERNANCE'

Discussion of these issues, in particular the question of democratisation as a conditionality, has evolved rapidly in recent years, closely following changes in policy and practice [*Anyang'Nyong'o, 1992; Barya, 1992; Healey and Robinson, 1992; Moore, 1993; ROAPE 1990, 1992; Sørensen, 1993*]. There are key questions in this connection as to the propriety of externally imposed political norms and the likely effectiveness of the conditionalities concerned. The discussion has been conducted increasingly with reference to the recently rediscovered concept of 'governance', which points to qualities comprising more than just proper administration and organisation (though certainly including these). Edgardo Boeninger, the Chilean minister responsible for political reform, formulated the concept in these terms:

A concept that has recently attracted attention is the role played by 'governance'... (H)ere we refer to governance as, first, identifying economic and social objectives, and second, charting a course designed to move society in that direction. Governance can then be defined as the good government of society. Good government guides the country along a course leading to the desired goal, in this case, development [*Boeninger, 1991: 1*].

'Governance', originally a legalistic concept, thus in principle acquires a political dimension, broadly oriented towards the way the political system is organised and how it is handled. Precise conceptual delineations are more difficult to formulate. Landell-Mills and Serageldin observe in this connection:

> 'Governance' is not a word that has been used extensively in the past by political scientists, but its recent appearance in popular usage has not been very rigorous. It has become in many ways both an all-embracing and a vague concept... In essence, therefore, governance may be taken as denoting how people are ruled, and how the affairs of a state are administered and regulated. It refers to a nation's system of politics and how this functions in relation to public administration and law. Thus, the concept of 'governance' goes beyond that of 'government' to include a political dimension [*Landell-Mills and Serageldin, 1991*].

It is striking how rapidly this term in recent years has been assimilated as a household word in development parlance and beyond. Its popularity in donor circles is probably best explained by its focus which implicitly places the onus for many failing development policies and projects on bad recipient-country management. It is notable that over the past few years discussions on 'governance' have focused partly on the question of what exactly the concept would or would not comprise. This is indicative, perhaps, of a rather unscientific procedure, while at the same time it demonstrates an apparent need for a conceptual category to accommodate an acute donor concern. Resolution of the question as to what should or should not be understood by 'governance' is not attempted here. The question itself, perhaps, is not particularly interesting. More relevant is the coincidence that against a backdrop of lack of clarity as to the concept's content – in particular the extent to which it should be considered 'political' – organisations such as the World Bank began a few years ago to determine their position regarding the formal adoption of criteria of 'good governance' – and if so, which criteria – in their package of conditionalities and directives. This coincidence may have had its 'useful' instrumental aspects for the organisations concerned: while there is conceptual ambiguity it may be a little easier in this controversial area to test one's way as to how far any package of conditionalities should go. Evidently the search has been for a conceptual demarcation which would ensure some influence over the entire sphere of development politics, policy-making and implementation, thus accommodating the political concerns and demands of donors, and making it possible to call for various concrete policy measures on the part of recipient governments. The decision ultimately adopted by the World Bank was to opt for a concept of 'governance' oriented towards 'depoliticised' management and accountability in terms of its own programmes whilst claiming a strategic convening role for itself in communicating the political concerns of lending countries to recipients, and moreover making continuation of its own aid programmes subject to observance of other donors' political preoccupations [*Gibbon, 1993: 55-6*].

The World Bank has adopted an increasingly prominent role in setting standards in these matters *vis-à-vis* various Western donors, while the latter have sometimes sought to articulate, however faintly, a position of their own within more limited margins [*Payne, 1992/93; Gibbon, 1993: 35-6*]. This tendency is related to the near impossibility for individual donors of indicating precise criteria for political reform whose observance will ensure particular envisaged effects. However, it has been observed, and apparently with some justification, that while 'the bilateral donors at present often refer to the World Bank's statements on good governance, this is probably more a case of hiding in the skirts of an international institution than a demonstration of the impact, or quality, of the Bank's ideas' [*Uvin, 1993: 67*].

For a proper understanding of the phenomenon of state formation under supervision and the related discussion about 'good governance', it should be observed that whereas this evidently touches on the problem of external involvement in the implementation of government policy, this is not necessarily the same. The numerous French administrators engaged in the bureaucracies of West African states, for example, might, at least in theory, execute policy that had been fully determined by the governments concerned. Their involvement in the execution and even in the *preparation* of policy need not affect the state structures or the direction of state formation processes. A similar qualification applies to dependency relations. Externally-directed state formation is derived from dependency relationships, and not conceivable without them. However, not every economic or even political dependency relation will lead inevitably to state formation under supervision. Examples abound of regimes which for many years faced no difficulty in qualifying for loans or other assistance simply by means of adopting a 'loyal' posture, especially during the Cold War. Their policy and political frameworks were never questioned in the process.

Space does not permit discussion of the extent of recipient governments' compliance with political conditionalities, and of donors' problems and dilemmas in enforcing them. Suffice it to note that the record so far is rather a mixed one, especially in terms of the demands for the adoption of multi-party systems. Finally it should be observed that the primary concern here is not a normative assessment of the relationships underlying this specific variant of state formation processes; it is an attempt to identify the phenomenon as such and to place it in a broader context.

V. CONDITIONALITIES AND POLITICAL CONTEXTS

For all the heightened concern with the promotion of 'good governance' in Third World countries, it is quite conceivable that one effect of the various external initiatives and involvements in this regard is, paradoxically, to reduce rather than strengthen Third World governments' capacity for policy-making and implementation. At the micro-level the externally-induced creation of autonomous institutions for improved management may undermine local government capacity. Diversion of aid flows via NGOs may similarly weaken the government departments charged with responsibility for the areas concerned. Demands for compliance with contradictory instructions from different donors may result in confusion and distortions in addition to overburdening qualified manpower which is in short supply. Above all, it is in the essence of conditionalities that the setting and assessment of standards of proper policy-management is shifted to various donor headquarters across the globe. Moreover, donor co-ordination increasingly sets the limits and targets for national policy-making, leaving the governments concerned with limited space for autonomous action. The price of enhancing external accountability may thus be the progressive erosion of policy-making capacity. Notwithstanding the powerful thrust of these new strategies, however, Yusuf Bangura aptly observes that :

> Neo-liberalism has no theory of the state or of state formation and offers limited clues by way of policy on how to respond to the problems of de-institutionalisation and the erosion of local level expertise. State systems have tended to further diminish in quality and reach in most countries where free market reforms have been attempted. Economic reforms cannot be effective in situations where the state is incapable of carrying out its primary roles of regulation, mediation and social protection [*Bangura, 1994: 298*].

From a broader epistemological perspective too the formulation of criteria of 'good governance' as 'conditionality' raises questions and issues of wider political implication. The strategy rests on the assumption that it is possible in principle to search for universally valid criteria of proper management and policy-making: 'good governance is good governance', no matter where or by whom (or for whom). This presumption, however, touches upon increasingly controversial issues within organisation theory, social philosophy, cultural history and other disciplines. Here, there is growing recognition that Western rationality-based premises of the phenomenon of modern bureaucracy, and even the Western model of liberal democracy [*Parekh, 1992*], represent discontinuity with other cultural traditions. Thus the question that asserts itself is whether it is possible to conceive of general standards of 'good governance' that would be acceptable to both external and internal political actors. This must be addressed, irrespective of the further question as to whether or to what extent the imposed nature of the instruments concerned is acceptable to recipient countries.

External re-emphasis of 'universal' conditions and structures for policy management and political organisation is bound to have a certain effect in concrete situations, although it is difficult to predict the precise nature of its impact on the complex network of political or organisational processes. It is equally conceivable, for example, that it will accentuate existing social tensions and conflicts, at least in the short run, as that it will assist their resolution. Whether there will be any positive effects in the longer run remains a very open question. As to the specificity of the contexts concerned, questions concerning their characteristics hardly figure in the formulation of conditions for 'good governance' – except as an assumption that they carry shortcomings to be overcome. At any rate, it must be expected that the total structure of externally-initiated policy measures will generate its own momentum on processes of political and administrative development, although analysis of its overall impact is likely to remain indeterminate.

This question can be approached from two other perspectives. The first of these is based on the fact that in many Third World situations, there is intensive and continuous exploration of new modes of structuring relations between state and society, and of different ways to give them significance. Such processes are usually problematic and difficult but, above all, require space and occasionally some cautious support. It remains most uncertain whether the introduction of external models for 'universal' good government as conditionalities is helpful in such situations.

The specific role and position of the state structure within or *vis-à-vis* civil society varies significantly according to societal and cultural context and it is only natural that in varying contexts there will be vast differences in the way these relationships are structured or restructured. In the words of Denis-Constant Martin:

> (T)here is no standard formula for fostering an acceptable level of state management and good governance; the road to such a destination is mapped out by cultural factors that vary considerably from place to place and are in no way unalterable; on the contrary, they keep changing under the pressure of both internal and external dynamics, which makes it all the more difficult to define them [*Martin, 1991: 15*].

The current package of policy prescriptions for 'good governance' appears to ignore these basic problems and fails to offer any answer to them. Again, this is why it is quite conceivable that externally devised and *a priori* standard models for organising government structures, which by their nature cannot take into account specific state-society relations, may have a negative rather than a positive effect. 'All things considered, it is most unlikely that good governance can be introduced from outside' [*Martin, 1991: 20*].

The second perspective is from that of external concern with the promotion of transparent organisation and management. 'Good governance' is often considered as a way of providing an 'enabling environment' for 'development' (development in this context almost certainly means the totality of donor-led development programmes). By implication, the basic responsibility for the lack of a favourable 'enabling environment' is placed with the governments of the developing countries concerned, ignoring the co-responsibility which international donor organisations carry. The inverse argument is kept entirely outside the scope of debate: namely, to what extent does a global 'enabling environment' support 'good governance' and what conditions should receive priority attention in this context? This is the kind of question which has been raised in the report of the South Commission [*1990*], in the manifesto of the Stockholm Initiative on Global Security and Governance, *Common Responsibilities in the 1990s*, in the UNDP *Human Development Report 1992*, and elsewhere. Again, it underscores how much the elaboration of the concept of 'good governance', and by implication the premises and direction of state formation processes, must be subjected to continuous critical assessment.

VI. CONCLUSION

Discussion and practice of external involvement with the development of 'good governance' undoubtably will continue to draw a good deal of attention in the next several years. Key questions are likely to focus on the development of specific norms of 'good' and 'bad' political management, and the formulation and application of sanctions which should be attached to such norms. Debate will continue on the tension between externally initiated, 'universal' standards on the one hand and the specificity of the role and position of the state structure and the cultural variations inherent in different contexts on the other. In the final analysis, the question which connects these different issues is: who determines the direction of future state formation processes in the countries concerned? The outcome will be determined largely through contests taking place in the 'field', on the basis of innumerable initiatives for new norms and adjustments that are being posed every day. But, while the final outcome still appears indeterminate, a further related question is looming: namely, whether an entirely new assessment of the ensemble of concepts of state formation will need to be debated in due course.

The growth of new institutional and political global relations and the establishment of new norms for the reorientation of state structures by dominant global centres may be viewed as a process of 'state' formation on a global scale. Pre-existing, formally autonomous state structures could be seen as being incorporated within an emerging global network of institutional and power relations. A trend towards globalisation, with increasing emphasis on the introduction of standard institutional norms and structures derived from Western models, seems unmistakable. However, this trend should perhaps be viewed more as an affirmation of new global power relations than as an effort to create more genuine global unification, or the establishment of a new political world order. In itself it implies neither cultural homogenisation nor democratisation at the level of global institutions, however desirable the latter may be [Held, 1992]. In many respects the trend instead goes together with increased tension and diversity. The growing gap between rich and poor on a world scale is one important dimension of this. To what extent and through what means globalisation will come about, therefore, will be determined largely by the outcome of the dynamic processes of confrontation between the power and logic of specific politico-cultural patterns on the one hand and the universalising demands of globally integrative structures on the other.

REFERENCES

Anyang'Nyong'o, Peter, 1992, 'Discourses on Democracy in Africa', CODESRIA Seventh General Assembly on Democratization Processes in Africa: Problems and Prospects, Dakar.

Bangura, Yusuf, 1994, 'Intellectuals, Economic Reform and Social Change: Constraints and Opportunities in the Formation of a Nigerian Technocracy', *Development and Change*, Vol. 25, No. 2.

Barya, John-Jean B., 1992, 'The New Political Conditionalities of Aid: An Independent View from Africa', paper presented at EADI Symposium, Vienna (April).

Boeninger, Edgardo, 1991, 'Governance and Development: Issues, Challenges, Opportunities and Constraints', World Bank Annual Conference on Development Economics paper, Washington DC.

Claessen, Henry J.M. and Peter Skalnik, eds., 1976, *The Early State*, The Hague: Mouton.

Doornbos, Martin, 1986,' "Big Man" and his Big Brother: Some Notes on Incorporation' in M.A. van Bakel, R.R. Hagesteijn and P. van der Velde (eds.), *Private Politics: A Multidisciplinary Approach to "Big Man" Systems*, Leiden: Brill.

Doornbos, Martin, 1990,'The African State in Academic Debate: Retrospect and Prospect', *Journal of Modern African Studies*, Vol. 28:2.

Gibbon, Peter, 1993, 'The World Bank and the New Politics of Aid', in Georg Sørensen, ed., *Political Conditionality*, London: Frank Cass.

Healey, J. and M. Robinson, 1992, *Democracy, Governance and Economic Policy: Sub-Saharan Africa in Comparative Perspective*, ODI Development Policy Studies.

Held, David, 1992, 'Democracy: From City-states to a Cosmopolitan Order?', *Political Studies*, Vol. XL.

Landell-Mills, Pierre and Ismail Serageldin, 1991, 'Governance and the External Factor', World Bank Annual Conference on Development Economics paper, Washington DC.

Martin, Denis-Constant, 1991, 'The Cultural Dimension of Governance', World Bank Annual Conference on Development Economics paper, Washington DC.

Mkandawire, Thandika, 1992, 'Adjustment, Political Conditionality and Democratization in Africa', CODESRIA Seventh General Assembly on Democratization Processes in Africa: Problems and Prospects, Dakar.

Moore, Mick, ed., 1993, 'Good Government?', *IDS Bulletin*, Vol.24, No. 1.

Overseas Development Institute, 1992, 'Aid and Political Reform', briefing paper (Jan.).

Parekh, Bikhu, 1992, 'The Cultural Particularity of Liberal Democracy', *Political Studies*, Vol. XL.

Payne, Julian H., 1992, 'Economic Assistance to Support Democratization in Developing Countries: A Canadian Perspective', *Development* (1992/93).

Review of African Political Economy,
    1990, Special Issue on 'Democracy and Development', No. 49.
    1992, Special Issue on 'Democracy, Civil Society and NGOs', No. 55.

Rudebeck, Lars, ed., 1992, *When Democracy Makes Sense: Studies in the Democratic Potential of Third World Political Movements*, Uppsala: AKUT Working Group for the Study of Development Strategies.

South Commission, 1990, *The Challenge to the South*, Oxford: Oxford University Press.

Stockholm Initiative on Global Security and Governance, 1991, *Common Responsibilities in the 1990s*, Stockholm: Prime Minister's Office.

Sørensen, Georg, ed., 1993, *Political Conditionality*, London, Frank Cass.

United Nations Development Programme, 1992, *Human Development Report 1992*, New York.

Uvin, Peter, 1993, ' "Do as I Say, Not as I do": The Limits of Political Conditiona-

lity', in Georg Sørensen, ed., *Political Conditionality*, London: Frank Cass.
World Bank, 1990, *The African Capacity Building Initiative: Towards Improved Policy Analysis and Development Management*, Washington, DC.

15

Conditionality, Democracy and Development

GEORG SØRENSEN

1. INTRODUCTION

This chapter addresses three controversies concerning political conditionality: the issue of double standards (or foul play) on the part of the recipient as well as that of the donor; the notion of democracy as a problem for policies which aim to promote the practice of democracy; and the relationship between democracy and economic development with special reference to Southeast Asia.

The donor countries are often accused of employing double standards in that political conditionalities are applied only when it is politically expedient and not when other, economic or security interests are at stake. This is true, of course. But this chapter seeks to demonstrate that double standards are also involved on the part of recipient countries. There is no moral high ground from which 'innocent' recipients can blame 'guilty' donors.

The thesis of this chapter is that the debate on democracy in the Third World is both one-dimensional and based on a Western concept. At the same time, however, a universally valid notion of political rights and civil liberties is gaining ground.

Finally, the issue of consequences for economic development in democratic regimes is considered. It is stressed that the debate remains unresolved: it cannot be maintained that democracy as a form of regime is a necessary precondition for economic development. Yet non-democratic regimes are not necessarily more successful in developing their economies than democratic ones. It is important not to draw misleading conclusions from the apparent economic success of authoritarian regimes in Southeast Asia.

II. CONDITIONALITY AND DOUBLE STANDARDS

Double standards on the part of the donor regarding political conditionality have been demonstrated often enough: donor countries pursue a number of interests in their relationship with recipients, of
which concern for democracy and good governance is only two items
on the list of priorities. Economic and security interests are major
considerations as well. China is the clearest (but not the only) example of this having led to a high Western tolerance for the abuse of
human rights. American decision-makers are not in agreement about
the proper weight to be attached to issues concerning human rights
and democracy [*Diamond, 1992: 44*]. According to Jack Donnelly,

> The prospects for a sustained American effort, though, are not
> bright. On issue after issue, public attention and US foreign poli-
> cy have typically lurched from crisis to crisis, punctuated by long
> stretches of neglect. ... In the absence of dramatic short-term suc-
> cesses, the likelihood that the public and government will once
> again lose interest in human rights issues is great. Hard economic
> times at home are likely to deflect attention even further
> [*Donnelly 1992: 272*].

It is probably the larger powers among donors which display these
competing concerns most visibly. Yet the problem is reflected too
among smaller, like-minded countries. Denmark, for example, has cut
back on bilateral aid to China for reasons concerning human rights;
but it continues to take part in projects through multilateral sources.
    It is against this background that Western donors are accused of
double standards or foul play. Possibly the clearest denunciation has
come from a Ugandan observer, John-Jean B. Barya:

> ... the new political conditionalities have nothing to do with a
> desire of Western countries to actually encourage democracy in
> Africa. For a long time Western countries supported dictatorship
> for instance in Zaire, Liberia, Uganda and Kenya. France distin-
> guished itself in supporting dictators with open military interven-
> tions on their behalf against popular opposition. With the col-
> lapse of Soviet-led state socialism Western countries can no
> longer justify their support for dictators who have hitherto been
> so-called "bulwarks against communism". The new conditionali-
> ties in the emerging unipolar world therefore are designed to
> serve, in the new situation, three purposes: one, to crush once and
> for all the ideology of socialism and to replace it unambiguously

393

with the ideology of free enterprise world-wide; two, to create a new credible source of legitimacy for hegemony and thereby ensure leverage over specific countries which are considered economically and politically useful to the West...; three, a "justification for the impending decline in Africa's share of global assistance as resource flows to Eastern Europe begin to mount" ([*Barya, 1992: 1n*]. The last sentence is from *Africa Recovery*, April-June 1990).

Double standards are easy to identify in the case of various donor interests. It is less commonly noted that they are also a problem on the recipient side. This springs from changes in sovereignty which accompanied the decolonisation of the Third World.[1]

Before the Second World War sovereignty was bestowed only on countries which were able to demonstrate a capacity for self-government. 'States historically were empirical realities before they were legal personalities'; in other words, a sovereign state consisted traditionally of 'a bordered territory occupied by a settled population under effective and at least to some extent civil – that is "civilized" – government' [*Jackson, 1990: 34, 38*].

Previously then, positive sovereignty (demonstrated capacity for self-government) preceded and was indeed a precondition for negative sovereignty (that is, legal recognition by other states and freedom from outside interference). Following decolonisation, however, this was no longer the case. There are two main elements in the new system of sovereignty: (a) the right to self-determination of ex-colonies, and (b) an entitlement of poor countries to a development assistance regime where economic aid flows from rich, developed countries to poor, underdeveloped ones.

The two elements are interrelated: the right of ex-colonies to self-determination created a number of states which have negative sovereignty without having positive sovereignty – Jackson uses the term 'quasi-states'. To become states with positive sovereignty they need development; hence the development assistance regime.

But this means that Third World countries want to have their cake and eat it too: to enjoy sovereignty in the form of freedom from outside intervention (that is, to be recognised as equals in the international society of states); and to enjoy development assistance (that is, to be recognised as unequals and therefore entitled to aid). In Jackson's words:

---

1. What follows draws heavily on the penetrating analysis by Jackson [*1990*].

The new ethics of international development are obviously difficult to reconcile with historical liberties of sovereign statehood. If developed states have obligations to come to the assistance of underdeveloped states – as is often claimed – they certainly have no corresponding rights to ensure that their assistance is properly and efficiently used by governments of the latter. ... There is a fundamental incompatibility, therefore, between classical liberal rules of reciprocity and commutative justice and contemporary doctrines of nonreciprocity and distributive justice. ... Southern governments have only rights and Northern only duties. The former have no obligations to use foreign aid properly or productively. The latter have no right to demand it [*Jackson, 1990: 44*].

This double standard of post-colonial international society is exploited to the limit by state elites of the Third World; hence the demand by leaders such as Mobutu, Moi and Banda to receive both their legitimate and rightful development aid funds and to enjoy their legitimate and rightful sovereignty in the form of freedom from outside interference.

In short, Northern governments pursue many different objectives in the South; human rights and democracy compete with other concerns. And Southern governments have several different interests *vis-à-vis* the North, centred around the twin goals of reaping maximum benefits while enjoying the greatest possible measure of autonomy. It is this complex territory that policies of political conditionality have to negotiate in order to meet the noble aspiration of serving human rights and the democratic desires of the peoples (rather than the state elites) of the Third World. The most productive starting point is to recognise that double standards and foul play can pertain to elite groups both amongst donors and recipients.

III. CONCEPTS AND MEANINGS OF DEMOCRACY

Normally, the form of government known as democracy is defined as follows:

meaningful and extensive *competition* among individuals and organized groups ... for all effective positions of government power...; a highly inclusive level of *political participation* in the selection of leaders and policies, at least through regular and fair elections ... and a level of *civil and political liberties* – freedom of expression, freedom of the press, freedom to form and join organizations... [*Diamond et al., 1988: xvi*].

AID AND POLITICAL CONDITIONALITY

However, many political systems in the Third World cannot meet these demands. This has led to various concepts of semi-democracy in order to identify systems which are not strictly authoritarian or democratic, for example the categories in Sklar [1983].

In contrast, there are theorists who are not satisfied with liberal democracy and who search for a democracy which involves more than 'political formalities'. Lars Rudebeck calls this broader concept 'people's power'.[2]

> People's power...is both social, political and economic, thus not limited to the level of political structure. We may think of people's power as emerging, when or if people jointly assume control of their own living situations. The concrete beginnings are local. The extension of people's power beyond more local levels is, however, inconceivable except in connection with democratisation [Rudebeck, 1988: 24; see also Beckman, 1989].

It is important to note that the discussion about the meaning of democracy, including the mainstream definition provided by Diamond et al., is informed by the development of democracy in Europe and North America; traditions with other roots, for example in the Third World, play an unobtrusive role.[3]

Yet even in the Western debate, there are very different conceptions. Two versions of liberal democracy are of special interest in this context. One stresses the strictly liberal elements: that is, a limited role for the state in an economy guided by market principles and open to international exchange. The other version stresses the democratic elements such as popular participation, the creation of an autonomous civil society and the accountability of rulers. One criticism of conditionality is that it has over-emphasised the former version of liberal democracy, thereby creating an economic and social environment inimical to the realisation of the democratic elements in the latter version. An editorial in the Codesria Bulletin claimed that the policy of liberalisation 'completely undermines Africa's sovereignty, creates and/or further strengthens authoritarian regimes who will have to implement an inherently anti-democratic set of socio-economic reforms entailed in the programme' [quoted from Barya, 1992: 3].

Most observers making democratic demands on the Third World are rather modest in their expectations, probably because they want to

---

2.   Both Rudebeck [1988] and Beckman [1989] analyse African experiences.
3.   For an introduction of such Third World notions of democracy, see Pye [1985] on Asia and Nursey-Bray [1983] on Africa.

be realistic. Richard Sandbrook, for example, found in 1985 that democracy did not have 'any real prospects in the limiting conditions of contemporary Africa'; all that could be hoped for was 'decent, responsive and largely even-handed personal rule' [*Sandbrook 1985: 157*].

Another important point relates to the broad concept of democracy, which forces us to admit that there can be democratic elements in the actions of non-democratic regimes. For example, the progressive military junta that took power in Peru in 1968 abandoned the democratic political system. Yet the military government also went on to launch more far-reaching measures against poverty and poor living conditions than had been seen under the previous, democratic government. Which regime is the more democratic: the one that upholds a democratic political system serving principally an elite, or the one which abandons democracy in order to promote the struggle for freedom from hunger, disease and poverty?

If we persist in the narrow, purely political definition of democracy, there is no doubt that the deposed regime is the democratic one; but in the wider context of discussing the preconditions for democracy, this is not unequivocal.

A similar problem arises when employing Rudebeck's concept of people's power. In the short term, there can be people's power at local level without political democracy at the national level.[4]

India provides another example of the possible discrepancy between a democratic political system at the macro level and democracy at the micro level. It is one of the most stable democracies in the Third World, having adopted a democratic constitution in 1950; for only one and a half years, during the so-called Emergency of 1975-77 declared by Indira Gandhi, has there been non-democratic rule.

However, democracy at the macro level of the political system has not meant its introduction in all localities. The Congress Party achieved its dominant position in India's vast countryside through alliances which enforced the traditional patterns of domination. Congress dealt with the electorate through 'existing patron-brokers who, as landowners and caste-leaders, had no desire to jeopardise their positions by transforming local social structures. In adapting to local conditions, the party thus increasingly became tied to age-old patterns of status and leadership' [*Scott, 1972: 137*; see also *Frankel, 1978; Vanaik, 1985* and *Bardhan, 1984*].

Against this background, it is not surprising perhaps that

---

4.   Cf. also Rudebeck's example of people's power in Mozambique in 1983 [*Rudebeck, 1988*].

democratic India has set in motion programmes which, while claiming to promote participation and welfare at local level, have had the opposite effect: making the poor majority even worse off and strengthening the traditional structures of dominance and subordination.[5]

In China, political democracy in the vein of India was never seriously under consideration. The CCP is a Bolshevik party: it did not propose to fight for the interests of all Chinese, but for the interests of workers and poor peasants against internal and external class enemies. Secondly, the democracy sought was in the form of leadership from above combined with some degree of participation from below, and with a special status accorded to the small faction of the population (less than one per cent in 1949) who were members of the party [Blecher 1986: 104].

At the same time, it can be claimed that the Communists within this overall structure of authoritarian socialist rule, promoted elements of democracy at the local level through what was called the mass line. The mass line took at least five different concrete forms.[6] First, leaders at grassroots and county level were given a higher degree of latitude in ensuring that higher-level instructions were in accordance with local needs, conditions and opinions; second, cadres were sent to the villages to work and live alongside the peasants, to share their experiences and learn from rural life; third, elections by secret ballot were held regularly at village, township, county and regional levels, providing a democratic and representative character to local government: 'The only restriction was the "three-thirds" principle, according to which one-third of offices were to be filled by CCP members, one-third by non-CCP leftists, and one-third by liberals...' [Blecher, 1986: 26]. Fourth, popular political expression in the form of the 'big character poster' (dazibao) was encouraged; and finally, the armed forces were to take part in civilian affairs under rules which required subordination to civil authority.

The difference between China and India at the local level is quite clear: the authoritarian Chinese government has encouraged structural reforms and systems of local participation which have done much more for democratic change at the micro level than the so-called reforms attempted by democratic India.

This is not to suggest that this contradiction between democracy (or lack of it) at the macro level and democratic tendencies (or lack of them) at the micro level can be widely generalised. The core of the

---

5.   For an example of such a programme, see Prakash and Rastogi [1986]; see also Sørensen [1991, Ch. 2].
6.   Cf. Blecher [1986:25n].

matter is that a macro framework of democracy does not guarantee its reality on the local level; while its authoritarian counterpart does not completely block democratic elements on the local level.

Such contradictions may be expected to become less pronounced in the long term and it can be argued that India's democracy has grown stronger at the micro level since independence while overall authoritarianism is increasingly prevalent in China. In other words, in the longer term, democracy at the macro and micro level condition and reinforce each other, but in the short and medium terms there may be discrepancies which must be taken into account in the struggle for democracy on all levels.

Assuming for the sake of the argument that some donor countries give a genuine high priority to the promotion of democracy in the Third World, should support be aimed at the macro or the micro level?

My personal preference is to concentrate on the micro level without completely disregarding the macro level. If focus is single-mindedly on the macro level, steps in the direction of a democratic political system cannot ensure change in the basic ways in which most sub-Saharan African states function: the form of personalised rule which has been analysed in detail by Richard Sandbrook [1985] and others.

The historical record confirms this. The formal constitutional superstructures which many colonial powers imposed on their African colonies quickly degenerated upon independence, precisely because they had no roots in the civil societies upon which they were imposed. What took their place was illegitimate personalised rule:

> This form of patrimonialism arises in culturally plural peasant societies where rulers have no constitutional, charismatic, revolutionary, or traditional legitimacy. A chief or strongman emerges and governs on the basis of mercenary incentives and personal control of his administration and armed force. Personal loyalty and fear are the mainstays of a personalistic government untrammeled by traditional or modern constitutional limitations [*Sandbrook, 1986: 323*].

In a sense, the argument here is a traditional Marxist one: lasting, qualitative changes in the political superstructure require similarly fundamental changes in its basis: the structure of the economy and civil society.

Again, the argument is not that the superstructure should be disregarded completely: the atrocities of Mobuto and others who rule through personal patronage should not merely be criticised; the criticism ought to be followed by economic and other sanctions directed towards securing respect for basic human and civil rights. But even successful efforts in this area do not in themselves change the mechanisms of personalised rule.

How is it possible to secure such qualitative changes in the basis? Unfortunately, there is no straightforward answer. Göran Hydén [1983] suggests the introduction of capitalism and market forces as the most efficient way of preparing for structural change in what he calls the traditional economy of affection. This may be true, but from a long experience with market forces we know that they do not necessarily benefit the poor.

My own proposal is neither very original nor dramatic. It involves the support of activities which aim at political, cultural, social and economic empowerment of the populace.[7] Denis Goulet aptly summarises the argument, drawing together the experiences in Sri Lanka and Brazil:

> When it is self-initiated by grassroots groups, participation aims primarily at improving the groups' own positions. ...Participation began largely as a defense mechanism against the destruction wrought by elite problem solvers in the name of progress or development. From there it has evolved into a preferred form of "do-it-yourself" problem solving in small-scale operations. Now, however, many parties to participation seek entry into larger, more macro, arenas of decision making. Alternative development strategies centring on goals of equity, job creation, the multiplication of autonomous capacities, and respect for cultural diversity – all these require significant participation in macro arenas. Without it, development strategies will be simultaneously undemocratic and ineffectual. Without the developmental participation of non-elites, even political democracy will largely be a sham [Goulet, 1989: 175n].

Thus, at the micro level genuine development and democracy in the broad sense are, if not identical, then closely interconnected. It is clear that there are many other examples of activities and projects which have been successful in terms of empowering participants, both in Africa and elsewhere.[8] In that sense, there is already a rich body of

---

7. A number of authors have made this suggestion already; perhaps the closest study is Guy Gran's book, *Development by People* [1983].
8. See for example Chambers [1983]; Tidemand [1988]; Fuglesang & Chandler, no year.

experiences to draw on. In the optimum situation, then, the national government itself gives priority to grassroots democracy, so that internal and external initiatives can support each other.

The expressed difficulties concerning meanings and levels of democracy should not be taken to mean that political conditionalities face insurmountable problems. Even if the relevance of multi-party and western political systems in a Third World context is a matter for debate, there is increasing unanimity on a universally valid core of civil rights and political liberties which any political system must meet in order to qualify as democratic.[9]

This is the starting point. The role of negative conditionality is thus to dissuade rulers, both in non-democratic and newly-democratised states, from abusing the human rights of their opponents. With the important exception of times of civil war and internal chaos, it is possible to define clearly a number of rights which must be respected and to identify the ruling groups which must be held responsible.[10]

But these considerations also highlight the need for positive measures aimed at strengthening groups in civil society (ethnic and kinship associations; self-help groups involved in housing, health-care, education, co-operatives both of consumers and producers; amnesty committees, civic associations, non-governmental organisations (NGOs) and professional associations). In the case of authoritarian regimes, such assistance is probably best channelled through NGOs. Projects to increase popular participation and empowerment are better managed by smaller organisations not linked closely with donor governments.[11] Assistance directed towards empowerment at the grassroots level working through NGOs solves some of the problems surrounding foreign aid in this area; but it should be emphasised that it creates a number of other problems.[12]

IV. DEMOCRACY, AUTHORITARIANISM AND ECONOMIC DEVELOPMENT

The economic success of authoritarian regimes in the Southeast Asian area has been used as a basis for the argument that some form of authoritarianism is conducive to the formation of strong states, capable of rapid economic development. If this is the case, is it necessary

---

9. That is, the rights and liberties set out by Diamond *et al.*[*1988*].
10. See also Nelson and Eglinton [*1992:41-43*].
11. See also Diamond [*1992*] and Clark [*1991*].
12. The most important dilemmas of NGO activity are summarised in Anheier [*1992*].

to adopt the position of some observers,[13] who consider democracy expensive in terms of development, since it leads to a decline of the state's strength, that is, its ability to pursue economic development. It would be somewhat embarrassing for the whole notion of political conditionality if it could be demonstrated that important dimensions of 'good governance' are best managed by authoritarian regimes; and this is a possible claim on the basis of the East Asian experience.

Yet there is no need for great concern in this regard. From a comparative perspective, the authoritarian economic successes stand out as quite extraordinary creations, especially in the context of the experiences of other countries. Indeed, there is no direct correlation between the form of regime and the outcome in terms of economic development. Thus, when the system of government (democratic or authoritarian) is regarded as the independent variable and economic development (defined for example as growth and welfare) as the dependent variable, categorical statements about expectation or prediction in terms of economic development are not possible.

In focusing on economic development, it is useful to distinguish between five types of regimes, three authoritarian and two democratic.[14] The authoritarian varieties can be summarised as shown in Figure 1.

FIGURE 1
TYPES OF AUTHORITARIAN SYSTEMS: CONSEQUENCES FOR ECONOMIC DEVELOPMENT

| Regime type | Aspects of economic development | | Country example |
	Growth	Welfare	
Authoritarian developmentalist regime	+	+	Taiwan China
Authoritarian growth regime	+	-	Brazil under military rule
Authoritarian state elite enrichment regime	-	-	Zaire under Mobuto

The distinctive feature of an authoritarian developmentalist regime is its capacity to promote both growth and welfare. The regime is directed towards reform and enjoys a high degree of autonomy from vested elite interests; it controls a state apparatus which has the bureaucratic and organisational capacity to promote development, and is run by a state elite ideologically committed towards encouraging economic development. This type of regime may be categorised as socialist, as in China, or capitalist, such as in Taiwan. Although often

13. See the summary of arguments in Sørensen [1993].
14. What follows draws heavily on Sørensen [1993].

seen as opposites, Taiwan and China have several characteristics in common, in addition to their authoritarian political systems. Taiwan, like China, advanced economic development through radical agrarian reform and the transfer of economic surplus from agriculture to industry. As in China, there has been a high degree of state involvement in the economy. There are only a few other examples of this type of authoritarian regime, and they are also from Southeast Asia. The most obvious ones are the two Koreas.

In the second category, the authoritarian growth regime promotes economic growth, but not welfare. Brazil, during military rule from 1964 until the present period of a return to democracy, provides a good example. Brazil exhibits the following typical characteristics: economic growth objectives are pursued with the aim of building a strong national economy (which, in turn, can provide the basis for a strong military power). The long-term interests (but not necessarily the immediate interests) of the dominant social forces are respected while the economic surplus necessary to promote growth is planned to come from the workers and peasants who make up the poor majority. It is a model of development which is explicitly oriented towards an elite, based on an alliance between local private capital, state enterprises and transnational corporations. The priority of the elite applies to the supply side (the emphasis on consumer durables) as well as to the demand side (capital intensive industrialisation, chiefly benefiting a minority group of skilled and white-collar employees and workers). The military regimes which imposed authoritarian rule in Uruguay, Chile and Argentina in the early and mid-70s attempted to advance models of economic growth with similar features. They were less successful in terms of growth; in contrast to Brazil, they opened their economies to external shocks which, until corrective measures were taken, led to de-industrialisation, that is, towards the dismantling of the existing industrial base. Nevertheless, these cases have a basic feature in common: the authoritarian regimes attempt to pursue economic growth one-sidedly in an alliance with elite interests.

The final type of authoritarian regime promotes neither growth nor welfare: its main objective is the enrichment of the elite which controls the state. This is reflected in the name: Authoritarian State Elite Enrichment, or ASEE regime. It is often based on autocratic rule by a supreme leader. The leader's actions may not be understandable judged by the standards of formal development goals set up by the regime, but they are perfectly coherent if seen in terms of patronage and clientelistic politics. It is clear that several African regimes, with their systems of personal rule as described in the previous section, fall into the category of authoritarian state elite enrichment regimes in so far as they combine personal rule with authoritarianism. One observer has described the system in terms of clan politics: 'The clan is a political faction, operating within the institutions of the state and the governing party: it exists above all to promote the interests of its members ... and its first unifying principle is the prospect of the material rewards of political success: loot is the clan's totem' (Cruise O'Brien, quoted from Hydén [*1983: 37*]). Hence, the defining characteristic of the ASEE regime is simply that the elite which controls the state is preoccupied with enriching itself. Other examples from Africa include the Central African Republic under Jean Bedel Bokassa and Uganda under Idi Amin. There are other examples outside Africa which have much in common with the ASEE type of regime: Haiti under Duvalier Senior and Junior (Papa and Baby Doc); Nicaragua under Somoza, and Paraguay under Alfredo Stroessner.

There is less material for a typology of democratic systems, simply because there are very few relatively stable democracies in the developing world. Other than very small countries with a population of less than one million, only Costa Rica (with a population of three million) has been a stable democracy for as long as India. Venezuela and Colombia have almost achieved similar stability. There is a common denominator between these examples and the majority of current transitions towards democracy. They are all democracies dominated by an elite. A brief description of India will help illustrate this point.

Indian democracy was achieved by a coalition of three main groups: the urban professionals, who had founded the Congress movement in 1885; the Indian business community in trade and industry, and the rural landowning elite. The masses of poor peasants supported the coalition's struggle for independence and democracy; they rallied behind Gandhi as the great leader, instrumental in forging this alliance between elite groups and the poor masses. Yet the support of the poor peasants did not really upset the rural elite. Gandhi's vision of the future of the Indian villages did not threaten their position; and it was they, not the landless peasants, who controlled the Congress organisation at the local level. Their continued dominance in the Indian democracy shaped and set limits to what could be achieved in terms of economic development, a process which has mainly served the interests of the privileged groups in the dominant coalition. The pre-eminence of their interests has impeded the capacity of Indian democracy to mobilise resources for economic growth and welfare improvement through basic agrarian and other reforms.

The majority of current transitions towards democracy are also transitions from above, that is, dominated by an elite. The risk is that this leads to 'frozen democracies' unwilling to transgress the narrow limitations imposed on them by the select factions who engineered the transition to democracy in the first place. The Indian experience of some 40 years of elite-dominated democracy demonstrates that such fears are well-founded; there has been economic development in India both in terms of growth and welfare, but as a whole the process has given insufficient benefits to the mass of poor people.

At the same time, it is important to emphasise another factor: democracy introduces a degree of uncertainty in the political process. It opens channels for popular pressure on the rulers. Even elite-dominated democracies may be directed towards more effective reform measures than have been the case in India. A good example of this is Costa Rica. Here democracy has also been based on political pacts between elite factions. Yet within these limitations, the dominant coalitions in Costa Rica have supported governments which have promoted substantial welfare programmes. This has resulted in major improvements in welfare, although the achievements in growth are less spectacular, especially during the crisis period in the 1980s.

Therefore, the question arises of why the elite-dominated democracy of Costa Rica fared relatively well in welfare terms. Several factors help to explain this. First, the nature of elite rule in Costa Rica during the 19th and early 20th centuries differed from most other countries in Latin America. The system did not place Indians and slaves under the control of a rural elite; there was an independent peasantry and a rural working class free from feudal ties binding its members to rural patrons like slaves. Second, the dominant stratum of coffee barons supported liberal values of religious freedom, freedom of the press, and the promotion of public education. A law enabling free, compulsory education had been passed in 1884. Good levels in education and open public debate led to a variety of groups and associations beingformed which made demands on the political system. Third, the democracy established after 1948 has gained a reputation for notably fair and honest elections in a political system which encourages negotiation and compromise. In dramatic contrast to its Central American neighbours, the Costa Rican army was abolished in 1949.

The case of Costa Rica demonstrates that elite-dominated democracies need not fare as poorly as India in terms of welfare and are capable of becoming more responsive to mass demands. On the other hand, the political background for this contains some very unusual features which are hard to find in other elite-dominated democracies.

The egalitarian values of the dominant coalition led to a social and political environment which was conducive to the organisation of popular forces at an early stage.

The example of Costa Rica demonstrates positively that there is no law stipulating that elite-dominated democracies cannot address issues of welfare. Unfortunately it appears hard to find the conditions which were instrumental in accomplishing this result in the other similar systems, including most of those currently in transition towards democracy in Latin America, Asia and Africa.

Mass-dominated democracies can be defined in contrast to elite-dominated systems. In the former, 'mass actors have gained the upper hand' and the pressure for reforms is from below, attacking the power and privilege of the elites. A prominent example is the Unidad Popular (Popular Unity) government under Salvador Allende in Chile between 1970 and 1973. The government was elected on a programme promising massive improvement for low-income and poor groups through increases in wages and better social and housing conditions. At the same time, there were to be measures making the economy more effective, directed towards faster growth while also increasing popular control. The policies aimed to redistribute land through agrarian reform, and to regain state control over the mineral sector through nationalisation, which was also foreseen for the largest enterprises in the private sector. While successful in its first year in power, the Unidad Popular had to face rapidly growing resistance from landowners, industrialists, and the middle classes. A process of radicalisation took place where an increasingly united opposition faced a government which was divided internally as to whether it should seek radical confrontation or moderate accommodation with its political adversaries. This culminated in 1973 in the military coup led by Augusto Pinochet. The experience underlines the fragility of mass-dominated democracies: they lead easily towards hostile confrontation which may result in a return to authoritarian rule.

The fate of the Unidad Popular government and other mass-oriented democracies in Latin America has led to rather pessimistic conclusions regarding future possibilities for such systems in the region, as we saw in Section II. Taking a broader perspective, it is possible to be more hopeful. It should be possible for mass-dominated democracies to proceed more cautiously towards reform and avoid the kind of widespread confrontation that took place in Chile. One example of this is the Left Front rule in West Bengal in India from 1977. At the same time, democracies have the capacity to transform. It is possible to see the development of most West European democracies since the 19th century as a process beginning with elite-dominated systems which transform gradually towards mass-dominated systems. The latter, in turn, are responsible for the welfare states built since the 1930s. The process of gradual transformation prepared the elite for acceptance of social reforms and policies encouraging equity.

The logic of this study of the various types of democratic systems is simple. It suggests that the prospects of economic development, and especially the likelihood of improvements for the underprivileged, depend on the nature of the ruling coalitions behind the democracies. Highly restricted, elite-dominated democracies may be virtually 'frozen' in that their room for manoeuvre in addressing welfare issues, and also in promoting resources for economic growth, is set within very narrow limits of continued support for the status quo. It has been argued earlier that most of the current transitions towards democracy are directed from above, that is, they are elite-dominated. Consequently, the pessimistic prospect of 'frozen democracies' resulting from many of them remains a convincing projection for future developments.

Mass-dominated democracies, on the other hand, contain the potential for substantial reform which can restrain vested interests. But the process risks leading to confrontation with elite forces and the subsequent undermining of democracy itself.

Yet there is a space in between these extremes, where relatively stable democracy and economic progress can work in conjunction. The elite-dominated systems are not necessarily locked in their frozen positions forever. They have the ability to change which may lead to greater responsiveness to popular demands. The Scandinavian welfare states are leading examples of countries which have undertaken this transformation.

In conclusion, transitions towards democracy do not guarantee a promised land of rapid economic development.The elite-dominated 'frozen' democracies seem to offer little hope of a process of economic development which can meet the aspirations and needs of the poor majority. The transitions themselves can lead to instability and the breakdown of authority involving a worse violation of human rights then before. The promise of democracy is not that of automatic improvement in other areas; it is the creation of a 'window of opportunity', a political framework where groups struggling for development and human rights have greater potential than before to organise and to express their demands. Democracy offers the opportunities; it does not offer guarantees of success.

The implications of these results for the notion of political conditionality ought to be clear: frail, elite-dominated democracies may be a political advance compared with outright authoritarianism, but there is little reason to expect that such democracies will be able to sustain strong states. The mere swing away from authoritarianism towards the creation of a thin layer of democracy in terms of multi-party systems and elections will not create the necessary basis for states with more developmental strength. This is achieved only through the long and difficult process of empowering the general population, creating a more solid basis for democratic rule. It is therefore more important to give positive assistance directed towards strengthening civil society rather than to impose negative conditionalities which are not sufficient to secure the necessary progress towards more consolidated democracies, less dominated by elite interests.

It is sometimes claimed on the basis of the apparent East Asian success that authoritarianism is necessary for the creation of strong, developmental states. This must be rejected. The more disquieting result of this investigation is that the democracy which is advancing currently in many developing countries may not accomplish that objective either. The challenge is to help frail, elite-dominated democracies to develop a secure, popular basis in a strong civil society. This may be the real difficulty facing future considerations of the notion of political conditionality.

V. CONCLUSION

I have tried to address some of the controversies which appear when considering policies of political conditionality. None of the conclusions renders policies of political conditionality impossible or even inapplicable. But a number of complex issues are indicated which must be taken into account if such policies are going to achieve real progress in terms of human rights and democracy.

REFERENCES

Anheier, H.K., 1992, 'The Political Economy of Non-Governmental Organizations in Africa: A Comparative Analysis', paper for the Inaugural Pan-European Conference on International Relations, Heidelberg, 16-20 Sept.

Bardhan, Pranab, 1984, *The Political Economy of Development in India*, New Delhi: Oxford University Press.

Barya, J.-J.B., 1992, 'The New Political Conditionalities of Aid: An Independent View From Africa', paper for the EADI Conference on The New Political Conditionalities of Development Assistance, Vienna, 23-24 April.

Blecher, Marc, 1986, *China. Politics, Economics and Society*, London: Frances

Pinter.

Chambers, Robert, 1983, *Rural Development. Putting the Last First*, London: Longman.

Clark, J., 1991, *Democratizing Development. The Role of Voluntary Organizations*, London: Earthscan.

Diamond, L., J.J. Linz, S.M. Lipset, 1988, *Democracy in Developing Countries. Volume Two, Africa*. Boulder, CO: Lynne Rienner.

Diamond, L., 1992, 'Promoting Democracy', *Foreign Policy*, 87, Summer.

Donnelly, J., 1992, 'Human Rights in the New World Order', *World Policy Journal*, Vol. IX, No. 2.

Frankel, Francine, 1978, *India's Political Economy, 1974-77*, Princeton: Princeton University Press.

Fuglesang, Andreas & Dale Chandler, no year, *Participation as Process – what we can learn from Grameen Bank*, Bangladesh, Oslo: NORAD.

Goulet, Denis, 1989, 'Participation in Development: New Avenues', *World Development*, Vol. 17, No. 2.

Gran, Guy, 1983, *Development by People. Citizen Construction of a Just World*, New York: Praeger Publishers.

Held, D., 1987, *Models of Democracy*, Cambridge: Polity Press.

Hydén, Göran, 1983, *No Shortcuts to Progress. African Development Management in Perspective*, London: Heinemann.

Jackson, Robert H., 1990, *Quasi-States: Sovereignty, International Relations, and the Third World*, Cambridge: Cambridge University Press.

Nelson, J.M., with S.J. Eglinton, 1992, *Encouraging Democracy: What Role for Conditioned Aid?*, Washington, DC: Overseas Development Council.

Nursey-Bray, P., 1983, 'Consensus and Community: The Theory of African One-party Democracy', in G. Duncan (ed.), *Democratic Theory and Practice*, Cambridge: Cambridge University Press.

Prakash, O.M. and P.N. Rastogi, 1986, 'Development of the Rural Poor: The Missing Factor', *IFDA Dossier*, No. 51, January-February.

Pye, Lucian W., 1985, *Asian Power and Politics: The Cultural Dimensions of Authority*, Cambridge, Mass.: Harvard University Press.

Rudebeck, Lars, 1988, 'Erosion – and conditions of regeneration', in Rudebeck, L. & C. Lopes, *The Socialist Ideal in Africa. A debate*, Uppsala: Scandinavian Institute of African Studies.

Sandbrook, Richard, 1985, *The Politics of Africa's Economic Stagnation*, Cambridge: Cambridge University Press.

Sandbrook, Richard, 1986, 'The State and Economic Stagnation in Tropical Africa', *World Development*, 14:3.

Scott, J.R., 1972, *Comparative Political Corruption*, New Jersey.

Sklar, R.L., 1983, 'Democracy in Africa', *African Studies Review*, Vol. 26, Nos. 3-4, Sept.-Dec.

Sørensen, Georg, 1991, *Democracy, Dictatorship and Development. Economic Development in Selected Regimes of the Third World*, London and New York: Macmillan and St. Martin's Press.

Sørensen, Georg, 1993, *Democracy and Democratization. Processes and Prospects in a Changing World*, Boulder, CO: Westview Press.

Tidemand, Per, 1988, 'Folkelig deltagelse og udviklingsplanlægning i Zimbabwes Communal Areas' ('Grassroots participation and development planning in Zimbabwe's Communal Areas'), *Den Ny Verden*, Vol. 21, No. 4.

Vanaik, A., 1985, 'India's Bourgeois Democracy', *New Left Review*, No. 154, Nov.-Dec.

Glossary

LIST OF SELECTED ACRONYMS AND ABBREVIATIONS

AI	Amnesty International
ABRI	Angkatan Bersenjata Republik Indonesia (Armed Forces of the Republic of Indonesia)
ACP	African, Caribbean and Pacific countries, signatories of the Lomé Conventions
ADB	African Development Bank
AKUT	Arbetsgruppen för studier av utvecklingsstrategier i Tredje Värden (Working Group for the Study of Development Strategies for the Third World – the universities of Stockholm and Uppsala)
ANAP	Anavatan Partisie (Motherland Party, Turkey)
ASEE	Authoritarian State Elite Enrichment
BADC	Belgian Administration for Development Co-operation
BBC	British Broadcasting Corporation
BITS	Swedish Commission for Technical Co-operation
BMZ	Bundesministerium für Wirtschaftliche Zusammenarbeit (Federal Ministry for Economic Co-operation, Germany)
CA	Current Account
CAP	Common Agricultural Policy (of the EC)
CAPMAS	Central Agency for Public Mobilisation and Statistics (Egypt)
CBE	Central Bank of Egypt
CCFF	Compensatory and Contingency Financing Facility
CCP	China's Communist Party
CCM	Chama Cha Mapinduzi (Tanzania – TANU)
CDA	Christen Democratisch Appèl (Christian Democrats, Netherlands)

CGI	Consultative Group on Indonesia
CGR	Central Government Revenue
CILSS	Comité Permanent Inter-états de Lutte contre la Sécheresse dans le Sahel
CIS	Commonwealth of Independent States
CODESRIA	Council for the Development of Economic and Social Research in Africa
COM	Commission (EC)
CPI	Consumer Price Index
D'66	Democraten 1966 (Netherlands)
DAC	Development Assistance Committee (OECD)
DANIDA	Danish International Development Agency
DDA	Direction de la coopération au développement et de l'aide humanitaire internationales (SDC – Switzerland)
DG	Directorate General (EC)
D-GIC	Directorate-General of International Co-operation (of the Ministry of Foreign Affairs, Netherlands)
DM	Deutsche Mark (German currency)
DOD	Debt outstanding and disbursed
DOM(s)	Département(s) d'Outre-Mer (French Overseas Department)
EADI	European Association of Development Research and Training Institutes
EBRD	European Bank for Reconstruction and Development
EC	European Community
ECA	Economic Commission for Africa
EEC	European Economic Community
EFTA	European Free Trade Association
EJDR	(The) European Journal of Development Research
EPC	European Political Co-operation
EPD	Evangelischer Pressdienst
EPTA	Expanded Programme of Technical Assistance
ERSAP	Economic Reform and Structural Adjustment Programme (Egypt)
ERP	Economic Recovery Programme
ESAF	Enhanced Structural Adjustment Facility
ESCWA	Economic and Social Commission for Western Asia
EU	European Union
EXPGRS	Export of goods and services
FAC	Food Aid Convention
FAO	Food and Agriculture Organisation

FINNFUND	Special Fund for Industrial Development Co-operation (Finland)
FORD	Foundation for the Restoration of Democracy (Kenya)
FRETELIN	Frente Revolucionaria do Timor Leste Independente (Revolutionary Front for an Independent East Timor)
FRODEBU	Front pour da démocratie au Burundi
GATT	General Agreement on Tariffs and Trade
GC	Government Consumption
GDI	Gross domestic investment
GDR	German Democratic Republic
GDS	Gross domestic saving
GNP	Gross National Product
GOLKAR	Golongan Karya (Functional Groups - Indonesian government party)
G7	Group of Seven (major powers)
G24	Group of Twenty-four
HIC	Highly Indebted Countries
HYV	High-yielding varieties
IBRD	International Bank for Reconstruction and Development (World Bank)
ICJ	International Court of Justice
IDA	International Development Association (World Bank)
IDS	Institute of Development Studies (University of Sussex)
IFDA	International Foundation for Development Alternatives
IGGI	Inter-Governmental Group on Indonesia
ILO	International Labour Organisation
IMF	International Monetary Fund
INGI	International Non-governmental Group on Indonesia
INPRES	Instruksi Presiden (Indonesia)
INTERFAIS	International System of Information on Food Aid (of the WFP)
INTRAC	International NGO Training and Research Centre
ITSH	Internal transport, storage and handling
IUED	Institut Universitaire d'Etudes du Développement (Genève)
KANU	Kenyan African National Union
LLDC	(List of) Least-developed countries (UN definition)
LDC	Less-developed countries/developing countries (DC)
MDAP	Mutual Defence Assistance Programme

MFA	Ministry of Foreign Affairs
MP	Member of Parliament
NATCAP	National Technical Co-operation Assessment and Programmes (UNDP)
NATO	North Atlantic Treaty Organisation
NCCK	National Christian Council of Kenya
NEF	Near East Foundation
ER	Nominal Exchange Rate
NIC	Newly industrialised countries
NMFA	Netherlands' Ministry of Foreign Affairs
NOR	Nichtregierungsorganisation (NGO)
NORAD	Norwegian Agency for International Development
NORDFUND	Special Fund for Industrial Development Co-operation (Norway)
NGO	Non-governmental organisation
NIEO	New International Economic Order
NJCM	Nederlandse Juristen Commissie voor Mensenrechten (Dutch Lawyers' Committee for Human Rights)
NOK	Norwegian kroner (currency)
NTB	Non-tariff barrier
NUPI	Norsk Utenrikspolitisk Institutt (Norwegian Institute of International Affairs)
OAU	Organisation of African Unity
OCDE	Organisation de Coopération et de Développement Economiques (OECD)
ODA	Official Development Assistance
ODF	Official Development Finance
ODI	Overseas Development Institute (London)
OECD	Organisation of Economic Co-operation and Development
OEEC	Organisation of European Economic Co-operation
OPEC	The Organisation of Petroleum Exporting Countries
OXFAM	Oxford Committee for Famine Relief
Packet-De	Deregulation, de-bureaucratisation, and decentralisation
PC	Private Consumption
PE	Public enterprise
PDI	Partai Demokrasi Indonesia (Indonesian Democratic Party)
PL480	Public Law 480 (United States)
PM	Prime Minister
PMO	Prime Minister's Office

PO	People's Organisation
PRI	Private Investment
PVDA	Partij van de Arbeid (Labour Party, Netherlands)
QR	Quantitative restrictions
RENAMO	Resistência Nacional Moçambicana
ROAPE	Review of African Political Economy
SADCC	Southern African Development Co-ordination Conference
SAF	Structural Adjustment Facility
SAL	Structural Adjustment Loan
SAP	Structural Adjustment Programme
SBA	Stand-by arrangement
SDC	Swiss Development Co-operation (DDA)
SDR	Special Drawing Rights (IMF)
SECAL	Sectoral Adjustment Loan
SEK	Swedish kronor (currency)
SFD	Social Fund for Development (Egypt)
SID	Society for International Development
SIDA	Swedish International Development Authority
SP	Socialist Party (Flemish)
SPA	Special Programme of Assistance (for Africa – World Bank)
SSA	sub-Saharan Africa
SWEDFUND	Special Fund for Industrial Development Co-operation
SUPER SEMAR	Surat perintah sebelas Maret
TANU	Tanganyika African National Union (later CCM)
TB	Treasury bill
TL	Turkish Lira (currency)
TOES	The Other Economic Summit
TOM	Territoire d'Outre-Mer (French Overseas Dependency)
UK	United Kingdom
UN	United Nations
UNCHR	United Nations Commission for Human Rights
UNCTAD	United Nations Conference on Trade and Development
UNDP	United Nations Development Programme
UNESCO	United Nations Educational, Scientific and Cultural Organisation
UNICEF	United Nations (International) Children's

	(Emergency) Fund
URT	United Republic of Tanzania
US	United States (of America)
USA	United States of America
USAID	United States Agency for International Development
USD	US dollar (US$)
USDA	US Department of Agriculture
USECA	US Economic Co-operation Administration
USSR	Union of Soviet Socialist Republics
VAT	Value added tax
VVD	Volkspartij voor Vrijheid en Democratie (Liberal Party, Netherlands)
WEED	Weltwirtschaft und Entwicklung
WFP	World Food Programme
WIDER	World Institute for Development Economics Research (of the United Nations University)

Notes on Contributors

Gouda Abdel-Khalek is Professor of Economics, Faculty of Economics and Political Science, Cairo University, Cairo.

Edward Clay is a Research Fellow (Economics), Overseas Development Institute, London. He was formerly director of the Relief and Development Institute, London.

Martin Doornbos is a Fellow, Institute of Social Studies, The Hague, and Professor of Political Science. He is editor of *Development and Change*.

Jacques Forster is Professor of Development Studies, IUED - Institut universitaire d'études du développement, Genève and previously its director (1980-92). He was for years a member of the EADI Executive Committee, during 1985-90 the Vice-President. He is a member of the International Committee of the Red Cross.

Mosharaff Hossain is Professor Emeritus (Economics), Dhaka University, Dhaka. He was a member of the first Planning Commission after Bangladesh's independence.

Karima Korayem is Professor of Economics, Faculty of Commerce, Girls Branch, Al-Azhar University, Cairo.

Oliver Morrissey is Associate Professor, Department of Economics, University of Nottingham, Nottingham.

Samuel S. Mushi is Professor, Department of Political Science and Public Administration, University of Dar es Salaam, Dar es Salaam.

Nico G. Schulte Nordholt is a Research Associate (Political Anthropology), Technology and Development Group, University of Twente, Enschede.

Robrecht Renard is Professor of Development Economics, College for the Developing Countries - RUCA, University of Antwerp, Antwerp. He was a member of the EADI Executive Committee for several years (1984-89).

Filip Reyntjens is Professor of Law and Politics, College for the Developing Countries - RUCA, University of Antwerp, Antwerp.

Mark Robinson is a Research Fellow, Institute of Development Studies, University of Sussex, Brighton.

Olav Stokke is currently the Director of Research and Deputy Director of the Norwegian Institute of International Affairs, Oslo. He is editor of *Forum for Development Studies* and, since 1979, the Convenor of the EADI Working Group on Aid Policy and Performance.

Georg Sørensen is Professor of Political Science, Aarhus University, Århus.

Peter P. Waller is Deputy Director of the German Development Institute, Berlin, and Professor of Geography. He has been a member of the EADI Executive Committee since 1990, during 1990-93 as Vice-President.

Stanislav Zhukov is a Senior Researcher (Economics), Institute of World Economy and International Relations (IMEMO), Moscow.

For Product Safety Concerns and Information please contact our EU
representative GPSR@taylorandfrancis.com
Taylor & Francis Verlag GmbH, Kaufingerstraße 24, 80331 München, Germany